Global Education Policy and International Development

Second Edition

ALSO AVAILABLE FROM BLOOMSBURY

Comparative and International Education, David Phillips and
Michele Schweisfurth
Education and International Development, edited by
Tristan McCowan and Elaine Unterhalter
Globalization and International Education, Robin Shields

Global Education Policy and International Development

New Agendas, Issues and Policies

Second Edition

**EDITED BY
ANTONI VERGER,
MARIO NOVELLI AND
HÜLYA KOSAR ALTINYELKEN**

Bloomsbury Academic
An imprint of Bloomsbury Publishing Plc

B L O O M S B U R Y
LONDON · OXFORD · NEW YORK · NEW DELHI · SYDNEY

Bloomsbury Academic
An imprint of Bloomsbury Publishing Plc

50 Bedford Square
London
WC1B 3DP
UK

1385 Broadway
New York
NY 10018
USA

www.bloomsbury.com

BLOOMSBURY and the Diana logo are trademarks of Bloomsbury Publishing Plc

First edition published 2012
Second edition published 2018

British Library Cataloguing-in-Publication Data
A catalogue record for this book is available from the British Library.

ISBN: HB: 978-1-4742-9602-1
         PB: 978-1-4742-9601-4
         ePDF: 978-1-4742-9604-5
         ePub: 978-1-4742-9603-8

Library of Congress Cataloging-in-Publication Data
Names: Verger, Antoni, 1975- editor. | Novelli, Mario, editor. | Altinyelken, Hèulya K., editor.
Title: Global education policy and international development : new agendas, issues and policies / edited by Antoni Verger, Mario Novelli and Hulya K. Altinyelken.
Description: Second edition. | London, UK ; New York, NY : Bloomsbury Academic, 2017. | Includes bibliographical references.
Identifiers: LCCN 2017019673 | ISBN 9781474296021 (hardback) | ISBN 9781474296014 (pb) | ISBN 9781474296045 (ePDF) | ISBN 9781474296038 (ePUB)
Subjects: LCSH: Education–Economic aspects–Developing countries. | Education and state–Developing countries. | Education and globalization–Developing countries. | Economic development–Developing countries. | BISAC: EDUCATION / Multicultural Education.
Classification: LCC LC67.D44 G56 2018 | DDC 379.72/4–dc23 LC record available at https://lccn.loc.gov/2017019673

Cover image © Majority World / Getty

Typeset by Integra Software Services Pvt. Ltd.

This book is dedicated to the life, work and memory of Margriet Poppema (10/07/1950–01/09/2016), a critical scholar, and a sadly missed colleague and friend.

Contents

List of Tables

List of Figures

1

Global Education Policy and International Development: A Revisited Introduction

Antoni Verger, Mario Novelli and Hülya Kosar Altinyelken

Chapter Outline

Introduction

Today, as we speak, similar education reforms and a common set of education policy jargon are being applied in many parts of the world, in locations that are incredibly diverse both culturally and in terms of economic development. Education policy programmes such as child-centred pedagogies, school-based management, teachers' accountability, public–private partnerships or conditional-cash transfer schemes, are being discussed and implemented everywhere, to the point that they have acquired the status of 'global education policies' (GEPs). More and more researchers, coming from different disciplines and sub-disciplines, such as comparative education, political sociology, anthropology and political sciences, are paying attention to the GEP phenomenon. Traditionally, scholars have used very diverse terms to refer to the globalization of education policy, such as 'policy diffusion', 'policy borrowing', 'policy transfer', 'policy travelling' or 'policy convergence', among others.

However, paradoxically, existing research on GEP does not always incorporate processes of globalization into its analytical framework, at least in a comprehensive way. Quite often, research on the topic does not provide an account of how and why policies are globally constructed and settled in global agendas. They are focused on the international dimension of the policy process, that is, they look at the transfer of policies 'within countries and across countries' (Stone 2004, p. 545) or as a 'boundary-crossing practice' (Peck and Theodore 2010, p. 169), but do not grasp the global dimension that education policy-making is now acquiring. Another habitual problem in the policy transfer literature is that it often implies a dichotomy between the local and the global 'levels' and represents them as separate layers of educational governance (Mukhopadhyay and Sriprakash 2011). When doing so, research fails to capture the complexity of global politics and the fact that different political scales are mutually constituted (Robertson et al. 2002). Furthermore, much research on GEP does not provide sufficiently rich empirical evidence on the interplay between processes of globalization and re-contextualization. Doing so is methodologically challenging, but if we attempt to understand education policies globally, the study of the complex relationships between global ideas, its dissemination and re-contextualization in local settings becomes a key task (Ball 1998).

This book contributes to addressing these and other challenges that globalization poses in education policy analysis. Its main objective is *to analyse the reasons, agents and factors behind the globalization of educational policy programmes*[1] *and, by doing so, reflect on the structures, processes and events through which a global education policy landscape is being constituted.*

Contributions to the book provide an in-depth theoretical and empirical understanding of educational change and education reform in an increasingly globalizing but diverse world. The case studies collected in the volume reflect, on the one hand, on the capacity of international organizations and other political actors to shape education agendas and disseminate education policies globally. On the other hand, they analyse the complex process of the re-contextualization of global policies at the country level and their effects on educational governance. In the different studies, authors look at the globalization–education relationship from multiple theoretical perspectives, including neo-institutionalism, constructivism, international political economy (IPE) and so on, and by applying different methodological approaches, such as comparative analysis, the vertical case study or discourse analysis. Despite their diversity, all chapters in this volume converge on the idea that processes of *globalization* have drastically altered the education policy landscape across the world and, more particularly, in the context of southern countries.

The book conclusions' section draws on the special contribution of professors Roger Dale and Gita Steiner-Khamsi. In their concluding remarks, these two distinguished scholars look at the GEP phenomenon and, in particular, the cases collected in the book, with the different theoretical lenses through which they look at the globalization–education relationship, and as a way to develop some crucial and original insights.

To a great extent, this book focuses on the global south due to the particular nature and intensity of global influences in this area. Developing countries, especially low-income countries, are often highly dependent on foreign expertise, information and, especially, financing (Rose 2007). In low-income contexts, there is a bigger presence of external actors, including international non-governmental organizations (INGOs), donor agencies and international organizations (IOs) that have a great capacity – both material and ideational – to set agendas and priorities in the countries they operate. In this sense, low-income countries' policy landscapes are much more penetrated than countries in more industrialized societies. Furthermore, developing states are not only the object of a more intense flow of external pressures, but usually depend on hindered capacities to mediate supranational policy pressures (Grek et al. 2009).

Taking globalization 'seriously'

While notoriously slippery and expansive (Rupert 2005), 'globalization' is a very well-established term in social sciences research. 'Globalization' can be broadly defined as a constitutive process of increasing interdependence between people, territories and organizations in the economic, political and cultural domains. The dominant processes of globalization can be characterized as hyper-liberalism in the economic domain, governance without government in the political domain, and commodification and consumerism in the cultural one (Dale 2000). Globalization is a very convenient concept for social scientists due to its euphemistic character and due to all the meanings it subsumes within it (such as capitalism, colonialism and Westernization). On occasion, referring to the *supranational* would be more accurate than to the *global*, since many of the trends we are witnessing in education policy are more intense at a regional scale than at the global one.

Taking globalization seriously implies capturing the multiple ways globalization affects education policy. In the following analysis, we detail a comprehensive, although not exhaustive, list of impacts of globalization in education policy.

- Globalization *generates new problems that education policy needs to address* (Ball 1998). Among them, the transformation of the labour market and the reorganization of work worldwide stand out. In a global economy, most countries aim at raising their international competitiveness by offering knowledge-intensive products and services, and new manpower profiles. Accordingly, they expand education and base educational content and processes on skills, competences and the notion of flexibility (Carnoy 2016).

- Globalization, or the 'idea of globalization' (see Hay 2006), *alters the capacity of welfare states* to address education and non-education problems via education policy, as well as the state's capacity to provide and finance education directly in a context of increasing and changing educational demand. To some extent, this is related to the fact that, in a more globalized economic environment, countries, as a way to compete for capital and export markets, change their taxation system towards a more business-friendly, low-taxation model.

- Globalization *revitalizes the role of international agencies* in the making of educational policy. Among them, international governmental organizations (IOs) with an explicit or implicit education mandate, such as the World Bank, the Organization for Economic Co-operation and Development (OECD) or UNESCO, stand out. However, globalization also brings new international players into education policy-making, most of which are non-governmental, including transnational corporations (TNCs) and philanthropic foundations, international consultants and transnational civil society coalitions (Verger et al. 2016a).

- The revitalized role of international players in educational politics contributes to the *deterritorialization of the education policy process* and to the 'national' territory, losing its centrality in such processes (see Robertson, Chapter 2 in this volume). Deterritorialization implies the redefinition of the scale, the space and the dynamics through which education policy is being negotiated, formulated and implemented. International players have an increasing capacity to settle education agendas and define the priorities of countries concerning education reform processes through advice and technical assistance, but also to impose certain policies via funding and aid conditionality.

- Neoliberalism, as the currently dominant political–economic ideology worldwide, frames many of the education policy ideas that circulate internationally (Ball 2012). Proposals such as the introduction of market mechanisms and logics (such as school choice and competition), the liberalization and privatization of the education sector, and the importation of management techniques and leadership styles coming from the corporate sector in public education, resonate strongly in the neoliberal policy landscape.

- Beyond the formulation and dissemination of policies, some IOs have the capacity to *transform the legal framework* of member countries and, by doing so, alter the rules of the game through which policies are being formulated. Some of the most remarkable cases here are the UNESCO conventions or the regional, bilateral and global trade agreements that are being negotiated in the context of the World Trade Organization (WTO) and in other trade *fora*. These types of agreements have the potential to modify a range of in-country 'regulatory barriers' to trade in education, including ownership, taxation, licensing or quality assurance rules (Kelsey 2016).

- The advances in *Information and Communication Technologies (ICT)*, which are, at the same time, cause and consequence of globalization, allow the intensification of the international circulation of policy ideas and the constitution of broader policy networks (Peck and Theodore 2010). The fast evolution of ICT is also transforming education practices and the patters of education delivery, testing and certification and reduces substantially the costs of cross-border distance learning and teaching (Yuan and Powell 2013).

- Globalization also creates a *transnational market of education provision* that complements and/or competes against national education providers. This emerging global market challenges some of the core functions of conventional education systems, such as 'nation building' (Robertson et al. 2002), and promotes English as the international educational *lingua franca* – especially in higher education, but not only.

- Finally, globalization also fosters the organization of *transnational social justice movements* that struggle for the realization of education as a global public good and its endorsement as a human right. These movements contest the neoliberal global education agenda and aim at promoting alternatives to it (Mundy and Murphy 2001).

In conclusion, globalization needs to be first and foremost understood as a new terrain, the new '*context of contexts*' (cf. Peck and Theodore 2010), of education policy. It defines the problems to be addressed and, at the same time, alters the capacity of the states to respond to these problems by themselves; it generates the conditions for the emergence of international actors and makes the transnational organization of policy networks more pressing; and it is a strategically selective and conflicting terrain for educational policy-making that is more conducive to certain education policy ideas and political actors than others.

Global education policy studies: Methodological considerations

Globalization has not only altered education policy, but also the way we think about and study education policy. GEP is an emerging area of research that *examines the different ways in which globalization processes, agents and events contribute to educational policy change on a range of scales, and with what consequences*. GEP studies raise important theoretical and methodological implications for education policy analysts. The shaping of this new area does not simply mean introducing globalization as a 'topic' onto the educational research agenda, but rather revising certain theoretical postulations, models of analysis and research methodologies (Green 2003). Many of these implications have to be seen in relation to the changing relationship between the state and education in a more globalized policy-scape.

The first and most obvious methodological implication is that globalization challenges the basic unit of analysis, the nation state, and, accordingly, the *methodological nationalism* that predominates in educational research and in comparative education in particular (Green 2003; Dale and Robertson 2007).

Based on a Westphalian understanding of political authority,[2] education policies have traditionally been developed within national settings. However, public policies are today the result of a 'combination of political forces, social structures, cultural traditions and economic processes entangled in a matrix of intersecting multi-level, multi-scalar (local, national, regional and global) sites and spaces' (Yeates 2001, p. 637). The concept of scale, instead of that of level, is helpful for this purpose because it allows an understanding of the production of space as a mutable product of social relations and struggle in which the global and the local are mutually embedded (see Robertson, Chapter 2 in this volume). A multiscalar conception of policy processes permits us to unpack the nature of global educational reform by exploring who controls what in which scale, from the local to the global, and the interrelationships therein (Dale 2005).

Secondly, globalization urges us to transcend *educationism* (Dale and Robertson 2007). This means that, when analysing new policy trends, policy changes and/or regulatory transformations in the educational field, we need to consider that these elements are in most cases shaped by extra-educational structures, events and processes (such as the prevailing welfare regime in a particular world region, the changing levels of poverty and social cohesion, societal values or the economic performance in a country). Comparative education is still strongly marked by a disciplinary parochialism that encourages researchers to base education policy studies on approaches that come exclusively from within the field of education (Dale 2005). To overcome this problem, many educational changes should be better understood as being embedded within interdependent local, national and global political economy complexes (Novelli and Lopes Cardozo 2008).

A third challenge concerns *methodological statism*, that is, assuming that the state is a rational and cohesive entity and that it has the monopoly over political action within the borders that delimit a territory. Overcoming statism implies, first, that the state cannot be understood as a monolithic unit of analysis, but as a range of diverse apparatuses that represent distinct material condensations of social forces (Hartmann 2007). In fact, the different (and differentiated) factions constituting the state usually push for diverging, and sometimes even contradictory interests and agendas both in international organizations and at the domestic level (Cox 1995). For instance, it is quite common that, within the same government, the minister of education and the minister of finance have very different preferences about the amount of public resources needed in the education system.

Overcoming methodological statism implies understanding that non-state actors are also relevant political agents in the governance of education (Dale and Robertson 2007). Recognizing the political relevance of non-state actors does not necessarily mean assuming that the state is becoming less powerful.

Rather, it means accepting that the role and functions of the state have been altered and redefined in the broad scenario of governance, that other players are actively participating at the levels of education policies and politics, and that the state is not as autonomous in relation to the definition of certain policy issues as it was in other periods (Hay 2006, see Box 1.1).

Box 1.1 Global governance, education and the state

The notion of 'global governance' aims at capturing an increasingly complex policy landscape in which state and non-state actors, which operate at a range of scales, gain political authority and presence in policy fields such as education. Global governance refers to the intensification of the interactions and the embeddedness between different scales in policy processes. According to Dale (2005, p. 132), 'What we are witnessing is a developing functional, scalar and sectoral division of the labour of educational governance.' Funding, provision and ownership of education are carried out by a broad range of supranational, national and subnational agents, including IOs, the state, the market, the community and/or the families. To a great extent, the global governance of education means the redefinition of the relationship between education and the state. In fact, the state today is less inclined towards the direct provision of education and more towards the establishment of standards and evaluation mechanisms that determine whether schools and universities are achieving standards effectively (Neave 1998).

Global governance refers to both 'formal institutions and regimes empowered to enforce compliance, as well as informal arrangements that people and institutions either have agreed to or perceive to be in their interest' (Commission on Global Governance 1995, p. 4). Indeed, currently, the activities of most states and, in particular, state social policies are framed and conditioned by a dense web of international legal and political obligations (Yeates 2001). These obligations include, in the case of education, legally binding agreements such as the above-mentioned GATS agreement or the UNESCO conventions, as well as non-binding declarations such as the Education 2030 Framework for Action or the Bologna Declaration, which have also triggered important educational transformations both in the South and in the North. Overall, beyond material resources and hard law, sociocultural norms and soft law are also powerful global governance devices with effective regulatory powers (Snyder 1999).

Bourdieu's concept of *field* contributes to overcoming some of the methodological 'isms' in the analysis of GEP sketched above (i.e. nationalism, educationism and statism). Thus, rather than understanding policy diffusion or transfer as the simple correspondence or influence between two levels (e.g. from the global to the local) or two institutions (e.g. IO-state or state A-state B), it is more accurate to consider that a global education field, which interacts with the broader social, political and economic fields, is being constituted (Vavrus 2004). The increasing political dimension acquired by international standardized tests such as Programme for International Student Assessment (PISA) or by educational development goals such as the sustainable development goals (SDGs); the constitution of global education funding mechanisms such as the Global Partnership for Education; or the growing cross-border flows of researchers, teachers and students are all tendencies that have generated growing awareness among policy-makers, scholars, students and practitioners of being part of a common 'global education policy' field.

Overall, fields are conflicting terrains. Different actors struggle for the transformation and/or reproduction of fields, and for positioning themselves in a central place in the field through the activation of networks, capital, institutions and/or ideas, among other social forces (Bourdieu 1999; Beckert 2010). Despite being open to the participation and involvement of a broad range of actors, however, a field is far from a flat terrain. In the GEP field, not all of the actors have the same power and capacity to mobilize the different types of capital that are necessary to promote their interests and ideas (Lingard et al. 2005). Key international players and policy entrepreneurs, with the capacity to transcend different scales at any moment, have more chance of introducing their ideas, preferences and languages in this field.

To sum up, globalization introduces new methodological and epistemological challenges in educational policy research. In fact, taking globalization seriously means the revision of the core questions that frame education policy research agendas and projects (Dale 2005). There are at least four main sets of interlinked research questions that can contribute to putting globalization at the centre of education policy studies. These questions allow us to analyse the whole GEP process: from the structural selectivity of certain policies to its actual implementation in particular contexts.[3] They are as follows:

1   What is the nature of the relationship between globalization and processes of educational change? Why is 'global education policy' happening?

2   How are global education agendas and global policy solutions formulated and constituted, and by whom? Why do certain policies and not others become selected and privileged in global agendas?

3   To what extent are GEPs being disseminated effectively? Why do local policy-makers and practitioners adopt them?

4   What are the mediating elements and institutions affecting the translation and re-contextualization of global policies to particular education contexts? What are the specific challenges associated with the enactment of GEPs in specific contexts, including dynamics of resistance? What are the local effects of GEPs in terms of educational processes, students and teachers' satisfaction, educational quality and equity and so on?

In the following sections we explore how the GEP literature has dealt with these different questions.

Theorizing global education policy

There are two main macro-approaches that broadly explore the relationship between globalization and educational policy, as well as what is the nature of the global drivers affecting educational change. We refer, on the one hand, to sociological institutionalism, represented in comparative education by the 'World Society' theory (also known as World Culture theory) and, on the other, to IPE approaches, that find in the 'Globally Structured Agenda for Education' one of its most remarkable formulations.

World society theorists argue that a single global model of schooling has spread around the world as part of the diffusion of a more general culturally embedded model of the modern nation state (Anderson-Levitt 2003). The need for nation states to conform to an international ideal of the rationalized bureaucratic state has led to a process of institutional isomorphism and convergence (Drezner 2001). According to this theoretical approach, nation states expand schooling as part of a broader process of adherence to world models of the organization of sovereignty (the modern state) and the organization of society as composed of individuals (the modern nation) (Meyer et al. 1997). Education is a key area for governments to demonstrate to the international community that they are building a modern state. World Society scholars have validated their thesis empirically by showing, for instance, that school expansion in African countries has not been so related to their level of development, industrialization or urbanization, but to how close these countries have been to colonial powers and Western influence (Meyer et al. 1992a).

World Society research problematizes the presumption that education measures are applicable globally, independently of the needs and capacities of the countries adopting them. They observe that education policies (but also health, fiscal policies, etc.) are being adopted in a quite routine way all around the planet due to external and internal legitimation reasons. This is something especially challenging for developing countries since, despite commanding fewer resources and organizational capacity than rich countries, they feel similar pressures to comply with educational reform imperatives (Meyer et al. 1997). Nonetheless, to these scholars, the main point is not whether state educational policy is exogenously influenced, but the fact that the state itself is an exogenously constructed entity.

World Society scholars have not traditionally focused on specific education policy reform models, but on the constitution of education itself as a world model. Nonetheless, these scholars have also conducted extensive research on international convergence around curricular contents (Meyer et al. 1992b) and, more recently, on institutional isomorphism in higher education policy (Ramirez 2006), lifelong learning (LLL) systems (Jakobi 2009), educational evaluation (Benavot and Tanner 2008), school decentralization (Astiz 2006) or multicultural education (Terra and Bromley 2012).

Some authors, despite not being strictly part of the World Society school, follow an analogous neoinstitutionalist and culture-centred approach to analyse education reform. This is, for instance, the case of Schriewer and Martinez (2004), who argue that decisions on education policy (and, more broadly speaking, the educational conceptions of decision-makers) are affected by the dissemination of a world-level developmental cultural account and education ideology. Based on Luhmann's work, these authors propose the concept of 'externalisation' to analyse the way policy-makers argue for the necessity of education reform based on external models.[4] Externalization can be subtle and does not refer to specific models, but to a web of norms and beliefs that make national constituencies more receptive to educational reform. Education reforms are thus embedded in a universalized web of ideas about development and social problems, 'a web of reciprocal references which takes a life of its own, moving, reinforcing and dynamising the worldwide universalisation of educational ideas, models, standards, and options of reform' (Schriewer 2000, p. 334).

International Political Economy theories do not put so much emphasis on cultural or ideational factors, but on economic ones as the main drivers of educational change. According to the Globally Structured Educational Agenda approach (GSEA), the world capitalist economy is the driving force of globalization and the first causal source of multiple transformations manifested in different policy sectors, including education (Dale 2000).

The World Society model has an implicit theory of the state in which legitimation, both internally and externally, is the main problem to be addressed by the state. In contrast, for the GSEA, apart from providing the basis of legitimation, the core problems of the state include supporting the regime of accumulation and providing a context for its reproduction (Robertson et al. 2002). The core problems of the capitalist state cannot all be solved together, and solutions to them tend to be rather contradictory. These problems and their tensions, which are exacerbated in the context of economic globalization, provide the dynamic of educational systems and condition importantly the state educational agenda (Dale 2000).

IPE approaches focus on the indirect effects of globalization in education, and not exclusively on the direct influences between countries or between IOs and countries. They suggest that the most important way globalization is affecting education policy is by altering the structural conditions in which education reform happens, including the conditions in which reform is framed and perceived by policy-makers as necessary. A good example of how globalization altered the structural conditions of educational governance can be found in the World Bank-/IMF-sponsored Structural Adjustment Programmes (SAPs) implemented in Latin American and African countries in the 1980s and 1990s. The SAPs had serious repercussions in education, first by lowering the public budget necessary to fund educational expansion and, second, by raising the levels of poverty and, consequently, the opportunity costs of schooling (Bonal 2002). The new social structure after the SAPs period became highly conducive to the emergence and implementation of Conditional Cash Transfer policies, which promote, via economic incentives, poor students attending school (see Bonal et al., Chapter 7 in this volume).

For IPE scholars, economic globalization and the competitive pressures associated with this phenomenon are provoking educational changes all around the planet. Globalization is putting governments under financial pressure to control inflation and the public deficit and, as a consequence, to reduce public spending growth and find alternative funding sources to cover educational expansion. In fact, many governments believe that, in a global economy, they have to reduce the rates of corporate taxation to avoid capital moving away from their jurisdiction. In this intensely competitive economic environment, finance-driven reforms such as privatization and decentralization become highly attractive (Carnoy 2016).

Furthermore, in a globalized economy, most political and economic actors, including state actors (Cerny 1997), aim to raise their economic competitiveness and performance, and perceive education and knowledge as key competitive assets for this purpose (Brown and Lauder 1996 and Carnoy and Rhoten 2002). This is also the case of individuals who increasingly conceive education as a 'positional good' (Marginson 2004) in a highly competitive and dualized labour market. These beliefs have spread to the extent that most countries and regions in the world today aspire to become 'knowledge economies'. The knowledge economy works as a powerful economic imaginary (Jessop 2008) or a 'political condensation' (cf. Ball 1998) that frames the preferences of a broad range of actors and guides the way they intervene in society. The knowledge economy ideal puts education at the centre of the economic strategies of governments due to its crucial contribution to the formation of knowledge-intensive manpower, applied research and knowledge transfer (Barrow et al. 2004). The knowledge economy is often associated with an educational reform jargon based on the principles of quality, learning, accountability and standards, and has effectively contributed to shaping education reform in countries as different as Denmark, Nepal and China (Carney 2009).

The emphasis given by IPE scholars to ideational factors such as the 'knowledge economy' shows that there is room for reconciliation between materialist and constructivist approaches when it comes to explaining educational change. Traditionally, for IPE scholars, ideas or cultural factors have been subordinated to material factors in understanding social and institutional changes, or have been simply neglected. The Cultural Political Economy (CPE) approach is an attempt to overcome such an ideational-material dualism in political analysis. CPE adds to conventional political economy a clear focus on semiosis (understood as all forms of social production of intersubjective meaning) and a rich account of the semiotic dimension of economic and political orders (Jessop 2008). CPE promotes a more critical understanding of the cultural embedding of broader economic, political and institutional transformations, and highlights the role of discursively selective 'imaginaries' and structurally selective institutions – such as an increasingly competitive capitalist state – in such transformations (Sayer 2001; Jessop 2010). In this volume, Lopes Cardozo and Novelli adopt a CPE approach to show how the appearance of the education in emergencies field is the consequence of economic interests and geopolitical factors, but also the globalization of humanitarian norms and discourses on education as life-saving.

Overall, IPE approaches are concerned with globalization's effects in education for two main reasons. First, globalization provokes neoliberal and efficiency-driven types of reforms that, among other implications, put education equity goals and values in the background (Carnoy 1999). Second, globalization implies the weakening of sovereignty and democratic control since, in a global education policy field, many important education decisions are being taken within or strongly influenced by diffuse networks of experts that have not been democratically elected (Moutsios 2010; Poppema 2012). However, IPE scholars also pay attention to the potential of social movements when it comes to counterbalance some of these dynamics and to reclaim and re-democratize education policy spaces (Stromquist 2015).

Setting education policies in global agendas: The key role of IOs and beyond

The two theoretical approaches described above focus on the structural conditions that favour the dissemination of global policies. However, GEP studies are also attentive to the more agent-level types of analysis concerning how policies are settled in global agendas, and by whom. As we show in this section, there is a range of research that pays attention to the structuring capacity of international organizations (IOs) and other types of transnational actors, as well as to how these actors alter decision-making dynamics in multiscalar policy systems.

Currently, a dense network of IOs interacts and competes to promote their educational discourses and preferred policy solutions within the GEP field. IOs play a key role in agenda-setting processes. According to the World Society approach, IOs contribute to policy convergence in education by spreading the Western system of political organization and state authority around the world (Meyer et al. 1992a). Certainly, IOs – including INGOs – might represent Western modernity broadly speaking. However, when we look at IOs policy preferences in more detail, we observe that they express divergent and even rivalling education agendas in relation to a broad range of policy-related themes and notions such as the knowledge economy (Robertson 2005), participation in education (Edwards and Klees 2015) and education for all (EFA; Chabbott 2003; King 2007).

For IPE theories, IOs are conceptualized as key transmitters of particular views of education and educational reform, basically instrumental and market oriented, to national contexts. Roger Dale (1999) systematizes a range of policy mechanisms activated by IOs and other external actors that allow them to frame and influence national and subnational education policies in a more or less coercive way (see Box 1.2). In recent decades, these global mechanisms have acquired more centrality than traditional mechanisms of bilateral influence such as 'policy borrowing' and 'policy learning' (Dale 1999). IOs need to be seen as both forums of cooperation and struggle between member nations, as well as autonomous policy actors in themselves. The most powerful states usually try to instrumentalize IOs to align these organizations with their own economic and geopolitical interests. However, IOs are neither exclusively at the service of member-states nor simply the extension of particular national interests. IOs' bureaucracies are also relatively autonomous sources of power with sufficient room of manoeuvre to interpret and redefine the broad political mandate of the organization, and to exercise power over their members accordingly (Heyneman 2003, Mundy and Verger 2015). The main sources of political power of IOs' bureaucracies are usually

Box 1.2 Global mechanisms of influence

- *Imposition:* External actors compel some countries to take on particular education policies (the classic example being the conditionality to credit of the World Bank, the IMF and other aid agencies to borrower countries).
- *Harmonization:* A set of countries mutually agree on the implementation of common policies in a certain policy area (e.g. the configuration of the European Space for Higher Education).
- *Dissemination:* External agents use persuasion and its technical knowledge to convince countries on the implementation of certain policies (e.g. through annual reports, best practices databases and technical assistance).
- *Standardization:* The international community defines and promotes the adhesion to a set of policy principles and standards that frame the countries' behaviour (e.g. international performance tests, such as PISA, contribute to the standardization of curricular content at the global level). *Installing interdependence* occurs when countries agree to achieve common objectives to tackle problems that require international cooperation (e.g. climate change, 'education for all').

Source: Adapted from Dale 1999.

informal and rely to a great extent on the legitimacy of the rational–legal authority that they represent, as well as on their control over information, data and technical expertise (Finnemore 1996). IOs' legitimacy relies also on their capacity to *technify* education problems and solutions. In other words, the capacity of influence of many IOs depends on their ability of portraying as technical, issues that are perceived as highly political and sensitive at the national scale. Once IOs are conceived as political or ideological agents – as has happened to the World Bank in several Latin American countries – their capacity of influencing national policy becomes substantially restricted.

According to Barnett and Finnemore (2004), IOs exercise power by organizing three types of apparently apolitical and technical actions: first, *classifying the world*, for instance by stratifying countries according to their level of performance in international evaluations such as TIMMS or PISA and, accordingly, putting governments under great pressure to introduce education reforms; secondly, *fixing meanings in the social world* by, for instance, defining what educational quality means, which is something that IOs can do explicitly, but also indirectly in the form of indicators and benchmarks; and thirdly, *articulating and disseminating new norms, principles and beliefs* by, for instance, spreading what they consider 'good' or 'best' practices in educational development.

Overall, the power of IOs does not only rely on disseminating specific policy solutions. Within the GEP field, power is also about the capacity to define the main priorities and goals of educational change, as well as what are the main problems that education systems should try to address. The global battle to define discussion on whether learning outcomes should be the main focus of educational reform globally that we have observed in the context of the so-called post-2015 debate[5] illustrates well how important it is to conceive the problems' definition moment as a core component of agenda-setting processes.

International actors other than IOs have also the capacity to influence and frame GEP by resorting to different forms of ideas (including norms, principled believes, and scientific evidence). We refer to actors – or networks of actors – such as epistemic communities (Chabbott 2003), transnational civil society networks (Mundy and Murphy 2001), international consultants (Gunter et al. 2015), policy entrepreneurs (Ball 2007; Robertson and Verger 2012) or international foundations (Srivastava and Oh 2010; Scott and Jabbar 2014). Under some circumstances, these types of actors can mould state preferences for various policy options, or help states to identify their interests and to position themselves in relation to certain policy matters, above all in moments of uncertainty. In fact, in many places, these new actors are becoming an integral part of emerging forms of global governance, and count on an increasing capacity to frame global policy agendas and to provoke processes of policy transfer and learning.

The power of non-state actors in international politics is not a new phenomenon; what has changed is the way these actors mainly interact with and within the global arena. Decades ago, non-state actors tried to influence international forums and agreements *through* the state (i.e. they interpellated one or more nation states as a way to make their demands heard in the international arena through the states in question). However, currently, multilateralism is moving away from an exclusively state-based structure, and civil society and private actors play an increasingly relevant role in multilateral structures directly. In this emerging 'complex multilateralism' (O'Brien et al. 2000), non-state actors have more spaces and opportunities to influence IOs without the necessary mediation of the state. Examples of 'complex multilateralism' in the educational sector can be found in the participation of INGOS and corporate actors in the board of the Global Partnership for Education (Menashy 2016), or in the increasing role of TNCs in educational aid structures (van Fleet 2012, Junemann and Ball 2015).

TNCs such as Microsoft are promoting educational programmes and establishing bilateral relations with Southern countries, as traditional donor countries would do (Bhanji 2008), or provide international organizations such as UNESCO with funds (Bull and McNeill 2007). These emerging forms of private authority in education are under suspicion due to the conflict of interests they generate – since private players are usually policy advocates and service providers at the same time (Junemann and Ball 2015). For instance, many ICT companies, such as Microsoft and Intel, conceive corporate social responsibility as a tool to open new markets abroad (van Fleet 2012), and big consultancy firms are advocating for PPPs in education using evidence-based arguments, but at the same time benefit from contracts for educational services provision all around the world (Robertson and Verger 2012).

The international actors we have referred to in this section (both IOs and non-state actors) have very different interests and reasons to become involved in the GEP arena. However, what many of them have in common is that they are knowledge-intensive entities, and that their main power source relies on knowledge and ideas (with TNCs and development banks being an exception to this premise due to the huge economic power they also count on). Thus, most of these non-state actors are gaining authority in global governance structures because of the scientific knowledge they possess, their track record for problem-solving and, in the particular case of civil society networks and social movements, their principle-oriented views to the problems they deal with (Keck and Sikkink 1998; Haas 2004).

However, being knowledge actors does not mean that international players are continuously innovating and/or producing new policy alternatives. Most of the time, policy entrepreneurs sitting in international foundations, think tanks or IOs act more as brokers and framers of policy ideas than as pure theorizers. They usually take already-existing policy practices, relabel them and sell them around. Many GEPs have started their journey in this way, being first formulated and implemented in particular countries. School-based management originated in the UK (Ball 2007), outcomes-based education in New Zealand (Spreen 2004) and charter schools in the United States (Bulkley and Fisler 2003). Since the most influential international policy entrepreneurs come from the Anglo-Saxon world, it does not come as a surprise that their policy *référentiels* come from Anglo-Saxon countries. There are some exceptions, however. For example, Conditional-Cash Transfer schemes started being implemented in different localities in Brazil and Mexico and later on became adopted and spread as a global model by the World Bank and other regional development banks (see Bonal et al., Chapter 7 in this volume).

Adoption: Why do policy-makers *buy* into GEP?

The adoption moment is the other side of the coin of international policy diffusion. For education policies to become effectively globalized, they need to be adopted and institutionalized in networks of practices by policy-makers and practitioners. Often, countries adopt GEPs and programmes because they are externally imposed via aid conditionality or coercion (see Box 1.2) or because nation states are inclined to adhere to world models of educational organization (as the world society theory would assume). However, national policy-makers have more room of manoeuvre in educational reform processes than some macro-theories predict, and often adopt GEPs in a voluntary way. Thus, in a globalized education policy field, it is more relevant than ever to understand – and to empirically explore – why it is that local policy-makers engage with GEPs, as well as what are the processes, reasons and circumstances that favour GEP adoption.

A rationalist approach to policy transfer would provide with a first type of answer to the policy adoption question. According to rationalistic policy transfer theory, local policy-makers would adopt and implement global policies because there is enough evidence showing that these policies 'work' or have worked well elsewhere. For rationalism, policy-makers are well-informed rational actors with sufficient time and capacity to scan the international education policy arena and choose the most suitable policy solutions for their educational systems. However, rationalism is insufficient to understand why there are so many education reform models that disseminate globally, despite there is not sufficient empirical evidence supporting the benefits of these models. Policies such as universal voucher schemes, high-stakes accountability or even some forms of child-centred pedagogies have been extensively criticized for their uneven and even negative impacts, but this has not prevented them from continuing to be internationally disseminated (Luke 2003; see Altinyelken, Chapter 10 in this volume).

A more nuanced answer to the GEP adoption question would be provided by critical constructivism and would say that policy-makers adopt GEP because they *perceive* that these policies work. Policy-makers could perceive that some global policy solutions are appropriate for their countries for educational, but also for political and economic reasons. The literature is very rich in explanations and hypotheses related to this alternative line of argument. These include explanations focusing on the persuasive capacity of global agents to frame policy decisions, but also explanations focusing on local actors that interact with the global arena as a way to gain political credibility and advance their pre-established policy preferences (Mundy et al. 2016; see Addey and Sellar, Chapter 5 in this volume). We explore in more detail these and other policy adoption factors in the following lines.

Framing matters. Policy entrepreneurs are very active promoters of global policy solutions. Currently, the GEP field is packed with a broad range of policy entrepreneurs that compete among themselves to make policy-makers aware of the educational problems they face and, more importantly, of the effectiveness of their policy solutions in addressing these problems. In general terms, more than the internal consistency of policy ideas, the way these ideas are framed and presented affect policy-makers' decisions on whether to buy or not to buy into a certain policy (Verger 2012). IOs and other types of policy entrepreneurs know this well and put a lot of resources and effort in knowledge dissemination and mobilization. Global policy ideas are launched and spread through highly distributed policy briefs, papers and reports, and in public or private events (seminars, workshops, report launches, etc.) that are usually well attended by national political leaders and policy-makers (see Avelar et al. in this volume). Despite IOs' use of an apparently neutral and technical discourse, at the same time they strongly advocate their proposals, often with great enthusiasm. To frame GEP in an appealing way, IOs need to present new policies in a clear and concise manner, and convince countries that these policies are most likely to be taken up if they are perceived as technically workable, and fit within their budgetary and administrative constraints (Kingdon 2002). Not surprisingly, many policy entrepreneurs highlight the cost-effectiveness and efficiency gains of the policies they are promoting.

However, framing strategies are often in dispute with scientific rigor. In order to sell their programmes and frame them in a more convincing way, policy entrepreneurs might on occasion need, more or less explicitly, to simplify reality (Ball 1998) and resort to different types of logical fallacy and argumentative shortcuts (Verger 2012). Indeed, the international travelling of education policies has been strengthened by the consolidation of the *evidence-based policy* approach (i.e. basing policy decisions on solid research that shows what kind of policies 'work'). Evidence-based policy is seen by many policy-makers and donors as a superior approach to taking policy decisions, and it has arguably many advantages over simply political- or ideological-based forms of decision-taking. Nonetheless, it is well known that evidence can be easily instrumentalized to support the adoption of certain policies instead of others. Especially in relation to contentious areas of policy research such as quasi-markets in education (Lubienski et al. 2014), accountability reforms (Reckhow et al. 2016) or incentivist policies (Scott and Jabbar 2014), think tanks, IOs and other types of knowledge brokers can sum up sympathetic data and subsidiary arguments in support of their pre-established policy preferences. Such cherry-picking practice means that research travels straight from ideology to policy recommendations, and uses science and evidence mainly as a legitimatory frame. Hence, according to Pawson (2006), rather than evidence-based policy, 'policy-based evidence' is a more common practice in many policy circles.[6]

In general, those policies that resonate best within the prevailing form of capitalist accumulation and the prevailing development policy paradigm will have more chances of being retained in global agendas and selected in particular countries (Dale 2000). From a semiotic perspective, neoliberalism and related policy discourses have become hegemonic and a sort of common sense. Ideas such as performance-based incentives, competitive funding, education as a competitiveness device and so on have been interiorized by many decision-makers and practitioners (Carney 2009). As a consequence, market-oriented principles and logics are shaping the parameters of policy-making in many countries (Taylor and Henry 2000). However, at the same time, governmental decision-makers often avoid hard-privatization policies (such as school vouchers) since these policies are very controversial and usually perceived as too ideological. That is why, to make these policies more normatively acceptable, most IOs promoting quasi-markets in education avoid using the 'privatization' concept and use instead more friendly concepts such as public–private *partnerships* (Robertson and Verger 2012).

Global status and deterritorialization. As pointed out earlier, the most well-known GEPs have a local origin, which is usually Western and, more precisely, Anglo-Saxon. For this reason, it is useful to think about GEPs as globalized localisms (cf. Santos 2005). Likewise, once a critical number of countries borrow a policy, it seems as though its particular origins vanish; the policy becomes *global* and is traded as a *global model* (Steiner-Khamsi 2010). The acquisition of 'global status' raises the attractiveness of policies and predisposes policy-makers to discuss educational reforms guided by them.

Nonetheless, the global prestige of the actors backing GEPs is similarly important. Usually, the most successful policy entrepreneurs are based in IOs that are located at the interstices of a range of influential social and policy networks (Campbell 2004). Indeed, in many countries, the opinion of a World Bank expert will be more considered than that of a scholar from a local university, even if both actors have a similar high-quality training and propose the same successful or failed policy ideas. The definitive move for a policy to become globally traded comes when a global institution that counts on high levels of exposure and good networks adopts it. On occasion, social networks are key to understanding this type of movement. For instance, outcomes-based education became a global policy in part because one of the promoters in New Zealand, Maris O'Rourke, became the director of education of the World Bank (Steiner-Khamsi 2004).

Windows of opportunity and GEP selectivity. Some scholars consider that policy-makers perceive importing new policies from elsewhere as necessary when the situation of their education systems is critical, or in the context of broader societal and economic crises. Phillips and Ochs (2003) use the concept of 'impulses' to refer to the preconditions for borrowing. Impulses include an eclectic set of elements such as internal dissatisfaction with the education system on the part of families, teachers and so on; the collapse or inadequacy of educational provision; negative external evaluation results; political change and the changing demands for education; and so on.

IOs play a key role in generating some of these aspects, especially when it comes to making governments and the public opinion aware of their educational problems and the need to implement reforms accordingly. International standardized tests such as PISA have generated a feeling of reform urgency even in powerful and economically developed countries such as Germany and Switzerland (Bieber 2010). In the global south, the fact that many countries are still far from reaching internationally agreed education development goals – such as the EFA goals in the past and, more recently, the SDGs – is opening political opportunities for many policy entrepreneurs trying to sell their policy prescriptions (see Sayed in this volume). For instance, educational corporations like Pearson are framing the desirability of investing in low-fee private schools in low-income countries by resorting to a humanistic rhetoric and to the key role that the private sector could play within global education compacts such as the SDGs (see Verger et al. in this volume).

Natural catastrophes and post-conflict settings also open important windows of political opportunity to advocates of educational reform. In these extreme situations (such as post-Katrina New Orleans and post-earthquake Haiti), education reform advocates benefit from a sense of reconstruction urgency and, accordingly, insufficient time and conditions for proper policy deliberation. Such conditions allow reformers to accelerate changes that, in a more stable situation, would be much more difficult to promote successfully (Verger et al. 2016b).

Instrumentalizing GEP. Steiner-Khamsi (2004, 2010), on the basis of intensive fieldwork in several Asian countries, concludes that local policy-makers have a double register in their education policy discourse; they speak differently to local constituents than to international donors. Policy-makers adopt the international language of reform as a way of securing international funds but, once they get these funds, they implement the type of reforms they consider more relevant and, somehow, go ahead with 'business as usual'. Thus, according to this scholar, more than *global policies*, what is being actually disseminated is a *global policy speak*. This is indeed a sceptical approach to globalization's effects in policy change that breaks with the usual hyperglobalist approaches that perceive developing countries as passive recipients of global policies.

Although following a different reasoning, Martens and Wolf (2009) also consider that countries can instrumentalize the global arena to advance certain policy reforms. According to them, countries approach global institutions to reduce transaction costs for problem-solving and policy formulation purposes, but also to gain leverage at the domestic level when it comes to advancing policy changes. From this point of view, global policy recommendations would be instrumentally invoked by policy-makers for legitimatory reasons and as a way of softening internal resistance. The Bologna process has been, to some extent, manipulated in this way by a range of European countries to advance pre-established governmental policy preferences (Huisman and Van Der Wende 2004). In her analysis of the political dimension of PISA, Grek (2007, p. 35) makes a similar point when she states that 'reference to "world situations" enables policy-makers to make the case for education reforms at home that would otherwise be contested'.

Re-contextualization and enactment

Research on the re-contextualization of GEP traces the different translations of policy programmes, and tries to find out about the multiple relationships that reconstitute such programmes in multiple scales (Mukhopadhyay and Sriprakash 2011). Experiences from the field tell us that we should question those hyperbolic arguments about globalization as a driver of global convergence of policy and practice in education.[7] Globalization is not an absolute project with identical effects in all places (Appadurai 1996; Robertson and Dale 2006). Although globalization presents common features around the world, the effects of globalization in education policy are mediated by domestic history and politics, and by the complex interplay of global and local forces, among other contingencies.

Several authors stress that borrowed policy ideas are modified, indigenized or resisted as they are implemented in the recipient countries (Phillips and Ochs 2003; Steiner-Khamsi and Stolpe 2006); as a consequence, global educational reforms tend to develop into multiform policy patterns (Schriewer 2012; Mundy et al. 2016). On their part, Peck and Theodore (2010, p. 170), who are key proponents of the so-called *policy mobilities* approach, consider that global policies mutate during their journeys and 'rarely travel as complete packages, they move in bits and pieces – as selective discourses, inchoate ideas, and synthesized models – and they therefore "arrive" not as replicas but as policies already-in-transformation'. Similarly, Ball (1998, 2016), considers that global policies are barely translated into policy practices in pristine form since policies are something more complex than a 'text' that is easily transferable across scales. Policies are also part of an often-disputed technical and political debate that is highly contingent and situated (see also Avelar et al., Chapter 3, and Edwards, Chapter 6, in this volume).

Overall, since imported education policies are locally mediated and re-contextualized through multiple processes, the consequences of transfer remains unpredictable (Beech 2006). By ignoring differences in contextual capacity and culture at national, regional and local levels, globalization has resulted in unintended and unexpected consequences for educational practice, and runs the risk of deteriorating education quality (Carnoy and Rhoten 2002). The development of global education programmes is often questioned for not taking sufficiently into account the social context and needs (Crossley and Watson 2003). In the literature, we find four main arguments that reflect on why the GEP re-contextualization can be so problematic, especially in developing countries. According to their different emphases, we call these explanations *material, institutional, cultural* and *scalar*.

Material. As Lewin (2007) notes, it is not appropriate to import models that might have worked in consolidated, well-funded, highly professionalized and well-regulated educational systems to places whose educational conditions are far from reaching these standards. Many developing countries often do not have the appropriate material and human resources to implement very costly and technically demanding global education programmes such as quasi-markets in education or high-stakes accountability policies. The World Bank often faces this issue with the projects it finances. The 2011 report of the World Bank's Independent Evaluation Group finds quite 'uneven results' in the Bank's portfolio of education projects, precisely, due to 'design and implementation weaknesses' including 'overly complex designs relative to local capacities' (IEG 2011, p. 13).

However, local policy-makers are often aware of the resources available and the material needs in their countries when engaging with GEP and, accordingly, adapt global discourses selectively. This is for instance the case of many African governments when embracing worldwide principles on LLL, since the governments conceive LLL as adult literacy and basic education, instead of higher education or alternative qualification frameworks as more industrialized countries do (Jakobi 2009). Bonal, Tarabini and Rambla (Chapter 7 in this volume) show how technical capacities, the economic resources available and, specifically, the final design of global policy models, in this case Conditional Cash Transfers, are key mediating factors in understanding the outcomes of these models in the terrain.

Institutional. Institutions of a different nature, including political institutions, shape the local retention and adaptation of global policy models. According to Taylor and Henry (2000), partisan politics and political ideology are the main reasons why nations do not deliver equally in the GEP field. Specifically, these authors show that government ideologies (market-liberal, liberal-democratic and social-democratic) represent a key filter when it comes to adopting and adapting the OECD recommendations in educational policy. Similarly, welfare regimes have also the potential to strategically mediate the trajectory of global education reforms, with liberal welfare states traditionally more inclined to promote market approaches, and social democratic welfare states more conducive to strengthen public education and citizens' participation in educational reforms.

The political participation tradition of a country (including the level of openness of the polity to social movements) or the presence of veto points in political architectures also explains whether GEPs have more chances of being enacted and modified. Global reform models are often selectively retained as the result of political conflicts and oppositional movements. Once a government announces its education reform plans, political actors and other stakeholders, according to their level of (dis)agreement with these plans, articulate strategies of opposition or support. The consequent negotiation and conflict may result in the transformation, partial displacement or total rejection of the initial government plans (Bardach 2006).

Historical institutionalism has a long tradition of studying the mediating role of institutional legacies and national regulatory frameworks in the adaptation of global education models. According to this approach, external models will not substitute existing institutions in a drastic way. Due to the path-dependent nature of institutions – and due to the fact that those actors that make up institutions have an interest in maintaining institutions as they are – gradual changes are more likely to occur. In comparative education, several studies emphasize the mediating role of political and socio-economic institutions in the re-contextualization of international policy frameworks such as education assessment systems (Benveniste 2002), decentralization reforms (Rhoten 2000) and skill formation regimes (Busemeyer and Vossiek 2016).

Cultural. Another group of scholars highlights how a range of cultural processes (such as interpretation and meaning-making) and cultural frameworks (including group identities and predominant public sentiments in a society) can mediate effectively GEP adoption and implementation. Anthropological policy studies have developed this approach by focusing on the relationship between, on the one hand, local knowledge, culture and identities and, on the other, dynamics of global policy translation and localization (Anderson-Levitt 2003; Phillips and Stambach 2008). Similarly to the policy mobilities approach mentioned above, this scholarship tradition shows that local actors, including local policy-makers, teachers, school principals and so on, always transform the official models they are handed through dynamics of interpretation and translation (Anderson-Levitt 2003, p. 4). One of the most recurrent outcomes of researchers adopting such a *global-policy localization* approach is that the real meaning of global policies varies radically in the different contexts where these policies penetrate (Vavrus and Barlett 2006).

Researchers that are part of this tradition usually resort to ethnographic methods as a way to 'trace connections across a human conceptualized space and time, to follow the turns and trajectories of people's relations and arguments, and to see where arguments intersect, how they stop and fragment, and when, by whom, and how they are diverted' (Stambach 2016, p. 500). Altinyelken (Chapter 10 in this volume) looks at how child-centred pedagogy (CCP) was re-contextualized in Uganda and Turkey from a similar perspective. Her study points to convergence at a superficial level and around new rituals that have emerged as a result of the dissemination of CCP. However, her findings indicate more strongly the persistence of divergences across countries as CCP was interpreted differently, the reform practices were embraced unevenly, and adaptations to classroom realities and student background have resulted in very distinct practices.

Scalar. The professionals who ultimately have to make new policies work (teachers, principals, local government officials, etc.) often perceive education reform as something imposed from above. This problem is more striking in the case of GEPs that have been defined, designed and/or negotiated at a supranational scale. Incrementalist approaches tell us that policy changes, to work out smoothly, need to be grounded on previous practices and advance progressively. As the gap between the new policy and the previous system becomes bigger, implementation processes become more problematic (Rizvi and Lingard 2010). This 'gap' is usually accentuated in relation to policies imported from elsewhere and initially designed by officials unconnected to local realities.

Following this type of reasoning, Steiner-Khamsi (2010, p. 331) argues that very often reform failures are not due to technicalities, limited funding or similar implementation problems. Rather, such failures reflect 'the fundamental contradictions that arise when (policy) solutions are borrowed from educational systems where the problems are entirely different.' Thus the main implementation problem can be found in the decoupling between the global policy, whose programme ontology has a universalistic pretension, and the local reality, with the particular configuration of problems that predominate.

Unterhalter (Chapter 4) observes how global targets inevitably oversimplify reality, as well as the complexity of the problems that policies are intended to address. The main issue here is thinking that by achieving a specific target, the problem that the target relates to has been solved as well. She shows how this 'political relaxation' effect happens in the case of the EFA gender parity target; once countries have achieved this target, decision-makers consider that they have solved the gender equity issues, which is something much more complex and difficult to measure and address in real situations.

Conclusion

GEP has become a rich study area that analyses how and why education reforms happen in an increasingly globalized policy space. Specifically, GEP studies focus on the settlement of global education agendas, and on the mobilization, translation and re-contextualization of these agendas in multiple scales of governance. GEP studies are also interested in analysing how global reform models are enacted in different educational realities, and in finding out about the main outcomes of these models in terms of quality and equity in education.

In this introduction, we have shown that the effects of globalization on education policy are multiple and cover very different dimensions. Nonetheless, it is also true that in an increasingly globalized policy field, it is not easy to distinguish whether educational reforms are exogenously or endogenously originated, or whether reforms are the result of international policy 'transfer' dynamics or the outcome of internal pressures and innovations. As we have seen, globalization has intensified the international flow and exchange of policy ideas; it has meant the constitution of influential transnational networks of experts and, overall, has contributed to rescale education agenda-setting and policy-making processes in an unprecedented way. The influence of these and other global developments in national education systems is not always easy to observe, distinguish and track empirically.

Overall, the GEP field resembles more a messy market of policy ideas that, albeit its hierarchical nature, is not structured according to very well defined centres of diffusion and receptive peripheries, but through more complex multiscalar dynamics. Furthermore, despite the education policy field is globalizing, policy convergence cannot be taken for granted as an outcome of the globalization of educational policy. Taking globalization seriously requires contemplating and researching the multiple policy trajectories that global education models follow. Such an endeavour compels researchers to have an in-depth knowledge of the specific contexts in which global policies are being disseminated and adopted, and infusing local institutions and actors – including policy-makers, social movements and so on – with agency and transformative powers. Putting scale and the agency of policy actors operating at multiple scales at the center of our research designs is key in current GEP studies.

The GEP phenomenon is being studied from very different theoretical, epistemological and methodological perspectives. Table 1.1 tries to make sense of the numerous theoretical approaches that configure GEP as a study area. Far from exhaustive, our classification focuses on those approaches that are more present in comparative education research and that we have presented in this introduction. We organize these approaches according to their main research focus (i.e. global drivers, policy adoption and/or re-contextualization), and to whether they put more emphasis on ideational or material factors in their explanations of education policy change.

Table 1.1 Mapping global education policy theories

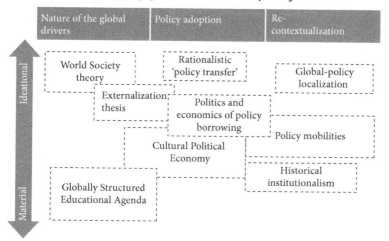

Finally, having laid out schematically the landscape of the different methodological and theoretical approaches on globalization, education policy and international development, it is perhaps fitting now to conclude that there remains a great deal of work to be done. Many of the debates outlined above, beyond their analytical dimension, have hugely important implications for social justice and the fulfilment of the right to education around the world. Globalization, far from producing a flat world, has increased inequalities both within and between countries, and has altered the cartography of contemporary social relations and education politics. Power and its unequal distribution are reflected throughout these pages, and challenge us to think beyond the current mainstream in the education/globalization relationship and to develop more inclusive, participatory and egalitarian educational policy processes. Hopefully this book can contribute to highlighting the fault lines upon which these principles can emerge.

Notes

1 By policy programmes we refer to 'technical and professional ideas that specify cause and effect relationships and prescribe a precise course of policy action' (Campbell 2004).

2 The basic rules of the Westphalian State are as follows: (1) Authority can be exercised only by a state over a defined geographical territory. (2) Each state is autonomous to develop its own policies. (3) No external actor can direct the state's priorities (Yeates 2001).

3 We do not mean here that each GEP research initiative should address all these questions, since doing so would require a huge amount of time, resources and data collection.

4 Here we find an important difference between World Society theory and externalization theory. World Society theory looks at the dissemination of global models in education from a hyperglobalist and top-down perspective. In contrast, the externalization theory entry point to GEP is the way local/national systems look at, adopt and transform global models and norms.

5 This is how the debate for the definition of the SDG agenda has been known in many policy and academic circles.

6 According to Pawson (2006), this way of using science and evidence to legitimate predefined policy preferences, instead of evidence-based policy, should be called 'policy-based evidence'.

7 World Society scholars are the most well-known advocates of the policy convergence thesis in comparative education. Despite admitting that some level of *loose coupling* between GEPs and local practices might prevail, only in the last few years have they started theorizing local variation more seriously (see Pope and Meyer 2016).

References

Anderson-Levitt, K. M. (2003). *Local meanings, global schooling: Anthropology and world culture theory.* Basingstoke: Palgrave Macmillan.

Appadurai, A. (1996). *Modernity at large: Cultural dimensions of globalisation.* Minneapolis: University of Minnesota Press.

Astiz, M. F. (2006). 'School autonomy in the province of Buenos Aires, Argentina: Evidence from two school districts'. *Comparative Education,* 42 (2), 203–223.

Ball, S. J. (1998). 'Big policies/small world: An introduction to international perspectives in education policy'. *Comparative Education,* 34 (2), 119–130.

Ball, S. J. (2007). *Education Plc: Understanding private sector participation in public sector education.* New York: Routledge.

Ball, S. J. (2012). *Global education inc: New policy networks and the neo-liberal imaginary.* New York: Routledge.

Ball, S. J. (2016). 'Following policy: Networks, network ethnography and education policy mobilities'. *Journal of Education Policy,* 31 (5), 1–18.

Bardach, E. (2006). 'Policy dynamics'. In M. Moran, M. Rein and R. E. Goodin (Eds.), *Oxford handbook of public policy.* Oxford: Oxford University Press, pp. 336–366.

Barnett, M. and Finnemore, M. (2004). *Rules for the world: International organisations in global politics.* Ithaca, NY: Cornell University Press.

Barrow, C. W., Didou-Aupetit, S. and Mallea, J. (2004). *Globalisation, trade liberalisation, and higher education in North America: The emergence of a new market under NAFTA?* Dordrecht: Kluwer Academic Publishers.

Beckert, J. (2010). 'How do fields change? The interrelations of institutions, networks, and cognition in the dynamics of markets. *Organization Studies,* 31 (5), 605–627.

Beech, J. (2006). 'The theme of educational transfer in comparative education: A view over time'. *Research in Comparative and International Education*, 1 (1), 2–13.

Benavot, A. and Tanner, E. (2008). The growth of national learning assessments in the world, 1995–2006. Background paper for EFA Global Monitoring Report.

Benveniste, L. (2002). 'The political structuration of assessment: Negotiating state power and legitimacy'. *Comparative Education Review*, 46 (1), 89–118.

Bhanji, Z. (2008). 'Transnational corporations in education: Filling the governance gap through new social norms and market multilateralism?' *Globalisation, Societies and Education*, 6 (1), 55–73.

Bieber, T. (2010). 'Playing the multilevel game in education-the PISA study and the Bologna Process triggering Swiss harmonisation'. In K. Martens, A. Nagel, M. Windzio and A. Weymann (Eds.), *Transformation of education policy*. Basingstoke: Palgrave Macmillan, pp. 105–131.

Bonal, X. (2002). 'Plus ça change … The World Bank global education policy and the post-Washington consensus'. *International Studies in Sociology of Educational*, 12 (1), 3–21.

Bourdieu, P. (1999). 'Rethinking the state: Genesis and structure of the bureaucratic field'. In G. Steinmetz (Ed.), *State/culture: State-formation after the cultural turn*. New York: Cornell University Press, pp. 53–75.

Brown, P. and Lauder, H. (1996). 'Education, globalisation and economic development'. *Journal of Education Policy*, 11 (1), 1–24.

Bulkley, K. and Fisler, J. (2003). 'A decade of charter schools: From theory to practice'. *Educational Policy*, 17 (3), 317–342.

Bull, B. and McNeill, D. (2007). *Development issues in global governance: Public-private partnerships and market multilateralism*. London: Routledge.

Busemeyer, M. R. and Vossiek, J. (2016). Global convergence or path dependency? Skill formation regimes in the globalized economy. In K. Mundy, A. Green, R. Lingard and A. Verger (Eds.), *Handbook of global policy and policy-making in education*. West Sussex: Wiley-Blackwell, pp. 145–161.

Campbell, J. L. (2004). *Institutional change and globalisation*. Princeton, NJ: Princeton University Press.

Carney, S. (2009). 'Negotiating policy in an age of globalisation: Exploring educational "Policyscapes" in Denmark, Nepal, and China'. *Comparative Education Review*, 53 (1), 63–88.

Carnoy, M. (2016). 'Educational policies in the face of globalization'. In K. Mundy, A. Green, R. Lingard and A. Verger (Eds.), *Handbook of global policy and policy-making in education*. West Sussex: Wiley-Blackwell, pp. 27–42.

Carnoy, M. and Rhoten, D. (2002). 'What does globalisation mean for educational change? A comparative approach'. *Comparative Education Review*, 46 (1), 1–9.

Cerny, P. G. (1997). 'Paradoxes of the competition state: The dynamics of political globalisation'. *Government and Opposition*, 32 (2), 251–274.

Chabbott, C. (2003). *Constructing education for development: International organisations and education for all*. New York: Routledge.

Commission on Global Governance (1995). *Our global neighbourhood*. Oxford: Oxford University Press.

Cox, R. W. (1995). 'Social forces, states, and world orders: Beyond international relations theory (1981)'. In R. W. Cox and T. J. Sinclair (Eds.), *Approaches to world order*. Cambridge: Cambridge University Press, pp. 85–123.

Crossley, M. and Watson, K. (2003). *Comparative and international research in education: Globalisation, context and difference*. London: Routledge Falmer.

Dale, R. (1999). 'Specifying globalisation effects on national policy: Focus on the mechanisms'. *Journal of Education Policy*, 14 (1), 1–17.

Dale, R. (2000). 'Globalisation and education: Demonstrating a "common world educational culture" or locating a "globally structured educational agenda"'? *Educational Theory*, 50 (4), 427–448.

Dale, R. (2005). 'Globalisation, knowledge economy and comparative education'. *Comparative Education*, 41 (2), 117–149.

Dale, R. and Robertson, S. (2007). 'Beyond methodological "isms" in comparative education in an era of globalisation'. In A. Kazamias and R. Cowan (Eds.), *Handbook on comparative education*. Netherlands: Springer, pp. 19–32.

Drezner, D. W. (2001). 'Globalisation and policy convergence'. *International Studies Review*, 3 (1), 53–78.

Edwards Jr., D. B. and Klees, S. J. (2015). 'Unpacking "participation" in development and education governance: A framework of perspectives and practices'. *Prospects*, 45 (4), 483–499.

Finnemore, M. (1996). 'Constructing norms of humanitarian intervention'. In P. J. Katzenstein (Ed.), *The culture of national security: Norms and identity in world politics*. New York: Columbia University Press, pp. 153–185.

Green, A. (2003). 'Education, globalisation and the role of comparative research'. *London Review of Education*, 1 (2), 84–97.

Grek, S. (2007). 'Governing by numbers: The PISA effect'. *Journal of Education Policy*, 24 (1), 23–37.

Grek, S., Lawn, M., Lingard, B. and Varjo, J. (2009). 'North by northwest: Quality assurance and evaluation processes in European education'. *Journal of Education Policy*, 24 (2), 121–133.

Gunter, H. M., Hall, D. and Mills, C. (2015). 'Consultants, consultancy and consultocracy in education policymaking in England'. *Journal of Education Policy*, 30 (4), 518–539.

Haas, P. M. (2004). 'When does power listen to truth? A constructivist approach to the policy process?' *Journal of European Public Policy*, 11 (4), 569–592.

Hartmann, E. (2007). 'Towards an international regime for the recognition of higher education qualifications – The empowered role of UNESCO in the emerging global knowledge-based economy'. In K. Martens, A. Rusconi and K. Leuze (Eds.), *New arenas of education governance: The impact of international organisations and markets on educational policy making*. New York: Palgrave Macmillan, pp. 76–94.

Hay, C. (2006). 'What's globalisation got to do with it? Economic interdependence and the future of European Welfare States'. *Government and Opposition*, 41 (1), 1–22.

Heyneman, S. P. (2003). 'The history and problems in the making of education policy at the World Bank 1960–2000'. *International Journal of Educational Development*, 23 (3), 315–337.

Huisman, J. and Van Der Wende, M. (2004). 'The EU and Bologna: Are supra- and international initiatives threatening domestic agendas?' *European Journal of Education*, 39 (3), 349–357.

IEG (2011). *IEG annual report 2011: Results and performance of the World Bank Group*. Washington, DC: World Bank.

Jakobi, A. P. (2009). *International organizations and lifelong learning.* Basingstoke: Palgrave Macmillan.

Jessop, B. (2008). 'Cultural political economy of competitiveness and its implications for higher education', In B. Jessop, N. Fairclough and R. Wodak (Eds.), *Education and the knowledge-based economy in Europe*, Rotterdam: Sense, pp. 13–39.

Jessop, B. (2010). 'Cultural political economy and critical policy studies'. *Critical Policy Studies*, 3 (3/4): 336–356. doi:0.1080/19460171003619741.

Junemann, C. and Ball, S. J. (2015). *Pearson and PALF: The mutating giant.* Brussels: Education International.

Keck, M. E. and Sikkink, K. (1998). *Activists beyond borders. Advocacy networks in international politics.* New York: Cornell University Press.

Kelsey, J. (2016). From GATS to TiSA: Pushing the trade in services regime beyond the limits. In M. Bungenberg, C. Herrmann, M. Krajewski, J. P. Terhechte, (Eds.), *European yearbook of international economic law 2016.* Springer International Publishing, pp. 119–151.

King, K. (2007). 'Multilateral agencies in the construction of the global agenda on education'. *Comparative Education*, 43 (3), 377–391.

Kingdon, J. W. (2002). *Agendas, alternatives, and public policies.* London: Longman Publishing Group.

Lewin, K. M. (2007), 'The limits to growth of non-government: Private schooling in sub Saharan Africa'. In P. Srivastava and G. Walford (Eds.), *Private schooling in less economically developed countries: Asian and African perspectives.* Oxford: Symposium, pp. 41–65.

Lingard, B., Rawolle, S. and Taylor, S. (2005). 'Globalising policy sociology in education: Working with Bourdieu'. *Journal of Education Policy*, 20 (6), 759–777.

Lubienski, C., Scott, J., and DeBray, E. (2014). 'The politics of research production, promotion, and utilization in educational policy'. *Educational Policy*, 28 (2), 131–144.

Luke, A. (2003). 'After the marketplace: Evidence, social science and educational research'. *The Australian Educational Researcher*, 30 (2), 89–109.

Marginson, S. (2004). 'Competition and markets in higher education: A "glonacal" analysis'. *Policy Futures in Education*, 2 (2), 175–244.

Martens, K. and Wolf, K. D. (2009). 'Boomerangs and Trojan horses: The unintended consequences of internationalising education policy through the EU and the OECD'. In A. Amaral, G. Neave, C. Musselin and P. Maassen (Eds.), *European integration and the governance of higher education and research.* Dordrecht: Springer Netherlands, pp. 81–107.

Menashy, F. (2016). Understanding the roles of non-state actors in global governance: Evidence from the global partnership for education. *Journal of Education Policy*, 31 (1), 98–118.

Meyer, J. W., Ramirez, F. O. and Soysal, Y. N. (1992a). 'World expansion of mass education, 1870–1980'. *Sociology of Education*, 65, 128–149.

Meyer, J. W., Kamens, D. H., Benavot, A. with Cha, Y. K. and Wong, S. Y. (Eds.) (1992b). *School knowledge for the masses: World models and national primary curricular categories in the twentieth century.* Washington, DC: Falmer Press.

Meyer, J. W., Boli, J., Thomas, G. M. and Ramirez, F. O. (1997). 'World society and the nation-state'. *The American Journal of Sociology*, 103 (1), 144–181.

Moutsios, S. (2010). 'Power, politics and transnational policy-making in education'. *Globalisation, Societies and Education*, 8 (1), 121–141.

Mukhopadhyay, R. and Sriprakash, A. (2011). 'Global frameworks, local contingencies: Policy translations and education development in India'. *Compare*, 41 (3), 311–326.

Mundy, K. and Murphy, L. (2001). 'Transnational advocacy, global civil society? Emerging evidence from the field of education'. *Comparative Education Review*, 45 (1), 85–126.

Mundy, K. and Verger, A. (2015). 'The World Bank and the global governance of education in a changing world order'. *International Journal of Educational Development*, 40, 9–18.

Mundy, K., Green, A., Lingard, R. and Verger A. (2016). Introduction: The globalization of education policy – Key approaches and debates. In *Handbook of global education policy*. West Sussex: Wiley-Blackwell, pp. 1–20.

Neave, G. (1998). 'The evaluative state reconsidered'. *European Journal of Education*, 33 (3), 265–284.

Novelli, M. and Lopes Cardozo, M. T. A. (2008). 'Conflict, education and the global south: New critical directions'. *International Journal of Educational Development*, 28 (4), 473–488.

O'Brien, R., Goetz, A. M., Scholte, J. A. and Williams, M. (2000). *Contesting global governance: Multilateral economic institutions and global social movements*. Cambridge: Cambridge University Press.

Pawson, R. (2006), *Evidence-based policy: A realist perspective*. London: Sage Publications.

Peck, J., and Theodore, N. (2010). 'Mobilizing policy: Models, methods, and mutations'. *Geoforum*, 41 (2), 169–174.

Phillips, D., and Ochs, K. (2003). 'Processes of policy borrowing in education: Some explanatory and analytical devices'. *Comparative Education*, 39 (4), 451–461.

Phillips, K. D. and Stambach, A. (2008). 'Cultivating choice: The invisible hands of educational opportunity in Tanzania'. In M. Forsey, S. Davis and G. Walford (Eds.), *The globalisation of school choice?* Oxford: Symposium Books, pp. 145–164.

Pope, S. and Meyer, J. W. (2016). Local variation in world society: Six characteristics of global diffusion. *European Journal of Cultural and Political Sociology*, 3 (2–3), 280–305.

Poppema, M. (2012). 'School-based management in post-conflict Central America: Undermining civil society and making the poorest parents pay'. In A. Verger, M. Novelli and H. K. Alitnyelken (Eds.), *Global education policy and international development: New agendas, issues and policies*, London: Bloomsbury, pp. 161–180.

Ramirez, F. O. (2006). 'Growing commonalities and persistent differences in higher education: Universities between globalisation and national tradition'. In H. D. Meyer and B. Rowan (Eds.), *The new institutionalism in education: Advancing research and policy*. Albany, NY: SUNY University Press, London: Bloomsbury, pp. 123–141.

Reckhow, S. and Galey, S. and Ferrare, J. J. (2016). Bipartisanship and Idea Brokerage in Education Policy Networks. *Political Networks Workshops & Conference* 2016. Available at: SSRN: http://dx.doi.org/10.2139/ssrn.2798935.

Rhoten, D. (2000). 'Education decentralisation in Argentina: A "global-local conditions of possibility" approach to state, market, and society change'. *Journal of Education Policy*, 15 (6), 593–619.

Rizvi, F. and Lingard, B. (2010). *Globalizing education policy*. London: Routledge.

Robertson, S. (2005). 'Re-imagining and rescripting the future of education: Global knowledge economy discourses and the challenge to education systems'. *Comparative Education*, 41 (2), 151–170.

Robertson, S. and Dale, R. (2006). 'Changing geographies of power in education: The politics of rescaling and its contradictions'. In D. Kassem, E. Mufti and J. Robinson (Eds.), *Education studies: Issues and critical perspectives*. Buckinghamshire: Open University Press, pp. 221–233.

Robertson, S. and Verger, A. (2012). 'Governing education through public-private partnerships'. In S. Robertson, A. Verger, K. Mundy and F. Menashy (Eds.), *Public private partnerships in education: New actors and modes of governance in a globalizing world*. London: Edward Elgar, pp. 21–42.

Robertson, S., Bonal, X. and Dale, R. (2002). 'GATS and the education services industry: The politics of scale and global reterritorialisation'. *Comparative Education Review*, 46 (4), 472–496.

Rose, P. M. (2007). *Supporting Non-state Providers in Basic Education Service Delivery*, paper commissioned by DFID Policy Division. Brighton: Consortium for Research on Educational Access, Transitions and Equity (CREATE). Research Monograph 4/2007.

Rupert, M. (2005). 'Reflections on some lessons learned from a decade of globalisation studies'. *New Political Economy*, 10 (4), 457–478.

Santos, B. S. (2005). *El milenio huérfano. Ensayos para una nueva cultura política*. Madrid: Trotta.

Sayer, A. (2001). 'For a critical cultural political economy', *Antipode*, 33 (4), 687–708.

Schriewer, J. (2000). 'World system and interrelationship networks: The internationalisation of education and the role of comparative inquiry'. In T. S. Popkewitz (Ed.), *Educational knowledge: Changing relations between the state, civil society, and the educational community*. Albany, NY: State University of New York Press, pp. 305–343.

Schriewer, J. (2012). 'Editorial: Meaning constellations in the world society'. *Comparative Education*, 48 (4), 411–422.

Schriewer, J. and Martinez, C. (2004). 'Constructions of internationality in education'. In G. Steiner-Khamsi (Ed.), *The global politics of educational borrowing and lending*. New York: Teachers' College Press, pp. 29–53.

Scott, J. and Jabbar, H. (2014). The hub and the spokes: Foundations, intermediary organizations, incentivist reforms, and the politics of research evidence. *Educational Policy*, 28 (2), 233–257.

Snyder, F. (1999). 'Governing economic globalisation: Global legal pluralism and European law'. *European Law Journal*, 5 (4), 334–374.

Spreen, C. A. (2004). 'Appropriating borrowed policies: Outcomes-based education in South Africa'. In G. Steiner-Khamsi (Ed.), *The global politics of educational borrowing and lending*. New York: Teachers' College Press, pp. 101–113.

Srivastava, P. and Oh, S. A. (2010). 'Private foundations, philanthropy, and partnership in education and development: Mapping the terrain'. *International Journal of Educational Development*, 30 (5), 460–471.

Stambach, A. (2016). Ethnography and the localization of global education policy. In *The handbook of global education policy*, pp. 490–503.

Steiner-Khamsi, G. (2004). *The global politics of educational borrowing and lending*. New York: Teachers' College Press.

Steiner-Khamsi, G. (2010). 'The politics and economics of comparison'. *Comparative Education Review*, 54 (3), 323–342.

Steiner-Khamsi, G. and Stolpe, I. (2006). *Educational import: Local encounters with global forces in Mongolia*. New York: Palgrave Macmillan.

Stone, D. (2004). 'Transfer agents and global networks in the "transnationalisation" of policy'. *Journal of European Public Policy*, 11 (3), 545–566.

Stromquist, N. P. (2015). Explaining the expansion of feminist ideas: Cultural diffusion or political struggle?. *Globalisation, Societies and Education*, 13 (1), 109–134.

Taylor, S. and Henry, M. (2000). 'Globalisation and educational policymaking: A case study'. *Educational Theory*, 50 (4), 487–503.

Terra, L. and Bromley, P. (2012). 'The globalization of multicultural education in social science textbooks: Cross-national analyses, 1950–2010. *Multicultural Perspectives*, 14 (3), 136–143.

Van Fleet, J. (2012). 'A disconnect between motivations and education needs: Why American corporate philanthropy alone will not educate the most marginalized'. In S. Robertson, K. Mundy, A. Verger and F. Menashy (Eds.), *Public private partnerships in education: New actors and modes of governance in a globalizing world*. London: Edward Elgar, pp. 151–181.

Vavrus, F. (2004). 'The referential web: Externalisation beyond education in Tanzania'. In G. Steiner-Khamsi (Ed.), *The global politics of educational borrowing and lending*. New York: Teachers' College Press, pp. 141–153.

Vavrus, F. and Bartlett, L. (2006). 'Comparatively knowing: Making a case for the vertical case study'. *Current Issues in Comparative Education*, 8 (2), 95–103.

Verger, A. (2012). 'Framing and selling global education policy: The promotion of PPPs in education in low-income countries'. *Journal of Education Policy*, 27 (1), 109–130.

Verger, A., Fontdevila, C. and Zancajo, A. (2016a). *The privatization of education: A political economy of global education reform*. New York: Teachers College Press.

Verger, A., Lubienski, C. and Steiner-Khamsi, G. (Eds.) (2016b). *World yearbook of education 2016: The global education industry*. New York: Routledge.

Yeates, N. (2001). *Globalisation and social policy*. London: Sage.

Yuan, L. and Powell, S. (2013). MOOCs and Open Education: Implications for Higher Education. A white paper. Bolton (UK): JISC CETIS. Available at: http://publications.cetis.ac.uk/2013/667.

2

Researching Global Education Policy: Angles In/On/Out...

Susan L. Robertson

Introduction

This chapter is concerned with *researching* global education policy. This is not at a straightforward task, particularly in the area of education policy studies. To begin with, it involves going beyond accounts of the global as 'outside/ exogenous' that acts upon, and shapes, education policy-making on what is describes as the 'inside/endogenous', or 'local'. This way of seeing reinforces a view of the global as abstract, homogeneous, structural and without agents or agency, whilst the local is concrete, diverse, agentic and imbued with democratic notions of bottom-up legitimacy, however tenuous or thin in reality. Researching global education policy means making visible methodological statist and nationalist assumptions of policy studies more generally, and the ways in which these assumptions continue to influence education policy analyses (Robertson and Dale 2008). What is increasingly clear is that to understand our changing social worlds, new epistemic paradigms are needed. It also involves us asking about the policy process itself, particularly when it is no longer only, or primarily, the nationally located state engaged in the making (and regulating) of policy and its implementation. And if this is the case, what then are the implications for thinking about policy as political, contested and public.

Yet invoking the need for a new epistemological paradigm, as opposed to articulating the basic elements entailed, are very different things, and the challenges are huge. How best to capture the complexities of education projects, policies and programmes that are now increasingly dispersed over what were once tightly managed boundaries around units of social life? How might we generate analyses of the moments and movements of education actors and policies (and their varying forms – ideationally, materially, institutionally) across time and in space that take into account policies as 'a complex, uneven and asymmetrical set of multi-layered cross-cutting processes and nodes of interaction' (Cerny 2001, p. 397)? How can we better understand the process of education policy-making and its implementation when it involves a range of actors who are geographically dispersed, engaged in diverse governance activities, and involving different accountability communities? And if education policy continues to be the '*authoritive* allocation of values', as Prunty (1984, p. 42) reminded us more than two decades ago, then questions of *authority*, as well as *whose* values are represented, *how, where, when*, and the relationships between competing sites of power, continue to be important ways of understanding education policy analytically, including when it invokes, and involves, the global in new ways.

Rather than engage in a major review of the extant literature in the education policy field, my entry point into the challenges posed above is to engage with methodological accounts of global education policy being advanced by a group of education scholars working in international development contexts (see Steiner-Khamsi 2004; Sobe and Ortegon 2009; Vavrus and Bartlett 2006; Bartlett and Vavrus 2011; Carney 2009, 2011). These writers challenge 'orthodox' comparative and international education approaches, and are engaged in a lively debate around different aspects of global education policy. A range of concepts have emerged to describe these processes, from 'borrowing and lending' to 'transfer', 'circulation', 'pipes' and 'mobilities'. Their challenge is to advance ways of 'seeing' and studying education policies transnationally which are theoretically and empirically sensitive to the specificities of space, time and sociality, without giving ground to what Marginson and Mollis call 'ultra-relativism' (2001, p. 588).

This chapter will therefore proceed in the following way. I will begin with some brief comments on these different ways of understanding the global in education policy. I then review contributions by Steiner-Khamsi (2002, 2004), Sobe and Ortegon (2009), Vavrus and Bartlett (2006), Bartlett and Vavrus (2011) and Carney (2009, 2011). These authors advance new ways of researching these global processes. My engagement with their work is intended to stimulate a dialogue with, and generate notes towards, a critical account which I hope is helpful for researching global education policy.

Locating the 'Global' in education policy

The question of how the 'global' features in education policy and how we might come to know the global in researching global education policy is dependent on how we understand each of the constituent elements – the 'global', 'education' and 'policy', and the relationships between them. I will be arguing that the global features in education policy in somewhat different, though related, ways, as a 'condition of the world', 'discourse', 'project', 'scale' and 'means of identifying the reach of particular actors'. As a *condition of the world*, this signals an ontological shift – a world that has profoundly changed as a result of neoliberalism as an organizing project, the advance of new technologies, the blurring of boundaries between national territorial states and so on. As a *discourse* in education policies, the global is invoked as a particular imaginary, often tied to ideas like a 'global knowledge economy', 'global village', 'global social justice' and so on. As a *project* in education policy, it is to propose, and set into motion by extending out into 'global' space, particular ways of framing 'education' problems and their desirable/preferred solutions (privatization, decentralization, 'Education for All', quality, etc.). As *scale*, it is to register the ways in which platforms for action are constructed – in this case the 'global' – from which particular actors, as global actors, claim the legitimate right to advance ideas, to represent constituencies, or to govern.

And finally, viewing the global as *reach* refers the horizon of action of particular institutions and actors engaged in different aspects of education policy work. These ways of understanding the global in education are not meant to be exhaustive. Rather, they are meant to indicate the rather different ways in which the global features, and the different methodologies we might deploy in attempting to make sense of the global in education policy. For instance, the global as discourse suggests we use some form of discourse analysis, whilst the global as reach, or spatial extension, suggests ways of understanding education policies as they move from one point of origin (local) through space to be fixed/altered/ in a new locality, or place. It is important to view concepts like the global and the local as relational. In other words, it is important not to essentialize some actors, such as the World Bank Group, located in Washington, United States, as *always* global. There are many activities of the Bank as an institution that are local, such as 'in-house' organizational policies. It is when the Bank's policies are promoted in distant locations that we might view the Bank's activity as global. This leads us to suggest that rather than see the global as operating in some stratosphere – up there – that we see them as *places* made up of a range of spatial relationships – some global, some local and so on. In other words, place is

> a meeting place of a whole series of complex networks and social relations. Its boundedness is understood not as forming a simple enclosure but as being permeated by the multiple relations that stretch across the globe. The specificity of place is not linked to a place-based identity, for places are traversed by unequal relations of power and struggles to contest these relations. (Massey 1994, p. 155)

Importantly, too, as Sobe and Ortegon (2009, p. 63) argue, our approaches to the global need to be attentive to the ways in which movement involves reciprocal, reversible and multiple vectors, forming dense, overlapping webs of relationships.

And what of 'education'? Or policy? It is clear that education as a sector, teaching as a profession and learning as a means of regulation/emancipation have been radically transformed; this is the outcome of political projects, like neoliberalism, the conception of education as a human right, or the creation of globally competitive knowledge economies. The division of labour in education that characterized post-war societies has been subject to major efforts, or policies, to unpick deeply embedded and institutionalized relationships, and to insert new ways of doing education. Not only has the global been invoked as the reason for policy, but education policies have been advanced by actors at new scales – the global, the regional, the local and the individual – in order to develop very different education sectors, teachers and learners. Finally, policy is both a medium and a message system. As medium, policies may take different forms, dependent on what kind of policy arenas we are looking at. As message system, policies are ideational. They have at their heart a set of ideas (values) about what the education as a social institution and set of practices should look like, including who is taught what, how and so on, and how these practices to be governed. With new actors in the education sector (such as for-profit firms), with different kinds of aspirations (such as making a profit, realizing a different kind of learner), means of accounting (such as shareholders) and scalar horizons, this demands new ways of thinking about education policy. Policy is also a process; they are never 'one off' and discrete events, but rather social practices that unfold over time and in space. Untangling these analytically and empirically and making decisions about the nature of the tools to be deployed are clearly challenges we face in doing global policy research.

Angles in/on: Researching the global in education policy and international development

As noted earlier, my intention is not to offer an exhaustive 'review' of different research approaches to global education policy in international development. Rather, it is to engage with the work of a small group of critical education researchers explicitly engaged in a range of education development sites and projects, to look at the way they are approaching these challenges.

The global as policy movement

Gita Steiner-Khamsi's (2002, 2004) work engages explicitly with the *movement* of education policies from one locality to another – that is, 'transnational borrowing and lending' (2004, p. 1) – and in the process becomes 'global'. As she notes, in much of the literature, what motivates the movement of education policies from one location to another is the (normative) view that we can learn from elsewhere. Stepping aside from what might best be viewed as a lesson-learning stance, Steiner-Khamsi proposes an analytical way forward; to focus on the 'why', 'how' and 'who' in the transfer of education policies. Whilst noting that this concern might be regarded as 'old hat' (2004, p. 4), she points out the 'global', as the 'out-there education policy trend', is now being mobilized by a new 'semantics of globalisation' (2004, p. 5) to legitimate the adoption of particular education policies to 'problems in-here'. These policies are not just discourses; rather they are real, and must be understood – not just as something borrowed – but as discourses that enter into local circuits that are then 'adapted, modified and resisted' (2004, p. 5). In other words, these policies are discourses that have real effects, though quite what effects cannot be known (only imagined) in advance. Drawing on cases that are presented in her 2004 edited book, Steiner-Khamsi offers some answers to the question of 'why' policies are moving from one location to another: for example, the 'certification' (or legitimation) of changes in one locality will reference an 'external' set of social practices; the export of policies and programmes as part of emerging trade within the education sector; the territorial practices of organizations who operate transnationally – 'leaving their mark'; when returns to investments in education are dependent on economies of scale – hence forms of going global; or as certain kinds of technologies (rankings) able to accelerate change. Why are global policies taken up in particular locations? A range of possibilities are presented: for example, referential networks operating in different locations which take up ideas because there is as shared outlook, or because they are part of a *similar* professional network, and so on. Steiner-Khamsi's methodological move is to focus on social networks, and network analysis, and these are clearly promising ideas and ways of viewing the movement of education policy. For example, a small network of global education policy entrepreneurs has been highly influential in advancing the World Bank's version of public–private partnerships in education (see Verger 2012). However this kind of analysis tends to favour an agency/actor account, as Sobe and Ortegon (2009) argues, and in doing so risks obscuring the complexity of the connections and inter-crossings that engender certain cultural forms and social patterns and not others.

Like network theory in general, with its eschewal of hierarchy (and scale theory), social network theory tends to lean towards a flat ontology of social sites. And in flattening out space, we also do not see the ways in which key actors concerned with education policy, the state and non-state actors (such as the World Bank Group [WB], the European Commission [EC], the Organization for Economic Co-operation and Development [OECD]), mobilize hierarchy as a means of legitimating rule. In other words, as Amin and Thrift observe: 'Those concerned with the politics of regulation and governance associated with globalization are right to note the very real and felt contest of jurisdiction between local, national and global state and non-state organisations' (2002, p. 396). What is important, however, is not to view scales as fixed, but as mutable; they are produced and reproduced by socio-economic processes and political struggles, with education policies selectively and strategically advanced to do precisely some of this kind of work. In other words, global education policies may well move along social networks, but they are also mobilized by social networks, as well as by hierarchically organized actors – such as the state and non-state actors – to advance projects of governing and rule.

The vertical case

If hierarchy can be shown to be ontologically important in social space, then to what extent does Vavrus and Bartlett's (2006, p. 95) approach which they call a 'vertical case' help us understand global education policy. Their approach is epistemological; that is, it is animated by a concern about *what* can be known about the world, and *how*. They are also particularly interested in comparison as a methodology; what can be known about specific localities which are, in turn, part of larger structures, forces and politics.

They argue that epistemologically, the aim of the vertical case is to 'grasp the complexity of the relationships between the knowledge claims among actors with different social locations as an attempt to situate local action and interpretation within a broader cultural, historical, and political investigation'. They are particularly concerned with the importance of 'context', but unlike case studies whose context is regarded as 'local' and 'situated', their context extends out to 'take account of historical trends, social structures, and national and international forces that shape local processes at this site' (Vavrus and Bartlett's 2006, p. 960). In other words, their extended view of context includes 'the global'.

Bartlett and Vavrus (2011) argue that the vertical case makes three important contributions. First, it insists on simultaneous attention to the micro, meso and macro-levels to enable 'vertical comparison'. Second, it emphasizes the importance of historically situating processes under consideration to enable comparing across time, or what can be viewed as 'transversal comparison'. Third, it emphasizes the importance of comparing how similar processes unfold in distinct locations in space – or 'horizontal comparison' (2011, pp. 1–2). In looking at learner-centred pedagogy (LCP) in Tanzania and Kenya using the vertical case methodology, their horizontal comparison with other sites suggests there is a common semantic clustering of codes at work in the policy arena, for instance strong discourses around 'secondary education for all', investments in technology and the need for a particular kind of pedagogy in secondary education to turn advance a competitive knowledge-based economy.

The strength of their vertical case is to move beyond what Bartlett and Vavrus (2011) call 'policy discourse', to developing the links between the production of policy discourses and the ways in which they are appropriated and practised in discrete though connected locations, and the relationships between these newer discourses and older, more deeply embedded, ones. In the case of Tanzania and LCP, Bartlett and Vavrus are able to detect an older 'socialist discourse' with its focus on education for self-reliance with a newer discourse that emphasizes competition, individualism and authority. They also show that the differences between Tanzania and Kenya in terms of LCP, and between different schools in each national setting (horizontal comparisons), is mediated by different training experiences, the outcome of different levels of engagement with the global economy.

There is a great deal of value in their approach for doing global education policy research – particularly their view of, and contribution to, undertaking 'transversal' and 'horizontal' comparisons, making visible their overlappings and asymmetries. In drawing our attention to the multilayered and cross-cutting processes and nodes of interaction, some recent and others less so, they provide us with a strong sense of both present and past, and of the complexities of what it means to refer to 'situatedness', or what Polanyi (1944) refers to as 'embeddedness'.

However, the implicit assumption in the idea of 'vertical comparison' is that the global is equated to the macro, and structural, a social force that the local (or micro) must face. Here we have an unhelpful pitting of structures (as global/macro) against agents (as local/micro). Yet, and I have noted earlier, following Massey (1994) we should think of places as made up of actors with local and global horizons of action. The question here for the education policy analyst ought to be: Whose values are allocated, how, and with what outcomes for education as a sector, for teachers and learners? That we have a way of viewing the 'global' is simultaneously lived, concrete and local is important for it emphasizes locality and place as a meeting point for complex networks and social relations that stretch out into global space.

Finally, we need here a way of finessing how we talk about different things in the social worlds we are studying that tend to be caught in a micro-meso-macro 'catch-all' which might refer to hierarchy and rule, structures and agents, the global and the local, the abstract and the concrete and so on. This is clearly a different order to the concept to the idea of macro as level of abstraction and that what we regard as abstract is necessarily derived from objects, structures and mechanisms (Sayer 1984, p. 140).

Scopic systems and the global

In a rather different contribution, Sobe and Ortegon (2009) draw attention to the work of Knorr Cetina (2008) and her problematization of networks for understanding currency markets. Knorr Cetina's argument is that the idea of the network does not capture the totality of what is at play, including the significance of heightened moments of reflexivity when multiple forms of information are presented simultaneously, then aggregated, articulated and projected and, in doing so, give it new meaning. She refers to these processes as 'scopic systems', that is, 'ways of seeing the global that tends toward a single collective' (Sobe and Ortegon 2009, p. 58). Sobe and Ortegon make use of this suggestive idea to think of the way in which education, both historically and in the present, has been projected globally as well as projecting globality. They point to International Expositions and World Fairs held in the late nineteenth century as examples of the ways in which objects were placed together, classified and then evaluated against a notion of an unfolding future given forward momentum by assumptions of progress and modernity. In this very moment, the world is presented as a singular world (Sobe and Ortegon (2009, p. 61).

Similarly, today there are a burgeoning array of scopic systems that gather together, place in hierarchies, and project globally, a singular education world – from the OECD's Programme in International Student Assessment (PISA), or their Teaching and Learning International Survey (TALIS), to global university rankings (Shanghai Jiao Tong, Times Higher, U-Multi-Rank), the World Bank's Knowledge Assessment Methodology (KAM) (Robertson 2009) and the recently launched SABER system to assess and rank school and teacher performance globally (Robertson 2012). What is significant about these scopic systems, argue Sobe and Ortegon (2009, p. 62), is 'the extent to which they function like an array of crystals that collects and focuses light on one surface'.

Yet it is important to note that scopic systems in global education policy take *fragments* (partial understandings) of knowledge about complex education processes, yet present them as *fractals* (a smaller version of a whole). In doing so, the complexity and diversity of education systems, and their need for diverse policy solutions to complex (and different) policy issues, also disappears.

Fractals (disguised fragments) act as a proxy, shorthand and lever for education policy problems/solutions; as a 'one-size fits all' diagnosis and solution. Their power as levers of policy reside in their capacity to project a singular solution to an imagined single problem (competition, efficiency, world class), and in doing so, diversity is made absent. Scopic systems in education are also forms of power in that they simultaneously *frame* education problems, offer a *desired* re/solution, project *outward* with considerable spatial extension, reinforce new social practices over time because of further rounds of data gathering and projection and tap into *emotions* (shame, pride) that change behaviour – deep inside national territorial states (Robertson 2012). These are powerful systems, which both state and non-state actors have mobilized as a new means for governing education systems. They are key sites of global education policy, as project, projection and propagation. What is important for ongoing studies of global education policy is to identify the different actors and interests involved in scopic systems, the values that are being advanced, the ways in which authority to govern is generated, and whether and how the processes are open to, and visible to, wider publics.

Policyscapes and the global as 'optique'

By far the more developed account for consideration in this chapter on researching global education policy is the recent work of Steve Carney (2009, 2011) and his concept of 'policyscapes'. Using what he describes as an *optique* of globalization, Carney advances 'an experiment in method' to derive accounts of the *experiences* of different countries in the *production* of globalization. In doing so, he aims to focus attention on the constitutive moment of globalization in particular places which he argues are being deterritorialized as a result of global processes. What is central, Carney argues, is the need to theorize the dynamics of space, and bring to the fore the specificities of education, and the implementation of education policy in particular places.

Carney's experiment is to study three places in one space; Denmark, Tibet/China and Nepal to 'present some of the lived consequences of these entanglements' (p. 6) in global education reform. As he argues: 'This interest in the entangled and co-produced experience of global education reform is lacking in many recent analyses of education policy.' Drawing from the work of Tsing (2005), Carney explores the '"friction" of global connectivity between these imagined worlds where "heterogeneous and unequal encounters" share "new arrangements of culture and power"' (p. 7). In a context of globally shared visions for education, and with the advance of neoliberal political projects privileging the market, new localities are emerging as; 'the embodiment of the practices that make certain de-territorialized displays of identity' (p. 8). In other words, localities are being reconfigured as global educational policies, institutional fabrics and other social relationships move across national territorial boundaries.

However, though Carney aims for an approach that he describes as 'mutually constitutive and dialectically constructed' (p. 7), he does not go far enough because of the limitations imposed by this particular conceptualization of globalization, one that tends to privilege flows, motion, instabilities and uncertainty, without attending to the *new* ways in which processes of fixity, reterritorialization, rebordering and reordering are at work (cf. Robertson 2011).

Given Carney's (and by implication on Bartlett and Vavrus's 2011) debt to Appadurai, and the idea of 'educational policyscapes' as a means for studying the globalization of education, it is important we look more closely at Appadurai's anchoring ideas. In a series of works, Appadurai (1996) popularized the idea of global flows, along with his locution 'scapes' (as in 'ethnoscapes', technoscapes, mediascapes, ideoscapes and financescapes), as 'different streams or flows along which cultural material may be seen to be moving across national boundaries' (1996, pp. 45–46). Scapes were therefore a means of superseding standard geographical thinking advanced by the nation state.

It was also a way of capturing what he saw to be the multiple, chaotic and disjunctive nature of flows, and the distributions and results of processes at any given time.

Whilst recognizing there have always been flows in the past, Appadurai insists the present is radically different. As he says, 'Globalisation has shrunk the distance between elites, shifted key relations between producers and consumers, broken many links between labor and family life, obscured the lines between temporary locales and imaginary national attachments' and 'broken the monopoly of autonomous nation states over the project of modernization' (1996, pp. 10–11). And if the past was 'placed' and 'localistic', the present is now a 'placeless locality of flows'. These transformations are the outcome of new information technologies and the speed of transport as well as the deep rupturing of modernity, its signs, and centres of power. For Appadurai, this opens the space for a new global imagination, drawing its energy, vitality and creativity from the unpredictable outcomes from 'disjunctures' between flows, and from the possibilities enabled by the faster pace of new technologies and the accelerated speed of transport.

Appadurai extends his argument for 'disjuncture' through the concept of 'deterritorialisation', as a process in the actual world *and* a conceptual break with a past constructed from the tightly bound containers of home and social life located within nation states. Processes of deterritorialization now permit diaspora-based ethnic politics to communicate and act across the globe, enabling, in turn, the diffusion of mediascapes and ideoscapes *beyond their narrow places into global networks*. Most importantly, deterritorialization makes the normal functioning of nation states problematic and contingent since their prime cultural challengers are transnational ethnic movements (Appadurai 1996, pp. 39–40).

However, there are a number of questions we need to ask about Appadurai's account of globalization which also feature in Carney's globalization *optique*. Appadurai's project is to advance a more dynamic, contingent and less static reading of contemporary social and political life by emphasizing movement, flows, disjunctures and the disappearance of borders. However, he is now in danger of veering in the opposite direction, so that power is now amorphous, history is obscured, there is an underdeveloped conception of the present and there are no boundaries that order difference (Heyman and Campbell 2009). And whilst Carney is concerned to see power as 'frictions' using the work of Anna Tsing (2005), these are the visible manifestations of power (as productive). A more complex view of power would lead us to search for absences (Santos 2004) as well as to focus on those events that generate events, or the rules and logics that structurally and strategically shape everyday social practices.

A sympathetic reading of Appadurai's work suggests that the focus on movement and radical rupture typified early work on globalization. More recently, scholars (Harvey 1999, 2006; Mittelman 2004) have pointed to the duality of change and continuity making up the transformation of the world order. For example, if we look at the global education policy landscape, we can detect longer-standing claims about education as a public good and public sector encountering more recent claims about education as a market, a private good and a services sector.

Secondly, Appadurai's understandings of transnationalism, as the extension outward from a particular locality into global networks, and whose horizons of action are now global, broadly aligns with Santos's (2004) understanding of globalization. However Santos goes further than this 'node on a global network' understanding by arguing that globalization can be understood as a localism that acquires for itself universal hegemonic status, so that all other contenders are deemed local. This way of thinking about globalization helps us work with a more complex view of power; as not only positionality in a network (Sheppard 2002), but where some localisms secure sufficient power and reach, including through scopic systems, which enables them in turn to determine the rules of the game.

Thirdly, Appadurai's transnational network metaphor of globalization places it *above*, and not *on*, the terrain that is also occupied by a range of actors, including the national territorial state, subnational actors and so on. The local and place are now dislodged by the global, as the key category in a hierarchy of categories to understand social life. In other words, he moves from the rejection of the localized and bounded to an opposite extreme. Several problems follow from this. The first problem is that the researcher is invited to see the world through a global optic that ontologically flattens space. Second, by viewing the world as having no boundaries; 'the global exists as a space that is neither here nor there; it has no distributed patterns, and has no internal relations reproducing convergence or differentiation. It is simply a space that is everywhere' (Heyman and Campbell 2009, p. 136). Ironically this encourages a homogenous view of social life, despite intending the opposite. In other words, this way of seeing the world encourages us to bypass a fundamental effect of flows; how they constitute, reproduce and reconstitute social life.

Fourthly, Appadurai conceptualizes the present (as global) and flows, whilst borders as realities disappear. This leads to his adoption of deterritorialization as a key organizing concept. Deterritorialization is the name given to the problematic of territory losing its significance and power in everyday social life. The effect here, however, is to conceptually end up in the same place as Kenichi Omhae's (1990) 'borderless world', or Thomas Friedman's (2005) 'flat earth'. And as O Tuathail (1999, p. 140) argues, 'Discourses of deterritorialisation tend to ascribe a unique transcendency to the contemporary condition, defining it as a moment of overwhelming newness. Such functionally anti-historical notions of deterritorialisation find a variety of different expressions in political, economic and techno-cultural knowledge.' The problem here of course is that these discourses have considerable ideological power and rhetorical force and 'are part of neoliberal ideology in that it strives to denaturalise and delimit the power of the state and naturalise and bolster the virtues of the market' (O Tuathail 1999, p. 147).

Angles out: Notes towards a critical processual account

In the opening paragraphs of this chapter, I posed a series of questions around researching global education policy, questions that have been at the heart of the different angles *in and on* global education policy that I have been exploring. In this section, I want to draw these insights together and look at what more we need to do in order to advance this research agenda. In this sense, it is an *angle outward*, or a potential way forward, taking with us – but moving on from – where we are. For instance, whilst social networks give us new insights into how education policies move through space, we need to keep in view hierarchical power, such as the way in which the state makes use of different scales (above, and below) govern those within its ambit.

Similarly, whilst the idea of flows as a metaphor helps us to grasp hold of the movement of education policies around the globe, it is clear that we must also be attentive to the new forms of bordering that are also at work. 'Flow speak' tends to 'detach global flows from the material and institutional conditions which underpin global culture' (Bude and Durrschmidt 2010, p. 482). And whilst recognizing that a new set of dynamics are at work reflected in distinctive developments in contemporary world history (Scholte 2005), it is not possible to imagine a world which is *only* borderless and deterritorialized in that the basic ordering of social groups and societies *requires* categories and compartments (Harvey 2006). More recently, researchers have begun to argue we need to study the other of movement and change, for instance 'stickiness' (along with slipperiness) (Markusen 1996), 'fixity' (along with motion) (Harvey 1999) and 'borders' (along with flows), as a corrective to too much of one over the other.

In studies of globalizing education policy-making, it is critical we see the collapsing of boundaries as accompanied by new bordering processes, giving rise to new ordering practices and subjectivities (cf. Robertson 2012). Sassen (2006) argues that new bordering practices are taking place within a context of dissolving or weakening boundaries. In his paper 'Europe as borderland', Balibar argues that, far from being at the outer limit of territories, 'these borders are dispersed a little everywhere, wherever the movement of information, people, and things is happening and is controlled – for example in cosmopolitan cities' (Balibar 2002, p. 71). In other words, when we conceive of globalization as partly enacted at various subnational scales and institutional domains, we can see a proliferation of borderings deep inside national territories. A focus on such bordering capabilities allows us to see a 'geopolitics of space' easily obscured in those accounts which assume the mutual exclusivity of the national and the global by the way in which we represent them as discrete hierarchical spaces (Sassen 2006). This has led Amin to argue: 'I have distanced myself from the territorial idea of sequestered spatial logics – local, national, continental and global – pitted against each other. Instead, I have chosen to interpret globalisation in relational terms as the interdependence and intermingling of global, distant and local layers, resulting in the greater hybridisation and perforation of social, economic and political life' (Amin 1997, p. 133).

In their different ways, the different analytical approaches raise direct and indirect questions about the national state and its role in global education policy. For instance, how is national state power challenged by scopic systems, or networks? And, whose interests are advanced by these representations of education, whose framings count, and with what consequences for fundamental questions that state education policy has historically been asked to account for (social justice, legitimation, issues of redistribution, the state–citizen contract, etc.)? What is entailed in the decentring of the national state? Furthermore, whereabouts is state power if education policy is dispersed over scales?

In order to bring to the fore the spatiality of state power, I have found Ferguson and Gupta's (2002) account of the spatiality of the modern nation state particularly helpful. They argue modern nation states used two sources of spatial imaginary and projection: 'vertical power' and 'encompassment' (2002, p. 982). Vertical power leads to the idea of the state as an institution 'above' civil society, the community and family. It is a powerful container of social and political life that not only sits above, but also encompasses in a series of radiating circles outward, from the family to the system of nation states. As Ferguson and Gupta (2002, p. 982) remark, 'This is a profoundly consequential understanding of scale, one in which the locality is encompassed by the region, the region by the nation state, and the nation state by the international community.' Such metaphors are powerful ideas; in relation to the national state, they reinforced a view of the state as possessing higher functions (reason, control, capacity for regulation) which were productive of social and political life.

If verticality and encompassment captures something of the geometry of state power in the modern nation state, what is the geography of the contemporary state? Theoretical work is still in its early stages, largely as this new geography has not yet stabilized in what Jessop (2002) has called a 'socio-temporal fix'. For the moment, let me point to two (somewhat different) lines of work emerging that may prove to be fruitful for the study of the globalization of education policy. The first focuses attention on the rescaling of the state (Brenner 2004, 2009) which has paralleled the rescaling of capital accumulation. Scales in this work are argued to be sites for political struggle as well as one of their key mechanisms and outcomes (MacLeod and Goodwin 1999; Jessop 2002). As Brenner observes, 'The rescaling of institutions and policies is now conceptualised as a key means through which social forces may attempt to "rejig" the balance of class power and manage the contradictory social relations of capitalism' (Brenner 2009, p. 126). This leads to the question of what post-national statehood might look like, and what might be the implication of this for education policy? Do the new learning metrics that are emerging to measure the realization the sustainable development goals and which are promoted by a mix of actors, including education corporations reflect something of this new post-national world?

Whilst the notion of the post-national in work by Jessop (2002) and Brenner (2009) is argued to be a tendential rather than a substantive concept, both make clear that it does not mean the national is marginalized, *but that the national itself is being redefined in relation to the other scales*. This kind of account contrasts with Appadurai's approach where, as we have seen, the national/local is absorbed into global networks. Jessop and Brenner's reading of the transformation of state space resonates with a growing body of work in the globalization of education – where it is possible to see education policies as simultaneously constitutive of new scales that contain newer social actors and relations (Europe, the European citizen, the European Higher Education Area, etc.), as well as being platforms from which to advance projects of rule, and projects that concern themselves with the development of globally competitive education systems and subjectivities (see Robertson et al. 2016).

A rather different kind of analysis of the geography of contemporary state power in modern Western neoliberal economies comes from John Allen and Cochrane (2010). They argue that whilst Brenner stretches the language of scale to take account of a new institutional complexity that views multiscalar power relations as multiple, overlapping, tangled and so on, in their view it does not quite grasp the changing geography of state power. Advancing a topological account of state spatiality, Allen and Cochrane draw attention to the state's reconfiguration of hierarchical power (or what Ferguson and Gupta called 'verticality') and the ways in which a more transverse set of political interactions, or *reach*, holds that hierarchy in place. They stress that it is not *extensivity* of reach that characterizes the new geography of state power but *intensivity*, serving to disrupt what is near or far, in turn loosening our sense of defined times and distances. As Allen and Cochrane argue: 'What is politically at stake ... is that such an approach is able to show how the state's hierarchical powers have not so much been rescaled or redistributed as reassembled in terms of spatial reach' (2010, p. 1073). Reach here means those arts of governing that enable the state to permeate and penetrate those spaces that hitherto had been unreachable. They add:

> It is *not* that state hierarchies have transformed themselves into horizontal networking arrangements, but rather that the hierarchies of decision-making that matter are *institutional* and not scalar ones ... In that sense, the apparatus of state authority is not so much 'up there' or indeed 'over there' as part of a spatial arrangement within which different elements of government, as well as private agencies, exercise powers of reach that enable them to be more or less present within and across ... political structures. (Allen and Cochrane 2010, p. 1074)

Drawing on Sassen's (2006) work, and her use of 'assemblage' to signal a new geography of state power, they suggest that different bits and pieces of institutional authority are drawn within reach of one another. State hierarchies, together with private agencies, partnerships and supranational institutions may, in that sense, be seen as part of a geographical assemblage of distributed authority in which power is continually being renegotiated. Public–private partnerships are one example of this reworking of institutional boundaries, sectors, and the redistribution and reassembling of authority. However future work will need to ensure that assemblages are not simply viewed as a coincidental, contingent activity. Rather assemblages will have their own forms of structural and strategic selectivity that produce and reproduce education sectors, forms of labour, learning and subjectivities. Allen also offers some useful cautions regarding how to approach the task of identifying the stuff of the assemblage; as he observes, there is no blueprint to follow, and we can easily end with thin description as we identify all that lies before us, or we focus on the obvious and self-evident and give them more primacy than those linkages and processes that are less visible and yet no less important or powerful. Approaching the task of empirically detailing the assemblage demands thoughtful conceptualization.

> A tangled bundle of co-existing logics, each beating its own rhythm, has first to be apprehended before it can be comprehended, The interactions between different logics, the different modes through which things work themselves out in practice, and the content of the relationships that hold assemblages in place have first to be specified in some way for us to grasp their looming shape and wider potential significance. (Allen 2011, p. 156)

My own sense, however, in examining the rescaling of education through global education policy, is that hierarchy continues to be invoked as a basis of authority and legitimacy to rule (e.g. the EC's determination to advance a European higher education area). These assemblages might be viewed as having particular territorial regimes; ones that need to be traced out in detail, including how modes of rule and claims to rights are navigated and negotiated. In education sectors, these include a new array of scopic systems, networks and hierarchical systems, cross-crossing, overlapping and extending out from particular meeting places. As a result, authority and sovereignty is no longer fused with the national scale but rather is unevenly spread. Finally, it would seem that both *extensivity* and *intensivity* characterizes the new geography of state power, and that these are not mutually exclusive categories. For example, scopic systems, like league tables, both generate a singular (statistical) representation of social activity and a hierarchical ordering to produce a moral judgement about social life; in doing so we can see these two elements working in combination, and with considerable effect.

Conclusion

This chapter set out to explore researching global education policy that avoids the cul-de-sacs that dog many explanations. This is a challenging and ambitious project, and it is evident the works reviewed in this chapter have made a significant contribution to. However, I have argued there is more to do, and that a critical, *processual* account might help advance the project further.

In arguing for a processual approach to the study of the globalization of education policy, I also want to point to risks, and political consequences, if we fail to historicize our accounts of transformations in the education sector, or inadvertently allow ourselves to be seduced by arguments that everything has changed and that now nothing is fixed in either meaning, sites, or sources of power and authority. Rather, our challenge must be to identify, and trace out, the sites, actors, institutions, scales, technologies of rule and consequences of new assemblages of education policy-making and practice which increasingly includes private forms of authority mobilized by powerful players.

I have also suggested that a processual account would be attentive to the new, and different, ways in which points of fixity, bordering and ordering are taking place in the education sector, as well as the changing spatiality of state power. Like Allen and Cochrane, I do not believe that the state is *not* a presence in our everyday lives. Far from it! The state has increasingly acquired for itself a new range of scales from which to act, as well as new tools and means of governing. In combination, this new spatiality of state power strategically advances educational projects that shape the lives and subjectivities of each of us, albeit in contested and mediated ways.

Our analytic accounts of global education policy must also be *relational* in three senses. First, in a strategic sense, in that policy is advanced in order to secure particular projects and interests. These interests are always in relation to others' interests. Second, flows themselves or 'scapes', may be discrete, but they are not disconnected. They overlap as well as interpenetrate the other. We see this very clearly at the current time with intense financialization of the education section, on the one hand, and the attempt to construct education as a trading sector, on the other. Education finds itself caught in the swirl of other flows, and is the object and target for new points of fixity. It is relational in a third sense' that is, policies that are being globalized enter into locations that are themselves circuits of flows anchored in social relations. Global education policy interventions not only generate potential frictions, but might, as Sassen (2006) argues, result in the emergence of 'new logics', and new 'tipping points', in turn altering the nature and shape of the education sector.

By way of a final conclusion, it is worth returning to Prunty's (1984) conceptualization of education policy as the authoritative allocation of values. In asking what difference does the global make, it is clear that it does. Not only have the sites and sources of authority been dispersed away from the national, but the state itself – and with it education as a public service – has been transformed. This has not been the result of a global steamroller; rather, it is the complex reworking, re/bordering and re/ordering of education spaces to include a range of scales of action. What are consequences of these developments, particularly in relation to whose interests are advanced? These are clearly empirical questions and ones that deserve urgent attention.

Questions for discussion

1   What are the main differences between ways of understanding the global?

2   Why does it matter how globalization is conceptualized for research purposes?

3   What are the main criticisms presented with regard to each of the different angles on researching global education policies?

4   What are the implications for understanding international development in a global context when flows along with points of fixity are considered?

5   Consider an education policy problem, and discuss what makes it global using the various arguments from the chapter.

References

Allen, J. (2011). 'Powerful assemblages'. *Area*, 43 (2), 154–157.

Allen, J. and Cochrane, A. (2010). 'Assemblages of state power: Topological shifts in the organisation of government and politics'. *Antipode*, 42 (5), 1071–1089.

Amin, A. (1997). 'Placing globalisation'. *Theory, Culture and Society*, 14 (2), 123–137.

Amin, A. and Thrift, N. (2002). *Cities*. Oxford: Polity.

Appadurai A. (1996). *Modernity at large: Cultural dimensions of globalisation*. Minneapolis, MN: University of Minnesota Press.

Balibar, E. (2002). 'World borders, political borders'. *PMLA*, 117 (1), 71–78.

Bartlett, L. and Vavrus, F. (2011). *Knowing Comparatively: Vertical Case Studies as an Approach to Policy as Practice*, a paper presented to CIES, Montreal, 1–5 May.

Brenner, N. (2004). *New state spaces*. Oxford: Oxford University Press.

Brenner, N. (2009). 'Open questions on state rescaling'. *Cambridge Journal of Regions, Economy and Society*, 2 (2), 123–139.

Bude, H. and Durrschmidt, J. (2010). 'What's wrong with globalization? Contraflow speak – toward an existential turn in the theory of globalisation'. *European Journal of Social Theory*, 13 (4), 481–500.

Carney, S. (2009). 'Negotiating policy in an age of globalization: Exploring educational policyscapes in Denmark, Nepal and China'. *Comparative Education Review*, 53 (1), 63–88.

Carney, S. (2011). 'Imagining globalisation: Educational policyscapes'. In World Yearbook of Education, Gita Steiner Khamsi and Florian Waldow (Eds.), *Policy borrowing, policy lending*. London and New York: Routledge.

Cerny, P. (2001). 'From "Iron Triangles" to "Golden Pentangles"? Globalising the policy process. *Global Governance*, 7 (4), 397–410.

Dale, R. and Robertson, S. (2011). 'Toward a critical grammar of education policy movement'. In World Yearbook of Education, Gita Steiner Khamsi and Florian Waldow (Eds.), *Policy borrowing, policy lending*. London and New York: Routledge.

Ferguson, J. and Gupta, A. (2002). 'Spatialising states: Toward an ethnography of neoliberal governmentality'. *American Ethologist*, 29 (4), 981–1002.

Friedman, T. (2005). *The world is flat: A brief history of the twenty-first century*. New York: Farrar, Straus & Giroux.

Harvey, D. (1999). *The limits to capita (new ed.)*. London and New York: Verso.

Harvey, D. (2006). *Spaces of global capitalism: Toward a theory of uneven geographical development*. London and New York: Verso.

Heyman, J. and Campbell, H. (2009). 'The anthropology of global flows: A critical reading of Appadurai's 'Disjuncture and Difference in the Global Cultural Economy'. *Anthropological Theory*, 9, 131–147.

Jessop, B. (2002). *The future of the capitalist state*. London: Polity.

Knorr Cetina, K. (2008). 'Micro-globalization'. In I. Rossi (Ed.), *Frontiers of globalization research: Theoretical and methodological approaches*. New York: Springer.

MacLeod, G. and Goodwin, M. (1999). 'Space, scale and state strategy: Rethinking urban and regional governance'. *Progress in Human Geography*, 23, 503–527.

Marginson, S. and Mollis, M. (2001). 'The door opens and the tiger leaps: Theories and reflexivities of comparative education for a global millennium'. *Comparative Education Review*, 45 (4), 581–615.

Markusen, A. (1996). 'Sticky places in slippery space: A typology of industrial districts'. *Economic Geography*, 72 (3), 293–313.

Massey, D. (1994). *Space, place and gender*. Cambridge: Polity.

Mittelman, J. (2004). *Whither globalisation: The vortex of knowledge and ideology*. London and New York: Routledge.

O Tuathail, G. (1999). Borderless worlds: Problematising discourses of deterritorialisation. *Geopolitics*, 4 (2), 139–54.

Omhae, K. (1990). *The borderless world*. New York: HarperCollins.

Polanyi, K. (1944). *The great transformation: The political and economic origins of our time*. Boston, MA: Beacon Press.

Prunty, J. (1984). *A critical reformulation of educational policy analysis*. Geelong: Deakin University.

Robertson, S. (2009). 'Producing" the global knowledge economy: The World Bank, The knowledge assessment methodology and education'. In M. Simons and M. Peters (Eds.), *Re-reading Education Policies*. Rotterdam: Sense Publishers, pp. 235–256.

Robertson, S. (2012). 'Placing teachers in global governance agendas'. *Comparative Education Review*, 56 (4), 584–607.

Robertson, S. L. and Dale, R. (2008). 'Researching education in a globalising era: Beyond methodological nationalism, methodological statism, methodological educationism and spatial fetishism'. In J. Resnik (Ed.), *The production of educational knowledge in the global era*. Rotterdam: Sense Publications, pp. 19–32.

Robertson, S., Olds. K., Dale, R. and Dang, Q.-A. (2016). *Global regionalisms and higher education*. Cheltenham: Edward Elgar.

Santos, B. D. S. (2004). 'Interview with editors'. *Globalisation, Societies and Education*, 2 (2), 1–12.

Sassen, S. (2006). *Territory, authority, rights*. Princeton, NJ: Princeton University Press.

Sayer, A. (1984). *Method in social science: A realist approach*. London and New York: Routledge.

Scholte, J. A. (2005). *Globalization: A critical introduction*, 2nd edn. New York: Palgrave Macmillan.

Sheppard, E. (2002). The spaces and times of globalization: place, scale, networks, and positionality. *Economic geography*, 78(3), 307–330.

Sobe, N. and Ortegon, N. (2009). 'Scopic systems, pipes, models and transfers in the global circulation of educational knowledge and practices'. In T. Popkewitz and F. Rizvi (Eds.), *Globalization and the study of education*. New York: NSSE/ Teachers College Press, pp. 49–66.

Steiner-Khamsi, G. (2002). 'Re-framing educational borrowing as a policy strategy'. In M. Caruso and H. E. Tenworth (Eds.), *Internationalisierung-Internationalisation*. Frankfurt: Lang.

Steiner-Khamsi, G. (2004). *The global politics of educational borrowing and lending*. New York: Teachers' College Columbia.

Tsing, A. (2005). *Friction*. Princeton, NJ: Princeton University Press.

Vavrus, F. and Bartlett, L. (2006). 'Comparatively knowing: Making a case for the vertical case study'. *Current Issues in Comparative Education*, 8 (2), 95–103.

Verger, A. (2012). 'Framing and selling global education policy: The promotion of public-private partnerships for education in low-income contexts'. *Journal of Education Policy*, 27 (1): 109–130.

3

Education Policy Networks and Spaces of 'Meetingness': A Network Ethnography of a Brazilian Seminar

Marina Avelar, Dimitra Pavlina Nikita and Stephen J. Ball

Introduction

Public sector reforms initiated since the 1980s have brought about a shift from welfare state government to neoliberal modes of governance, known as the shift 'from government to governance' (Rhodes 1994). Centred on processes of deregulation and privatization, these reforms have introduced new ways of organizing and delivering both services and policy. This has led to a move away from state-centred systems of governing towards a *heterarchical* form that relies on networks of actors (institutions and individual agents) actively engaged in processes of policy-making, which is sometimes referred to as *network governance* (Rhodes 2007). This means that new actors are increasingly involved in policy-making and service delivery, connected in complex, ever-changing, opaque and polycentric networks. These new policy networks have attracted the interest of scholars around the globe and present challenges for researchers, demanding new research approaches, methods and theories.

This chapter aims to contribute to a growing body of literature which is exploring the shift 'from government to governance' in education policy, and particularly the increasing role of private actors, such as businesses, venture capitalists, corporations and others within 'new philanthropy' (Ball 2008). We draw on recent studies that have been working to clarify *how* business and new philanthropy are operating in and through global polycentric education policy networks (Ball and Junemann 2012; Olmedo 2014; Au and Ferrare 2015; Junemann and Ball 2015, among others). So this paper aims to understand *how* global policy networks work and *how* individuals invest their labour to animate these networks and, within this, we carefully look at the relevance of events for global education policy networks.

Policy networks join up diverse actors in many ways and involve both pragmatic social relations and the constitution of moral and epistemic communities (Ball and Junemann 2017). To maintain and animate these networks, actors interact both virtually and face-to-face. Events and meetings, such as seminars, become key sites, or network nodes, for policy-making. They are 'sites of knowledge exchange' and 'sites of persuasion', where relationships are built or strengthened, and policy discourses are shared. Thus, it becomes fundamental that policy analysis pays attention to the 'wheres' of policy (Ball and Junemann 2017).

Although such policy issues have been previously researched, drawing on interview and documentary data, this chapter highlights how the qualitative method of network ethnography can contribute to the study of global policy networks. Network ethnography draws on online material, interviews and ethnographic field notes (e.g. attendance at an event). All of this begins with the construction of a network of actors (known as nodes) where the lines connecting them (known as ties) represent shared information, knowledge and social capital. In this chapter, we will look at one specific network of actors within the space of an event, a seminar called 'Paths for the Quality of Public Education: School Management', which took place in São Paulo, Brazil in September 2015. This seminar, organized by a group of Brazilian private actors (foundations and advocacy coalitions), illustrates very well the use of events to promote the meeting of international representatives from government, business and philanthropy to discuss education policy. In what follows, a discussion of research concepts (policy networks and mobilities) and research method (network ethnography) is followed by a presentation of data regarding an illustrative case: a seminar on education policy and the policy relations represented at this event. The chapter concludes with some analytical considerations, focusing on how events are key sites for policy-making, including public and private actors, and how studying events might shed some light on how global education policy networks operate.

Policy networks, policy mobility and spaces of 'meetingness'

Governance and networks have become buzzwords in policy analysis that are now used extensively across different fields to reflect contemporary changes in politics and the state. Governance refers to 'a *new* process of governing [...] or the *new* method by which society is governed' (Rhodes 1996, pp. 652–653), which can be conceived of as an ongoing shift from the hierarchical and formal authority of the government towards the informal authority of networks (Bevir et al. 2003). This 'new process' is often referred to as *network governance*, which is currently a central concept used in policy sociology studies. Together with bureaucracy and markets, network governance is one of the three contemporary public policy organizational forms which are present in different configurations in different local and national settings around the globe.

The term 'network' refers to both a *conceptual device* used to 'represent a set of "real" changes in the forms of governance of education, both nationally and globally' and to a *method*, as 'an analytic technique for looking at the structure of policy communities and their social relationships' (Ball 2012, p. 6). We will elaborate here on the use of networks as a conceptual device in conjunction with the policy mobility approach and in the following section we will further explore the use of networks as a method.

The policy mobility approach offers a critical orientation to the global movement of policies. It represents an alternative to the concepts of policy transfer, convergence or learning (Sabatier 1991; Haas and Haas 1995; Stone

2004, p. 547). These concepts derive from what Peck and Theodore (2010) refer to as 'orthodox views of policy transfer', in which authors usually assume a rational choice on the part of policy actors, presuming there is a tendency for good policies to drive out bad ones. In contrast, the policy mobility approach is part of a 'new generation of critical policy studies' (2010). Though heterogeneous, these are rooted in critical epistemologies and assume that 'policy actors and actions are understood to be politically mediated and sociologically complex. As such, the beliefs and behaviours of policy actors are embedded within networks of knowledge/expertise (many of which are translocal and transscalar), as well as within more "localised" socioinstitutional milieux' (Peck and Theodore 2012, p. 23). Not all aspects of these 'unorthodox' approaches to global policy analysis are new and distinct (see Dale 2005 and Steiner-Khamsi 2004), but drawing from Peck and Theodore we will briefly sum up some of the main features of these new critical policy studies. First, it is assumed that policy formation and transformation are socially constructed processes and fields of power. Second, actors are not seen as 'lone learners', but members of epistemic communities. Third, mobile policies rarely travel as 'complete packages', but are moved in bits and pieces. Fourth, policies move in a 'complex process of nonlinear reproduction', mutating and morphing as they move. And fifth, mobile policies do not move across a flattened space of transaction, but they move in 'transscalar and interlocal' spaces that are increasingly complex within new forms of uneven economic development. In sum, 'in contrast with the orthodox literature on policy transfer, the governing metaphors in critical policy studies are not those of transit and transaction, but of mobility and mutation' (Peck and Theodore 2010, p. 170).

Besides highlighting the power relations present in the movement of policies, the mobility turn also emphasizes the role of mundane activities of policy work, the labour involved in policy movement, especially how 'the bases of such [physical, corporeal] travel are new ways in which social life is apparently "networked"', that is 'life is networked but it also involves specific co-present encounters within certain times and places'. In this sense, 'meetingness, and thus different forms and modes of travel, are central to much social life, a life involving strange combinations of increasing distance and intermittent co-presence' (Urry 2003, pp. 155–156). Urry's *mobilities paradigm*, although primarily applied to social networks, pertains to 'an alternative theoretical and methodological landscape' (Urry 2007, p. 18), which can prove fruitful once applied to policy analysis.

The mobility turn emphasizes movement in its multiple configurations and variations, from physical movement of materials and people to digital or virtual movement of other goods (e.g. information, ideas, even of power). It 'connects the analysis of different forms of travel, transport and communications with the multiple ways in which economic and social life is performed and organized through time and across various spaces' (Urry 2007, p. 6). Thus, the movement and labour invested in different activities, including policy-making is stressed. This allows us to consider how 'very "costly" meetings, communications and travel through time–space' are central to networks, and are 'necessary to "form" and to "cement" weak ties at least for another stretch of time' (Urry 2007, p. 231). By 'meeting', he refers to 'both the highly formalized with "agendas", structure and timetables and the informal to where the specific space and time are planned in advance to where they are negotiated en route' (p. 232). In these spaces of meetingness 'network members, from a range of backgrounds, come together, where stories are told, visions shared, arguments reiterated, new relations made, partnerships forged, and commitments made' (Ball).

In paying attention to people and policies in movement, mobilities research require methods that allow us to access and observe social relationships and interactions in the most direct sense. This means 'observing directly or in digitally enhanced forms mobile bodies undergoing various performances of travel, work and play'. Options would include 'mobile ethnography', 'time-space diaries' and 'cyber-research', methods that stimulate the memory or methods that would capture the 'atmosphere of place' or 'transfer points' (Urry 2007). The following section outlines network ethnography, the method we employ and which seems to be aligned best with this particular theoretical approach.

Network ethnography and following policy

The study presented here has employed a particular version of ethnographic research called network ethnography, as deployed policy sociology scholars who are interested in the diverse interactions among public and private actors in education policy-making and service delivery. Ball and Junemann (2012); Junemann and Ball (2015); Olmedo (2014); Hogan, Sellar and Lingard (2015); and Au and Ferrare (2015) have employed network ethnography as an appropriate method of investigation of the participation of business and new philanthropy in education governance. This combines the basic elements of ethnographic research with techniques from Social Network Analysis (SNA) 'in which researchers aim to construct the network governance structures through which organizational and individual actors shape educational policies and reform movements' (Au and Ferrare 2015, p. 11). To do so, the method consists of 'a mapping of the form and content of policy relations in a particular field [...] towards anthropological version of network analysis with an emphasis on the understanding of the contents, transactions and meanings' (Ball and Junemann 2012, p. 13).

Originating in Harvard's sociology department and while multidisciplinary was in its early stages (psychology, sociology and social anthropology), SNA developed using mathematics to depict, measure and conceptualize social relations (Prell 2012). Despite its strength in creating, measuring and presenting social relations, SNA has been criticized by Howard (2002, p. 550) of failing 'to capture detail on incommensurate yet meaningful relationships', as it is not helpful in 'uncovering and identifying culture' (p. 560). It can also be short of the 'rich information' that researchers can have access to only by participating in the context one is researching, while it 'has also limited use in revealing stories of mobility within communities' (2002). Network ethnography aims to address these shortcomings, by combining field observations and narratives (typical ethnographic tools) with the tools of mapping social relations from SNA. In Howard's (2002, p. 561) words, 'Network ethnography is the process of using ethnographic field methods on cases and field sites selected using social network analysis.' By using the method of network ethnography, it becomes possible to capture the detail and meaning of the active policy relations and the relations and interactions, practices and meanings these actors share, as well as their influence on and participation in the policy process (Ball and Junemann 2012). Furthermore, as the networks of governance grow in scope and influence, the focus on policy networks is increasingly relevant, with the contribution of SNA being that 'it gives primacy to social relations and embeds social actors within these networks of relations' (Au and Ferrare 2015).

Ball and Junemann (2012) describe a set of three main activities employed in network ethnography: first, 'extensive and exhaustive internet searches' around the primary actors of the studied network; second, interviews with individuals identified at the online stage; third, the participation and observation of events as key sites of policy making and network maintenance. Throughout the three activities, 'policy network' graphs are built as a tool to identify relevant individuals, institutions and relations regarding specific policies or networks. Drawing on these data, networks are addressed 'narratively' and 'discursively' with a focus on network histories and their evolution. The network graph becomes a research tool that supports the 'following' of people and tracking of policy developments. The graph is not a research 'product', or the end point of analysis in itself, it is not simply a matter of finding network structures and applying measures as in more orthodox versions of SNA.

With the aim of exploring how network ethnography can be applied to the field of global education policy studies, this chapter explores one single event, the seminar 'Paths for Public Education Quality: Education Management', to analyse the labour that is involved in network governance and the global mobility of policies and discourses. Starting from the event's programme, the speakers and presenters were 'followed' online, meaning that they were tracked through spaces, places and interactions before the event. We searched for previous events they had spoke at, official meetings they (co)attended, and institutions or projects they had supported or had supported them, and they had worked or collaborated with. As Peck and Theodore (2010) describe it, this involves 'following processes, practices, discourses, technologies or networks, thereby connecting sites, scales, and subjects' (p. 171). This allowed us to better understand the 'social in the social networks' (Ball 2016). Data were collected from multiple online sources, especially institutional websites (governments and foundations) and newspapers (reporting meetings and events). Some interviews were then carried out to extend online findings and offer a view from inside the network (Ball and Junemann 2012). Here we draw on two of these interviews: one with a project manager at the Lemann Foundation and one with the director of the Natura Institute. The interviews were semi-structured, with questions focused on specific relations and partnerships identified during online searches. For the present chapter, we did not conduct on-site observations, but rather watched the videos of the seminar presentations that were made available on the Unibanco Institute website.

We would like to raise some crucial methodological considerations here regarding network ethnography in general and the study of events in particular, and their significance for the analysis of policy networks with a global reach. First, if we accept that 'education policy analysis can no longer be limited to within the boundaries of the nation state, what scholars such as Jessop and Brenner call "methodological territorialism"' (Ball 2012), it becomes necessary to find new methodological approaches. Network ethnography replaces a focus on boundaries and structure with attention to flows and relationships. It requires us to attend to spaces of policy, in, between and beyond the limits of the nation state. Second, in using network ethnography, researchers direct their attention to specific people and institutions, together with their practices – the *whos, hows* and *wheres* of policy. This allows us to address the materiality of policy mobility and avoid the abstraction of structural studies that oversimplify the global movement of policies and discourses. Third, global networks are fluid, unstable and vast. The fast-changing composition and the global reach of a policy network create immense challenges for education policy researchers. Thus, the study of an event offers a bounded case within a complex global policy network, making research more feasible and focused. Furthermore, attention to events is one form of response to the increasing opacity and elusiveness of new modes of policy activity and governance. Network ethnography in this sense can identify social relations and connections and shared rationalities, interests and agendas.

The seminar 'Paths for the Quality of Public Education: School Management'

The seminar entitled 'Paths for the Quality of Public Education: School Management,' held in São Paulo in September 2015, was organized by the Instituto Unibanco[1] and the newspaper *Folha*,[2] with the support of Insper[3] – that is a big national bank and a large national newspaper, supported by a higher education institution that was created and is directed by new philanthropists in Brazil. The organizers were able to employ their financial and social capitals in the organization of this event: the former, to fund the seminar, and the latter to invite high-profile speakers and policy-makers, and ensure intense media coverage. This event was chosen for the current research due to three main aspects: the relevance of the organizing institutions; the size and importance of the event; and the presence of international speakers, which was strategically presented as the 'comparative aspect' of the seminar. According to the official website, the seminar aimed at 'promoting the dialogue between the Brazilian experience of school management and international cases that reached relevant improvements in student learning results'. It is an interesting example of 'meetingness' in education policy-making, within a large event that promoted the encounter of national and international actors from government, business and new philanthropy. It illustrates the changing nature of face-to-face meetings, which are 'less concerned with traditional (one-way) presentations of information and passive learning and more with building and sustaining networks and exchanging social goods' (Urry 2007, p. 165).

The main 'international' speakers were Barry McGaw, from Australia, Michael Wilshaw and Anthony McNamara, from England, and Mary Jean Gallagher, from Canada. Each of these speakers brought a 'symbolic association with specific locations [that] evokes a grounded form of authenticity, implies feasibility, and signals an ideologically palatable origin story' (Peck and Theodore 2010, p. 170). Among the Brazilian speakers, there were representatives from the Ministry of Education (MEC), state and municipal secretariats of education, multilateral organizations, universities and foundations. Amongst these national speakers, two 'cases'[4] were highlighted at the seminar programme: Sobral (and its state Ceará) and the state of Goiás. The first case has been increasingly used by new philanthropists in Brazil as a 'policy story' (Ball 2016) or a compelling argument for education reform. The second case has been discussing the privatization of school management according to the models of the American Charter Schools and English Academies. These state representatives are a receptive audience to the possibilities of further reform and are willing receivers or emulators. The seminar speakers are presented in the table below:

Mary Jean Gallagher	Vice minister of Education from the province of Ontario
Barry McGaw	Melbourne University, former president of the Australian Curriculum, Assessment and Reporting Authority (ACARA), also worked at Organization for Economic Co-operation and Development (OECD)
Michael Wilshaw	Chief of Inspections at OFSTED (UK)
Anthony McNamara	International Associate in National College for Teaching and Leadership (NCTL), UK
Renato Janine	Minister of Education – MEC
Manuel Palácios	Secretary of Basic Education – MEC
Claudia Costin	Senior Director for Education – World Bank
Francisco Soares	President of the Anísio Teixeira National Institute of Educational Research and Studies (INEP)
Julio Cesar C. Alexandre	Secretary of Education – Sobral Municipal Secretariat of Education
Mauricio Holanda Maia	Secretary of Education – Ceará State Secretariat of Education
Raquel Teixeira	Secretary of Education – Goiás State Secretariat of Education
Ricardo Henriques	Executive Superintendent of Unibanco Institute
Pedro Malan	Vice President of Unibanco Institute Council
Ricardo Paes de Barros	Professor at Insper, Cátedra Instituto Ayrton Senna

These speakers were 'followed' digitally, with the intention of finding pre-existing relationships, previous meetings and events they had co-attended and their participation in other related movements or projects. Below you will find a policy network graph built with the data collected online and designed with the software Gephi. The network nodes (individuals or institutions) are connected by edges, which can represent co-presence in previous events (as speakers), financial investments and/or partnerships (institutional or in projects). We emphasize here that this is a qualitative take on social network analysis. Thus, this graph has been used to guide us in the process of collecting data and qualitatively analysing this network, with a focus on how actors operate and the labour employed in this policy network.

Following the graph, there is a brief analysis of the network relations within which the speakers are located, with some description of those relations that are represented graphically. We cannot attempt here an exhaustive account of all the people and relations represented at this event, but rather offer a purposeful analysis. We will focus on two aspects of this network: firstly,

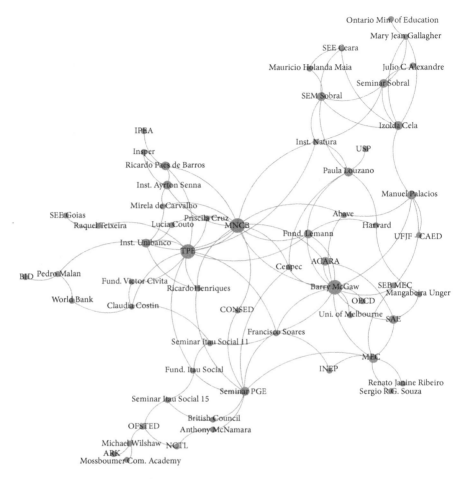

FIGURE 3.1 *Network of pre-existing relationships at the seminar*

we discuss an undisclosed presence at the event, the advocacy coalition *Movement for the National Common Base (MNCB)*. Although not made known in the seminar programme, many of its members, institutional or individual, were at this seminar. We draw on this example to argue how events are spaces for policy influence and dialogue, and how this can be done with little accountability and transparency. Second, we discuss the series of events that joined up the seminar speakers, and how they had met in previous meetings.

Events as spaces for policy advocacy: The Movement for the National Common Base

The Movement for the National Common Base (MNCB, or referred to as 'Movement') was well represented at the seminar. Many speakers and institutions at the seminar, from Brazil and other countries, were supporters or related to MNCB. The Movement is an increasing active presence in education policy conversations in Brazil. Its members have privileged access to spaces of policy-making but its efforts and engagement with policy remain mainly opaque.

This seminar was held amid debates over the needs and purposes of a standardized national curriculum in Brazil, which have mobilized different interest groups. At the moment, Brazil does not have a mandatory curriculum, but rather a 'National Curricular Parameter' (NCP), created during the 1990s, which presents curricular guidelines. Nonetheless, critics question how 'non-mandatory' the NPC is, arguing it has characteristics of a 'curriculum' rather than 'guiding principles'. Thus, there has been an ongoing debate about 'what', 'how' and 'who' should decide on teaching and learning in Brazil (Galian 2014). In this context, at the beginning of the 2010s the creation of a standardized and mandatory curriculum, the so-called National Curricular Common Base (NCCB, or simply referred to as 'Base') started to gain greater support in Brazil. New philanthropy actors created in 2013 the advocacy group called MNCB that has been a significant participant in the debate.

MNCB is constituted of both people and institutions. The 'institutional supporters' of the movement include new philanthropy (family or corporate) organizations, research organizations and education civil servants associations. The decisions of MNCB are taken in group meetings, where members can voice opinions. MNCB is funded by Lemann Foundation, Natura Institute and the bank Itau BBA, while Lemann Foundation is the 'executive secretariat', with the task of carrying out the decisions taken by the group. The institutional supporters include research associations (ABAVE and CENPEC), new philanthropy, both family and corporate (Foundations Lemann and Roberto Marinho, and Institutes Ayrton Senna, Inspirare, Natura and Unibanco), education civil servants associations (CONSED and UNDIME), a corporate advocacy coalition (Todos Pela Educação) and an NGO (CEDAC).

The concept of international comparisons and 'benchmarking' is fundamental for MNCB. Its work draws upon curriculum examples from other countries, namely the United States, Canada, England, Chile and Australia. Besides the institutional supporters, MNCB has international individual and institutional partners. In this context, Barry McGaw and ACARA are key international partners. ACARA was hired as a consultant for MNCB, and has produced commissioned studies. Barry McGaw is part of its list of 'international dialogue', with scholars that produce studies and deliver presentations for MNCB. Mary Jean Gallagher is part of an education reform effort of Sobral, supported by Natura Institute. Natura Institute has been working on issues of curriculum reform in Sobral since 2014, which is to be used as a case or a 'policy story' for the MNBC. Thus, here we see a concatenation of activities which exploit a 'policy window', created by the receptiveness of state governments, to piloting education policies, with the more general goal of constructing a policy story that will support advocacy at the national level. The director of the Natura Institute described their intention in an interview:

> In Sobral we are helping them to reconsider their curriculum. So to do that, the first step is to know what exists 'out there' (outside Brazil). Then the work Ontario did concerning curriculum was relevant, so we brought here a person from there to talk to them. [...] And every benchmarking that was done, for this project in Sobral, was made available to MNCB, for the specialists to study. So we try to link one thing to the other, we never do anything isolated. (Interview Natura Institute, São Paulo, May 2016)

So although the event was about school management, most of the speakers were related to MNCB. They were direct supporters, MNCB project consultants, or had worked for institutions that support it (like TPE and Itau BBA). When asked about this representation from MNCB at the seminar, a project manager from Lemann Foundation replied:

> Unibanco Institute is a member of the Movement. So if it is going to do a seminar of education that will discuss curriculum, it will make use of the Movement's network. I think it is one of the differences of the Movement, that we really created a body with many tentacles, in a good way. So if one is doing an event, it will ask the others who is the best speaker to invite, and in the end the members of the Movement are all in the same events. (Interview Lemann Foundation, São Paulo, April 2016)

As MNCB has organized itself as a network with many powerful foundations as members, it is able to populate and steer events, and in doing so, reach more people and disseminate policies and discourses. A small group of foundations can, together, arrange events with policy-makers and choose speakers who support their policy agenda, within their epistemic community. So, as the interviewee puts it, it is always the same group of people that populate these policy events, shaping discourses and delimiting what is thinkable and unthinkable. By not being announced in the programme and news, MNCB's presence and labour are neither transparent nor accountable to citizens. New philanthropists can organize such events by applying their economic and social capitals, and invite relevant policy-makers under the safeguarding of offering a formative event, where international specialists 'gather to share best policy practices'.

The backstory: Many events assembling a network

The analysed seminar was one amongst many others that, together, were used to create and maintain policy relations and incite a climate for change. Before the seminar, the international speakers Mary Gallagher, Barry McGaw and Anthony McNamara had previously been to Brazil at other events or meetings with Brazilian institutions and individuals also present at this seminar. We will briefly describe some of the previous contacts between speakers to illustrate this role and importance of meetings and the dense connection among seminar speakers.

In June 2015, about two months before the seminar, Sobral's Municipal Government promoted an event focused on 'Education Management and Curriculum Reformulation' where Mary Jean Gallagher was the keynote speaker. In the same week she held meetings with the state secretary of education, the state university and signed a collaboration agreement between Sobral and Ontario. The event was organized by the municipal and state governments together with Natura Institute. This institute has a long-standing relation with Sobral, since 2013, and aims to make Sobral a 'showcase' of educational policies for Brazil. After supporting the city in implementing 'full-time'[5] schools, Natura Institute started to invest in a curricular to reform Sobral. The project started after a meeting held in São Paulo with Sobral's mayor, Natura Institute and Votorantim. Not long after, in May 2015, Paula Lozano, a consultant from Lemann Foundation, was hired by Natura Institute and presented a 'diagnostic study' together with a proposal for a new curriculum for Sobral.[6]

McNamara spoke at a large seminar organized by CONSED with support of new philanthropy, including Itau Social, CENPEC and Natura Institute. The event was held in 2014, with speakers from the Brazilian Ministry of Education, INEP, Unibanco Institute and CEDAC. Following from this event, a selection of thirty Brazilian head teachers undertook a two-week-long course in England with McNamara at the NCTL.

Most importantly, Barry McGaw has been visiting Brazil since 2011, when he spoke at a seminar organized by Itau Social, where Claudia Costin also spoke. In 2013, he presented a lecture at the ABAVE biannual meeting and offered an interview to CENPEC (interviewed by Paula Lozano). McGaw also visited Brazil in July 2015, less than two months before the seminar, to attend meetings with the Brazilian Ministry of Education – including the Brazilian seminar speakers Renato Janine, Manuel Palácios and Francisco Soares. After attending meetings in Brasília (the capital of Brazil), McGaw went to São Paulo for meetings with new philanthropy institutions, in particular the Lemann Foundation.

So Gallagher had met state and municipal representatives in a seminar, funded by Natura Institute. McNamara also had met new philanthropists and state representatives in another seminar organized by CENPEC and Itau. McGaw had met federal representatives in an official government visit, and then new philanthropists from MNBC in another seminar. This sequence of meetings illustrate that 'networks have a history', that meetings 'join-up' networks, and that at events are spaces where 'the past, the present and possible futures co-exist' (McCann and Ward 2012). There might be, and there are likely to be, other spaces, virtual or face-to-face, where these actors maintain such relationships. However, these events are traceable only though scattered, traces of opaque and fast-changing policy relations.

Regarding this use of events by foundations in their policy work, a project manager from Lemann Foundation stated in an interview:

Since we started this process [with MNCB] we have organised many meetings. Twice already we have taken a group of 50 people for a week long immersion at Yale university. Back in 2013 that was how we started, we took a group of people to Yale to discuss curriculum, and there the Movement was created. Then last year [2015] we did it with people that were starting their mandates in January, state secretariats, federal deputies, state deputies, governors [...] Every year there is a seminar Lemann-Stanford here in Brazil. They bring specialists from there to discuss education themes. This year it is going to be in June, the theme is the Base. Last year we had an enormous seminar in July with all the writers of the Base. We brought specialists from Australia, one from the American Common Core of Mathematics and from Chile, so this kind of activity is very common.

And he/she added:

Only this year, the ACARA team has come to Brazil twice. Once in January, and then they do a bunch of meetings, a lot of discussions to help us solve the main issues, exchange ideas, talk with the Movement. But also talk with Congressman, talk with the Base writing team and talk with everyone that is important in this debate. They came back recently, two weeks ago, and stayed for over a week again in a series of important meetings, and the agenda is this: what is the biggest challenge now? Say 'challenge A', and then how Australia dealt with this challenge, with strategies A, B and C. Without the ambition of incorporating their solutions exactly the same way, but expecting they might inspire our solutions here in Brazil. So we do this very often. Barry came because at the time he was ahead of ACARA and we were at this point of discussing. It all happens very often, we do this many times and works really well. (Interview Lemann Foundation, São Paulo, April 2016)

In this extensive quote, the interviewee clearly explains how the use of meetings and events is a deliberate strategy for Lemann Foundation and MNCB; it is a fundamental part of how they operate. First, as she indicates, people are brought to Brazil or taken elsewhere to 'discuss matters of interest'. Such meetings, that often involve carefully selected values, are spaces attentively crafted for policy-making. Seminars are planned to gather the chosen people: the selected 'specialists', who will rehearse and reinforce the funder's beliefs, are brought together with 'everyone that is important in this debate', or the policy-makers and supporters needed to advance their agenda. Second, one journey is often exploited to the full by scheduling series of meetings. So a public seminar can be a small part of a larger set of meetings, but it is the part that surfaces to the public amid other blurry activities that are not easily accessible. Third, in the case of ACARA and MNCB, there is a mobility of policy strategies. The 'specialist' comes as a 'consultant', who will offer advice regarding specific challenges one is facing. So new philanthropies from one place draw not only on policy examples from elsewhere, but also on the means used to achieve such policies.

We would argue that in such opaque and sprawling policy networks, researchers are unlikely to identify the relevant people, institutions and relations, or to know what questions to ask in interviews without the prior conduct of deep internet searches and an understanding of connections between actors in a network. Secondly, as some of these relations might be somewhat controversial, identifying such relations before interviews is a leverage. Once relevant relation are identified, they can be better understood through interviews.

Conclusion

Recently, researchers (Ball and Junemann 2012; Olmedo 2014; Au and Ferrare 2015; Junemann and Ball 2015, among others) have set out to 'understand and explain how neoliberalism "gets done in practice", that is to unpack the mechanisms by which neoliberal discourses and rationalities take shape and transform our everyday lives and experiences' (Olmedo 2014, p. 576). Within the new heterarchical governance arrangements, networks of public bodies, private actors, individuals and institutions, networks that even transcend the boundaries of nation states, become the field within which such mechanisms operate and flourish. It is 'by paying attention to these agents of neo-liberalism [that] it becomes possible to think about how power and "expertise" flow between nations and how policy entrepreneurs, NGOs, think tanks and commercial providers of education "do" globalization' (Exley et al. 2011, p. 213). Events are one space of global interaction and activity, of dissemination of ideas and practices, of network building and capital strengthening. Taking a seminar as our focal point, we are able to see how policy-makers use events as an opportunity to reiterate, re-contextualize and disseminate global education policy discourses, or 'education solutions' as they refer to them.

In particular, the seminar described in this chapter is an example of how events provide the platform and space for these actors to 'do' neoliberalism and enact network governance. 'Thought leaders' and 'policy entrepreneurs' from different countries, such as Canada, the United Kingdom, Australia and Brazil, meet in these events with more traditional policy actors and new philanthropists to discuss education problems, policies, partnerships and investments and to mediate and translate transposable policy models. These are 'sociologically complex actors [...] whose identities and professional trajectories are often bound up with the policy positions and fixes they espouse' (Peck and Theodore 2010). In this sense, the choice of invited speakers makes evident the policy models the organizers aim to promote. The policy entrepreneurs bring with them 'models that emanate from the "right" places invoke positive associations of (preferred forms of) best practices [...] they connote networks of policy-making sites, linked by overlapping ideological orientations' (2010, p. 171).

Invitations to such events are also a reflection of embodied network capital, that is, 'the real and potential social relations that mobilities afford' (Urry 2007, p. 196) as well as an opportunity for a further reshaping and reinvestment and enhancement of this capital. The international speakers of our event, Mary Jean Gallagher (Canada), Barry McGaw (Australia) and Anthony McNamara (England), had been in Brazil months before the event, building relations with Brazilian actors also present in the seminar. In this sense, although the international speakers are presented as representatives of 'international best cases', they are also products of previous networked relations that depend on different kinds of capitals, including financial and network capital. In this sense, policy networks have a history. As McCann and Ward (2012, p. 48) put it, these events are 'relational sites where the past, present and potential future of a policy can co-exist. Past "successes", current "problems" and future "scenarios" are discussed comparatively'. We would argue that not only the past, present and possible futures of a policy co-exist in events, but also the past, present and future of policy networks. In such events, actors bring to bear the relations they have built over time; they engage with network members building new relations and have the possibility of initiating or being recruited to new policy endeavours.

Regarding methods for the study of global education policy, within a network ethnography approach events offer researchers a window into vast and blurry policy networks. They are often spaces where policy relations become visible, at least fleetingly. Therefore, events enable us to find connections that would not be apparent otherwise. So far, we have shown the labour involved in assembling the network. This labour might involve travelling to sites of policy, meeting over conference calls or investing time and money in maintaining social relationships, formal and informal, as well as, more publically, writing reports and blogs, giving newspaper interviews and speaking at public events. Having access to this network labour is challenging to researchers. Nonetheless, here we have shown *following the policy* to be a productive research tool. By following policy, it was possible to see some aspects of the labour involved in the global mobility of curriculum policies, such as network members co-attending previous events, having meetings with state policy-makers and presenting their policy 'solutions' to different audiences. By *following actors*, it was possible to identify previously unknown relations between actors and institutions, such as between MNCB and ACARA, and their development over time. These relations, the interactions that take place among them and the spaces of policy in which they are enacted are, we suggest, part of a reconstruction of the mix between bureaucracy, markets and networks that constitutes educational governance and concomitantly the reform of the state. It is not always the case that events and relations translate directly into policy and practice but they contribute to a series of moves and actions that make change possible.

Within a global setting where everything is in a state of flux, where technologies have created an intricate networked society and communications happen instantly and most of the times 'behind the scenes', it is important for researchers to be able to think and work within a framework that can accommodate such rapid change and inherent opacity. In this chapter, we have drawn upon work in progress to showcase how research within the mobilities paradigm, in general, and network ethnography as a method, in particular, can help address these issues. We argue that the mobilities paradigm can provide the conceptualizations and methods to enable research that aims to explore how education policy is made and governance done in a global context. Network ethnography offers techniques that are fit-for-purpose in the post-government world of policy.

Questions for discussion

1   Have you ever encountered an education event like the one analysed in this chapter? Before reading this chapter, did you think they were relevant for policy-making or policy analysis? And after reading it, has your opinion changed?

2 In what ways, in theory and practice, does mobilities research differ from more traditional forms of policy analysis?

3 What are the contributions of network ethnography to the analysis of global education policies?

4 What are the strengths and weaknesses of analysing events for policy analysis?

Notes

1 Created in 1982, this institute is part of the social investment of the bank Itau-Unibanco, which works mainly with secondary school.

2 Brazilian newspaper, the second in circulation in the country.

3 Non-profit private institution of higher education and research. Co-created by Lemann, Sicupira and Telles, in its councils there are relevant new philanthropists.

4 Brazil, as a federation, organizes its education in three administrative levels: federal, with higher education, state level, with primary and secondary education, and municipal, with primary education. States and municipalities have reasonable scope to decide upon education policies.

5 Full-time schools are the ones where children spend the entire day in school, differently from what happens in the majority of Brazilian schools, where children spend either the morning or afternoon.

6 This is not publicly available at the present time.

References

Au, W. and Ferrare, J. J. (2015). *Mapping corporate education reform: Power and policy networks in the neoliberal state*. New York: Routledge.

Ball, S. J. (2008). 'New philanthropy, new networks and new governance in education'. *Political Studies*, 56 (4), 747–765. doi:10.1111/j.1467–9248.2008.00722.x.

Ball, S. J. (2012). *Global education inc: New policy networks and the neo-liberal imaginary*. Oxon: Routledge.

Ball, S. J. (2016). 'Following policy: Networks, network ethnography and education policy mobilities'. *Journal of Education Policy*, 31, 1–18.

Ball, S. J. and Junemann, C. (2012). *Networks, new governance and education*. Great Britain: The Policy Press.

Bevir, M., Rhodes, R. A. W. and Weller, P. (2003). 'Traditions of governance: Interpreting the changing role of the public sector'. *Public Administration*, 81 (1), 1–17. doi:10.1111/1467–9299.00334

Börzel, T. A. (1998). 'Organizing Babylon – On the different conceptions of policy networks'. *Public Administration*, 76 (2), 253–273. doi:10.1111/1467-9299.00100.

Dale, R. (2005). 'Globalisation, knowledge economy and comparative education'. *Comparative Education*, 41 (2), 117–149.

Exley, S., Braun, A. and Ball, S. (2011). 'Global education policy: Networks and flows'. *Critical Studies in Education*, 52 (3), 213–218. http://doi.org/10.1080/175 08487.2011.604079.

Galian, C. V. A. (2014). 'Brazilian curriculum parameters and the development of curricular proposals in Brazil'. *Cadernos de Pesquisa*, 44 (153), 648–669.

Haas, P. M. and Haas, E. B. (1995). 'Learnign to learn: Improving international governance'. *Global governance*, 1 (3), 255–285.

Hogan, A., Sellar, S. and Lingard, B. (2015). Network restructuring of global edu-business. In W. Au and J. Ferrare, *Mapping corporate education reform: Power and policy networks in the neoliberal state,* London: Routledge, pp. 43–64.

Howard, P. N. (2002). 'Network ethnography and the hypermedia organization: New media, new organizations, new methods. *New Media & Society*, 4 (4), 550–574. doi:10.1177/146144402321466813.

Jessop, B., Brenner, N. and Jones, M. (2008). 'Theorizing sociospatial relations'. *Environment and Planning D: Society and Space*, 26 (3), 389–401. doi:https://doi.org/10.1068/d9107.

Junemann, C. and Ball, S. (2015). *Pearson and PALF: The mutating giant.* Brussels, Belgium: *Education International.*

Knox, H., Savage, M. and Harvey, P. (2006). 'Social networks and the study of relations: Networks as method, metaphor and form'. *Economy and Society*, 35 (1), 113–140. doi:https://doi.org/10.1080/03085140500465899.

McCann, E. J. (2008). 'Expertise, truth, and urban policy mobilities: Global circuits of knowledge in the development of vancouver, Canada's "four Pillar" drug strategy'. *Environment and Planning A*, 40 (4), 885–904. doi:https://doi.org/10.1068/a38456.

McCann, E. and Ward, K. (2012). 'Assembling urbanism: Following policies and "studying through" the sites and situations of policy making'. *Environment and Planning A*, 44 (1), 42–51.

Olmedo, A. (2014). 'From England with love… ARK, heterarchies and global "philanthropic governance"'. *Journal of Education Policy*, 29 (5), 575–597. http://doi.org/10.1080/02680939.2013.859302.

Peck, J. and Theodore, N. (2010). 'Mobilizing policy: Models, methods, and mutations'. *Geoforum*, 41 (2), 169–174.

Peck, J. and Theodore, N. (2012). 'Follow the policy: A distended case approach'. *Environment and Planning A*, 44 (1), 21–30.

Prell, C. (2012). *Social network analysis: History, theory and methodology.* London: Sage.

Rhodes, R. A. W. (1994). 'The hollowing out of the state: The changing nature of the public service in Britain'. *The Political Quarterly*, 65 (2), 138–151. doi:10.1111/j.1467-923X.1994.tb00441.x.

Rhodes, R. A. W. (1996). 'The new governance: Governing without government1'. *Political Studies*, 44 (4), 652–667. doi:10.1111/j.1467-9248.1996.tb01747.x.

Rhodes, R. A. W. (2007). 'Understanding governance: Ten years on'. *Organization Studies*, 28 (8), 1243–1264. doi:10.1177/0170840607076586.

Sabatier, P. (1991). 'Political science and public policy'. *PS: Political Science and Politics*, 24 (2), 144–156.

Steiner-Khamsi, G. (2004). *The global politics of educational borrowing and lending*. New York: Teachers College Press.

Stone, D. (2004). 'Transfer agents and global networks in the "transnationalization" of policy'. *Journal of European Public Policy*, 11 (3), 545–566. doi:10.1080/13501760410001694291.

Urry, J. (2003). Social networks, travel and talk. *British Journal of Sociology*, 54 (2), 155–175. doi:10.1080/0007131032000080186.

Urry, J. (2007). *Mobilities*. Cambridge: Polity Press.

Further reading

Ball, S. J., Junemann, C. and Santori, D. (2017). *Edu.net: Globalisation and education policy mobility*. Taylor & Francis.

Sheller, M. and Urry, J. (2006). 'The new mobilities paradigm'. *Environment and Planning A*, 38 (2), 207–226. doi:10.1068/a37268.

Williams, P. (2002). 'The competent boundary spanner'. *Public Administration*, 80 (7), 103–124. doi:10.1080/0007131032000080186.

4

Silences, Stereotypes and Local Selection: Reflections for the SDGs on Some Experiences with the MDGs and EFA

Elaine Unterhalter

Chapter Outline

Introduction

Addressing gender inequality has been a key concern of global policy on education and poverty for many decades (Unterhalter 2007; Rizvi and Lingaard 2010; Unterhalter 2016). At the apex of the global initiatives from 2000 to 2015 stood the Millennium Development Goals (MDGs) with three out of eight goals addressing these areas – MDG1 deals with poverty, MDG2 with universal primary education and MDG 3 with gender equality and the empowerment of women. A second major global framework, put in place in 2000, the Dakar Platform for Action on Education For All (EFA), had goals on education and gender and, while not explicitly concerned with poverty, implicitly addressed this because of the very large numbers of poor children out of school or not flourishing within. In September 2015, the UN General Assembly adopted seventeen Sustainable Development Goals (SDGs). The SDGs comprised an expanded range of goals, targets and indicators. SDG4 addresses all phases of education from early years to higher. A number of other goals and targets entail aspects of education. The MDGs had separated out different goals, paying little attention to how they might affect each other (Waage et al. 2010). Some features were perverse, for example the focus only on primary education made it difficult to formulate plans for the technical and higher education needed to fulfil other goals (Unterhalter 2014). The SDGs attempted to remedy this shortcoming.

Attempts to implement the MDGs and EFA elicited a huge literature, summarized and assessed each year in the UNESCO Global Monitoring Reports (UNESCO 2015). However, relatively little research was conducted on interlinking gender, education and poverty, although girls' education became a particular focus for interventions (Sperling and Winthrop 2015; Unterhalter 2016).

This chapter explores how global policy frameworks like the MDGs and EFA were understood in a range of local settings, how these understandings bear on practice and what reflections on this tell us about approaches to framing global obligation for the engagement with the SDGs. The analysis develops partly through discussion of some conceptual literature on global policy frameworks. It also draws on data from the *Gender, education and global poverty reduction initiatives* (GEGPRI) research project conducted between 2007 and 2011,[1] which looked at understandings of global gender, education and poverty policy in two countries – South Africa and Kenya – and a number of global organizations. In such a short space, it is impossible to do justice to the nuance of the large body of data collected for this project, and a fuller exploration of a number of themes is made in other publications from the project (e.g. Dieltiens et al. 2009; Karlsson 2010; Unterhalter and North 2011a,b; Unterhalter et al. 2012).

Conceptualizing global frameworks

Global policy frameworks like the MDGs, EFA and the SDGs have generated a rich literature which considers the nature of claims made for global compact and the forms of realization that emerge. The debate about global obligation has moved from assessing whether this is feasible and desirable (Wallace Brown and Held 2010), through discussing how to achieve a transformation of unjust structures (Paul et al. 2006), what level of sufficiency in education or poverty reduction is required and whose obligations were entailed (Brock 2013; Young 2013). Central to this debate is a concern with the ethical form of the political relationship between global, national and local bodies, and the ways in which the contours of context are important to distilling the shape of relationships.

In trying to distinguish different approaches to global obligation associated with the policy languages of a number of UN gatherings which gave prominence to gender, education and poverty reduction, I have identified differences between a minimalist conception of securing only universal primary schooling, gender parity and reduction in poverty for a portion of the population, and a maximalist vision of global responsibility and engagement with rights, capabilities and gender equity and some of the historical contexts in which each emerges (Unterhalter 2007, 2012, 2016). Similar points were made in assessments of the MDGs. Gore (2010, p. 71) considered the MDGs to represent a shift from a 'procedural conception' of international society with a 'common respect for a set of rules, norms and standard practices' such as those associated with the Universal Declaration of Human Rights or the Beijing Declaration on Women and Gender, to a 'purposive conception', where the stress is on a 'co-operative venture to promote common ends'. For Gore, a procedural conception entails a maximalist view of development. Here aspects of equality and flourishing are goals for rich and poor countries. A purposive conception is associated with a minimalist view, which ensures the most deprived cross a threshold of adequate provision. This might mean earning a dollar a day or completing a primary cycle of schooling. In commenting on the SDGs, Gore (2015) has written that there are opportunities to try to undertake development in a transformative way, but also many forces pushing for business as usual.

By implication both the procedural and the purposive approaches face a problem relating to the nature of the social contract that underpins them. The more demanding the social justice content of the procedural approach, the more difficult it becomes to secure full human rights or gender equality through agreements at all levels, from multinational conventions, to national governments, down to local assemblies. The more minimal the purposive agreement, the easier it might be for governments to sign up. However, this begs the question of whether governments are able to implement purposive agreements and how these are understood at subnational level. This point was often made in relation to the difficulties of realizing the MDGs in many countries in Africa, which came to the project in 2000 from a very low base (Vandemoortele 2009). A separate question is whether the purposive agreements associated with the MDGs represent a wide enough range of ideas of well-being, and whether a more expansive purposive arrangement is feasible (Waage et al. 2010). The SDGs have tried to address these problems by giving a greater role to national and regional processes of accountability, and developing some key cross-cutting themes, notably 'leave no one behind'. Education also acts as a form of aspiration to support sustainability and equity, as outlined in the first Global Education Monitor (UNESCO 2016)

The rationale for the MDG approach, initially formulated by an inner circle of development assistance specialists, and then later endorsed by the majority of governments and international organizations, was that in focusing on a particularly delimited purposive development strategy, which just met some limited but universally agreed targets, many of the contentious issues of value associated with development could be bracketed somewhere else. The consensus on achieving sufficiency, it was suggested or implied, would be an important form of global glue to support poverty reduction, gender equality, education and health expansion, but the detail of the policy direction in these larger areas was not to be specified by global compact (Vandemoortele 2011; Fukuda Parr and McNeill 2015). In an early article on the MDGs (Unterhalter 2005), I argued they might open the way for a wider engagement with rights, capabilities and equality, that is that they could be seen as necessary, but not sufficient to enable such a process to unfold. Thus, while the political liberalism associated with the purposive agreements might offer a way through the difficulties with the comprehensive ethical visions associated with the procedural view, it might be the case that the overlapping consensus, which holds together the purposive view is concerned with very minimal social provision, so that the gradations of crossing a line regarding level of schooling or income do not sufficiently open up further ethical actions and claims on national and international bodies, but in fact close them down. In my most recent work on this theme (Unterhalter 2015, 2016), I note a slippery feature of this process, where claims are made to act to deepen concerns with equality and rights, while at the same time legitimating relationships which increase inequalities and injustice.

The empirical data conducted for the GEGPRI project of negotiations with gender, education and poverty reduction initiatives in Kenya and South Africa investigated engagements with the MDG and EFA process. In conclusion, I reflect on what this suggests about the prospects for work on forms of global obligation linked with the SDGs

Kenya and South Africa: Context and methods

The GEGPRI project aimed to examine empirically initiatives engaging with global aspirations to advance gender equality in and through schooling in contexts of poverty. Between 2007 and 2011, data were collected in ten research sites. These comprised government bodies: the National Department of Education in South Africa and the Ministry of Education in Kenya, a provincial department of education in each country, and a school in each country in a matched neighbourhood on the edge of a large city serving a poor population. Data were also collected from non-statutory bodies – a non-governmental organization (NGO) working on questions of poverty and schooling in a rural setting in each country, and an NGO working at the national level engaged in discussions with global networks. A number of interviews were conducted with staff working on gender and education in selected global organizations. Research methods comprised documentary analysis, interviews and focus group discussions (133 hours), observations, field notes and report-back meetings. The research was conducted over three years to enable some documentation of change. In all research settings, engagements with global frameworks were examined, and the meanings attributed to gender, poverty and education explored. In analysing the data for this chapter, I look at the kinds of claims people make about global obligation.

Kenya and South Africa were selected as the research settings because both countries had put in place policies to address poverty reduction, the expansion of education and gender equality. Both were active players in relation to the global policy frameworks. However, there were some differences. In this period South Africa was a member of the UN Security Council and the G20, lauded as one of the BRICS. Kenya was the recipient of a substantial aid package, but subject to constant international scrutiny regarding corruption and threats of violence.

South Africa and Kenya are very unequal societies, with high Gini coefficients and large populations of very poor people living close to people who are comfortably or very wealthy. Both have active women's movements, with different emphases. In South Africa, gender equity has enjoyed policy attention since 1994. In early post-apartheid policy, discussion of gender equity in education expressed an early promise of non-discrimination and equality of opportunity. This orientation moved through a phase with stress on gender neutrality to a period where gender was seen as a moral issue closely associated with sexuality, and aspects of race and identity. In Kenya, the movement for more gender equity in policy came from the bottom-up through women's rights groups mobilizing on a wide range of issues from political leadership to environmental degradation, and from the top-down through global institutions engaging in different ways with ruling elites. A gender and education policy was developed in 2007, and gender equity figures prominently in the policy language associated with aid relationships. The Constitution, adopted in 2010, set up a number of important structures, such as an influential Gender Commission, to keep gender equality under review. These similarities and differences between the two countries suggested potential to yield rich insight into engagements with global policy.

Negotiating global frameworks

In line with many studies on global policy transfer (Steiner-Khamsi 2004), the data indicated there were only a partial connection between practice in global, national and local sites and the procedural approach to global policy. The stress was rather muted on a full ethical dimension of global policy, which brought together ideas about rights, substantive equality and responses to poverty. More common than reflections on procedural discussion and engaging with purposive implementation was a limited instrumental concern to 'cross the line' of sufficiency with regard to poverty or school enrolment. Often this was accompanied with over-simplified ideas that gender was mainly about numbers of girls and boys, not social relations or power. The more reflective engagement with procedural agenda was articulated by staff working in global organizations, and some by individuals in the South African national and provincial departments of education who were networked into global discussion. The further national implementation moved away from a global hub, generally close to a capital city. The less the language and frameworks of the global policy discourse in its most substantive procedural form was used, the more limited the discussion of gender, education and poverty became. These restricted meanings, sometimes reflecting difficulties in thinking about gender, education and poverty *together*. Sometimes they reflected a concern to establish professional social distance from what were seen as the deficits of an excluded group, such as poor families or girls who did not attend school.

Purposive, rather than procedural?

In nearly all the sites where data were collected, the global frameworks, to the extent that participants were aware of them (in the rural NGO and school sites sometimes knowledge was limited), were most often understood in terms of measuring or accounting for performance. However, in some sites and for some individuals, the purposive framework opened up more procedural concerns. Thus, while the argument is often made that global frameworks are re-contextualized in national settings, sometimes following global directives and sometimes diverging from them (Cowen 2006; Rizvi and Lingaard 2010), placing the data from the different sites side by side we see particular kinds of engagement, sometimes dutiful, sometimes dismissive and sometimes expansive and critical.

The national departments

In the two national departments, the MDG and EFA frameworks were important for officials, as a 'guiding tool' or as a mechanism for exchanging information up and down the hierarchies of government (Kenyan National Ministry Official 1, 17/10/2008; South African National Department Official 23, 10/11/2008). In Kenya, partly because of the importance of a substantial aid package for the whole ministry, which drew heavily on the MDGs as frameworks, it was claimed the MDGs ensured a level of accountability to the global community by government and NGOs.

> Let me say, those goals and MDGs, they are very good because ... these goals keep the government and NGOs, all of us, on our toes. If we had no goals, we would go back and be in our own comfort and pretend everything is OK. (Kenyan National Ministry Official 5, 21/05/2008)

Officials acknowledged that working within the frameworks generally meant that there was little space for discussion and reflection on gender, other than through a concern with school enrolment:

> The Ministry is doing much more than that – the gender policy – because there are many things that the Ministry is doing to coordinate the MDGs ... When we are moving towards parity – and we want to have parity in enrolment – the Ministry from the top is addressing the MDGs. (Kenyan National Ministry Official 01, 17/10/2008)

By contrast, in South Africa, there was a sense that the national education priorities connected with the MDGs and EFA, but were not being driven by them. Indeed, a number of officials thought that deepening engagement with gender and poverty was needed, not because this was required by the global policy frameworks, but because of wider ethical concerns prompted by local complexity. One South African official said:

> People often look at that kind of data [collected for MDG and EFA reports] and say 'we've achieved gender parity – in a sense that those don't apply to us'. But in a way that has been the problem, because they are very generalized and they have help[ed], but now they don't help enough. Because actually what needs to be done is actually quite complex, it is multi-faceted. We have to deal with really difficult issues that are not about saying we have just achieved this particular international benchmark. (National Department of Education Official 13, 20/10/2008).

For another South African official, the MDG approach of using indicators could be useful in addressing issues, for example gender-based violence, but the fact that there was no indicator on this in the MDG or EFA framework meant this was not being done:

> We don't have an indicator on how many girls are raped in schools. We're not tracking that. So what is not measured does not get done. What is measured gets done. It's about the indicators. What we have found is that indicators drive what becomes important. At an international UNESCO level, the MDGs, EFA, influence must be at the level of indicators. (National department focus group discussion, 19/08/2008)

It can be seen that while the purposive approach was used in both national departments, for some officials in South Africa this went together with reflections on how global frameworks might support more procedural engagements. The reasons this wider perspective was not voiced in Kenya, and was only articulated by some officials in South Africa, may be associated with the professional backgrounds of staff in the two departments (Unterhalter and North 2011a) or the ways in which members of the research team were seen by participants (Makinda and Yates 2011). What is important to note for the argument is that in the national departments there were a range of responses regarding how the global frameworks were seen, but the language of the purposive approach was particularly compelling.

The provinces

In the two provinces, there was a strong sense that the global policy frameworks were set somewhere at a political distance, and that officials were tasked to deliver on behalf of national departments. In South Africa, a provincial official gave an account of a top-down process between tiers of government negotiating action on global goals:

They [the MDGs and EFA] are very important in the sense that we are not a province in isolation to the national mandates or international mandates because it becomes the programme for implementation for all government departments. At the beginning of the year or when financial period starts, these frameworks ... are always tabled to all government departments. (South African Province Official 2, 06/02/2009)

This managed response, following a line of command in respect of a global directive, sits slightly uncomfortably with the descriptions provincial officers gave of their work on education, gender and poverty initiatives, and with a sense of enormously inadequate human, financial and policy resources to take forward what they believed in (Karlsson 2010). One official eloquently confessed that she could never fulfil the expectations associated with the MDGs in the face of widespread poverty:

We have been to those places, we took old clothes, our clothes, to give those. How do you feel when you drive your car passing? You see those people selling mangoes. How do you feel? You are busy telling people that 'no, we are addressing the millennium goals'. In what way? How do you do it? (South African Province Official 3, 23/02/2009)

In Kenya, provincial officers felt the MDGs had been made a long way away from their day-to-day experiences. Some had heard about the MDGs, but did not know what they were. An officer said:

I tell you the first time I heard about the MDGs and you will not believe, it was last year when I went for a Ministry of Planning had a dissemination kind of workshop organized at the province here. I went to represent my boss and that's the first time I heard about MDGs and really it's like they belong to other people. (Kenyan Province Official 2, 16/09/2008)

A number of provincial officials articulated their responsibility to implement the MDGs, but felt achieving them was far-fetched. Some argued that the top-down communication of the policies was responsible for difficulties in implementation. Communities, it was claimed, find it hard to own the otherwise good policies because they are viewed as alien. One officer said, 'we were just told "here are the papers come out with the proposals, vet them, send them to us"' (District Official 2, 28/11/2008). Apart from MDG 2, many participants at the district level did not foresee the realization of the other MDGs by 2015. They stressed the challenges of achieving universal primary education because of poverty, drought, understaffing and overcrowding of schools, the long-distances children had to travel from home to school, and what was repeatedly called 'culture', that is, the lack of engagement with schooling by some communities. In contrast to the confidence of their South African counterparts about working to achieve the MDGs at the national level, Kenyan provincial officers appeared pessimistic. While South African provincial officials saw the MDGs as a top-down exercise that largely did not matter one way or the other to their work, for the Kenyan officials there seemed to be a sense that the very ambition of the MDGs in the face of the difficulties they encountered was a mockery. One official said:

> Another thing to this MDG. We are operating like crisis as far as the human resource is concerned. For us we have a number of schools actually [and not enough teachers]. Even sometimes we doubt the quality of the curriculum that we are offering. (Kenyan District Official 7, 24/11/2008)

One provincial official expressed incredulity about the monitoring associated with EFA. When a member of the research team asked for the provincial figures on teachers by gender, the request was greeted with scorn:

> Where do you think you can get such information? Does it really exist? Are you researching all the 22 districts in this province? ... I have not seen it. And I do not think there is an officer who is allocated that duty of collecting the information here. And I am not interested to know since I do not know what the end users of that information would be. (Kenya field notes, 17/09/2008)

These data exist at the national level and are reported to UNESCO as part of its work on monitoring EFA. It is not clear how they are collected with accuracy at the provincial or district without the involvement of local officers. But the response indicates both exasperation at the lack of staff to carry out many different administrative tasks and very limited interest in knowing about gender, teacher deployment and a global framework of accountability.

Thus, for provincial officials in both countries the global frameworks were primarily understood in their purposive form, while the wider procedural issues about rights or equality were viewed either sympathetically or exasperatedly as impossible to address adequately.

The schools

This sense of professional distance from engagement with the MDG project was even more pronounced at school level. Teachers were aware of the poverty children experienced, but in the South African school, where a feeding scheme was in place, there was a stronger sense of the school's involvement with aspects of poverty, while teachers in Kenya tended to see the problem of hunger as a responsibility of the children's families. The deputy head noted the effects of hunger on learning, but was unable to venture a view on what should be done:

> There is a slum near the school [...] The children go without food the whole day. The children come from very poor homes and this is affecting their performance. If a child is hungry especially in the afternoon, the child may not understand anything. (Deputy head teacher, date not known, 2008)

In both schools, gender was seen largely as a matter of equal numbers of girls and boys enrolled or taking responsibility as class monitors or members of sports teams. The South African principal (2008/03/25) described gender equality as being 'like a quota' and maintaining a 'balance' and a teacher as being 'in the equal' (Teacher 1, 2010/07/26). In Kenya, there was a similar sense that gender equality was parity:

> We encourage teachers to be gender sensitive, for example, at parade we encourage the girls to work hard and tell them that they can perform well. The whole staff in our school usually tries to make the boys and girls feel that they are equal and even when they are choosing prefects' body they know how to mix boy and girl ... If the game captain is a boy, then we have a girl assisting, so we balance. (Head teacher, 29/05/2009)

In both countries, teachers noted the effects of gender and poverty on families, but were not able to explain how they might intersect and the kinds of support they and the school might provide to help to effect change. In South Africa, absenteeism among girls was associated with poverty and the sexual division of labour in the household:

> We find that there is a grade 7 learner who is a boy and there is a grade 5 learner who is a girl. They are coming from one family. If there is a problem at home which needs somebody to stay at home, you know who will stay: the girl; because she will look after this. [...] From grade 5 upwards girls have to do mother's work at home. (South African deputy principal, 2010/09/15)

Similar connections were noted in Kenya:

> For the past five years is the fact that parents have given priority to their boy child. The boys are taken away to boarding and private schools that are numerous around this school. (Kenyan teacher 13, 2008)

It can be seen that the effects of gender inequalities and poverty were very evident to the teachers, but they lacked a language of policy and practice to connect them. The MDGs and EFA, to the extent they knew of them, were considered remote and spoken about in the public media with little bearing on the things that people experience or have capacity to effect:

> I do heard about it [MDGs and EFA] but I've never given my time to get an explanation about it because it's never touched [me]. I've never get the real explanation about it. (South African principal, 2008/03/25)

In Kenya, there was a similar sense of policy handed down from somewhere far away.

> I have only heard some of the Millennium Development Goals like universal primary education. I think it was declared in Dakar. (Teacher 14, 12/06/2010)

EFA and the MDGs had blurred together for one teacher, but she was one of only a handful who knew about the global policy framework. What these excerpts indicate is that teachers' sense of their work is about enrolling and retaining children in school. Wider connections between education, ending poverty and achieving gender equality are harder to make and do not appear as part of everyday discussion of practice at school. The global policy frameworks appear as far away, partly because the acronyms and processes are unfamiliar, but partly also because the ethical connection between ideas and institutional levels is not readily available to teachers. Provincial officials stressed purposive, rather than procedural, meanings of global goals because their work entailed that they were responsible for results, but other perspectives (negative and positive) were available to them. The teachers in these schools, in contrast, did not voice a wider language of procedural aspiration. This may be partly because of the dynamic of how they saw the research team composed of elite outsiders from universities. It may also partly be because that language was not an everyday or familiar discourse. What was more readily available to them was a language of critique of poor families for keeping children, particularly girls, out of school.

The rural NGOs

Teachers' limited engagement with a procedural approach to development was echoed by staff employed in the rural NGO, working in context of harsh poverty, limited access to transport and worsening livelihoods because of lack of water and disputes over land. Each NGO had established a particular niche. In Kenya, the NGO provided training for teachers and school management committees, some school infrastructure and learning materials. This education stream went together with work on health, livelihoods and a strong advocacy focus around ethnic rights. In South Africa, the NGO ran an after school club to encourage reading for children, a number of holiday programmes to accelerate learning and a literacy group for mothers. Both thus complemented the work of the government in engaging with global policy on EFA and the MDGs.

In Kenya, the concerns of a global development community were communicated to the NGO primarily through aid relationships.

In South Africa, the donor did not appear to be 'pushing' gender or poverty reduction. NGO fieldworkers in Kenya spoke of their work being networked with global, national and local NGOs and being multilateral and bilateral. This sense of a connection through funding to a wider policy community was not that clearly articulated in South Africa, although one of the facilitators had represented the NGO at a number of international meetings. Evidently there is not just one global policy framework, and many international relations involving NGOs do not draw on the concerns of the MDGs or EFA.

For participants interviewed in the NGOs in both countries, the global policy framework was either something they had heard of very generally or not at all. In South Africa, most of the six village-based facilitators who participated in a focus group discussion (05/06/2009) had only heard of the global goals by name and did not know what they meant. Village-based NGO officials reluctantly recognized that gender equality was a legal right in the national Constitution (I, 05/06/2009), and that there were policies governing these rights in schools. But gender was not part of the NGO remit, even though much of their work was with women. A village facilitator said: 'The NGO never talks about the global goals' (Local NGO staff member 2, 03/06/2009).

In Kenya, there was a similar sense that the organization's priorities were not being framed by or linked to the global policy framework. One NGO worker said, 'There are so many policies around here [...] we don't disseminate those policies' (staff member 5, 19/05/2010). On the MDGs the view was one of indifference and distance. One NGO worker noted sceptically, 'Another issue is whether the people own the global declarations. The issue is not even whether they own the MDG's but rather understand, comprehend and know them.' In another exchange with an interviewer, the issue of how the MDGs could be discussed at the grassroots was raised. The view was that the MDGs were too particular and that the nature of the work which the organization did was general and integrated with its own programme of education, not the steer from the MDGs:

While the NGO saw itself advocating to the Kenyan government to do more on the provision of schools, and on water and land policy, it did not see this as associated either for good or ill with an external process. They talked about a loose network with external actors or something 'whereby we share out what is really happening what is not working', so we can 'tailor make or change activities' (L staff member 01, d). The organization was thus being driven by its perception of need on the ground. Many NGO workers did not mention the global gender, education or poverty reduction framework. They stressed 'policy for the pastoral communities' (staff member 01), indicating a strong sense of local priorities that separated them from global and many national frameworks.

Thus, in contrast to the teachers at the school for whom some elements of EFA, particularly regarding enrolment and attainment, are very much part of daily practice, NGO workers not formally employed in schools see their remit as linked to local priorities with which national or global frameworks have only a contingent relationship. They might make gestures towards these frameworks in order to secure aid, but the discursive frame is not immediately familiar.

The global NGOs

A different language is spoken in NGOs located in large cities which network on a regular basis with global organizations. Both organizations, where data were collected, comprised the national offices of international NGOs working on education and gender in many countries. Both were active in promoting the MDGs and EFA nationally through workshops, circulating information, advocacy with national government, other NGOs and CSOs, and were directly involved in poverty reduction initiatives, such as supporting school vegetable gardens, distributing sanitary towels and, in education programmes for girls, supplementing the work of schools.

For both organizations, the MDGs and EFA were central to their mission and were strongly associated with rights and gender equality. The connections that were difficult for teachers and rural NGO workers to make came easily:

> Our starting point is that gender inequality is a key factor in poverty. Inequalities of race and imbalances of power between various socio-economic groups – whether racial, caste, or of course gender, are quite key. We make a very direct relationship between those two. If you want to address poverty, you must address inequalities and imbalances of power and gender inequalities are part of that. You must look both at public inequalities but also at inequalities in the household – how power is distributed. (South African National NGO staff member 12, 09/12/2010)

The MDGs were seen to complement this:

> I think our work is already targeting aspects of the MDGs and the MDGs came along and happened. There were goals that were set, and I think the MDGs whether they were implemented or not is not necessarily going to change the way [the NGO] is focused ... I tend to see the MDGs as a bit more of, it is a way to create more awareness, it's a potential way to get more government commitment and things like that. (South African National NGO staff member 2, 23/07/2009)

The NGO in Kenya, although aware that the MDGs were difficult to realize, still took them as a focal point in work at national and community levels.

> We usually sensitize the community members on importance of MDGs or education on that matter. (Kenyan National NGO staff member 3, 19/03/2009)
> When you look at societies one of the worst challenges facing the societies when it comes to opportunities towards the MDGs is pastoralist societies. But you will see a lot of challenges when you go to [rural area]. There are a few like distance to school, insecurity, and cultural perception. But you will still see that the willingness of us being there. So I would say when we talk about the MDGs, there is hope. (Kenyan National NGO staff member 8, 19/03/2009)

Thus, for both organizations the MDGs were an important component of how they oriented their work, but they did not form a straitjacket requiring particular results, as some government officials appeared to feel. This was most evident in the ways in which they explored a range of meanings of gender considerably beyond those expressed in the MDGs and EFA.

In the NGO studied in South Africa, 'Gender' was considered a technical term, suggesting projects needed to include men, which was considered obfuscating as the priority for the organization was women's rights:

> [Gender]It allows us to link women's economic empowerment, their reproductive roles with questions of resource equality and distribution – and the patterns that take place in one but are parallel to the contributions that are being made in another area. (South African National NGO 12, 09/12/2010)

It can be seen that, unlike government officials at national and provincial level, NGO workers, were comfortable with the MDGs and EFA as one of a number of strategies they can attach to rights, empowerment or local meanings. The purposive stress is not pre-eminent for them, possibly because they do not have the responsibility for results-based development.

There was considerable congruence between the views of staff in the global NGOs in Kenya and South Africa and those in multilateral organizations and global civil society networks in Europe and North America. Often these groups shared education backgrounds and had many opportunities for networking in person or through electronic discussions. In the global organizations, all participants except one – who said their work was locally defined – recognized that global frameworks were important in their work.

> What I think they have been useful for actually is uniting civil society, especially within education around a sense of global obligation. And the EFA declaration still has tremendous power in the global campaign for education movement and I think it's one reason why [it] doesn't suffer from some of the big ideological fractures that go on in other global coalitions because that baseline if you like, there is no serious dissent about that as the baseline. (International civil society network 5, 23/12/2008)
>
> I believe that global targets are extremely important because they allow for, if you will, international peer pressure ... I think that it is important that the international community has set certain standards and certain minimally acceptable behaviours with regard to their populations in general and also with regard to their children. (Multilateral Institution 8, 27/06/2008)

Despite differences in terms of which frameworks participants identified with most closely as individuals and as institutions, all recognized the MDGs as playing a key role in shaping international policy and action on gender and education. While, for some, the MDGs could leverage action, a more critical view was that the MDG framework with its stress on gender parity, curtailed work on women's empowerment.

> For me, for the type of work that I do, they are useful because ... [it] forms a framework that can push us. It can help us engage with government, because governments have agendas they wish to meet ... It can help us engage with partners on a more local level. We have a mandate. (Staff member, Bilateral Institution 3a, 03/03/2008)

It can be seen that in global organizations, as in the global NGOs, there is a confidence to work the MDG and EFA agenda regarding gender, education and poverty in ways they find strategic and satisfactory. They feel a sense of ownership of the agendas and possibility to use them in ways that advance their ideas about gender equality, education and addressing poverty.

Conclusion

The data suggest that the MDGs and EFA catalysed some connections of social policy, vocabularies and particular kinds of organizations. But this stopped short of building a broad global advocacy movement concerned with human rights and gender equality that reached down to district education officers, primary school teachers or rural NGO staff. In these organizations, the MDGs and EFA appeared as other people's projects, and on that basis it was difficult to engage in substantive discussion about poverty, rights and gender equality. Exploration of these ideas and a ready conceptual vocabulary came much more comfortably to some staff in government and those working in global NGOs and multilateral organizations.

A process of networking connected only certain staff in national departments of education, national NGOs and global organizations in a critical procedural reflection on development. In the national and provincial departments in South Africa, heightened capacity and confidence to define and reflect on education interests and agendas were evident. Purposive claims of governments and the pressures these claims place on staff were evident in the ways in which provincial officials and teachers express their connection to global frameworks. In the local rural NGO in both countries, neither purposive nor procedural vocabularies are deployed, and the stress is on local needs.

There was a contrast between those employed in global and national organizations who take the global frameworks as part of the landscape of their work, and who feel they can work both on and with the policy, and those who feel the frameworks and the vocabulary of rights and substantive equality, which they articulate, are not their project. Partly, these are differences of location, communication technologies and the meetings, both actual and virtual, which have created a global community concerned with the MDGs and EFA. The second group, if they used the internet, did not do so for work. Their professional horizons with regard to poverty and gender tended to be framed more by the national press, radio and participation in church. They had limited purchase on the global discussion of frameworks. All those in the first group are graduates, and many are postgraduates, while most of those in the second group have post-school-diploma-level qualifications. These are also differences of location, so that in South Africa, which is less answerable to global agendas in their purposive form, there is more confidence to consider a procedural language by some government officials.

What does this tell us about what might unfold with the SDGs? The political philosophical literature (Wallace Brown and Held 2010) highlights debates concerning conflicts of interest, procedural reason and the nature of mutuality and right. The data suggest that confidence in procedural reason and mutuality was most apparent for those whose professional biography and location supported the expression and examination of a vision of global obligation. Many more people participated in discussion of the SDGs, compared to the MDGs. It is possible that those who responded to surveys and commented on the SDGs overrepresented those constituencies which felt attached to an agenda of global obligation and underrepresented those who felt distant from this

Advocates of global connection are able to articulate, in the sense of express, such a project because their work articulates, in the sense of connects, the global, the national and the local. By contrast, those whose professional identities are squeezed by demands they fulfil certain purposive visions of a global education project, do not easily debate issues of right or mutuality, and more frequently portray the world in terms of conflicts of interest and disarticulation from a global gender, education or poverty reduction project. Practice clearly frames how meanings of global obligation are negotiated. It thus appears difficult to assume engaged work on addressing the connection between education, gender equality and poverty without critical, procedural reflection on practice in the light of global, national and local policy. Whether the SDG project will be able to go beyond this binary remains to be investigated. It is early days, and the landscape of financing, aid and professional education to allow this to happen is uncertain (UNESCO 2016)

In my view, these tensions concerning the nature of the procedural are linked. In going around the problem of securing widespread agreement for a procedural approach concerned with rights and equality, to stress 'a better way' of a minimal purposive achievement, the process of building the space for procedural reflection stopped in its tracks. This halt has been accentuated by some of the catastrophic failures around security issues in the Middle East, and the austerity measures introduced to address the global financial crisis after 2008. In the place of critical discussion of rights and equalities and consideration of the reasonable grounds on which they might rest has come a stress on meeting targets. This might get minimal achievement of social development, but it does not enhance processes of dialogue, reflection, strengthening of professional insight or enhancing critique. Indeed implementing the purposive approach appears to work easily with silences, stereotypes and particular forms of local selection. To bring the procedural reflection down from ideal theory to real-life implementation what is needed is the hubbub of comment, examination of the reasonableness of claims, negotiation around plurality and critical reflection on the significance of local context in the intersection of gender, poverty and education. To some extent the SDG agenda may have opened this up, but these are fragile spaces in which powerful interests can undermine transformational initiatives (Unterhalter 2016, 2017a,b).

Questions for discussion

1 What is similar and different about the ways in which different groups interpreted gender in EFA and the MDGs? What do differences of location and perspective suggest for taking forward the SDG agenda?

2 What notion of global obligation underpins the SDGs? How do the recent changes in the global context affect how the gender, education and poverty components of the SDGs might be addressed?

Note

1 GEGPRI was funded by the UK Economic and Social Research Council (ESRC) Award no. RES 167-25-260 under a partnership with the UK Department for International Development (DFID). The project ran from September 2007 to March 2011. The Institute of Education, University of London, held the award and co-investigators were engaged in work for the project at the University of the Witwatersrand, University of KwaZulu-Natal and the Catholic University of Eastern Africa. My thanks to all the members of the project team for the collaboration on the project, without which this chapter could not have been written.

References

Brock, G. (Ed.) (2013). *Cosmopolitanism versus non-cosmopolitanism: Critiques, defenses, reconceptualizations*. Oxford: Oxford University Press.

Dieltiens, V., Unterhalter, E., Letsatsi, S. and North, A. (2009). 'Gender blind, gender-lite: A critique of gender equity approaches in the South African Department of Education'. *Perspectives in Education*, 27 (4), 365–374.

Fukuda-Parr, S. and McNeill, D. (2015). 'Post 2015: A new era of accountability?'. *Journal of Global Ethics*, 11 (1), 10–17.

Gore, C. (2010). 'The MDG paradigm, productive capacities and the future of poverty reduction'. *IDS Bulletin*, 41, 70–79.

Gore, C. (2015). 'The Post-2015 moment: Towards sustainable development goals and a new global development paradigm. *Journal of International Development*, 27 (6), 717–732.

Karlsson, J. (2010). 'Gender mainstreaming in a South African provincial education department: A transformative shift or technical fix for oppressive gender relations?'. *Compare*, 40 (4), 497–514.

Makinda, H. and Yates, C. (2011). 'Social exclusion and violence: researchers' experiences of vertical and horizontal disconnections in conducting naturalistic inquiry in Kenya', paper presented to UKFIET Conference, Oxford, 13–15 September.

Paul, E. F., Miller, F. D. and Paul, J. (Eds.) (2006). *Justice and global politics*. Cambridge: Cambridge University Press.

Rizvi, F. and Lingaard, B. (2010). *Globalizing education policy*. Abingdon: Routledge.

Sperling, G. and Winthrop, R. (2015). *What works in girls' education: Evidence for the world's best investment*. Washington: Brookings Institution Press.

Steiner-Khamsi, G. (Ed.) (2004). *Global politics of educational borrowing and lending*. New York: Teachers' College Press.

UNESCO (2015). *Global monitoring report 2015: Education for all 2000–2015. Achievements and challenges*. Paris: UNESCO/Oxford University Press.

UNESCO (2016). *Global education monitoring report. Education for people and planet*. Paris: UNESC/Oxford University Press.

Unterhalter, E. (2005). 'Global inequality, capabilities, social justice and the millennium development goal for gender equality in education'. *International Journal of Educational Development*, 25, 111–122.

Unterhalter, E. (2007). *Gender, schooling and global social justice*. London: Taylor Francis Routledge.

Unterhalter, E. (2012). 'Mutable meanings: Gender equality in education and international rights frameworks'. *Equal Rights Review*, 8, 67–84.

Unterhalter, E. (2014). 'Walking backwards to the future: A comparative perspective on education and a post-2015 framework'. *Compare*, 44 (6), 852–873

Unterhalter, E. (2015). 'Global inequalities, multipolarity, and supranational organizations engagements with gender and education'. *Journal of Supranational Policies of Education (JOSPOE)* (3), 10–28.

Unterhalter, E. (2016). 'Gender and education in the global polity'. In Mundy, K., Green, A., Lingaard, B. and Verger, A. (Eds.), *Handbook of global education policy*. New York: Wiley.

Unterhalter, E (2017a). 'Global injustice, pedagogy and democratic iterations: Some reflections on why teachers matter'. *Journal of Curriculum Studies*, 49 (1), 24–37, DOI: 10.1080/00220272.2016.1205141.

Unterhalter, E. (2017b). 'Negative capability? Measuring the unmeasurable in education'. *Comparative Education*.

Unterhalter, E and North, A. (2011a). 'Responding to the gender and education millennium development goals in South Africa and Kenya: Reflections on education rights, gender equality, capabilities and global justice'. *Compare*, 41 (4), 494–511.

Unterhalter, E. and North, A. (2011b). '"Girls" schooling, gender equity, and the global education and development agenda: Conceptual disconnections, political struggles, and the difficulties of practice'. *Feminist Formations*, 23 (3), 1–22.

Unterhalter, E., Yates, C., Makinda, H. and North, A. (2012). 'Blaming the poor: Constructions of marginality and poverty in the Kenyan education sector'. *Compare*, 42 (2), 213–233.

Vandemoortele, J. (2009). 'The MDG conundrum: Meeting the targets without missing the point'. *Development Policy Review*, 27, 355–371.

Vandemoortele, J. (2011). 'The MDG story: Intention denied'. *Development and Change*, 42 (1), 1–21.

Waage, J., Banerji, R., Campbell, O. et al. (2010). 'The millennium development goals: A cross sectoral analysis and principles for goal setting post 2015'. *The Lancet*, 376 (9745), 991–1023.

Wallace Brown, G. and Held, D. (2010). *The cosmopolitanism reader*. Cambridge: Polity.
Young, I. M. (2013). *Responsibility for justice*. Oxford: Oxford University Press.

Further reading

Barrett, A. M. (2016). 'Measuring learning outcomes and education for sustainable development: The new education development goal'. In W. Smith (Ed.), *The global testing culture: Shaping education policy, perceptions, and practice*. Oxford: Symposium, pp. 101–114.
DeJaeghere, J. (2015). 'Reframing gender and education for the Post-2015 agenda'. In S. McGrath and Q. Gu (Eds.), *Routledge handbook of international education and development. Abingdon:* Routledge, pp. 63–77.

5

Why Do Countries Participate in PISA? Understanding the Role of International Large-Scale Assessments in Global Education Policy

Camilla Addey and Sam Sellar

Introduction

This chapter examines why countries participate in international large-scale assessments (widely referred to as ILSAs). ILSAs are a relatively new phenomenon that has significantly affected the way in which education is now understood globally, including what is valued in education and how education policy and practice is informed and evaluated. Studying how ILSAs are mobilized in different contexts, and how they have emerged and spread, has become an important task for studies of global education policy and international development. The central argument of this chapter is that countries participate in ILSAs for multiple and diverse reasons. These reasons must be examined on a case-by-case basis, but can be broadly informed by global education policy theories. The chapter draws on the analysis of empirical data and develops a framework of reasons for ILSA participation in different contexts, with a focus on the participation of low- and middle-income countries.

The history of ILSAs can be traced back to the middle of the twentieth century, when discussions about the need to measure educational outcomes were sponsored by UNESCO. In 1960, the International Association for the Evaluation of Educational Achievement (IEA) conducted its Pilot Twelve Country Study, which initiated a series of assessments that led to the commencement of its influential Trends in Mathematics and Science Study (TIMSS) in 1995. Thorn (2009) states that the work of Educational Testing Service and Statistics Canada (the Organization for Economic Co-operation and Development (OECD)'s main partner in its first ILSA endeavours) set the example of what could be measured by ILSAs with the Young Adult Literacy Assessment[1] in 1985 and the National Adult Literacy Survey in 1992, combining 'advances in psychometrics, reading theory and large scale assessment with household survey methodologies' (2009, p. 5). The Canadian Survey of Literacy Skills Used in Daily Activities was conducted in 1989 and demonstrated that ILSAs could produce comparable data across different languages and cultures (Thorn 2009).

In 1994, the OECD implemented its first international large-scale assessment, the International Adult Literacy Survey (IALS), which measured the prose, document and quantitative literacy skills of 16- to 65-year-olds across twenty-two countries. Other regional assessments also emerged in the 1990s. In 1997, the OECD began developing its Programme for International Student Achievement (PISA), which was first conducted in 2000 in forty-three countries and was implemented by over seventy countries in 2015. PISA has become the most well-known and influential ILSA and is currently expanding to low-income countries through PISA for Development (PISA-D). PISA-D offers PISA in a format designed to be more useful for low- and middle-income countries, and the OECD is paving the way to a single global indicator to measure progress in relation to the post-2015 UN development agenda. In 2003, the UNESCO Institute for Statistics (UIS), a latecomer to the ILSA phenomenon, began developing an IALS-equivalent assessment, the Literacy Assessment and Monitoring Program (LAMP), to assess literacy and numeracy skills across a greater variety of languages, cultures, scripts and numerical systems (Guadalupe 2015).

The number of ILSAs and the level of participation have grown significantly over the last fifteen years, and increasingly include low- and middle-income countries (Bloem 2013, 2015). In the context of ILSA expansion, it is necessary to understand the rationales behind participation and how these assessments are affecting global governance, policy and practice in education.

Theorizing participation in ILSAs

Participation in ILSAs can be understood in terms of new modes of global governance that shape the way that people think about education and the way that education systems operate (Sellar and Lingard 2014; see also Woodward 2009). Epistemological governance describes processes that shape ideas and values. This form of governance comprises both 'the incarnation of a community of countries sharing overarching values' and 'the realm of research, knowledge and ideas' that inform policy and practice (Woodward 2009, p. 6). The concept of epistemological governance describes how 'soft power' (Nye 2004) can be exercised through a common way of thinking within what Haas' (1992) calls epistemic communities. Infrastructural governance describes the development of new systems. This form of governance involves the joining up of various policy technologies, data sets and organizations to establish new mechanisms of governance, such as data infrastructures in education that span both national and global spaces (Anagnostopoulos et al. 2013; Sellar 2014). Mayer-Schönberger and Cukier (2013, p. 96) have argued that 'we are in the midst of a great infrastructure project ... [t]he project is datafication'. We can understand this datafication as an 'operating system' for education policy globally (Easterling 2014). Together, infrastructural and epistemological governance constitute new modes of global governance in education and ILSAs are an important part of this phenomenon (Sellar and Lingard 2014).

In addition to the notion of global governance, the rationales for participation in ILSAs can be analysed drawing on Verger's (2016) theorization of policy diffusion and adoption processes, according to which there are three main types: rationalist, normative emulation and political economy approaches, including cultural political economy (CPE) (Verger 2016; see also the introduction in this volume). Rationalist approaches begin from the assumption that policy-makers can and do look for policies that have been demonstrated to be effective elsewhere and that appear most optimal policy for their particular circumstances. The epistemological mode of governance that operates through the production of research-based knowledge for policy is an example of this rationalist view. Normative approaches, of which World Culture Theory is a prominent example (Meyer et al. 1992), focus on the desire of policy-makers to conform with international norms and models. When epistemological governance operates through the establishment of international communities with shared values it constitutes an example of this normative approach.

Verger (2016) argues, however, that these two approaches do not enable a fine-grained analysis of policy adoption processes and that critical constructivist and CPE approaches can address this gap (Jessop 2010; Robertson and Dale 2015). The CPE approach focuses attention on three stages of policy adoption: variation, selection and retention (Verger 2016). Variation occurs when established policy positions are challenged and a window for policy change is created (Kingdon 1984). The crises that can be produced by poor performance as measured by ILSAs provide a good example of variation. Selection occurs when policy-makers decide on the nature of the problem and the required policy solutions. Here, evidence-based policy discourses, which reflect rationalist approaches, may be used to promote or identify particular solutions. Finally, retention occurs when selected policies are institutionalized and affect practice.

Rationalist approaches to policy are often reflected in policy-impact studies and evaluations commissioned by international organizations to show the benefits of participation in ILSAs (e.g. Gilmore 2005, Abdul-Hamid et al. 2011). ILSA data are often promoted as evidence of what does and does not work in education. International organizations like the OECD, UNESCO and the World Bank tend to understand educational policy in rationalist terms when they claim that ILSA data can be used for policy reform and as a valid instrument to evaluate and compare educational performance. Lockheed (2013) argues that the World Bank, along with other donor and aid agencies, is an important advocate for ILSAs in developing countries, driven by an interest in accountability and international benchmarks, given their mandate to identify educational funding opportunities and monitor progress in aid and loan recipient countries. Indeed, ILSAs have become a requirement for low- and middle-income countries to monitor the efficiency of national education systems, the expenditure of educational aid and the effect of human capital investment on economic growth.

A normative emulation approach theorizes global education policy diffusion as primarily a process of state legitimization. Countries adopt global policies to 'demonstrate internationality' (Steiner-Khamsi, forthcoming) and to present themselves to the international community as modern and responsible states. A number of scholars have studied the participation of countries in ILSAs from this perspective. For example, Grek (2009) has shown that countries are interested in measuring their performance relative to OECD countries, but also as a way to be 'put on the map'. Kamens (2013) also suggests that countries join ILSAs for the prestige of competing and benchmarking against the exclusive club of wealthy OECD countries, adding that ILSAs 'make ministers and ministries look good at international conferences and events … for actively pursuing modern values' (2013: 128). This resonates with Wiseman's (2013) argument that joining ILSAs provides countries with a form of legitimacy and credibility that comes from belonging to a group of countries that emphasize the value of public education. Addey (2015) argues that while participation may be justified in terms of technical capacity building and as a way to measure global competitiveness, empirical data in Laos and Mongolia show participation in ILSAs to be part of a 'global ritual of belonging'. Indeed, Addey (forthcoming) argues global prestige is conferred to countries for simply joining the OECD's assessments, however poor the results might be.

International performance indicators are also promoted as a way of ensuring mutual accountability and transparency (Nóvoa and Yariv-Mashal 2003). This has led to the institutionalization of an international audit culture that has legitimized global evaluations and assessments and strengthened norms relating to performance measurement. Indeed, Kamens has argued that international testing is a 'requirement for all, rich and poor. In this new environment accountability and transparency are believed to be the routes to progress and social development' (2013, p. 118). This has given rise to governance by comparison, which involves particular policy agendas being adopted under peer pressure to compete and conform with high- performing countries (Novoa and Yariv-Mashal 2003; Martens 2007; Grek 2009).

Rationalist and normative approaches explain how ILSAs are positioned as part of global mechanisms of cognitive governance (e.g. the shared value of measuring and comparing educational performance) and normative governance (e.g. evidence-based policy). However, Verger (2016) argues that a CPE approach can complement these views. For example, this perspective draws attention to the unintended uses of ILSA data for policy. Policies made in relation to ILSA data often use the data to support predetermined reform narratives, rather than being based on what the data show. The majority of these policy uses are linked to the reference societies created by international rankings and the improving or declining performance of countries. These policy uses include: top-ranking performers becoming policy borrowing reference societies (Steiner-Khamsi and Waldow 2012); the so-called 'policy shocks' that open reform windows (Ertl 2006; Wiseman 2013); heightened attention to movements in the rankings (Sellar and Lingard 2013); and changes to educational curricula and national tests to improve performance. Addey (2015) employs this third theoretical approach to show how policy actors in Laos and Mongolia use ILSAs as a form of 'scandalizing and glorifying' performance (Steiner-Khamsi 2003) according to internal political agendas.

Countries thus participate in ILSAs for many reasons and use ILSA data for multiple purposes. Indeed, participation in ILSAs often involves multiple rationales and these may change between or during implementations. Rationales for participation can be fruitfully analysed using a combination of theoretical tools and must be understood relationally. Thus, while we focus on low- and middle-income countries here, we also examine the participation of wealthier OECD countries to understand how this creates imperatives for others to join the ILSA community. The framework developed below adds empirical detail to this theoretical discussion and shows how rationales for ILSA participation, in real situations, cut across rationalist, normative and CPE approaches to explaining policy adoption.

A note on methodology

The chapter builds on three empirical studies of ILSAs. The first examined developments in education policy globally, with a focus on PISA, and included more than fifty interviews (coded as SNAG) conducted between 2011 and 2014 with policy-makers, analysts and senior managers in Australia, in England and at the OECD.[2] The second study examined the ILSA participation of low- and middle-income countries using case studies of LAMP in Laos and Mongolia, with approximately thirty interviews (coded as WhyJoin) conducted in 2012 in both countries and at the UNESCO Institute for Statistics (Addey 2014). The third study focuses on changing global policy actors and policy processes in Ecuador and Paraguay through the development and implementation of PISA for Development.[3] Approximately twenty interviews (coded as P4D4Policy) were conducted at the OECD, at The Learning Bar,[4] and in Ecuador and Paraguay in 2015 and 2016.

Each of these research projects used semi-structured interviews as the primary mode of data generation. To ensure anonymity, participants are identified in terms of their study code, country or organization and an interviewee number. Other contextual information has been omitted for confidentiality reasons. Data were also collected in the form of ethnographic notes (coded as EN) while participating in seminars and conferences with policy-makers, technical experts and academics involved in developing, researching and using ILSAs. Relevant policy documents also provide a backdrop to the analysis. The analytical framework presented here has been developed inductively from analysis of these data, and excerpts of interview data are included to provide illustrative examples.

Understanding participation in ILSAs

The analysis that follows is structured according to seven categories that affect participation in ILSAs: (1) evidence for policy; (2) technical capacity building; (3) funding and aid; (4) international relations; (5) national politics; (6) economic rationales; and (7) curriculum and pedagogy. These categories are by no means hermetically sealed from each other; the boundaries are fuzzy and the data below illustrate multiple and potentially overlapping rationales can inform participation in any given case.

Evidence for policy

Governments and ILSA-administering organizations often justify participation based on the need for data to provide evidence for policy-making. For example, a senior bureaucrat in a national education department explained:

> Ministers are absolutely clear that [for] every policy that is developed they want to see underlying evidence not just from the national side, also the international level. [...] We are in even more international surveys than previously and doing more within those international surveys as well. (SNAG_UK#1)

Participating to increase the evidence base for policy reflects a rationalist understanding of policy. For example, data are often used to make comparisons with top performing educational systems and to set internal policy agendas, as described by a former minister in Argentina: 'We were convinced of the necessity to know both the absolute and the relative worldwide positions of Argentine students in order to be able to better design educational policies' (EN_Ar#1).

Increasingly, educational policy agendas and policy targets are being set in terms of global rankings and evaluated in terms of international performance, as described by an Australian policy-maker:

> Our results have been a little bit uncomfortable and trending a little bit down ... Other countries are going past us. So that's had an influence on policy, explicitly. And the ... government now has goals at a certain level and all

work relating to the new school reforms, they are all towards achieving that result; precisely because the government wants us to restore our standing higher up in the scales. (SNAG_Au#2)

Australia has now set national targets for future performance on PISA. Similarly, Paraguay established its educational objectives in terms of PISA levels: universalizing level 2[5] and reaching level 3 or higher on average in its National Development Plan 2030 (2014: 44). Referring to these educational objectives, Ecuadorian policy-makers were clear that PISA performance is not their primary aim; rather, their focus is on improving education more broadly:

> Some countries reform their curricula and their standards to perform well in PISA. Our objective is not to perform well in PISA, our aim is to obtain information that will allow us to take the right political decisions. (P4D4Policy_Ec#35)

Again, we can see a rationalist approach to policy-making here. ILSA data are also often used as evidence to justify the need for reform and to shift the terms of political debate. For example, referring to the newly elected government in Mongolia (2012), a high-level policy-maker stated, 'There are new people and they want to change and so they need data' (WhyJoin_Mon#16). This points to a process of variation or the creation of policy windows.

We can thus see that ILSA data may be used as evidence for policy according to rationalist logics (making the right decisions), but may also be used to destabilize perceptions of current policy and performance (variation) to legitimize reform or inaction that is more closely tied to internal political agendas, substantiating Luhman's (1995, 1997) externalization theory of subsystems using reference points from other educational systems to produce legitimacy (Schriewer 1988; Waldow 2012).

Technical capacity building

Participation in ILSAs may provide an opportunity to acquire innovative and sophisticated statistical methodology (e.g. Item Response Theory) and build capacities to develop national large-scale assessments. Although it is often assumed that this is exclusively a rationale for participation in low- and middle-income countries – as in Cambodia, Paraguay and Ecuador – capacity building in psychometrics has also been a rationale for OECD countries such as France. However, ILSA capacity building is contingent upon policy and political stability issues.

Look at the case of Guatemala ... they were part of loads of capacity building sessions, then the World Bank arrived ... and then a whole set of things happened with the President, and bang! The minister changed and they all left, the whole team was gone. (P4D4Policy_Ec#38)

Capacity building goes beyond the technical aspects of assessment to include sharing of educational challenges and experiences, in particular sharing of policy ideas at ILSA meetings (Grek 2014). In 2015, the head of the OECD Directorate for Education and Skills described the value of PISA primarily in terms of providing learning and knowledge sharing opportunities:

The global purpose is simply to allow those countries to engage with global best expertise. It isn't really about the scores, the scores would be a product of this. But the idea really is to connect the expertise in those countries with the best expertise which is around anywhere in the world, and that has been the motivation for those countries to join. And that is the vehicle for integrating countries in the global education community. (P4D4Policy_OECD#100)

Substantiating this view, a senior policy actor in Paraguay argued that not only is PISA a capacity building opportunity, but also an opportunity to learn from others. Although the capacity building rationale is primarily a technical issue here, the transfer of statistical capacity and the sharing of educational policy and practice are not separate issues. Rather, these processes are closely linked by the values that are encoded in the conceptual and methodological assumptions ILSAs are built upon and the knowledge sharing that takes place during such activities.

ILSAs can be seen as a desirable option when national assessments are either non-existent or of poor quality. In other cases, national assessments may be revised in line with ILSAs, or national assessments may be developed based on ILSA frameworks and methodologies or using ILSAs as a reference point. A senior staff member at the OECD explained the value of aligning national and international assessments: 'I always encourage countries to actually link those two up ... Some countries have actually done some very thoughtful work in getting those metrics somehow synchronised. I think that's what you need to get because the stories are different' (SNAG_Au#3).

In the case of Ecuador, the results of PISA-D were described as a way to legitimize national assessment instruments because it showed similar learning outcomes to national assessments: 'The closeness of the national and international assessments will give legitimacy to our national assessment' (P4D4Policy_Ec#37). It is worth noting that before implementing an ILSA, impact may already be seen where countries develop their national assessments with reference to ILSA frameworks.

The OECD promotes the view that both national assessments and international benchmarking are needed to adequately monitor educational performance. The dynamic created between differences in performance as measured by national and international assessments is important to understand when assessing reasons for participation. An OECD senior staff member argued:

> If you look back at the initial papers on PISA, it says very clearly, PISA is done to enrich national assessments ... If you have a very strong national assessment, obviously you are going to draw from both, PISA will give you an extra edge but not much, if you have a very weak national assessment or no national assessment or any other source of information, then it becomes a lot more relevant ... What we should be aiming for is both. Countries should have excellent national assessments combined with participation in international assessments. (P4D4Policy_OECD#30)

For example, a senior policy actor explained that although Paraguay has data from a national assessment and a regional assessment, both are curriculum-based assessments. He argued that participating in PISA-D, a competency-based assessment, is a new way for Paraguay to approach standardized assessments and to understand what can be assessed.

Participation for capacity building purposes is often conceived as a technical process only, but it also contributes to epistemological governance and normative policy emulation. ILSAs allocate values and thus the capacity building and learning that they generate are also a value-laden form of normative governance. Building capacity, aligning assessment approaches and creating systems for data management can also be seen as forms of infrastructural governance and PISA has been particularly influential in this regard (Sellar and Lingard 2014).

Funding and aid

Participation of low- and middle-income countries in ILSAs is often linked to funding and aid. Participation fees and implementation costs are frequently covered by international donors or bilateral aid schemes. Donors often require ILSA data to benchmark progress and, in a less direct manner, ILSAs are used to display commitment to accountability and transparency, which can increase donor approval. ILSA data are also used as evidence to obtain funds for education activities and are likely to become a key criterion in the future allocation of education aid.

Staff from international aid agencies describe low- and middle-income country participation in ILSAs as donor driven (Lockheed et al. 2015); however, we argue that a single rationale rarely explains participation and that no country takes part in ILSAs without also being driven by other purposes. For example, Mongolia participated in TIMSS 2011 with World Bank funding but returned the funding after the pilot phase when the government decided it no longer suited its agenda, as described by a World Bank officer:

> They had to give back the $600,000 USD they had not used for TIMMS. They stopped TIMMS because they said it was not a good type of assessment ... The two official reasons they gave were the timing was not right because they were in a transition to Cambridge educational system ... And that it was not mainstreamed because we were using consultants and not the Education Evaluation Centre, so there was no capacity building. (WhyJoin_Mon#26)

From the perspective of CPE, this example illustrates that despite aid conditionality, participation may still not be sustained as a policy position. The example also shows how rationales for participation can shift during an implementation, especially since implementations take place over several years and governments may change. Moreover, it demonstrates that aid conditionality is not always an important factor in decisions to participate or not. Understanding not only how countries fund their participation, but also what implications participation has for obtaining aid or complying with aid schemes, is an important element in determining the specific interrelated set of factors that drive participation in particular cases.

International relations

Pressure to engage in global education policy has often been dichotomized between external and internal factors, although they are often two sides of the same coin. For analytical purposes, we have differentiated between rationales that are tied to international relations and others that are more explicitly linked to national politics, which we discuss in the following section. This is particularly important in terms of understanding participation as a matter of normative emulation in relation to the international community.

Countries may participate in ILSAs as part of a broader nation-building narrative; to make a statement about political or economic status; to align their values with an international community; as a criterion for access to political, economic or trade entities; or due to pressure created by their status as signatories to global commitments. Countries often participate as a duty or responsibility, and non-participation may not be an option even when data are not relevant to a country's specific educational policy challenges. For example, in 2016 Mexico stated that, as an OECD member, it cannot leave PISA, even though the value of further implementations has been questioned.

International relations purposes for participation include factors related to membership in international organizations that administer ILSAs or initiatives which have been pledged by countries. In such cases, participation is undertaken as a responsibility, as described by a Mongolian policy actor: 'Because Mongolia really values literacy, it is our duty to [participate] since Mongolia is a big player in literacy and also started the United Nations Literacy Decade' (WhyJoin_Mon#28). Participation here appears to be valued as a process more than as a means to generate internationally comparative data. When participation is about the 'club' a country joins, participation can become a 'global ritual of belonging' (Addey 2015). Seeking recognition from a larger international community is both a form of cognitive governance and normative emulation.

An interviewee in Paraguay argued that non-participation in PISA-D was not an option unless they were willing to be excluded from the global community:

> I don't think there is any explicit sanction, but there is a connotation that one is outside of something. It's like the feeling of being auto-excluded … Not being on the information map in the 21st century is unbearable. (P4D4Policy_Py#45)

Not only does Paraguay's participation in PISA-D substantiate the global ritual of belonging, but high-level policy actors are clear about the importance of belonging to this international community in political terms, which then needs to be justified to the public in technical terms.

Closely linked to the global ritual of belonging is the use of international assessments to generate national statistics, as a global stamp of approval of an entity as a state, or as a way to gain recognition from the international community. A UIS staff member explained that '[t]he rationale for participating is obvious, it is part of the nation building, it was to put Palestine out there, and we have LAMP, therefore we must be a country' (WhyJoin_UIS#2). Participation is often related to economic and political status claims, but may also be used as a way to legitimize domestic educational policy and practice, as stated by a high-level policy actor in Europe: 'If you don't have data from international assessments, it feels bad and it looks bad, you are just an empty line, it looks like you are not doing anything in education' (EN_#2).

This leads to the question of non-participation. What are the benefits of non-participation? To what extent is it possible to not participate? Being an 'empty line' is less strategic than participating and ranking poorly, as suggested by a senior English policy-maker in relation to PISA-D:

Maybe countries don't want to see how badly they are doing. It will be discouraging and depressing and a negative experience for them, but I think you have got to be honest. I think the majority of countries probably do want to be on that spectrum, and not on a different one; even if they are at the bottom. (SNAG_UK#4)

Participation in ILSAs has clearly become a powerful global political technology with which countries increasingly feel compelled to engage. This rationale can be understood in terms of normative approaches to policy diffusion and in terms of epistemological governance.

National politics

Participation may also be prompted by pressures associated with national politics, which might come from ministries and institutions not directly related to education and can also be a response to special interest lobbies (e.g. French banks lobbied for France to take part in the 'finance literacy' section in PISA), media pressure or public opinion. Where forms of New Public Management have been implemented, ILSAs may be implemented as regulatory tools to measure progress towards performance targets.

Scandalizing with comparatively 'bad' data can be a means for political parties to win support or put the spotlight on weak performance and discredit opposition groups (Steiner-Khamsi 2003; Addey 2015). As described by a senior Mongolian policy-maker:

I think the new government will use LAMP for the next elections: 'They said education and literacy were like this, but look, LAMP shows this, we are now bringing change.' They will use it in a political way. (WhyJoin_Mon#20)

Countries may also apply pressure to modify ILSAs in ways that enable the 'glorification' of performance (Steiner-Khamsi and Stolpe 2006). A good example of this tactic is the shift to the measurement of literacy as a continuum, which avoids the concept of illiteracy and uses poor literacy as the lowest level. A senior policy actor in Mongolia recounts how LAMP can help to improve literacy statistics by changing the scale on which literacy is measured:

From 1990 we had a decade of new problems like poverty, school drop outs, low HDI, everything was getting worse so we needed to find a way to increase these numbers, change the bad results, and LAMP meets our needs. (WhyJoin_Mon#17)

Here we see an example of what is perhaps one of the most important factors relating to ILSA participation: the pressure that it places on governments, politicians and policy-makers. A senior policy-maker in Ecuador explained how politicians, well aware of these pressures, joke about PISA: 'A minister said the best scenario is to take office is the day after the PISA results and to leave the day before the students take the PISA exams' (P4D4Policy_Ec#35). This shows how PISA has become a kind of high-stake evaluation of ministerial performance. In Laos, the need for international data also responded to the need to account for progress that had been domestically produced through promises and electorate expectations, as suggested by a senior policy advisor:

> There is a lot of public rhetoric in the media. For example, the Vientiane Times[6] always promising the goals were going to be achieved by 2015. So now they have almost got to stand up for what they promised, sending out political messages which actually put pressure on themselves. (WhyJoin_ Lao#9)

Participation in certain ILSAs is taken for granted by political parties whose agendas tend to be aligned with ILSA values and may be rejected by others. In fact, newly elected governments often revise or differently emphasize participation in ILSAs in comparison to previous governments. For example, the emphasis on ILSA data shifted dramatically in the United Kingdom with the shift from Labour to the Coalition government in 2010. A CPE approach can offer theoretical purchase on the questions of how national political issues create variation, how new policies or reform directions are selected and whether or not these changes are retained.

Economic rationales

ILSAs are seen as a key measure of human capital and as a proxy indicator for global economic competitiveness and this is a view that the OECD supports. Murphy (2010) argues that economic competitiveness concerns are built into ILSA narratives to stimulate fears of being outcompeted. In 2015, the director of Education and Skills at the OECD observed:

> I remember when Brazil joined PISA in 2000, many people said 'We are a poor country, so why do you want to measure us against...?' But we live in a global economy, and that is also a new dimension now, the idea of globalization has arrived at the door steps of anyone. You go to a market in Mexico and you can find products from China. Suddenly workers in Mexico compete with workers in China, so naturally it makes sense to compare the skills of people. (P4D4Policy_OECD#100)

Almost all countries participating in ILSAs express interest in comparing with chosen reference societies to quantify the competitiveness gap, but also to understand what skills are valued in educating citizens for the global labour market. A policy-maker in Laos commented:

> With globalization ... we cannot say we are alone and that we don't need the others, we are connected to the world. International migration for labour means we need to link to other countries' curriculum. We do not drop Lao way of doing things but we have to adapt to the world. (WhyJoin_Lao#14)

ILSAs are also used to represent 'skills pools' and attract national and international investors, as described by a senior policy actor in Mongolia:

> We saw that the Mongolian skills were lower at the end of secondary school but we need to be like European students. Mongolian students need to be globally competitive. There is huge foreign investment here, investors want to recruit, but our skills are not at level, so we really need to look at where we are in the world. (WhyJoin_Mon#20)

The participation of Paraguay in PISA-D is said to have been influenced by the business sector, as a senior Paraguayan policy actor explained: 'An influential protagonist in the last years in Paraguay is the business sector, they created an organization, "Together for Education", which brings together business owners and very powerful people from the media, and they are very pro-PISA' (P4D4Policy_Py#42). Similar situations can be found elsewhere, including the USA where a number of corporate-sponsored lobby groups and philanthropies promote PISA.

ILSAs have thus become an important instrument within what Brown and Tannock (2009) call the global war for talent – the competition between nations for the most valuable human capital. The OECD has positioned PISA as the best way countries can measure how well educational systems prepare their students' 'capacity to face life at a global level' (P4D4Policy_Py#44) and to identify policy solutions. Economic rationales for participation can be understood from both rationalist (evidence to improve economic performance) and normative emulation perspectives (attracting business investment by demonstrating the quality of human capital).

Curriculum and pedagogy

Improving curriculum and pedagogy is a common rationale for pursuing policy reforms based on ILSA data. For example, Japan has modified its national curriculum to incorporate PISA-like approaches, and countries such as Mexico and Canada (Prince Edward Island) have used teacher and student manuals to embed test preparation in classroom teaching. In these cases, participation in ILSAs has encouraged alignment between national or school-level curriculum and pedagogy and the conceptions of knowledge and learning embedded in ILSA designs.

Often, however, changes to curriculum and pedagogy based on ILSA participation are driven by a desire to improve test-performance or internal political agendas and are only loosely based in the evidence generated by ILSAs. This may be a result of the prominence of PISA over other assessments. Whilst TIMSS and PIRLS measure how well students have acquired the taught curriculum, PISA measures the capacity to apply skills learnt over the first fifteen years of life both in and out of school. There is thus only a loose relation between curriculum and PISA performance, as a PISA-D contractor explained:

> Countries set their benchmarks to become number five in the world rankings, and they then revise their curriculum. But that is not what PISA says and it will not change the scores in the next PISA round. There is such a weak link between what is taught and PISA. (P4D4Policy_TLB#34)

Technical concerns about whether and how ILSAs can inform better teaching and learning practices are increasingly voiced by those most concerned that participation in ILSAs give something back to education at the level of the classroom. However, in the case of PISA it is not clear how ILSA data can sensibly inform changes at this level. This is one reason for the OECD developing the PISA-based Test for Schools, which has been designed to provide school-level data that are not available from participation in main PISA.

The aim to improve curriculum and pedagogy through ILSA participation can be understood from rationalist, normative emulation and CPE perspectives. A rationalist approach would emphasize the aim to improve curricula and adapt them to the needs of the global economy. A normative emulation approach would emphasize isomorphism of skills-oriented curricula globally, whilst a CPE approach draws attention to national political contests over curriculum control and the instrumentalization of ILSAs for this purpose.

Conclusion

In this chapter, we have outlined seven different categories that can be used to understand ILSA participation and dissemination: (1) evidence for policy; (2) technical capacity building; (3) funding and aid; (4) international relations; (5) national politics; (6) economic rationales; and (7) curriculum and pedagogy.

Each category highlights a particular area of concern that can affect the decision to participate in ILSAs. These categories can be understood according to different theories of policy diffusion and adoption – namely, rationalist, normative emulation and CPE approaches (Verger 2016) – and according to theories of global governance.

Drawing on the empirical data, our chapter shows that: participation is rarely driven by one factor alone; the decision to participate has to be understood in the particular context in which the decision is taken; rationales can change between and during implementations; it is not only access to data that drives participation, but the process of ILSA participation itself; and rationales for ILSA participation are often not discrete and cannot be assumed simply on the basis of income or level of development.

In relation to the latter point, it is widely assumed that lower- and middle-income countries participate in ILSAs for different reasons than wealthier countries. However, our empirical data does not support this thesis. For example, technical capacity has been identified as a rationale for participation in low- and middle-income contexts, but higher-income countries also participate to learn the most advanced assessment methodologies. If a distinction is to be made on the basis of income level, the following analysis can be made. First, in contexts where the relative cost of participation is higher than in wealthier OECD countries, participation may rely on external funding, but is often driven by other rationales and is not necessarily determined by this funding. Secondly, the majority of low- and middle-income countries are participating in ILSAs as latecomers. These countries are often aware of the poor policy relevance ILSAs have shown in other low- and middle-income countries and are primarily interested in ILSA participation for legitimation purposes rather than for the performance data. This would suggest that low- and middle-income countries are greatly driven by rationales that can be understood and explained from a normative emulation perspective.

Thus, although ILSA participation is frequently justified in terms of the dominant rationalist narrative of 'better data for better policies', the empirical evidence presented in this chapter deepens our understanding of the growing phenomenon of ILSAs. The analytical framework we have developed provides an insight into the complexity through which the global education landscape is being constituted and suggests the sociopolitical contexts in which ILSAs are adopted are transforming the intended uses of ILSAs. The multiple rationales for participation show how ILSAs can easily serve many different purposes, thus contributing to the rapid growth of the ILSA phenomenon over the last fifteen years.

Understanding how ILSAs have developed and spread so rapidly, and the meanings they acquire in each context, deepens our understanding of the central role ILSAs play in new modes of global governance. ILSAs are constituting a new form of infrastructural governance as they spread capacities to generate, collect, manage and analyse education data across countries around the world (Sellar and Lingard 2014). This infrastructure 'joins up' national assessments of education and lubricates the global governance of education through comparisons of national performance (Novoa and Yariv-Mashal 2003; Woodward 2009). Moreover, by participating in ILSAs, countries demonstrate that they share the values of an international community (cognitive governance) and produce evidence and knowledge for policy-making (normative governance). Participation in ILSAs thus also facilitates modes of epistemological governance that are producing alignment of assessment and other educational practices across countries around the world. Although countries participate in ILSAs for diverse reasons, they consent to common ILSA values of the need for more reliable, comparative data in education and, by doing so, contribute to generating ILSA-based policy knowledge.

Questions for discussion

1 What is the balance between political, educative and technical rationales for global education reforms? Can these different dimensions even be disentangled?

2 To what extent are ILSAs contributing to global education policy becoming an increasingly political and economic matter rather than an educative one?

3 Of all the reasons for ILSA participation presented in this chapter, which have more explanatory power? Similarly, which global education policy theories help understand the global dissemination of ILSAs?

Acknowledgements

The authors are deeply grateful to Néstor López, Bob Lingard and Antoni Verger for their valuable feedback on this chapter.

Notes

1 This is the first large-scale education assessment to use a household survey methodology.

2 The SNAG data draw on a Discovery Project (DP1094850) titled *Schooling the Nation in an Age of Globalisation: National Curriculum, Accountabilities and*

their Effects, which was funded by the Australian Research Council (ARC). The chief investigator of this project was Professor Bob Lingard, and it was based at The University of Queensland.

3 The P4D4Policy research project is supported by the Fritz Thyssen Foundation.

4 Canadian private company contracted to develop the PISA for Development background questionnaires.

5 Level 5 is the highest (students score above 625) and describes students who can manage 'sophisticated' reading literacy, whilst level 1 (students score between 335 and 480) is the lowest level and describes students who can complete the least complex reading literacy tasks (like locating a single piece of information in a text).

6 A state-run English daily paper in Laos.

References

Abdul-Hamid, H., Abu-Lebdeh, K. et al. (2011). *Assessment testing can be used to inform policy decisions*. Washington, DC: World Bank.

Addey, C. (2014). Why do countries join international literacy assessments? An Actor-Network Theory analysis with cases studies from Lao PDR and Mongolia. School of Education and Lifelong Learning. Norwich, University of East Anglia. PhD thesis.

Addey, C. (2015). 'Participating in international literacy assessments in Lao PDR and Mongolia: A global ritual of belonging'. In M. Hamilton, B. Maddox and C. Addey (Eds.), *Literacy as numbers: Researching the politics and practices of international literacy assessment*. Cambridge: Cambridge University Press.

Addey, C. (forthcoming). 'The assessment culture of international organizations: From philosophical doubt to statistical certainty through the appearance and growth of international large-scale assessments'. In C. Alarcón and M. Lawn (Eds.), *Pupil assessment cultures in historical perspective*. Frankfurt am Main: Peter Lang.

Anagnostopoulos, D., Rutledge, S. A., and Jacobsen, R. (2013). *The infrastructure of accountability: Data use and the transformation of American education*. Cambridge, MA: Harvard Education Press.

Bloem, S. (2013). *PISA in low and middle income countries*. Paris: OECD Publishing.

Brown, P. and Tannock, S. (2009). Education, meritocracy and the global war for talent. *Journal of Education Policy*, 24 (4), 377–392.

Easterling, K. (2014). *Extrastatecraft: The power of infrastructure space*. London and New York: Verso.

Ertl, H. (2006). 'Educational standards and the changing discourse on education: The reception and consequences of the PISA study in Germany'. *Oxford Review of Education*, 32 (5): 619–634.

Gilmore, A. (2005). *The impact of PIRLS (2001) and TIMSS (2003) in low- and middle-income countries: an evaluation of the value of World Bank support for international surveys of reading literacy (PIRLS) and mathematics and science (TIMSS)*. Amsterdam: International Association for the Evaluation of Educational Achievement.

Gobierno Nacional Paraguay. (2014). Plan Nacional de Desarrollo Paraguay 2030. Asuncion.

Grek, S. (2009). 'Governing by numbers: The PISA "effect" in Europe'. *Journal of Education Policy*, 24 (1): 23–37.

Grek, S. (2014). 'OECD as a site of co-production: European education governance and the new politics of "policy mobilisation"'. *Critical Policy Studies* 8 (3): 266–281.

Guadalupe, C. (2015). 'How feasible is it to develop a culturally-sensitive large-scale, standardised assessment of literacy skills?'. In M. Hamilton, B. Maddox and C. Addey (Eds.), *Literacy as numbers*. Cambridge: Cambridge University Press, pp. 111–128.

Haas, P. (1992). 'Introduction: Epistemic communities and international policy coordination'. *International Organization* 46 (1): 1–35.

Jessop, B. (2010). 'Cultural political economy and critical political studies'. *Critical Policy Studies*, 3 (3–4), 336–356.

Kamens, D. H. (2013). 'Globalization and the emergence of an audit culture: PISA and the search for "best practices" and magic bullets'. In H. D. Meyer and A. Benavot (Eds.), *PISA, power, and policy the emergence of global educational governance*. Wallingford/GB: Symposium Books.

Kingdon, J. W. (1984). *Agendas, alternatives, and public policies*. New York: Longman.

Lockheed, M. (2013). 'Causes and consequences of international large-scale assessments in developing countries'. In H. D. Meyer and A. Benavot (Eds.), *PISA, power, and policy the emergence of global educational governance*. Wallingford/GB: Symposium Books.

Lockheed, M., Prokic-Breuer, T. et al. (2015). *The experience of middle-income countries participating in PISA 2000–2015*. Paris: OECD.

Luhmann, N. (1995). *Soziale Systeme*, Stanford University Press.

Luhmann, N. (1997). *Die Gesellschaft der Gesellschaft*, Suhrkamp.

Martens, K. (2007). 'How to become an influential actor – The "comparative turn" in OECD education policy'. In K. Martens, A. Rusconi and K. Leuze (Eds.), *New arenas in education governance*. New York: Palgrave Macmillan.

Mayer-Schönberger, V. and Cukier, K. (2013). *Big data: A revolution that will transform how we live, work, and think*. Boston and New York: Basic Books.

Meyer, J. et al. (1992). 'World expansion of mass education, 1870–1980'. *Sociology of Education*, 65, 128–149.

Murphy, S. (2010). 'The pull of PISA: Uncertainty, influence, and ignorance'. *International Journal of Education for Democracy*, 3 (1), 28–44.

Nóvoa, A. and Yariv-Mashal, T. (2003). 'Comparative research in education: A mode of governance or a historical journey?' *Comparative Education*, 39 (4), 423–438.

Nye Jr., J. S. (2004). *Soft power: The means to success in world politics*. New York: PublicAffairs.

OECD (2013). *OECD skills outlook 2013: First results from the survey of adult skills*. Paris: OECD Publishing.

Robertson, S. and Dale, R. (2015). 'Toward a 'critical cultural political economy' account of the globalising of education'. *Globalisation, Societies and Education*, 13 (1), 149–170.

Schriewer, J. (1988). The method of comparison and the need for externalization: Methodological and sociological concepts. In J. Schriewer and B. Holmes (Eds.), *Theories and methods in comparative education*. New York: Peter Lang, pp. 25–86.

Sellar, S. (2015). Data infrastructure: A review of expanding accountability systems and large-scale assessments in education. *Discourse: Studies in the cultural politics of education,* 36 (5), 765–777.

Sellar, S. and Lingard, B. (2013). 'PISA and the expanding role of the OECD in global education governance'. In H. D. Meyer and A. Benavot (Eds.), *PISA, power, and policy the emergence of global educational governance.* Wallingford/GB: Symposium Books.

Sellar, S. and Lingard, B. (2014). 'The OECD and the expansion of PISA: New global modes of governance in education'. *British Educational Research Journal,* 40 (6), 917–936.

Steiner-Khamsi, G. (2003). 'The politics of League Tables'. *Journal of Social Science Education* 1: http://www.jsse.org/index.php/jsse/article/view/470.

Steiner-Khamsi, G. (forthcoming). Focusing on the local to understand why the global resonates and how governments appropriate ILSAs for national agenda setting. In C. Addey, S. Sellar et al. The rise of international large-scale assessments and rationales for participation. *Compare: A Journal of Comparative and International Education.*

Steiner-Khamsi, G. and Stolpe, I. (2006). *Educational import, local encounters with global forces in Mongolia.* New York: Palgrave Macmillan.

Steiner-Khamsi, G. and Waldow, F. (Eds.) (2012). *World yearbook in education 2012. Policy borrowing and lending in education.* New York: Routledge.

Thorn, W. (2009). International Adult Literacy and Basic Skills Surveys in the OECD Region. OECD Education Working Papers. Paris: OECD Publishing.

Verger, A. (2016). 'The global diffusion of education privatization: Unpacking and theorizing policy adoption'. In K. Mundy, A. Green, B. Lingard and A. Verger (Eds.), *The handbook of global education policy.* London: Wiley.

Waldow, F. (2012). Standardization and Legitimacy: Two central concepts in research on educational borrowing and lending. In G. Steiner-Khamsi and F. Waldow (Eds.), *World Yearbook in Education 2012. Policy Borrowing and Lending in Education.* New York: Routledge.

Wiseman, A. (2013). 'Policy responses to Pisa in comparative perspective'. In H. D. Meyer and A. Benavot (Eds.), *PISA, power, and policy the emergence of global educational governance.* Wallingford/GB: Symposium Books.

Woodward, R. (2009). *The organization for economic co-operation and development (OECD).* Abingdon: Routledge.

Further reading

Bloem, S. (2015). 'PISA for low- and middle-income countries'. *Compare: A Journal of Comparative and International Education,* 45 (3), 481–486.

Kamens, D. H. (2013). 'Globalization and the emergence of an audit culture: PISA and the search for "best practices" and magic bullets'. In H. D. Meyer and A. Benavot (Eds.), *PISA, power, and policy the emergence of global educational governance.* Wallingford/GB: Symposium Books.

Lockheed, M. (2013). 'Causes and consequences of international large-scale assessments in developing countries'. In H. D. Meyer and A. Benavot (Eds.), *PISA, power, and policy the emergence of global educational* governance. Wallingford/GB: Symposium Books.

6

School- and Community-Based Management as Global Education Policy: History, Trajectory, Continuity

D. Brent Edwards Jr.

Introduction

Notions of school- and community-based management have been popular around the world, but particularly in the education-for-development field, for many decades in one form or another. While these terms and their changing definitions over time will be further discussed in what follows, suffice to say that these forms of school management have – like the other reforms addressed in this book – achieved the status of a global education policy. Indeed, they have been promoted in multiple ways by the most influential international organizations working on issues related to education, including, for example, the World Bank and UNESCO, as well as other regional development banks, think tanks and international non-governmental organizations. A key purpose of this chapter is to explain how these reforms achieved global status. At the same time, an objective is to place this global education policy into historical context. In specific terms, the objectives of this chapter can be stated as follows:

- Explain the various meanings of the concept of decentralization over time, and its relationship to the concepts of community-based management (CBM) and school-based management (SBM).

- Characterize the difference between CBM and SBM and address the recent emphasis on the latter over the former.

- Highlight the importance of the country context for the emergence of a global education policy.

- Underscore the role of mechanisms of promotion in relation to global education policy.

- Present the findings of a case study of a CBM programme from El Salvador that went on to become a global education policy, explaining the trajectory of this policy from its origins to its location in the global reform agenda.

In attempting to accomplish this objective, the present chapter examines these policy ideas from multiple perspectives and moves through multiple sections. First, it situates CBM in long-term perspective by discussing it in relation to trends in decentralization generally in the post–Second World War context. Second, it presents and critically discusses the trajectory of a specific CBM reform that emerged from El Salvador in the early 1990s and went on to become a global education policy. This reform was known as EDUCO, or Education with Community Participation. Importantly, the case of EDUCO addresses not only the origins, implementation and evolution of the policy, but also the mechanisms of promotion engaged by the World Bank and other international organizations to widely promote the EDUCO model, wherein parent councils had the legal responsibility for hiring and firing teachers. The EDUCO case is presented because it can be considered the most extreme, well-known and widely promoted example of CBM to have arisen and taken hold in the education-for-development field. Finally, this chapter reflects on how community participation lives on under the label of SBM, in addition to commenting on how such reforms continue to be promoted and funded by international organizations.

Theoretically, the findings presented in this chapter have been informed by the international political economy perspective on global education policies (see discussion of this perspective by the editors of this volume in the introduction). In short, this theoretical perspective directs attention to the political–economic structural conditions that constrain a country, for example, as well as to the role of international organizations vis-à-vis country-level constraints and the mechanisms through which those organizations influence policy-making and policy diffusion at the national and international levels, respectively. Methodologically, the findings discussed in the sections below are the result of work completed over six years (2009–2015). Specifically, the discussion of decentralization in long-term perspective is the result of a broad literature review of 126 studies of decentralization (see Edwards and DeMatthews 2014, for more). However, the majority of the chapter – that is, all findings related to EDUCO – is the result of a multi-year case study of the origins and trajectory of this policy, with this research entailing both archival work and 157 interviews with actors at the local, national, and international levels and from relevant governmental and international organizations (for more, see Edwards forthcoming, 2013, 2015, 2016, and Edwards et al. 2015).

Decentralization in long-term perspective[1]

SBM and CBM are an extension of the long-term trend of decentralization. In the post–Second World War period, the meaning of decentralization has changed over time, with at least three identifiable periods – the first spanning 1950s–mid-1970s, the second lasting from the mid-1970s to early 1980s and the third beginning in the mid-1980s. Each is characterized in what follows.

Wave 1: Independence and the establishment of national education systems

Globally, a wave of independence from colonial powers swept the world in the 1950s and 1960s. In this context, generally, decentralization can be seen as the transference of power from the centre to the periphery of the world system. In the words of Cohen and Peterson (1999), 'In the early 1960s proponents of decentralization focused on using the intervention to assist colonies in beginning a transition to independence, achieving political equity, and responding to rising demand for public goods and services' (p. 1). By extension, for public services broadly and for education specifically, new nation states then set out to establish national education systems, an important feature of 'modern' nations. The establishment of such systems reflected decentralization in that they meant expansion of both government oversight and educational provision at the subnational level.

Wave 2: Administrative decentralization (mid-1970s–early 1980s)

During the second period of decentralization, in the education sector, the overarching concern was with 'administrative development', that is, extending the state apparatus further down from the level of centralized ministries. Planners approached education systems as complex organizations and created reform strategies for their improvement based on rational and technical logic. At the same time, many educational systems experienced challenges, problems that one would expect to accompany a period of rapid expansion of education. For example, many school systems were described as disorganized, in disarray, and unwieldy.

In this context, decentralization to the subnational level emerged in some countries as an attractive policy option to improve the quality of the education system. In a number of cases, where some form of administrative decentralization either already existed or was then being implemented, matters of both politics and organizational capacity altered or hampered the reform as designed. This was the case in parts of Africa and Latin America, as well as Papua New Guinea. In contrast to later forms of decentralization in developing countries, which would concentrate on the community level, these policies focused on provincial-, regional- or state-level administration. Moreover, they highlighted the fact that decentralization to these levels was a process inescapably bound up in politics and complex organizational dynamics, despite the best efforts of central planners at rational planning.

Wave 3: Neoliberal decentralization (mid-1980s)

This third phase began in the mid-1980s and has been characterized by the promotion of decentralization policies by international development organizations in order to, in the words of Cohen and Peterson (1999), 'facilitate more efficient and effective production and provision of public goods and services and to establish market-oriented economies in which public sector tasks can be privatized' (p. 2). Certain features of the broad reform context have facilitated the predomination of such a focus in the third period. The economic and political landscape changed internationally with the election of President Reagan in the United States and Prime Minister Thatcher in the United Kingdom, both of whom privileged neoliberal policy prescriptions across all areas of government and society. The Reagan and Thatcher governments reflected and embodied a neoliberal perspective on education reform that had been gaining momentum for many years (Whitty and Edwards 1998; Harvey 2005). Their elections, thus, had the effect of shifting the dominant global discourse around the role of the state and the provision of public services such that neoliberal policy prescriptions were elevated. The state and the centralized bureaucracies that had developed were now defined as the problem, with the latter being seen as large and ineffective in nature (Harvey 2005). The World Bank echoed the rhetoric of the times and extended its application to the realm of development work (Edwards 2012).

In education, the idea of decentralization, as Schiefelbein (2004) puts it, 'was transformed into a simple and appealing message: *devolving responsibilities to local schools would increase their performance, technical capacity might be retrieved, and corruption would disappear*' (p. 362, italics in original).[2] Because of the push during this time for fundamental institutional reform of governments along neoliberal lines and with an eye to 'good governance', decentralization prevailed over a range of other education reform strategies as a primary intervention of choice (Whitty and Edwards 1998; Edwards 2012). Community-level decentralization based on relations of accountability between the community and the school and for reasons of efficiency was an option that would resonate with the international trends of the times; the decision to preference this education reform was an ideological one made as part of the wider shift in thinking on the role of the state described earlier.

Central America is perhaps the region that adopted decentralization reforms which most closely mirrored the trend described by Cohen and Peterson (1999). In the 1990s and 2000s, in El Salvador, Guatemala, Honduras and Nicaragua, legally responsible councils with membership of between five and fifteen were made up of parents (along with the principal and one or two teachers in Nicaragua) at the community level who volunteered their time to manage the school. The primary responsibility of these councils was to hire, fire and motivate (i.e. 'hold accountable') teachers through the application of pressure and the threat of being terminated (teachers worked on one-year contracts). The school councils also purchased necessary educational materials with government-provided funds; they could also spend a discretionary portion of the money allotted to them, if there were any additional funds. Where this was not the case, and where the initial funds provided by the central government were insufficient, communities were expected to either raise the funds they required from external sources or else provide the contributions themselves (Di Gropello 2006).

Because of the significant responsibilities given to parents at the community level, these reforms fall under the label of CBM arrangements and were thought to be more efficient and cost-effective for central ministries of education for a number of reasons. These reasons were: they relied on voluntary (i.e. unpaid) councils to manage schools; they concomitantly reduced or eliminated the need for intermediate levels of bureaucracy; they incentivized the school councils to spend the allotted funds on the most efficacious mix of inputs; traditional schools would have to compete with schools under decentralized management; and community contributions (either in cash or in kind) would increase. The school council arrangement was also thought to be more effective because it addressed the principal–agent problem by relocating the management of teachers to the community level, thereby incentivizing the teachers to reduce absenteeism and perform better (Edwards 2012). In that such decentralization has been pursued primarily for its ability to enhance efficiency and effectiveness through accountability and competition, it reflects the principles of neoliberal decentralization (Edwards and Klees 2015). (Note that the logic and features characterized here for CBM reflects the logic of EDUCO.)

Although Central America stands out, the reach and popularity of neoliberal decentralization has been extensive. Indeed, many countries in other world regions have also pursued community-level education management decentralization since the mid-1980s, and especially during the 1990s. This is particularly true in sub-Saharan Africa, South and Southeast Asia and Latin America – though it should be noted that countries in these regions have, in practice, relinquished control to the community level in varying degrees (see Edwards and DeMatthews 2014 for further discussion of where and how this model has been adapted and implemented in practice). Despite what we know about decentralization, studies have tended not to trace the origins or trajectory of those models of CBM that have been held up as global exemplars.

Community-based management as global education policy: The case of EDUCO

Context of EDUCO's emergence

Because the background to EDUCO's emergence has been extensively documented in other publications (see, e.g., Edwards 2015; Edwards et al.

2015), only the essential characteristics of the political–economic context will be reviewed here. To that end, there are three features that need to be acknowledged. The first is the fact of civil war (1980–1992) and the effect this had on the country's politics. Specifically, not only was the Salvadoran government caught in an ongoing war with the Farabundo Martí National Liberation Front (FMLN) – a coalition of five rebel groups fighting for socialist reform of the land, economy and social services – but this conflict triggered the involvement of the United States, which was operating from a Cold War mindset. In all, during the civil war, the United States channelled $6 billion in military, economic and social aid to El Salvador (Robinson 2003), with $533 million in military aid arriving in 1985 alone (Booth et al. 2006). The United States thus held significant influence in Salvadoran politics, particularly as a result of the military and economic aid, without which it is doubtful the government would have been able to remain in power or to prevent the economy from collapsing (Montgomery 1995).

Dovetailing with the first issue was the second: that is, the international promotion of neoliberal ideology and reform by the Reagan administration, notably through the United States Agency for International Development (USAID) (Harvey 2005; Klein 2007). This organization, as a major player in El Salvador during the 1980s, funded the establishment and rise of Salvadoran think tanks that supported the foreign policy preferences of the United States. These think tanks then lent credibility to neoliberal reform principles (e.g. market deregulation, privatization of state agencies, austerity measures, shrinking of governmental agencies and elimination of state planning) by hosting famous economists (including the 'Chicago Boys') and by helping to elevate the profiles of Salvadoran economists and businessmen, who then promoted and employed the technocratic and neoliberal approaches to policy that resonated with USAID. In these ways, USAID was instrumental in transforming the national political context of El Salvador during the 1980s.

The third and final aspect of relevance here relates to the election in 1989 of the right-wing candidate for president, Alfredo Cristiani. Beyond having his campaign supported by USAID, he came from one of the think tanks that had been funded by this same organization. Moreover, when he transitioned to the presidency, he brought with him 'at least 17 business leaders and persons linked with [the USAID-funded think tank]' (Segovia 1996, p. 55). As the culminating political development of the 1980s, Cristiani's election had serious implications for the subsequent period of governmental reform. In particular, under the label of modernization, his election signalled that all governmental reform would have to accord with the market-based principles of accountability, efficiency and effectiveness. This state of affairs was a far cry from the agrarian reform and social welfare programmes that had been pledged by José Napoleón Duarte, president during 1984–1989 who represented the Christian Democrat party.

The constraints and interests that shaped EDUCO's rise

In 1990, after ten years of war, 37 per cent of children aged 7–14 were out of school, and statistics were much worse in rural areas, where government-provided services were often unavailable (MINED 1990). While responding to this situation was one of the first priorities of the Cristiani administration, it is important to note that there were multiple actors vying for influence at this point in time. Moreover, it is essential to highlight that the Ministry of Education (MINED) did not have control of large portions of the country, particularly in the northern regions along the Honduran border, where the FMLN and affiliated rural communities were following an approach to education – known as 'popular education' – that had its roots in liberation theology and which reflected the educational philosophy of Paulo Freire in that it taught students to identify and to mobilize against the political–economic structures that contributed to their oppression (Hammond 1998). Importantly, though, beyond the critical nature of this educational approach, the informal schools in these areas (and even beyond) were staffed by parents who worked in exchange for donations from the communities. These schools, thus, by default, were community-controlled, -managed, -staffed and -financed. Furthermore, in that they represented a challenge to the authority of the MINED, the new minister of education as of 1990 saw it as one of her goals to incorporate these communities into the official education system going forward.

With the above characteristics in mind, consider the following inter-institutional dynamics. First, after conducting a needs assessment mid-year 1990, a key consultant from UNESCO, who had previously worked on indigenous rights in Bolivia, recommended to the minister of education that the government build on the community-based model she had observed while collecting data for her study. For the minister of education, however, this was initially seen as an untenable suggestion because it implied building on the educational model of the FMLN. Additionally, the idea that rural parents could manage schools was seen as unrealistic.

The World Bank was equally sceptical of this suggestion at first. This is important to note not only because this organization later became a passionate advocate of the CBM idea, but also because the World Bank was at the centre of many of the reforms being considered once Cristiani entered office, both within and outside education. Indeed, the World Bank was in the midst of negotiating a structural adjustment loan at the same time that the minister of education was exploring options for funding education reform. The implication is that serious education reform could not be pursued without buy-in from the World Bank, since this institution would be the one to fund it.

Although initially favouring a reform model based on the voucher system in Chile, the representatives of the World Bank working in El Salvador began to see the opportunity that community management offered. This change of heart was prompted by two developments. First, the UNESCO consultant showed through the implementation of a pilot programme in early 1991 that rural, uneducated parents could, in fact, be trained to hire and pay teachers. Second, the World Bank staff in El Salvador recognized that a model of educational management based at the community level would represent an extreme form of decentralization, and one that resonated with the principles of neoliberal decentralization. To that point (1991), the decentralization of state functions had only been envisioned at the state or district level. Thus, by extending the idea of decentralization to the community level, the World Bank would be able, if successful in El Salvador, to promote and sell a model where the community was thought to hold the teacher accountable, and in a way that was seen as novel since the community would be formally responsible for hiring and firing the teachers (who worked on a one-year contract renewable at the discretion of the school council, itself made up of five parents elected from the surrounding community). Ultimately, then, this idea took the principles of accountability, efficiency, effectiveness and extended them in a way that generated significant excitement on the part of the World Bank. (See the description of CBM at the end of the 'Wave 3' section above for more on the assumptions and features of the EDUCO model.)

Once the World Bank saw the potential of the community-based model, it put significant financial and technical resources behind the programme – initially $10.3 million and $69.3 million overall in conjunction with the Inter-American Development Bank (Edwards 2013). The World Bank also began to promote the programme in terms of neoliberal principles, sanitizing its critical origins, and thereby allowing the policy to be mobilized more easily within the larger context of neoliberal globalization (Ball 2016). The minister of education, for her part, went with this idea because it met the conditions that constrained her: that is, (1) it expanded educational access, (2) it aligned with the neoliberal principles that were to guide all reforms in El Salvador at that time, (3) it had the blessing of the World Bank, and (4) it incorporated and undermined the FLMN communities (because these communities, which suffered from insufficient resources, were not only required to join the EDUCO programme if they wanted government funding, but they were also required to hire qualified teachers, which necessarily precluded them from hiring their own popular education teachers, who did not have the proper certifications). Teachers unions did not block the reform because, among other reasons, it would only affect teachers who worked in EDUCO schools. Later on, efforts to form a union of EDUCO teachers began in 2001. Over the next ten years, these efforts would bear fruit in that a union was formed but also in that this union would work together with other teachers unions to pressure to remove hiring authority from parent councils (SIMEDUCO 2011).

Before proceeding, it should be noted that the implementation of this policy was not in doubt. All the dominant organizational and political actors agreed on this policy choice, and so it was only a matter of time and effort. Going forward from 1991, when the first education loan was approved, the World Bank provided close monitoring of the programme as well as guidance at each step in the process. By 1994, thousands of communities had been integrated into the EDUCO programme. Concretely, while the programme began in 1991 with six communities, in 2004, EDUCO had 7,381 teachers and 378,208 students.[3] Approximately 55 per cent of rural public schools, which make up two-thirds of all schools in El Salvador, would operate under the EDUCO programme (Gillies et al. 2010). However, beginning in 2011, following the election in 2009 of the first left-wing president since the end of the civil war, the EDUCO programme began to be phased out. Teachers can no longer be hired and fired by parents, and the MINED has sought, with limited success, to implement a school governance approach that allows schools to be more inclusive, with the school at the centre of culture and with extended hours for extracurricular activities (for more, see Edwards et al. forthcoming).

Mechanisms and pathways of promotion

Through prior research, various mechanisms and pathways have been revealed via which EDUCO was promoted internationally (Edwards 2013, forthcoming). Here, mechanisms are defined as the 'underlying entities, processes, or structures which operate in particular contexts to generate outcomes of interest' (Astbury and Leeuw 2010, p. 368). On the other hand, pathways, following the discussion by Samoff (2009), can generally be thought of as more directly observable avenues through which institutions such as the World Bank exercise their influence. The findings that follow enumerate both underlying mechanisms (i.e. dissemination, certification, policy entrepreneurs, global reach) and more specific pathways of influence (which can be thought of as materializations of the underlying mechanisms). Together, the mechanisms and pathways focus on the various means through which EDUCO has been promoted in the context of the global governance of education. Examples of each can be found in Table 6.1.[4]

Table 6.1 Mechanisms and pathways of EDUCO's global promotion

Mechanism/ Pathway	Select Examples
Dissemination – publications	– 1996 – A UNESCO Bulletin on meeting the EFA goals in Latin America mentions the EDUCO programme as an example of decision-making power being transferred to the local level.– 1999 – EDUCO is identified in a regional UNESCO Bulletin as a strategy for providing quality education to underprivileged and/or excluded youth.– 2000 – In the Primary and Secondary Education Strategy of the Inter-American Development Bank, EDUCO is mentioned as an exemplar of reform based in local management and accountability.– 2001 – In a report by a conservative education think tank – the Partnership for Education Revitalization in the Americas – EDUCO is underscored for its potential to address issues of educational coverage.– 2004 – In its flagship publication, the World Development Report, the World Bank spotlights EDUCO as the prime example of public service decentralization in education along lines of accountability and for reasons of efficiency and effectiveness– 2009 – A World Bank review of school-based management highlighted and classified the EDUCO programme as one of the stronger models because community members are responsible for 'hiring, firing and monitoring teachers' (Barrera-Osorio et al. 2009, p. 7).– 2011 – In a review of evidence on accountability mechanisms in education, the World Bank again focused on the EDUCO programme as one of the 'stronger' examples.
Dissemination – International events	– 1997 – A regional seminar for Central America is financed by the World Bank to disseminate the lessons of EDUCO.– 1998 – The Inter-American Development Bank features EDUCO at its 1998 meeting of the board of governors in Cartagena, Colombia.– 2001 – At an international workshop in Lima, Peru, co-financed by the World Bank and titled the 'International Workshop on Participation and Empowerment for Inclusive Development,' the case of EDUCO is highlighted by the World Bank.– 2003 – At an international workshop sponsored by the Organization of American States (OAS) to promote knowledge sharing among countries, a Salvadoran MINED representative presents on EDUCO.– 2004 – World Bank consultants from El Salvador present on the successes of the EDUCO programme at a conference in Shanghai, China, themed 'Reducing Poverty on a Global Scale: Learning and Innovating for Development.'

Mechanism/ Pathway	Select Examples
Dissemination – Study tours	Governmental study groups came from at least twenty-two countries, including: Argentina, Bangladesh, Bolivia, Brazil, Chad, Chile, Colombia, Dominican Republic, Equatorial Guinea, Ghana, Guatemala, Honduras, Madagascar, Mauritania, Mauritius Islands, México, Morocco, Nicaragua, Panama, Paraguay, Senegal and Thailand.
Dissemination – Champion travel	EDUCO representatives travelled at least to Afghanistan, Bolivia, Brazil, China, Colombia, Guatemala, Honduras, Mexico, Spain and the United States.
Certification	– 1997 – EDUCO wins the President's Award for Excellence from the World Bank and is labelled a flagship programme of this institution.
Policy entrepreneur transfer	The World Bank hired a key EDUCO staff person from the MINED, with this person then writing and traveling to further present about the EDUCO programme.
Global reach	The World Bank engages consistently in order to seek out and remain aware of the emergence of relevant education models, policy windows or favourable reform contexts. In the case of EDUCO, the words of a long-time World Bank education specialist speak to this mechanism: EDUCO – the Bank did not invent EDUCO. The Bank saw it, and had a person in the right place at the right time – look at it, brought it to the Bank, the Bank study it, analyze it, learn what it was, and once we were comfortable with it, push it. It's not the way you think. It's not that we have the 'semilla germinal' (original idea) – no, because we are, like the holy spirit, almost everywhere. Many times, we have the right people in the right place at the right time, and we take advantage of it. (Edwards 2013, p. 279)

Source: Adapted from Edwards (2013) and Edwards and Loucel (2016).

- *Dissemination*: This mechanism refers to the ways that international organizations spread an idea. Though it can refer to various methods for idea dispersal (including other forms of dissemination mentioned below), it often refers to the way that international organizations highlight and promote a reform idea through different types of publications. While the World Bank has been the primary organization to engage this mechanism in relation to EDUCO, other international organizations have as well, as can be seen in Table 6.1 and in the examples mentioned in the follow section of this chapter.

- *Knowledge production*: Once the EDUCO programme had been scaled up, the World Bank – either directly or through its consultants – produced six impact evaluations on this programme's outcomes between 1994 and 2005. Though subsequent reviews of these studies have cast doubt on their validity and have offered alternative explanations for the observed outcomes (Edwards 2016; Edwards and Loucel 2016), these studies nevertheless were, at the time of publication, very impactful in that they provided the basis for proponents and others to highlight the effectiveness of the EDUCO programme and justify its continuity. These studies claimed, for example, that EDUCO produced better language test scores, reduced student absenteeism and enhanced student retention (see Edwards and Loucel 2016, for further discussion of and full references to these studies).

- *International events*: Conferences and workshops, among other kinds of events, have been used to promote EDUCO. This mechanism refers, for example, to those international events wherein actors have presented on or highlighted the EDUCO programme.

- *Study tours*: The MINED of El Salvador had an open-door policy when it came to study tours. Delegations of representatives from other countries would come to El Salvador to learn about the EDUCO programmed first hand, with these trips often financed by the World Bank. These tours started in 1992, and by the late 1990s, the MINED had received more than twenty delegations.

- *Champion travel*: The World Bank also sent Salvadoran officials to other countries to represent and advocate the EDUCO programme. For example, members of the EDUCO office would be called on to address concerns that illiterate rural parents should not be trusted with the management of schools and teachers.

- *Certification*: The World Bank has infused legitimacy to EDUCO by certifying and showing its approval of the programme in various ways. Two prime examples occurred in 1997, when the World Bank conferred to it the 'President's Award for Excellence' and labelled it a flagship programme.

- *Policy entrepreneur transfer*: While the World Bank also transferred its own staff to the Salvadoran government to advance its policy priorities (Edwards 2013, forthcoming), when it comes to EDUCO promotion internationally, this mechanism refers to the fact that the World Bank hired from El Salvador a key champion of the EDUCO programme as a consultant, with this person thus being certified by this institution as they wrote about and further promoted EDUCO at international events.

- *Global reach*: Global reach allows the World Bank to stay plugged, for example, into political changes and reform opportunities as they arise in various countries. The mechanism of global reach is one with which organizations such as the World Bank engage consistently in order to seek out and remain aware of the emergence of policy windows or favourable reform contexts. In this way, the World Bank was able to strategically extol the benefits and relevance of EDUCO as it engaged with other low-income countries.

EDUCO in the global agenda

As a result of the activation of the above mechanisms and pathways, EDUCO has become a global education policy model, in the sense that it has been widely promoted, discussed and embraced – particularly in those spaces and by those organizations involved in negotiating and setting the priorities and policies for the global education reform agenda. That is, in addition to being widely promoted by the World Bank in the ways enumerated above, EDUCO's status as a global education policy is further reflected in the fact that is has been featured and cited by other high-profile and international organizations with significant reach around the world. Consider a few examples (from among many more):

- *United Nations Task Force on Education and Gender Equality, 2005:* The report of this task force identified EDUCO as 'probably the most celebrated case of successful parental control', as well as a key strategy for improving primary school effectiveness (Birdsall et al. 2005, p. 67).

- *United Nations Children's Fund, 2007:* A report suggests that the EDUCO experience can provide lessons for decentralization in emergency or post-conflict settings in Africa (Beleli et al. 2007).

- *Brookings Institution, 2008:* A report on improving development effectiveness spotlights EDUCO and the fact that the school council 'hires, monitors, retains or dismisses teachers' (Hartman and Linn 2008, p. 47).

- *Global Partnership for Education 2009:* This entity focused on EDUCO as a 'way to ensure that the community contributes to improved educational outcomes' (Global Partnership for Education 2009, p. 96).

- *UNESCO, 2009 and 2011:* The Global Monitoring Reports in both 2009 and 2011, which addressed education governance and education in conflict-affected contexts (UNESCO 2008, 2011), highlight EDUCO.

Interestingly, in addition to achieving global status, EDUCO has also been interpreted or emphasized differently, depending on the institution in question that is highlighting the programme, and often for reasons that have nothing to do with the original goals of the programme. In looking at the evidence on EDUCO, they have found – or have chosen to see – lessons related not only to instituting community involvement in education as a means to improved outcomes (Global Partnership for Education 2009), but also to extending system coverage rapidly (UNESCO, n.d.), achieving educational and gender equality (Birdsall et al. 2005), providing education in post-conflict contexts (Beleli et al. 2007; UNESCO 2011), and ensuring the provision of education as a human right (UNESCO 2007). In that the example of EDUCO can be selectively underscored, the programme has become symbolic. Development professionals and policy-makers invoke EDUCO as a way to lend credibility to the points they wish to advance.

From CBM to SBM: Community participation lives on as global education policy?

As Edwards and Loucel (2016) report, an education specialist from the World Bank with over twenty years of experience in El Salvador and other countries explained that the lessons from EDUCO have become part of 'international knowledge', such that development practitioners and governmental functionaries in other countries are unaware that they are following the example of El Salvador. In his words:

Most development agencies now have learned about those models that happened, you know, more than 20 years ago, [like CBM in El Salvador] ... 20 years later [they] are well known processes, not only in the Bank but in the United Nation's Children's Fund, USAID, the Japan International Cooperation Agency ... they evolved from El Salvador, and they have become now part of *international knowledge* that some of our younger staff, the newer countries that are developing community participation programmes don't know that that evolved from El Salvador. My staff worked with Afghanistan, you know, they don't know. The ministry of education didn't know that what they call community participation schools and all these operational processes, that, you know, in organizational management, in financial transfer, in planning, that it evolved from this tiny nation [of El Salvador]. (Edwards and Loucel 2016, p. 25)

Notably, however, the language around community participation in education has changed. SBM is now consistently employed to refer to a range of forms of community involvement (see, e.g., Barrera-Osorio et al. 2009). CBM implied that the locus of control resided with the parents, with the key being that parents had the power to hire and fire teachers. The change in language may be due to the fact that, with a few exceptions (e.g. Guatemala, Honduras, Kenya, Madagascar, Zambia), most countries have not been amenable to granting such authority to parents in practice; it is easier for development banks and for politicians at the country level to achieve agreement for the purposes of lending and reform around less extreme versions of community participation (Di Gropello 2006; Krishnaratne et al. 2013). As the World Bank (2007b) explains:

> While some programs transfer authority only to school principals or teachers, others encourage or mandate parental and community participation, often in the form of school committees. Most SBM programs transfer authority over one or more activities. These could be: budget allocation; the hiring and firing of teachers and other school staff; curriculum development; the procurement of textbooks and other educational material; infrastructure improvement; and the monitoring and evaluation of teacher performance and student learning outcomes. (p. 3)

Thus, while EDUCO contributed to popularizing the notion of CBM – and while EDUCO garnered significant attention – due to its extreme form of decentralization, more mild forms of have endured in practice under the label of SBM, with these forms often being more symbolic and entailing less control for parents. Moreover, SBM is attractive to governments because of the commonplace and extractive – if also unofficial – expectation that community members support school maintenance and school finance by contributing of labour and materials and by paying fees (Edwards and DeMatthews 2014).

The implication, then, is that community participation, if not CBM specifically, does in fact live on as a global education. That is, CBM has been absorbed by discussion of community participation more broadly, with that participation encapsulated by SBM. Evidence of this can be found in the fact that, during 2000–2006, 11 per cent[5] of all projects – or 17 out of 157 projects – in the World Bank's education portfolio supported SBM, representing $1.74 billion (or 23 per cent of total education financing for this institution) (World Bank 2007a, p. 2). Other international organizations also continue to demonstrate a focus on community participation by advocating SBM. Aside from the publications mentioned in the previous section, consider that, as of 2016, the Japanese International Cooperation Agency is supporting SBM in west Africa (Burkina Faso and Niger), the Asian Development Bank is engaged in SBM in Cambodia, German Corporation for Technical Cooperation is facilitating SBM in Kosovo (and previously did so in Namibia, Edwards and Mbatia 2013), the UK Department for International Development funds SBM in Nigeria (in addition to producing a systematic review of the evidence on SBM; Carr-Hill et al. 2015) and USAID included community participation as a focus in its 2011 education strategy document.

Conclusion

In reflecting on the series of related issues raised this chapter, a number of points can be underscored. When it comes to global education policy, it is important to place the ideas into long-term context and to be sensitive to the ways that overriding concepts (like decentralization) and their implied meanings have changed over time. Likewise, it is necessary to take into account the nature of and the changes to the country context. This is particularly necessary when considering that the World Bank has supported other CBM and SBM reforms elsewhere that have not achieved the same global status. The difference in the case of EDUCO may be that it was not a case of simple policy imposition by the World Bank but rather a case wherein three dimensions converged – namely, (1) national political–economic structures, (2) national actors constraints and interests, and (3) international actor preferences for reform. That is, as described in this chapter, the EDUCO case demonstrates the ways that geopolitics and international organizations are, at times, and particularly in small countries, able to shape the context to be predisposed to certain reform ideas. However, as noted, this study highlights the fact that national-level interests matter and suggests that programmes associated with international agendas will not be adopted (at least not in an enduring or meaningful way) by the country in question if they do not align with national actor constraints. The EDUCO case further reveals the various and mutually reinforcing mechanisms of promotion that international organizations can engage to promote a given programme or model in an attempt to locate that policy in the global education reform agenda. Of course, the mechanisms discussed here are made more possible (1) where national-level actors see the value in participating in these mechanisms and (2) where credible evidence exists related to the effectiveness of the underlying programme (see Edwards and Loucel 2016, for more on this point).

Separately, it is important to remain aware of the ways that the example of EDUCO – even where it is not explicitly mentioned – is now contributing to – and has been appropriated by – advocates of SBM. Moreover, the fact that SBM advocates draw on the CBM experience of EDUCO as justification for the former shows the loose logic and imprecise reasoning that tends to characterize promotion of global exemplars. To advance their own interests, international actors are often eager to build on the legitimacy of renowned programmes and will seek to claim similarity to them – though a closer look at the details may reveal differences in programmed design with significant implications that render comparisons and residual credibility impossible.

Despite these insights, a number of issues remain for future contemplation and investigation. These include, for example, (1) the ways that 'participation' has been co-opted and sanitized by many in the development industry of its more critical and progressive meanings; (2) the consequences, effects and experiences of CBM and SBM policies in practice at the local level; (3) the possibility and strategies by which transnational civil society can combat the emergence and invocation of global education policies that arguably have negative implications (particularly for the most vulnerable) in practice; and (4) the ways in which acceptance of such global education policies and the means by which they are engendered work in the service of a reform ideology that diverts our attention away from alternative approaches to education policy specifically and development generally (Klees and Edwards 2014; Verger et al. 2014). It is hoped that the critical approach to global education policy in this chapter is a first step to broaching these questions.

Questions for discussion

1   Based on this chapter, what are the various ways that decentralization has been conceptualized in the post–Second World War period?

2   In what ways did international organizations influence the 'climate of reception' or the reform context in El Salvador during the 1980s and 1990s?

3   What are the differences in emphasis between 'popular education' and community-based management, as discussed in this chapter?

4   In what ways do the mechanisms of promotion of EDUCO work together and reinforce one another?

5   Can you identify examples of other global education policies that have been interpreted, promoted or borrowed selectively to fit the purposes of the organization or actor doing the interpreting, promoting or borrowing?

Notes

1   For additional references related to the trends described in this section, see Edwards and DeMatthews (2014).

2   See Edwards (2012) for a more detailed explanation of how this thinking developed, particularly within the World Bank.

3   While the EDUCO programme was initially only intended as a strategy to provide education at the preschool level and in grades 1–3, it was subsequently expanded in 1994 to cover through grade 6 and then again in 1997 to cover through grade 9 (Meza et al. 2004). After 2005, even some high schools became EDUCO schools (Gillies et al. 2010).

4   See Edwards (2013, forthcoming) for a discussion of other mechanisms of international influence that impacted the EDUCO programme.

5   Other World Bank publications put the percentage even higher, at 48 per cent of projects during 2001–2005 and 78 per cent projects during 2006–2009 (World Bank 2010, p. 28).

References

Astbury, B. and Leeuw, F. L. (2010). 'Unpacking black boxes: Mechanisms and theory building in evaluation'. *American Journal of Evaluation*, 31 (3), 363–381.

Ball, S. J. (2016). 'Following policy: Networks, network ethnography and education policy mobilities'. *Journal of Education Policy*, 31 (5), 549–566.

Barrera-Osorio, F., Fasih, T., Patrinos, H. and Santibánez, L. (2009). *Decentralized decision-making in schools: The theory and evidence on school-based management*. Washington, DC: The World Bank.

Beleli, O., Chang, V., Fegelson, M., Kopel-Bailey, J., Maak, S., Mnookin, J., Nguyen, T., Salazar, M., Sinderbrand, J. and Tafoya, S. (2007). *Education in emergencies and early reconstruction: UNICEF interventions in Colombia, Liberia, and Southern Sudan*. Princeton, NJ: Woodrow Wilson School of Public and International Affairs.

Birdsall, N., Levine, R. and Ibrahim, A. (2005). *Toward universal primary education: Investments, incentives, and institutions*. UN Millennium Project, Task Force on Education and Gender Equality. London: Earthscan.

Booth, J., Wade, C. and Walker, T. (2006). *Understanding Central America*. Boulder, CO: Westview Press.

Carr-Hill, R., Rolleston, C., Phereli, T. and Schendel, R. (2015). The effects of school-based decision making on educational outcomes in low and middle income contexts: A systematic review, 3ie Grantee Final Review. London: International Initiative for Impact Evaluation (3ie). Available at: http://r4d.dfid.gov.uk/pdf/outputs/SystematicReviews/61233_dfid-funded-decentralisation-review.pdf.

Cohen, J. and Peterson, S. (1999). *Administrative decentralization: Strategies for developing countries*. West Hartford, CN: Kumarian Press.

Di Gropello, E. (2006). *A comparative analysis of school-based management in Central America*. World Bank Working Paper 72. Washington, DC: World Bank.

Edwards Jr., D. B. (2012). 'The approach of the World Bank to participation in development and education governance: Trajectories, frameworks, results'. In C. Collins and A. Wiseman (Eds.), *Education strategy in the developing world: Understanding the World Bank's education policy revision*. Bingley: Emerald, pp. 249–273.

Edwards Jr., D. B. (2013). The development of global education policy: A case study of the origins and evolution of El Salvador's EDUCO program. Unpublished dissertation, University of Maryland, College Park.

Edwards Jr., D. B. (2015). 'Rising from the ashes: How the global education policy of community-based management was born from El Salvador's civil war'. *Globalisation, Societies and Education*, 13 (3), 411–432.

Edwards Jr., D. B. (2016). 'A perfect storm: The political economy of community-based management, teacher accountability, and impact evaluations in El Salvador and the global reform agenda'. In W. Smith (Ed.), *Global testing culture: Shaping education policy, perceptions, and practice*. Oxford Studies in Comparative Education. Oxford: Symposium, pp. 25–42.

Edwards Jr., D. B. (forthcoming). *The trajectory of global education policy: Community-based management in El Salvador and the global reform agenda*. New York: Palgrave Macmillan.

Edwards Jr., D. B. and Mbatia, P. (2013). 'Education decentralization and school clusters in Namibia: Technical, institutional, and political dimensions'. In A. Verger, H. Kosar-Altinyelken and M. de Koning (Eds.), *Global managerial education reforms and teachers: Emerging policies, controversies and issues in developing contexts*. Brussels: Education International, pp. 55–73.

Edwards Jr., D. B. and DeMatthews, D. (2014). 'Historical trends in educational decentralization in the United States and developing countries: A periodization and comparison in the post-WWII context'. *Education Policy Analysis Archives*, 22 (40), 1–36.

Edwards Jr., D. B. and Loucel, C. (2016). 'The EDUCO Program, impact evaluations, and the political economy of global education reform'. *Education Policy Analysis Archives*, 24 (49), 1–50.

Edwards Jr., D. B., Victoria, J. A. and Martin, P. (2015). 'The geometry of policy implementation: Lessons from the political economy of three education reforms in El Salvador during 1990–2005'. *International Journal of Educational Development*, 44, 28–41.

Edwards Jr., D. B., Martin, P. and Flores, I. (forthcoming). 'Education in El Salvador: Past, present, and prospects'. In C. M. Posner, Chris Martin and

Yvonne Martin (Eds.), *Education in México, Central America and the Latin Caribbean*, Continuum.

Gillies, J., Crouch, L. and Flórez, A. (2010). Strategic review of the EDUCO Program. USAID. Retrieved from: http://www.equip123.net/docs/e2-EDUCO_ Strategic_Review.pdf.

Global Partnership for Education (2009). *Six steps for abolishing primary school fees: Operational guide.* Washington, DC: World Bank.

Hammond, J. (1998). *Fighting to learn: Popular education and guerrilla war in El Salvador.* New Brunswick, NJ: Rutgers University Press.

Hartmann, A. and Linn, J. (2008). Scaling up: A framework and lessons for development effectiveness from literature and practice. Brookings Global Economy and Development Working Paper Series. Available at: http://www .brookings.edu/research/papers/2008/10/scaling-up-aid-linn.

Harvey, D. (2005). *A brief history of neoliberalism.* New York: Oxford.

Klees, S. and Edwards Jr., D. B. (2014). 'Knowledge production and technologies of governance'. In T. Fenwick, E. Mangez and J. Ozga (Eds.), *World yearbook of education 2014: Governing knowledge: Comparison, knowledge-based technologies and expertise in the regulation of education.* New York: Routledge, pp. 31–43.

Klein, N. (2007). *The shock doctrine: The rise of disaster capitalism.* New York: Picadur.

Krishnaratne, S., White, H. and Carpenter, E. (2013). Quality education for all children? What works in education in developing countries, Working Paper 20. New Delhi: International Initiative for Impact Evaluation (3ie).

Meza, D., Guzmán, J. and de Varela, L. (2004). EDUCO: A community-managed education program in rural areas of El Salvador. Ensayo presentado en la Scaling Up Poverty Reduction: A Global Learning Process and Conference, Shanghai, 25–27 May 2004.

MINED (1990). Servicios educativos a niños pobres Salvadoreños de 0 a 14 años [Educational Services for Poor Salvadoran Kids from 0 to 14 Years of Age]. San Salvador: MINED.

Montgomery, T. (1995). *Revolution in El Salvador: From civil strife to civil peace*, 2nd edn. Boulder, CO: Westview.

Robinson, W. (2003). *Transnational conflicts: Central America, social change, and globalization.* New York: Verso.

Samoff, J. (2009). 'Foreign aid to education: Managing global transfers and exchanges'. In L. Chisholm and G. Steiner-Khamsi (Eds.), *South-South cooperation in education and development.* New York: Teachers College Press, pp. 123–156.

Schiefelbein, E. (2004). 'The politics of decentralisation in Latin America'. *International Review of Education*, 50 (3), 359–378.

Segovia, A. (1996). 'Macroeconomic performance and policies since 1989'. In J. K. Boyce (Ed.), *Economic policy for building peace: The lessons of El Salvador.* Boulder, CO: Lynne Rienner, pp. 51–72.

SIMEDUCO (2011). *Ya no estamos dormidos*. San Salvador: Instituto de Derechos Humanos de la Universidad 'José Simeón Cañas'.

UNESCO (2007). *Educational governance at the local level.* Paris: UNESCO.

UNESCO (2008). *EFA Global Monitoring Report 2009: Overcoming inequality: Why governance matters.* Oxford: Oxford University Press.

UNESCO (2011). *EFA Global Monitoring Report 2011: The hidden crisis: Armed conflict and education*. Paris: UNESCO.

Verger, A., Edwards Jr., D. B. and Kosar-Altinyelken, H. (2014). 'Learning from all? The World Bank, aid agencies and the construction of hegemony in education for development'. *Comparative Education*, 50 (4), 1–19.

Whitty, G. and Edwards, T. (1998). 'School choice policies in England and the United States: An exploration of their origins and significance'. *Comparative Education*, 34 (2), 211–227.

World Bank (2007a). *Guiding principles for implementing school-based management programs*. Washington, DC: World Bank.

World Bank (2007b). *What do we know about school-based management?* Washington, DC: World Bank.

World Bank (2010). *World Bank support to education since 2001: A portfolio note*. Washington, DC: World Bank.

Further reading

Altschuler, A. and Corrales, J. (2012). 'The spillover effects of participatory governance: Evidence from community-managed schools in Honduras and Guatemala'. *Comparative Political Studies*, 45 (5), 636–666.

Amin, A. (2005). 'Local community on trial'. *Economy and Society*, 34 (4), 612–633.

Bray, M. (2001). Community partnerships in education: Dimensions, variations, and implications. Paris: UNESCO. Available at: http://unesdoc.unesco.org/images/0012/001234/123483e.pdf.

Edwards Jr., D. B. and Klees, S. (2015). 'Unpacking participation in development and education governance: A framework of perspectives and practices'. *Prospects*, 45 (4), 483–499.

Mansuri, G. and Rao, V. (2004). 'Community-based and –driven development: A critical review'. *The World Bank Research Observer*, 19 (1), 1–39.

7

Conditional Cash Transfers in Education for Development: Emergence, Policy Dilemmas and Diversity of Impacts

*Xavier Bonal, Aina Tarabini
and Xavier Rambla*

The context for the emergence of CCTs

For the last decades, international organizations have broadly commented the connection between poverty reduction and the potential of the worst-off for resilience. In the late 1980s, UNICEF responded to the alarming perverse effects of Structural Adjustment Programmes (SAPs) claiming for 'adjustment with a human face' underpinned by social emergency funds (Cornia 2001). One of the most visible reactions to the failure of SAPs was the identification of poverty alleviation as the most salient objective of international organizations in shaping the global agenda for development. The 2004 World Development Report, *Making Services Work for Poor People*, is a clear example of the inclusion of poverty alleviation vis-à-vis economic growth as the central priorities for development. The report is also an example of the idea of 'activating' the poor for them changing their own situation. Thus, the role of policy in this framework consists in empowering the poor and giving them the necessary facilities to take advantage of existing economic and social opportunities. The centrality of poverty reduction was also visible when *Poverty Reduction Strategy Papers* (PRSP) became the most significant instrument through which international organizations would support governments in fighting poverty. PRSP became in fact a necessary instrument for highly indebted poor countries to keep borrowing funds from international finance organizations and a new form of conditionality.

Thus, in the decade of 2000 the World Bank (WB) advised donors and governments to manage social risk by assessing the vulnerability to potential poverty-producing shocks and providing the necessary economic and social resources so that the victims withstand these shocks (Holzmann et al. 2003, p. 10). The idea is normally associated with a hypothetical 'generative mechanism' (Pawson 2006) grounded on social capital theories: the point is that the poor may improve their multidimensional deprivation by enacting their own social networks and expressing their voice in social policy consultation bodies (Narayan 1999; Atria 2003).

This understanding of poverty reduction gives of course a central role to education as one of *the best* policies. If poor people have to be empowered to develop social capital, there is nothing like education. Actually, education is one of the central strategies in PRSP and has also remained one of the central sectors in the WB's lending portfolio. Since the Millennium Development Goals (MDGs) were established, the Bank's support for education permanently increased to reach $5 billion in 2010 (World Bank 2011, p. vi). Between 2010 and 2015, the global financial crisis impacted on the WB lending in education to reach an annual average of $3.5 billion.[1]

That is the context in which Conditional Cash Transfer Programmes (CCTs) in education emerged. Interestingly enough, these programmes were neither part of any system of lending conditionality nor of the global agenda for education development of international organizations. CCTs are an example of inverse policy travelling, from the bottom to the top. State or federal governments in Brazil and Mexico initiated CCTs in education at a large scale in the mid-1990s. In Brazil, the State of Brazilia started the first *Bolsa Escola* in 1995. After two years the *Bolsa Escola Federal* was initiated. *Progresa* – then renamed *Oportunidades* – started in Mexico in 1997. Therefore, the WB did not promote the two most important CCT programmes in the world. The WB was actually very reactive to these new policies by closely observing and evaluating processes of implementation and their impacts (Peck and Theodore 2010).

One of the reasons of this passivity can be explained by the focus of the Bank's lending in investment and infrastructure, on the one hand, and on school supply policies on the other. The WB never financed current costs of education and concentrated its project lending activity in capital costs. Neither did WB include CCTs among their policy recommendations. The Bank has contemplated demand-side policies like school vouchers or educational loans, but never included CCTs as a good policy practice to enhance school access or school performance.

Interestingly enough, this is not the case anymore since the Bank is currently supporting programmes like *Bolsa Familia* in Brazil. There might be different reasons for this change but a plausible one has to do with the adequacy of CCTs within the framework of the anti-poverty agenda for development. CCTs are designed as a policy tool to break the intergenerational reproduction of poverty through education and as a method of empowering the poor to overcome their fatalities. In this sense, CCTs do fit with the ideas of the WB and other international organizations about fighting poverty by bypassing the inefficient state of developing countries and by putting resources directly to those mostly needed. It is not surprising therefore that the Bank underlines CCTs as one of the good demand-side interventions to enhance equity in education systems (World Bank 2011).

This is especially significant since CCTs have not showed a clear impact in school performance. What we know today is that there is mixed-evidence about the effects of CCTs in several educational dimensions. There is evidence of substantial gains in school access or in access to school meals (a very important effect in contexts of extreme poverty). Some authors even value positively the effects of CCTs in reducing child labour (Rawlings 2005). On the other hand, other authors have expressed doubts about how useful these programmes are to improve learning and performance (Schwartzman 2005). Significantly, by looking at Bangladesh, Brazil, Colombia, Guatemala, Honduras, Indonesia, Malawi, Mexico and Nicaragua, Reimers et al. (2006) found out that the logical framework of CCT programmes was often focused on attainment, assistance and enrolment, but its instantiation was seldom concerned with dropout, learning, quality of instruction, repetition and promotion and school improvement. In short, this sample of experiences shows that the alleged impact of these programmes on other sectors beyond social protection ultimately remains unclear, at least in the area of a so celebrated realm as education policy has become.

In spite of this uncertainty, one significant policy question that remains unanswered is whether CCTs are or are not worthy as a tool to break the reproduction of poverty. The answer to this question is not at all easy. It depends on how a CCT programme is designed, who are the beneficiaries and how do we assess the impacts of these programmes. Although the last question is particularly important – and would spell out the many limitations of impact evaluation methodologies – in this chapter we will concentrate on the first two. We argue that the uncertain effects of CCTs programmes have a strong relationship with two sets of factors. On the one hand, policy-makers face substantial dilemmas when designing CCTs. Options taken in the programme design may be decisive to understand the orientation of the programme and its effectiveness in terms of school access, school performance and other effects. On the other hand, the social conditions of educational demand explain why different families and different pupils react differently to the same type of inputs. The transfer can have a completely different impact depending on who is the beneficiary, even when all of them are poor.

In this chapter we explore the main dilemmas that policy-makers have to face when designing a CCT programme. The argument highlighted can be considered as generic, although reflections and examples are mainly taken from the analysis of the *Bolsa Escola* programmes (PBE) developed in Brazil (both in its federal and local forms), from the mid-1990s and until they were absorbed by the federal programme *Bolsa Familia* (PBF) in the year 2003. The dilemmas, shortcomings and possibilities of a CCT programme can be found in the realm of institutional design, in the technical processes of selecting and covering the beneficiaries and in the implementation systems developed. Our analysis will encompass all of these dimensions, and it is thus fed by the empirical evidence available in the different evaluations of the programme, sometimes performed by specialists from international institutions (UNESCO, World Bank, ILO), other times by professionals from academic institutions, and yet others by personnel from the programme itself. We have also added as fodder for our analysis the studies that our research group conducted in the 2000 decade,[2] and we shall especially take into account the evidence from a study about the impact of PBE on the conditions of educability of the beneficiaries of the town of Belo Horizonte.[3]

The chapter is structured as follows. In the next section, a description of the PBE is provided, with special attention to the variations between the federal and the municipal versions of the programme. The third section explores technical dilemmas involved in the programme design and also introduces reflexions on the changes brought after the implementation of the PBF. The fourth section provides examples about how different the impact of the transfer can be depending on the social and living conditions of beneficiaries. Finally, a concluding section underlines the main absences in mainstream evaluation when assessing CCTs programmes and provides guidelines for a 'realistic' evaluation of CCTs (Pawson 2006).

Characteristics of the *Bolsa Escola* programme

The PBE was a demand-side education programme based on income transfers to poor families, conditioned by their children's attending school. This programme was part of the Minimum Income Guarantee Programmes initiated in Brazil in the first half of the 1990s, and unlike other similar programmes implemented in Latin America (such as the Mexican *Oportunidades* programme), from the very start it was developed in a decentralized fashion on a municipal scale.

The programme was first implemented in 1995 in the Brasilia region with the aim of achieving three goals: (1) increasing the families' standard of living in the short term; (2) lowering child labour rates; and (3) optimizing children's staying in school with the ultimate goal of reducing future poverty. The highly favourable diagnoses on the earliest proposals implemented and the spread of the debates on this type of programme drove many other municipal governments – many of them governed by the PT (Workers' Party) – to develop education-associated minimum-income programmes, which became widespread in the country during the second half of the 1990s.

The ways the programme was implemented on a municipal scale showed differences in both design and management; however, generally speaking both their goals and the criteria used to choose the population converged. In terms of the goals, there was a general consensus with those set by the pioneering programme in Brasilia, with the exception of slight changes that corresponded to specific characteristics of the different towns. In terms of the selection systems, the programmes shared a series of criteria including family income, children's ages and time living in the town, with potentially eligible families being those with a per capita family income lower than a certain predefined level (generally, the poverty line) with at least one school-aged child and a minimum time of residence in the town that fluctuates from one to five years. The families that met the requisites and were accepted for participation in the programme received a monthly income transfer[4] conditioned on their child's regular attendance at school.

Starting in 1997, and in the light of the success of the municipal experiences, a type of federal programme began to be implemented under the government of F. H. Cardoso, initially created to provide financial support to poor towns with difficulties implementing the programme autonomously. In 2001, the federal PBE spread to a nationwide scale, leaving its management and implementation in the hands of the town education councillors, with the financing and monetary transfers to the beneficiaries remaining under the aegis of the National Secretariat (Tarabini and Bonal 2004). In the case of towns that already had a PBE, agreements were reached between both local and national administrations to make possible a fit between both programmes (as took place in many towns, including Belo Horizonte).

Table 7.1 summarizes the main characteristics of the municipal PBE in Belo Horizonte, and its comparison with the federal programme is explained in the following text.

Table 7.1 Design of the municipal PBE in Belo Horizonte

Start of programme	1997
Selection criteria	Per Capita Family Income < average minimum salary Children aged 7–14 (6–15 starting in *2001*) Minimum time residing in town: 5 years *Priority given to families with minors living in situations of social risk.
Value of the transfer	R$168 per month per family (equivalent to €71 in 2011)
Conditions	Children's minimum attendance of 85 per cent
Timeframe	Indefinite
Management and implementation	Municipal Education Secretariat
Budget	1.67 per cent of the municipal education budget
Methodology of Family Assistance	Socio-educational actions Education and professional training for young people and adults; Special attention to families with minors in situations of social risk

Until the end of 2001, the PBE in Belo Horizonte operated in the town autonomously, managing to assist a total of 9,311 families. In 2002, the federal PBE started to be implemented in the city, with prior agreement by both administrations aimed at resolving the main differences between them, namely the age of the children and the value of the monetary transfer. In terms of the former, the only difference was the age range set by both programmes, with the municipal PBE setting a range of 7 to 14 compared to the federal PBE's range of 6 to 15; the solution entailed adapting the municipal criteria to the ages used by the federal programme, thus broadening its scope to include families with children from ages 6 to 15. In terms of the latter, the difference was greater, since the Belo Horizonte PBE transferred a set monthly amount (R$ 168 equivalent to €71) per family, while the Federal PBE assigned a variable benefit according to the number of children in each family (R$15 for one child, R$30 for two and R$45 for three or more, equivalent to €6, €12 and €19, respectively). Based on this difference, the decision was taken to create a financial agreement (*Bolsa Consorciada*) between both entities, in which the resources needed to maintain the transfer to families benefiting from the Belo Horizonte PBE would be shared. Thus, since 2002, the federal government financed the R$15, R$30 or R$45 provided for in the design of its programme, while the municipal government put up the remaining amount until reaching the ceiling of R$168 per family. This agreement not only allowed the value of the benefit for the families participating in the municipal programme to be maintained, it also freed up municipal resources to increase the number of families aided by the programme.[5]

The agreement between both entities, however, only affected the families previously participating in the municipal programme, and under no circumstances did it exclude autonomous intervention by the federal programme. Both programmes coexisted in the city since 2002, aiding different populations and each making the corresponding transfers.[6]

In 2003, and due to the federal government change in Brazil, the PBE suffered an important modification: it was incorporated into a new targeting programme, the PBF. This modification supposedly brought changes both in the functioning and in the features of the programme. The PBF is part of the *Fome Zero Programme*, a public policy aimed to combat hunger and social exclusion in the country and the key project of Lula da Silva's social policy. Such a programme has unified all the income transfer programmes existing in the country (*Bolsa Escola, Bolsa Alimentação, Auxilio Gas* and *Cartão Alimentação*), and it meant, in general terms, the disappearance of the PBE as an independent programme. On average, the PBF transfers R$77 per family per month (equivalent to €25) and thus increases substantially the amount of the transference provided by the federal PBE (Tarabini 2008b). At the same time, the programme introduces a triple-approach action that includes education, health and feeding. This approach allows the programme to go beyond the educational conditionality and includes additional benefits for pregnant women, little children or food subsides. Moreover, the merger of the previous independent programmes has reduced administrative costs and bureaucratic complexity for both the beneficiary families and the administration of the programme. Before the unification of the programmes under the PBF, each of them had its own implementing agency, information system and financing source. This meant that it was possible for one family to receive benefits from all the programmes simultaneously, while another, with exactly the same socio-economic profile, could be excluded from all of them (Soares 2010, p. 2).

Despite the generalization of the PBF, for a few years this programme co-existed with some of the old independent programmes, like local PBE. In fact, many municipal modalities of the PBE have maintained a monetary transfer higher than the one provided by the PBF and have provided complementary actions and benefits much broader than those provided by the new programme. In these cases, some municipal councillors have established agreements with the federal government in order to articulate the PBF with the remaining municipal modalities of the PBE. These agreements have followed the same logic used under the implementation of the Federal PBE. During the last years, however, a number of municipal modalities of the programme disappeared (including the Belo Horizonte PBE), so did the benefits provided by them.

Nowadays, the PBF has been consolidated as the main national strategy to fight against poverty in Brazil. Moreover, as Draibe (2006) indicates, 'It has monopolized pro-poor policies in the whole country.' In 2006, it benefited eleven million families in the whole country, an 18'6 per cent of the total population (Villatoro 2007). Its estimative cost is a 0.5 per cent of the gross national product (GNP) and approximately 2.5 per cent of the total government expenditure (Lindert 2006).

Finally, it is important to notice the role of the WB in the programme. The WB's loan for the programme in its first phase (2004–2009) was US$572 million, while in its second phase (2010–2015) it increased to US$200 million. There is no doubt that the WB's involvement in the PBF does not only indicate the priority given to targeting in the WB portfolio, but also its growing influence in shaping the directions that targeting programmes have to follow.

Dilemmas in the PBE: An analysis from the standpoint of supply

In this section, we shall analyse the shortcomings and possibilities of the PBE from the standpoint of its institutional design, identifying certain dilemmas on whose resolution the equity and efficacy of the programme may depend. First, we shall refer to the dilemmas linked to the process of targeting and the coverage of benefits, secondly to the options related to the amount of the benefit and, finally, to the possible consequences derived from investing greater or lesser efforts on monitoring and family assistance measures.

Dilemmas of targeting and coverage: Who benefits?

In the experiences of targeting programmes, three criteria operate to delimit the beneficiary population: territorial criteria, criteria of vulnerability and institutional criteria. The experiences undertaken in the region have tended to use one of these criteria (or the combination of several of them) to choose the target population. The efficacy of the programmes and volume and characteristics of the population excluded from them largely depend on this selection process.

In the case of the PBE, the targeting method was based on a combination of territorial and vulnerability criteria, while institutional criteria were totally excluded.[7] The first phase of targeting in both the federal programme and its municipal variants was based on the territorial criterion, dependent on which zones with high levels of social exclusion were identified as places to which intervention should be targeted. Once the high-priority territories were established, the second phase of targeting entailed identifying the potential beneficiaries based on gathering information about families' economic status and calculating a vulnerability index.[8]

The available evaluations of the different modalities of the PBE all coincide in highlighting that the targeting was appropriate and that the selection process tended to be targeted to the neediest people in each territorial area. Sabóia and Rocha (1998), for example, evaluated the PBE in Brasilia and claimed that the targeting of the programme was effective, simultaneously arguing that the scoring system used to definitively select the families was an essential factor in ensuring sound targeting. The same conclusion can be found in the evaluation Lavinas et al. (2001) performed of the municipal programme in Recife.

The evaluations also stress certain recommendations to ensure a sound selection process, such as setting up mechanisms to avoid fraud, adjusting the scoring systems to the local reality and regularly reviewing the living conditions of the beneficiaries through systems of *recadastramento* (Sabóia and Rocha 1998; Rocha 2000; Alves Azeredo 2003). The increase in mechanisms ensuring the efficacy of the selection process may, however, generate excessive monitoring and control costs that on certain occasions might consume high proportions of the budget and thus significantly decrease the percentage earmarked for the transfers (Alves Azeredo 2003).

Moreover, in recent years CCT programmes have developed major improvements in their targeting, monitoring and evaluation components, thus generating important gains in terms of selection criteria and the reduction of fraud. In the case of the PBF, Lindert (2006) identifies the following improvements: launching a formal network system (*rede de fiscalizaçao*) for overseeing, auditing and controlling fraud of Bolsa Familia payments; initiating steps to improve the Unified Register System (*Cadastro único*) by reducing duplicate benefits, revising eligibility criteria and so on; and strengthening citizen social control by publishing online (*Portal da Transparencia* in the programme's website) the names of every person enrolled in the programme and the amount of the transference given to them and so on. Moreover, some evaluations agree to consider the PBF as one of the best targeted programmes in the world, because it succeeded in including *only* the poor (Soares et al. 2007).

On the other hand, it is important to take into account some risks linked to the geographical targeting associated to some CCTs. As Lavinas (2000) indicates the main risk of this targeting criterion is creating a 'fallacious ecology' by regarding the entire territorial unit as if it displayed social homogeneity (Brodershon 1999). To rectify this fallacy, one can operationally resort to defining very small territorial units that tend to minimize the lack of homogeneity.[9] This, however, does not avoid the fact that small pockets of poverty might remain outside the programme if they are located in territories with average values on the social indicators. Still, it should be pointed out that despite the criticism, the territorial criterion is one of the mechanisms with the lowest costs and with the most available information.

Finally, the criteria of targeting must inevitably be related to the programme's coverage capacity. Indeed, the different modalities of the PBE tended to generate situations of 'over-targeting', that is, of selection amongst the population that met the requisites to be beneficiaries, but that for budgetary reasons remained excluded from the programme. This need to select amongst the potential beneficiaries is usually resolved by creating a hierarchy of the scores earned on the indexes of vulnerability, thus attempting to ensure priority attention to the most vulnerable families. This process, which is ethically indisputable, may, however, have consequences on the efficacy of the transfer in terms of its potential impact on creating income autonomy. Some evaluations have pointed out that the PBE enabled many families to escape from destitution, though not poverty (Lavinas 2000). Only a small percentage of families, in certain municipal programmes, managed to change their living conditions enough to rise above the threshold of poverty. Paradoxically, sound targeting might reduce the efficacy of the programme in terms of the possibilities of effectively reducing poverty and generating better conditions of educability in the children. Thus, it could happen, as gathered from Lavinas' (2000) evaluation, that the efficacy of the programme, measured in global terms based on the number of families that manage to rise above the threshold of poverty, lies directly in the programme's coverage, or in the ethically questionable decision of excluding the indigent population from the programme in order to concentrate on families closer to the threshold of poverty. However, if we centre our measurement of the efficacy of the programme on the capacities of the indigent families to generate income autonomously based on receipt of the benefit, the problem goes beyond the targeting process, and other factors that hamper a qualitative change in the living conditions of these families to take place must be examined.

This tension between targeting criteria and coverage capacity is very well expressed by Soares (2010a) for the case of the PBF. According to the author, the limit of eleven million beneficiaries defined by the programme was clearly insufficient to cover the entire eligible population. Estimates indicate that about two million families who should also be receiving the benefit were in fact excluded of the PBF. Although in 2009 an increase in coverage was approved – expanding it from the initial pre-fixed target of 11 million families to a new target of 12.5 million – this change seems not to be enough. According to Soares (2010b), in order to include the families at poverty risk, the PBF should cover approximately fifteen million families.

The dilemmas mentioned might also have an effect on the social cohesion between the populations that do and do not benefit from the programme in the poor communities where it is implemented. The situations of over-targeting could generate a logical disgruntlement between those families that remain excluded from the programme despite the fact that they meet the requisites for access. Likewise, the discretional nature of whether one was a beneficiary of the federal or the municipal varieties of the PBE generated a logical disgruntlement between the families benefiting from the federal modality, who do not understand why they received less than other families who found themselves in an identical situation of poverty. Here we can identify one of the most obvious contradictions present in the discourses about education and poverty. While these discourses are placing increasing importance on community social cohesion as a mechanism to combat poverty (World Bank 2001, 2004; Putnam 2004), due to their very design the targeting programmes with their limitations on coverage generate breaches that make this social cohesion difficult to achieve.[10]

Dilemmas about the benefit: What amount to transfer?

Many of the previous dilemmas can arise in circumstances of 'fixed benefit', that is, they do not directly depend on the amount of the benefit transferred. There are other dilemmas, however, that do have a direct relationship with the amount of the transfer. The decisions in this realm are important since the programme's efficacy in achieving its goals largely depends on them. A first factor to take into account centres on what has been called by many authors the 'trade-off between breadth and intensity' (World Bank 2004). Indeed, targeting programmes debate between the breadth of the coverage and the intensity of the benefit, and both the PBE and the PBF are no exceptions.

The federal PBE variant, for example, offered broad coverage but a scant benefit (R$45 at most, equivalent to €19), while the municipal variant in Belo Horizonte offered a higher benefit (R$168, €71), which consequently hindered the programme's chances of breadth (although that obviously depends on the amount of resources invested). Broader coverage can ensure greater equitability in access to the benefit but lower efficacy in achieving the goals, and conversely, a higher amount transferred may enable certain families to escape from their situation of poverty and generate mechanisms for creating income autonomy, but it could also generate inequality amongst sectors of the population that meet the eligibility conditions yet do not manage to be aided by the programme.

Within a context of clear financial limitations (on both a federal and municipal scale), the choice of either type of strategy clearly involves a political decision. One of the considerations to be borne in mind when setting the amount of the benefit thus entails defining the goal to be achieved with the transfer. For example, a transfer may be chosen that manages to situate the families above the poverty line, or one may be chosen according to the opportunity cost associated with attending school (Sedlaeck et al. 2001). What is more, another criterion that can be used might arise from evaluations of the programme that make it possible to determine the relationship between the amount transferred and the educational career of the beneficiaries, thus determining the amount of the transfer not only based on the families' overcoming their material poverty but also based on knowledge of the relationship between the transfer and achievement of the goals, such as school attainment and the eradication of child labour. The consideration of which goals are given top priority is thus fundamental for resolving the dilemma of the transfer, and as a result, for considering to what extent a targeting programme like the PBE is exclusively envisioned to palliate the problems of lack of schooling and poverty (or even as an instrument of social control) or as a social policy that strives to use education as a key mechanism in the struggle against chronic poverty. Choosing one decision over the other will provide objective criteria for setting the amount of the transfer and assessing the coverage needs based on criteria that are not exclusively conditioned by the available budget, a predominant criterion in almost all the targeting programmes.

The PBF aims to increase both the coverage and the benefit of the previous programmes like the PBE, an objective that has been certainly accomplished. Nevertheless, considering that the PBF is the main national anti-poverty policy, the volume of resources available for the programme is still modest (Soares 2010a).

Finally, the disjunctions are also related to the fixed or variable nature of the transference. The majority of versions of the PBE have opted for a fixed transfer, although the federal modality of the programme introduced a variable transference depending on the number of 'eligible' children within the family unit. The PBF opted for a combination of the two options, according to the families' poverty level. As we have indicated, poor families receive a variable transference depending on the number of children, while extreme poor families also receive a monthly fixed stipend. Other programmes, such as Mexico's *Oportunidades*, have chosen a variable transfer according to indicators such as the number of children, sex and educational level.[11] The decision for either type of option generally has to do with the added costs that might be involved in introducing variability in the systems of selecting and monitoring the beneficiary population. The choice of the simple transfer model, recommended by some authors (Sedlaeck et al. 2001), may enable administrative costs to be saved; yet it might also lead to problems of equity and efficacy. The problems of equity are the result of offering identical amounts to family units with very different circumstances in terms of the ways they experience poverty. The problems of efficacy are derived from witnessing the impact of very different transfers amongst the beneficiary families. Below we shall examine this issue in more depth when we examine the programme's shortcomings and possibilities from the standpoint of the demand.

Dilemmas about monitoring and assistance: Is the transference alone enough?

A final set of dilemmas present in the design of the PBE centres on the least quantifiable but no less important terrain of ensuring its efficacy. These are measures that the programme can incorporate for the purpose of assisting and monitoring the beneficiary families. This is one of the realms in which the more help-oriented or redistributive orientation of the programmes can be seen (Tarabini 2008b). Logically, the chances for a greater breadth and/or intensity of the programme depend on the funds earmarked for the assistance measures, yet an efficacious use of the transfer can also break with the circle reproducing poverty.

The decisions in this area are indicative of the possible political orientations the programmes might have with respect to defining poverty and the mechanisms needed to combat it. In other words, the more comprehensive the monitoring and family assistance measures, the greater the inter-sectorial actions related to the programme; likewise, the more actions there are parallel to the transfers aimed at increasing the quality of the educational process, the more evidence there will be that the programme's design does not restrict the concept of poverty solely to material factors but extends it to other dimensions as well. Underpinning the design, then, is some kind of interpretation of the relationship between education and poverty, or, what amounts to the same, the choice of a vision of the relationship as either exclusively unidirectional (in which education is conceived as a causal factor in the situation of poverty) or recursive (in which education and poverty mutually influence each other). The more funds are earmarked to actions such as adult literacy, visits to health care centres, occupational training policies, meetings with the beneficiary families and follow-up of the students' school career, the closer the programme will approach a recursive vision of the relationship between education and poverty, in which factors that could determine the possibilities for taking advantage of the educational experience are as important as school attendance and the quality of the education.

The variants of the PBE differed considerably in their planning of the monitoring measures and complementary actions for the beneficiaries.[12] The municipal modality of Belo Horizonte and the federal modality could be identified as the two extremes along the existing continuum of different modalities: the former was limited to targeting and ensuring the income transference and left the design of the monitoring and assistance services to the municipalities, while the second applied a broad, diverse assistance methodology which included actions in the labour, social, educational and personal realm. In this regard, the PBF is clearly inspired in the municipal modalities of the PBE and articulates the monetary transference with several complementary actions for beneficiary families. These actions, oriented to maximize the effects of CCTs in reducing poverty, could be both specifically designed to attend PBF families or other existing programmes and include four main categories: access to knowledge (young and adult literacy programmes, vocational training, etc.), access to employment and income (professional qualification, access to microcredit, etc.), improvement of housing and infrastructure (basic services programmes) and rights of citizenship (programmes related to the exercise of civil and political rights) (http://mds.gov.br/assuntos/bolsa-familia).

The reflections in this section point to the possible political options that underpin the characteristics of the supply of the programmes. However, the efficacy of the programme in terms of meeting the goals does not only depend on the political orientation implicit in their design. Our studies highlight how the impact of the transfer has different effects according to the social conditions of the beneficiaries and their representations of poverty and education. The efficacy of a targeting programme, thus, must be seen based on the characteristics not only from the supply side but also from the demand side, and especially from the standpoint of the possibilities that the transfer and other complementary actions may alter the conditions of educability of poor students.[13]

Conclusion

For the last decade, CCTs have become a 'fast social policy' in the developing world. Different programmes have extended, especially in Latin American countries, but there are also recent experiences in Asia and some African countries. Interestingly enough, these programmes are part of the South-South travelling policies. Indeed, the first world has also learned from the Mexican or Brazilian experience, as it is illustrated by the CCT programme developed in New York City (Peck and Theodore 2010). Whether these programmes can be considered a progressive or regressive social policy is a very controversial issue. Are CCTs a good policy for the poor? Are they redistributive or are they part of the new faces of neoliberalism in social policies? Do they have positive effects for poverty alleviation? This chapter has shown that to answer this debate some specifications about these programmes are required. The first one refers to aspects related to programme design. Actually, by looking at the programme design we can infer the 'programme ontology'. That is, the values underlining specific public policies are implicit in the very design of the programme. In the case of the PBE and the PBF, we have looked at aspects like the programme extension, the value of the transfer, the targeting system, the follow-up monitoring procedures or the support methodology. We have observed significant differences among programme modalities, and we have illustrated tensions and dilemmas that policy-makers face when designing a CCT programme. Within this diversity, it would be a mistake to qualify or disqualify CCTs programmes as inherently 'good' or 'bad' policies for the poor. To know more about the effects of these programmes, we have observed how they are 'appropriated' by those that benefit from the transfer. Again, there is a notable diversity of impacts, which depend on the wide diversity of educational demand. Although all the beneficiaries are poor, they differ in the way the experience poverty. Their family structure and characteristics are different, so are the educational contexts of poor children, the different forms of using the non-school time and the school cultures where they attend. These factors are decisive to understand what we call 'conditions of educability'. The existence of the transfer means nothing if we cannot observe the role it can play within specific living conditions.

Reflecting conditions of educability is a necessary task to know more about the nature of CCTs and their usefulness as a tool to reduce the intergenerational reproduction of poverty. Focusing only in the educational results of beneficiaries is a very reductionist policy evaluation methodology to debar these programmes as efficient social policies. There are effects that can be assessed only in the long term, especially those that cannot be directly considered strictly 'educational' effects. Actually, conditions of educability point out 'what else' is necessary for a child to learn at school besides the transfer. While in some cases a few more interventions are necessary, there are cases requiring an intensive follow-up methodology and a multidimensional supportive strategy to help children to learn at school.

Observing conditions of educability is also useful to conclude that CCTs might be a very poor social or educational policy when they are not included within a larger strategy to reduce poverty through education. Those approaches that see CCTs as a non-expensive and useful social policy ignore that reducing poverty is undoubtedly an expensive objective. Most determinants of poverty require intensive intervention methodologies, among which CCTs can be an important one, but not the only one.

Questions for discussion

1   Which particularities of CCT programmes have as a global education policy? What is an inverse policy travelling?

2   What do you think about conditionality? Is it a good mechanism to ensure educational efficiency? Are there moral dilemmas associated to it?

3   Make a hypothetical design of a CCT programme to be implemented in the country X. What dilemmas will you face? Which pros and cons can you identify?

4   Which direct and indirect effects of CCT programmes on education and the conditions of educability can you identify?

5   Are CCT programmes in education enough for fighting poverty? How would you design an inter-sectorial policy for poverty reduction?

Notes

1   Data from http://smartereducation.worldbank.org/sep/ (Accessed 15 November 2010).

2   See the studies by Tarabini and Bonal (2004).

3   The project entitled *Una evaluación de los efectos educativos y sobre el trabajo infantil del programa municipal Bolsa Escola de Belo Horizonte (An evaluation of the educative effects and on the children's work of the* Bolsa Escola *municipal programme in Belo Horizonte)* was financed by the AECI (Spanish International Cooperation Agency) as part of the 'Intercampus' programme for Inter-University Cooperation between Spain and Iberoamerica (reference A/1605/04).

4   The monetary transfer tended to vary between one-half and one minimum salary.

5   Despite the agreement reached to finance the transfer, the selection process, implementation and monitoring of school attendance all remained under the control of the Municipal Education Secretariat.

6   In 2004, there were a total of 25,152 beneficiaries of the PBE in Belo Horizonte, 11,514 of them from the municipal variety of the programme (under the financial agreement with the federal government) and 13,638 solely from the federal one.

7   In educational policy, targeting based on the institutional criterion entails choosing those schools whose characteristics show situations of higher social risk and vulnerability. They are thus programmes that directly intervene on the educational supply and that, generally speaking, do not include transfers that are dependent on school attendance.

8   In the case of the PBF there is no territorial criterion for selecting areas of intervention. Nevertheless, and based on ex ante poverty estimates, the programme establishes a maximum level of beneficiaries for each municipality (municipal quotas). According to Lindert et al. (2007), one of the main benefits of municipal quotas is to keep mayors from registering populations indiscriminately.

9   In the case of the Belo Horizonte programme, for example, the town's map of social exclusion was used to focalize based on eighty-one planning units corresponding to the new regional units into which the city is divided. See the detailed explanation of the process in Bonal and Tarabini (2006).

10 The PBF intends to avoid this problem by including in the design of the programme both poor and extreme poor families and by planning a different benefit for them. In the first situation (poor families with per capita income below R$140, equivalent to €59), the programme gives a monthly stipend of R$22 (€9) per child attending school, to a maximum of three children. In the second situation (extremely poor families with per capita income less than R$ 70 per month, €29), the programme plans an additional flat sum of R$ 68 (€29), called 'Basic Benefit' and with no conditionality.

11 The transfer increases the more children a family has, when the beneficiaries are girls, and when the students are in secondary school.

12 For an in-depth explanation of the monitoring measures in the Belo Horizonte programme, see Bonal and Tarabini (2006).

13 See Bonal and Tarabini (2016) for a review of the impact of the PBE on students' conditions of educability.

References

Alves Azeredo, T. M. (2003). *Programa Bolsa Escola de Belo Horizonte: uma constribuçao para a avaliaçao economica, sob a ótica de eficácia, eficiencia e sustentabilidade*, Doctoral thesis. Departamento de Gestao Economica e Administraçao Pública. Belo Horizonte: Fundaçao Joao Pinheiro.

Atria, R. (2003). 'Capital social: concepto, dimensiones y estrategias para su desarrollo'. In *Capital social y reducción de la pobreza en América Latina y el Caribe*. CEPAL. Santiago de Chile: CEPAL.

Bonal, X. and Tarabini, A. (2016). 'Being poor at school: exploring conditions of educability in the favela'. *Education Policy Analysis Archives*, 37 (2), 212–229.

Brodershon, V. (1999). 'Focalización de programas de superación de la pobreza'. In *Derecho a tener derecho: infancia, derecho y política social en América Latina*. Montevideo: Instituto Internacional del Niño (IIN) y UNICEF.

Cornia, G. A. (2001). 'Social funds in stabilization and adjustment programmes: A critique'. *Development and Change*, 32, 1–32.

Draibe, S. (2006). 'Brasil: Bolsa Escola y Bolsa Familia'. In E. Cohen and R. Franco (Eds.), *Transferencias con responsabilidad. Una mirada latinoamericana*. Mexico DF: FLACSO.

Holzmann, R., Sherburne-Benz, L. and Tesliuc, E. (2003). *Social risk management: The World Bank's approach to social protection in a globalizing world*. Washington, DC: The World Bank.

Lavinas, L. (2000). 'The appeal of minimum income programs in Latin America'. *Programme for Bellagio Meeting on Socio Economic Security*. ILO, Bellagio, 6–10 March 2000.

Lavinas, L., Barbosa, M. L. and Tourinho, O. (2001). *Assessing Local Minimum Income Programes un Brazil*. Geneva: ILO, Brazil Regional Office, World Bank & IPEA.

Lindert, K. (2006), 'Brazil: Bolsa Escola Program. Scaling-up cash transfers for the Poor'. In OECD-WB (Ed.), *Emerging good practice in managing for development results: Sourcebook*. Washington, DC: OECD-WB, pp. 67–74.

Lindert, K., Linder, A., Hobs, J. and de la Brière, B. (2007). 'The nuts and bolts of Brazil's Bolsa família program: Implementing conditional cash transfers in a decentralized context'. *World Bank Social Protection Discussion Paper*, 79, 1–147.

Narayan, D. (1999). 'Bonds and bridges. Social capital and poverty'. Policy Research Working Paper 2167, pp. 1–50.

Pawson, R. (2006). *Evidence-based policy: A realist perspective*. London: Sage Publications Ltd.

Peck, J. and Theodore, N. (2010). 'Recombinant workfare, across the Americas: Transnationalizing "fast" social policy'. *Goforum*, 41 (2), 195–208.

Putnam, R. (2004). 'Education, Diversity, Social Cohesion and Social Capital'. OECD Meeting: *Rasing the Quality of Learning for all*. Dublin, 18–19 March 2004.

Rawlings, L. B. (2005). 'A new approach to social assistance: Latin America's experience with conditional cash transfer programmes'. *International Social Security Review*, 58 (2–3), 133–161.

Reimers, F., Silva, C. S. and Trevino, E. (2006). 'Where is the "education" in conditional cash transfers in education?' UIS Working Papers, 4, 1–80.

Rocha, S. (2000). 'Applying minimum income programs in Brazil two cases of studies: Belém and Belo Horizonte'. *IPEA texto para discussao*, 746.

Sabóia, J. and Rocha, S. (1998). 'Programas de garantia de renda minima-linhas gerais de uma metodologia de avaliaçao a partir da experiencia pioneira do Paranoá, no Distrito Federal'. *IPEA texto para discussao*, 582, 1–37.

Schwartzman, S. (2005). 'Education-oriented social programs in Brazil: The impact of Bolsa Escola'. Paper submitted to the *Global Conference on Education*

Research in Developing Countries (Research for Results on Education). Prague: Global Development Network, March–April 2005.

Sedlaeck, G., Gustafsson-Wright, E., Ilahi, N. and Lannon, M. (2001). *Brazil: As assessment of the Bolsa Escola Programs*. Washington, DC: World Bank.

Soares, F. V., Ribas, R. P. and Osório, R. G. (2007). 'Evaluating the impact of Brazil's *Bolsa Família*: Cash transfer programmes in comparative perspective'. *Evaluation Note,* 1. Brasilia: Policy Centre for Inclusive Growth.

Soares, S. (2010). 'Targeting and coverage of the Bolsa Família Programme: What is the meaning of eleven million families', International Policy Center for Inclusive Growth (IPC-IG), *One Pager,* 117.

Tarabini, A. (2008b). *Educación, pobreza y desarrollo: agendas globales, políticas nacionales, realidades locales*. Doctoral thesis. Sociology Department. Bellaterra-Barcelona: Autonomous University of Barcelona. Available at: http://www.tesisenxarxa.net/.

Tarabini, A. and Bonal, X. (2004), 'Bolsa Escola: una revisión de sistemas de evaluación de los programas de garantía de renta mínima en educación'. Paper presented at *X Encuentro de Latinoamericanistas Españoles Identidad y multiculturalidad*, Salamanca (Spain), 13–14 May.

Villatoro, P. (2007). 'Las transferencias condicionadas en América Latina: luces y sombras', Paper presented at *Seminario Internacional. Evolución y desafíos de los programas de transferencias condicionadas*. Brasilia, 20–21 November.

World Bank (2001). *World development report 2000/2001. Attacking poverty.* Washington, DC: Oxford University Press.

World Bank (2004). *Inequality in Latin America and the Caribbean: Breaking with History?* Washington, DC: World Bank.

World Bank (2011). *Learning for all: Investing in people's knowledge and skills to promote development. World Bank Groups Education Strategy 2020.* Washington, DC: World Bank.

Further reading

Barrera-Osorio, F., Bertrand, M., Linden L. and Perez-Calle, F. (2011). 'Improving the design of conditional transfer programs: Evidence from a randomized education experiment in Colombia'. *American Economic Journal of Applied Economics*, 3 (2), 167–195.

Filmer, D. and Schady, N. (2011). 'Does more cash in conditional cash transfer programs always lead to larger impacts on school attendance?' *Journal of Development Economics*, 96 (1), 150–157.

Fiszbein, A., Schady, Norbert, Ferreira, Francisco, H. G., Grosh, Margaret, Keleher, Niall, Olinto, Pedro and Skoufias, Emmanuel (2009). *Conditional cash transfers: Reducing present and future poverty.* World Bank Policy Research Report. Washington, DC: World Bank.

Gee, K. A. (2010). 'Reducing child labour through conditional cash transfers: Evidence from Nicaragua's *Red de Protección Social'. Development Policy Review,* 28 (6), 711–732.

Glewwe, P. and Kassouf, A. L. (2012). 'The impact of the Bolsa Escola/Familia conditional cash transfer program on enrollment, Dropout rates and grade promotion in Brazil'. *Journal of Development Economics*, 97 (2), 505–517.

Hanlon, Joseph, Armando, B. and David, H. (2010). *Just give money to the poor: The development revolution from the global south*. Sterling, VA: Kumarian Press.

Saavedra, J. and García, S. (2013). *Educational impacts and cost-effectiveness of conditional cash transfer programs in developing countries: A meta-analysis*. CESR Working Paper No. 2013–007.

8

Global Policies, Local Meanings: The Re-Contextualization of Competency-Based Education Reforms in Mexico

Rosanne Tromp

Chapter Outline

Introduction

Increasingly, new policy ideas emanate from the global education arena. Competency-based education (CBE) is an example of what Verger et al. (2012, p. 18) call a 'global education policy' (GEP). Stated briefly, CBE focuses on what learners can do with their knowledge rather than what they know. The focus is on objective and observable outcomes that can be measured (Smith and Patterson 1998). During the last two decades, CBE has been surging in popularity and is now linked to discourses on quality education. Its worldwide appeal is that in an era of a global knowledge economy, CBE is perceived to be the approach that produces human capital, in the form of knowledge, skills and attitudes of students entering the workforce. This is seen as having the potential to enhance countries' competitive advantage in the global marketplace (Vidovich and Sheng 2007). CBE is thus linked to economic growth, but also to social cohesion and cultural diversity (Opertti and Murueta 2010).

Around the world, international organizations, countries and schools scramble to develop their own versions of CBE (Griffith and Lim 2014). For example, the Organization for Economic Co-operation and Development (OECD) employs *competencies* as the measure of student academic achievement in the standardized evaluation Program for International Student Assessment (PISA) (OECD 2005). In countries as diverse as the Netherlands, Chile, Mali (Bourgonje and Tromp 2011), Uganda and Turkey (Altinyelken, this volume), curricula of basic and higher education are being reformed on the basis of competencies. However, while a global interest and national adoption of CBE can be witnessed, research also suggests that local contexts shape heterogeneous policy meanings, teaching and learning practices (Vidovich 1997; Power et al. 2004; Braun et al. 2011).

There is a growing interest in studying how global policies such as CBE re-contextualize, yet most studies focus on one phase of the policy process, for example, the translation of GEP in policy texts (cf. Mausethagen 2013). Moreover, while research shows a global convergence of policy discourses, it is not sufficiently clear how local contingencies produce different meanings and practices (Anderson-Levitt 2012), nor does research provide sufficiently rich empirical evidence of the re-contextualization of global policy discourses in local places (Verger et al. 2012). Thus, to understand how education reforms that draw on global ideas are enacted, and with what consequences, this chapter argues that the re-contextualization of education policy needs to be studied in different contexts and *all the way through* from international to (sub) national scales. Particularly, it constructs a multiscalar study of the processes of meaning-making and enactment of the 2009–2011 Mexican competency-based curricular reform to primary education.

Drawing on a broader study that examined global education reforms in Mexico (Tromp 2016), this chapter analyses the re-contextualization of CBE in the Mexican educational system. During the 2007–2012 administration, Mexico reformed its primary education curriculum on the basis of competencies, arguing that this would 'raise the quality of education so that students improve their level of educational achievement, have a means of accessing better well-being and thus, contribute to national development' (SEP 2007, p. 11). At the same time, several Mexican education researchers, teachers' unions and teachers contested the potential of competency approaches to increase the quality of education. For them, CBE was imposed by international financial institutions and it was irrelevant for the Mexican context (Ornelas 2008a,b; Navarro Gallegos 2009, 2011).

The argument in this chapter is based on in-depth fieldwork conducted between June 2012 and June 2014 which consisted of three main methods. First, policy document analysis of Mexican competency-based curricular reforms produced between 2002 and 2012 was carried out to understand the ways in which CBE was interpreted in these reforms. Secondly, 124 group and individual interviews were conducted with different policy actors (such as Ministry of Education officials, teachers' unions, academics and teachers) that operated at the international and the Mexican national, state and school scales. Participants were selected by purposive sampling, and interviews were conducted in Spanish, without the use of a translator. The main aim of the interviews was to understand how education actors perceived the position of Mexico in relation to the global education arena and how they interpreted and enacted the reform. Thirdly, observations were conducted at events during the reform processes, such as teacher training sessions, Ministry of Education reunions and teachers' union protests, as well as in twelve schools that were located in different socio-economic contexts in the states of Durango and Michoacan. Both states show similar socio-economic inequality. However, their political contexts differ vastly, as these are made up of different political parties as well as teachers' unions which draw on different political and socio-economic ideologies. A focus on these two states helps to analyse how context (structural aspects) and agents (e.g. MoE or teachers) mediate global education policies.

The findings show that while CBE resonated with education actors' social imaginaries of quality teaching and development at the national scale and the state of Durango, CBE clashed with imaginaries at the state scale of Michoacan. Subsequently, whereas it was adopted in the first cases, it was rejected at the Michoacan level. Nevertheless, at the level of teachers, the reform was not interpreted positively by all teachers in Durango, nor was it interpreted negatively or rejected by all teachers in Michoacan. In addition, competency practices in the classroom were shaped differently by available resources, both material and human.

The ideological work of the re-contextualization of global policy ideas

As it moves, it morphs.

(Cowen 2009, p. 315)

In order to situate the particular Mexican case, this first section briefly outlines the broader literature about the re-contextualization of education reforms into localized practices. Education policy scholars have argued that although globally similar education policy ideas are being adopted (Verger et al. 2012, p. 3), these policy ideas are rarely re-contextualized into education practices in the same way (Ball 1998). They instead 'map onto local practice in contingent, contested, inflected and thus unpredictable ways' (Burbules and Torres 2000, p. 102). Thus, as global policy ideas travel, they transform.

Policy ideas can therefore be conceptualized as floating signifiers. Floating signifiers are concepts that are 'open to interpretation' and obtain their meaning as they become fixed within education policy discourses, understood as a particular way of representing certain aspects of the world (signified) (Rear and Jones 2013, p. 375). Education policy discourses in turn draw on different social imaginaries (Urciuoli 2008). Imaginaries are 'collective social facts with which people define themselves and construct their relations to others, and build a world in and through modernity' (Rizvi 2006, p. 194). They bring together factual and normative aspects of policies and enable people to develop a shared understanding of the problems to which policies are proposed as solutions (Rizvi 2006, p. 198). Because signifiers – or global policy ideas – can be interpreted within different discourses (which in turn reflect different imaginaries), they can mean either the 'evil that has to be expelled' to some or the 'final road to progress' to others (Buenfil-Burgos 2000, p. 2).

Social imaginaries also provide with authority some interpretations of policy ideas over others. Globally, a neoliberal imaginary has become dominant (Rizvi 2006), which provides meaning to many of the education policy ideas that circulate (Ball 2007 in Verger et al. 2012). However, the neoliberal imaginary of globalization has also given rise to different imaginaries, which now co-exist (Appadurai 1996).

The processes of re-contextualization of GEP, that is, the reinterpretation of policy ideas as they become fixed within different discourses and imaginaries, are continuous. Rather than separating between distinct phases of policy-making and implementation, processes of translation, adoption and rejection take place by policy actors *along* the policy trajectory. Processes of multiple interpretability are highly political, with some education policy actors having more power to define dominant discourses than others. These 'key policy interpreters' (Ball 1994, pp. 17–18) actively try to shape the meaning of signifiers, according to their interests. Every instance of use of the signifier can be viewed as an attempt by the agents of the discourses to subtly transform the meaning of the term (Rear and Jones 2013, p. 375). Apple (2008, p. XI) refers to this as 'ideological work'. The positionality of key interpreters is configured differently at different scales of government. Therefore, this chapter traces the re-contextualization of CBE 'vertically' as well as in multiple political and socio-economic contexts.

CBE: From global education policy to Mexican education policy

CBE as global education policy

Before GEP ideas are re-contextualized in local contexts, they need to penetrate international policy agendas. How did CBE obtain the status of global policy? A review of the literature reveals that although it has been around since the 1960s, a new impulse to the popularity of competency approaches to education was seen in the 1990s. The rapid growth in technology, international competition and new trade agreements, developments that are sometimes described as the transition to the knowledge and information society (Kouwenhoven 2003), sparked an interest in education that focuses on practical skills such as the capacity to innovate and adapt (Argüelles 2000). CBE is proposed in the context of economic growth (Ananiadou and Claro 2009), as well as life-long learning (Commission/EACEA/Eurydice 2012). It also fits the outcomes-based trend, in the context of increased demand for accountability and efficiency of education (Biemans et al. 2004). At the same time, CBE proponents link it to a growing concern with citizenship and human rights issues (Keating-Chetwynd 2009).

Since the 1990s, at the international scale, the idea of basic or key competencies is promoted by organizations such as the OECD, the EU and UNESCO. These organizations denote the competencies that all students should develop in order to participate successfully in modern schools, work and life. Examples include competencies such as speaking the mother tongue, problem solving skills and basic mathematics (Farstad 2004). Globally, the OECD promotes a perspective to competencies that is dominantly informed by a human capital perspective. Instead, UNESCO promotes a competency discourse which emphasizes the importance of diversity and democracy (Opertti and Murueta 2010).

CBE models initially reappeared in the United Kingdom, Europe, Australia, Canada and New Zealand, and subsequently, travelled to Asia and Latin America. For example, in the late 1990s, South Africa started to experiment with its own model of competency or outcomes-based education (OBE). Research shows that the South African version of OBE was an amalgam of early debates about competency education in Australia, Canada and New Zealand (Brown 2015). Similarly, towards the end of the 1990s, Chinese reformers looked to North American competency models in an attempt to promote a more holistic approach to education (Kipnis 2006 in Ngok and Chan 2015).

Mexico in the global education arena

In order to understand why CBE was adopted in the particular Mexican context and how it re-contextualized, a brief description of how Mexico has imagined itself in the global arena is necessary. Towards the end of the 1980s, Mexico moved away from the welfare state and Keynesian economic model of revolutionary nationalism (Quezada Ortega 2001, p. 107) and social liberalism was adopted as the social imaginary of reforms, a euphemism for neoliberalism.[1] Mexico signed important trade agreements (e.g. NAFTA in 1994), and it became part of the OECD in 1994. Within the context of the wider economic modernization policies came a particular way of conceiving education and its role in society (Arnaut and Giorguli 2010, pp. 660–661). The dominant view became one in which education was subordinate to economic needs, inscribing on education a managerial administration. The main goals of Mexican education reforms since the 1990s were to improve quality, equity and relevance, which replaced the prior goals of investment in expanding education and nationalist education for social cohesion (Ornelas 2004, p. 399).

In 2000, the change of power to the centre-right wing National Action Party (PAN), after seventy-one-year reign of the Institutional Revolutionary Party (PRI), generated high expectations for change in the educational field (Miranda López 2004). Nevertheless, the administration continued the basic reform patterns designed in the 1990s (Ornelas 2004). Interestingly, the neoliberal education reforms started in the 1980s did not diminish the power of the teachers' union *Sindicato Nacional de Trabajadores de la Educación* (SNTE), Latin America's largest union. This union rapidly adopted the latest neoliberal globalization jargon (Street 2003), and its members enjoyed higher income and benefits, while its leaders gained more influence (Ornelas 2008a, p. 446).

Today, Mexico's economy is the fourteenth biggest economy in the world and the fourth largest in the Americas after the United States, Canada and Brazil (IMF 2014). It is also one of most unequal countries within the OECD. More than fifty-three million people live in multidimensional poverty, and while the richest man in the world is from Mexico, more than twenty-three million Mexicans do not earn enough to acquire a basic food basket (Esquivel Hernandez 2015).

CBE in Mexican education policy

It is within these economic aims described above that the introduction of the global policy idea of CBE in Mexico should be understood. In the 1990s, the Mexican government introduced a labour competency approach to vocational education and training, funded by the World Bank and the Inter-American Development Bank. This approach borrowed heavily on experiences with the National Vocational Qualifications in the United Kingdom (de Anda 2011). Over successive years, competency-based curricula were introduced to all levels of education, from preschool to university. The idea of key competencies, which was promoted at the international scale, was reflected in Mexican curricular reforms. In preschool and secondary education, a competency approach was introduced that focused on the competencies that favour continuous learning. It placed an emphasis on Spanish and mathematics, but also included transversal competencies, such as creativity and intercultural awareness (SEP 2004, p. 22).

Despite the enthusiasm for CBE within the national Ministry of Education (MoE), CBE reforms attracted critique from within academia and the dissident teachers' union *Coordinadora Nacional de Trabajadores de la Educación* (CNTE).[2] Critics interpreted competencies as narrow behavioural skills, framed by a managerial and neo-behaviourist discourse inspired by neoliberal imaginaries, and they critiqued the role of international actors in Mexican policy. Moreover, research suggests that teachers enacted CBE in heterogeneous ways, for example due to lack of teacher training (Reyes and Pech Campos 2007, p. 181) and infrastructure (Rothman and Nugroho 2010), or on the basis of different views and interests (Diaz-Barriga and Barrón 2014).

The translation, adoption and rejection of CBE in the curricular reform to primary education

In 2007, the only level of education that had not become competency based was primary education. To create a knowledge-based education system, 'a comprehensive reform, focused on the adoption of an educational model based on competencies that meets the development needs of Mexico in the twenty-first century' (SEP 2008, p. 5) was undertaken.

Once the preparation of the curriculum texts was finalized, the revised curriculum was piloted in the 2008–2009 academic year in 4,723 primary schools. In the following academic year, the implementation started in all Mexican schools in years 1 and 6, and in 2010–2011 in years 2 and 5. In 2011, all years of primary education were expected to implement the reformed curriculum. Teachers were invited to participate in yearly training courses from 2008 to 2011.

In the next section, the translation of CBE in the curricular texts is discussed. Subsequently, the interpretation and enactment of CBE is analysed *all the way through* from the international to the local Mexican level.

Translation of CBE in the curricular texts

An important articulatory moment within the processes of re-contextualization of the global policy idea in the Mexican curricular reform was its definition within the curricular texts. Within the curricular documents, the meaning of the signifier *competencies* was defined as

> [k]nowing to do (skills) with knowing (knowledge), as well as the assessment of the consequences of the impact of that doing. In other words, the manifestation of a competency reveals the putting in practice of knowledge, skills, attitudes and values to achieve purposes in a given context. (SEP 2008, p. 36)

In the curriculum, competencies acquired meaning within contrasting competency discourses. On the one hand, a set of broad *competencies for life* was defined, which were to be developed throughout basic education. The competencies for life emphasized the following competencies: continued learning; information and situation management; and living together in society. The Mexican competencies for life are an adaptation of the internationally promoted idea of basic competencies. Also, the curricular texts defined a *graduate profile*. This profile outlined the individual competencies that Mexican students were expected to have developed upon completing basic education. It was intended as a reference for the organization, development and evaluation of learning. The profile emphasized the importance of speaking and writing skills, as well as English and digital or information and communication technology (ICT) skills.

On the other hand, the curriculum specified *subject-specific competencies* and *expected learning outcomes,* which described in detail the knowledge, skills and attitudes/values that all students were supposed to develop in the different subjects. An extra set of *curricular standards* was added to the last version of the curriculum, which are 'descriptions of achievements and define what students are expected to be able to show' (SEP 2011, p. 29). These standards were to form the basis of national (*Evaluación Nacional de Logros Académicos en Centros Escolares* (ENLACE)) as well as external evaluations such as PISA. The MoE stated that the curricular standards define a type of global citizenship, as a product of the domination of skills and languages that allow the entry of Mexico into the knowledge economy. The curricular texts explicitly stated that the standards respond to the recommendation of the OECD in 2007 to Mexico to increase its scores on PISA, which, in a hyperbolic way, was presented as a 'global educational consensus' (SEP 2011, p. 85).

The above policy document analysis shows how CBE acquired meaning within different competency discourses in the Mexican curricular reform to primary education. Nevertheless, the specification of large amounts of standards and detailed expected learning outcomes favours a narrow interpretation of CBE. This leads to a fragmentation of curricular content, and does not favour the holistic development of students. Such a narrow interpretation of competencies is reinforced by a focus on testing. Lastly, the specification of competency standards for Spanish, English, mathematics, sciences, ICT skills and reading shifts the focus away from indigenous education, as well as other elements such as gender and diversity that are difficult to measure.

CBE accommodated agendas of international and national actors

Within the Mexican MoE, competencies were argued to be an integrated set of knowledge, skills, attitudes and values, and it had a positive connotation. Policy-makers explained that the competency approach in the reform was about the mobilization and application of this set to day-to-day life situations. The Spanish word for competency is *competencia*, which can mean both competency and competition. Contrary to some critical voices, the MoE emphasized that competency education was not about competition. A senior MoE official explained that

[t]he competency approach has nothing to do with competition. It is a holistic conceptualization of education, which is about putting in practice interrelated sets of knowledge, skills, attitudes and values for the resolution specific problems of personal, public and professional life. (I-NA6, Mexico City, 14 November 2012)

This interpretation was backed up by the national teachers' union SNTE. Although policy-makers within the MoE acknowledged that CBE emerged from the business sector and vocational training, they emphasized that the curricular reform to primary education took a 'competencies for life' approach, which was applicable to basic education:

> In Mexico, as in the rest of the world I presume, the competency approach comes from the workplace, factories, industry, the service sector. But those who critique it just stay with these origins. The theoretical discussions we have here are about how you move from the job skills approach to the life skills approach, which is totally different. (GI-NA1, Mexico City, 4 December 2012)

The appeal of CBE for the Mexican national MoE can be explained through the existence of a rationale that reproduced the view of Mexico as being part of the global knowledge economy and global education arena. Within the MoE, CBE aligned with the perceived demands of the knowledge economy, and as Mexico was seen as part of this, it was argued that they had to adopt CBE. The perceived knowledge economy established the need to change the focus of education towards an approach that develops skills in order to construct rather than reproduce knowledge. One Mexican senior policy-maker argued during a group interview that

> [k]nowledge and education content are losing validity, because of the rapid generation of scientific and technological knowledge. So, you can't focus any longer on trying to teach all those knowledges, you have to focus on teaching them the tools to construct and search knowledge. The competency approach attends to this social need. (GI-NA1, Mexico City, 4 December 2012)

The appeal of CBE as a policy idea was also reproduced at the national level not only because it aligned with Mexican agendas of economic growth, but also because it was flexible enough to morph it into something locally sellable. National policy-makers actively promoted the idea that competency education could be adapted to Mexican local contexts. As the emphasis of CBE is on the specification of outcomes, it was argued that urban and rural teachers alike could choose the best way to achieve these outcomes in ways that were contextually relevant. Promoting a view of competencies in this way thus worked as an 'acceptable compromise' (Steiner-Khamsi 2012, p. 459) between the perceived international demands and local contexts for education actors at the national level.

The interpretation of CBE within the Mexican national MoE was closely aligned with the OECD approach. Both the OECD and the MoE emphasized that the OECD had not been involved in the actual writing of the curricular reform, but that their participation had been at the level of conducting analyses, contributing ideas and sharing experiences. One senior MoE official argued that '[t]he competency approach in Mexican education comes from the views of the OECD' (I-NA8, Mexico City, 19 December 2012). For example, the competencies specified in the 'Definition and Selection of Competencies' project (DeSeCo[3]) were mentioned as having shaped the curricular reform. PISA as a measure of quality, developed by the OECD, also played a key role in defining the meaning of CBE in the curricular reform.

Within the dominant interpretation of the MoE, there was some 'room for maneuver' (Gale 1999, p. 394) for different interpretations at the national scale. For example, for UNESCO-Mexico, the emphasis of the administration on standardized evaluations PISA and ENLACE, which was a recommendation of the OECD, emphasized fractured knowledge outcomes (I-IN1, Mexico City, 22 November 2012). This overshadowed the development of a more holistic competency approach, which UNESCO promoted. Nevertheless, the inclusion of broad competencies in the reform by the MoE got UNESCO on board, while at the same time the MoE was able to push for their agenda to increase national scores on standardized tests.

These examples show how competencies can be thought of as a floating signifier, which the MoE as key policy interpreter actively changed through the ideological work described above. They aimed to change the meaning of the signifier to take on a meaning of competencies for education and life, rather than skills for the work place. This enthused education actors with different agendas (such as economic growth and the development of broad competencies) for the curricular reform.

Delegitimizing alternative meanings of CBE at the national level

Despite their ideological work, the interpretation of CBE by the MoE did not appeal to all educational actors. At the national scale, critique of CBE was articulated by the national section of the dissident teachers' union CNTE as well as various education researchers. According to these actors, competencies were measurable behaviouristic objectives which were aligned with the needs of the labour market. They argued this would lead to increased competition. According to the Union actors interviewed, CBE was imposed on Mexico by international financial organizations, and the reform was not developed in participatory ways. Moreover, they saw that CBE aligned with neoliberal economic imaginaries, which clashed with their socialist imaginaries. However, the Mexican MoE actively kept out this interpretation of CBE at the national level, for example by portraying the CNTE as illegitimate and motivated by political rather than educational interests.

Attempts of the MoE to define the meaning of CBE were also directed 'vertically', that is, towards actors positioned at different scales of government. During the processes around the reform, the MoE was sometimes confronted with the rejection of the idea of competencies by teachers or state MoE personnel, on the basis of the critique described above. A senior policy maker recalled that

> [t]he problem with mentioning competencies in Mexico is that it is incendiary, because competencies were identified with competition, and perceived as training for work. Competencies were linked to international organizations, similar to the word quality, and there was a very unwelcoming view of international organizations. (I-NA2, Mexico City, 6 December 2012)

Some teachers also questioned whether reforming the curriculum on the basis of the complex competency-based approach was the best way to improve the quality of Mexican education. For them, improving the quality of education was first and foremost related to dealing with conditions of structural inequality.

However, rather than being taken seriously, these teachers' critiques were rejected by the national MoE and they were portrayed as uninformed and conservative, defying change. Rather than the curricular reform itself, the MoE perceived uncooperative teachers as obstructing its success. As such, critique to the reform was depoliticized. An in-depth analysis of the minutiae of the policy process shows that, in order to co-opt the critique of CBE, the Mexican MoE emphasized the role of the Swiss educationalist Philippe Perrenoud, who was critical of CBE, as an important intellectual behind the Mexican curricular reform (rather than, for example, the role of the OECD). In addition, in order to promote an understanding of CBE as the development of holistic competencies for life, rather than for work, in the curricular reform texts the term 'UNESCO' was used over the terms 'OECD' and 'economic growth'.

These examples formed part of the attempts of the MoE to prevent an interpretation of competencies as being about competition in order to minimize ideological resistance to the curricular reform. They evidence the ideological work that the Mexican national MoE undertook to shift the meaning of the floating signifier *competencies* within the curricular reform in order to accomplish their objectives, such as complying with international and national agendas of economic growth. Whereas this formed an acceptable compromise for those operating within imaginaries of the knowledge society, for those operating within socialist imaginaries it did not.

Resonance and rejection of CBE at the state scale

The reinterpretations of the meaning of CBE at the state scale represented another important articulatory moment in the processes of re-contextualization of CBE. The interpretation differed between the states of Durango and Michoacan, with each having different socio-economic and political contexts. In Durango, from 2008 to 2012, when the Mexican states were called to pilot and implement the curricular reform, the political context at the state scale was aligned with the national MoE.[4] The political situation in Durango was characterized by a close collaboration between the MoE and the state chapter of teachers' union SNTE on the matter of pedagogical and educational issues.

The socio-economic imaginaries of integration into the global knowledge economy that shaped the competency-based reform resonated with the existing imaginaries and agendas at the scale of the Durango state. One senior policy-maker in the state MoE explained that

[t]his is a trend that responded to a need – not just in Mexico but in the whole world – for a new way of educating individuals because we had to respond to a rapidly changing global reality. (I-ST10, Durango, 5 June 2013)

The idea of competencies was more aligned with the interpretations of competencies found at the national scale, such as competencies being an integrated set of knowledge, skills and attitudes, favouring a learner-centred and life skills approach, and it being relevant for the Durango context.

The MoE had been able to influence and shape the way the national curricular reform developed in Durango. For example, during the sessions for feedback to the reform that the national Mexican MoE organized, the Durango MoE participated to adjust the exercises that were aimed at developing certain expected learning outcomes to the Durango context. Within their state, the MoE supported the development of the reform with resources, teacher training sessions and events about the reform. During these events, the reform was heralded as the 'educational hope for Mexico' (I-ST10, Durango, 5 June 2013).

On the other hand, from 2008 to 2012, Michoacan was headed by the left-of centre Party of the Democratic Revolution (PRD), which was different to and far to the left of the PAN that was in power at the national scale. The PRD was generally critical of policies emanating from the national MoE. In Michoacan, a dominant role was played by the dissident teachers' union CNTE. On the basis of their majority in the Michoacan union congress since the 1980s and consequent ability to mobilize teachers for strikes and protests, the CNTE was able to influence decisions of the Michoacan MoE.

The CNTE and the MoE critically reinterpreted CBE as narrow vocational skills (rather than as an integrated set of knowledge, skills and values) imposed by external financial interests. Importantly, competencies were thought not to be relevant, mainly because the material and socio-economic context of Michoacan (and Mexico in general) differed from the contexts in which, the CNTE argued, CBE had originated. The CNTE rejected the socio-economic imaginaries that gave competency education meaning in the curricular reform, which clashed with their socialist imaginaries, as the following quote by a CNTE activist illustrates:

> The problem is that the shrewd pragmatic bourgeoisie takes a fashionable term such as competencies and they give it a specific use. They link it to competition. They interpret it in a way that you have to demonstrate the set of knowledge, abilities, skills, values because you have to apply it in the world of work. (I-ST40, Morelia, 26 April 2013)

Within this context at the state level, the CNTE was able to play a role as a key policy interpreter of CBE. The CNTE did not allow the Michoacan state MoE to participate in the curricular reform feedback and training sessions at the national level. Moreover, teacher training sessions in the reform within the state were obstructed by the CNTE, textbooks were burnt and their delivery to teachers obstructed. Those who supported the national policy ran the risk of getting in trouble with the CNTE. To prevent the 'bourgeois message of the neoliberal curricular reform' (I-ST46, Morelia, 30 April 2013) from being spread, the union resorted to the reprinting of the prior 1993 curricular reform textbooks. The outcome of the ideological work of the CNTE meant that the curricular reform was not supported politically, financially or practically at the Michoacan state scale.

In a nutshell, the above discussion illustrates how the different political contexts at the state scales of the re-contextualization of CBE differently shaped its meanings and enactment.

Teachers' heterogeneous interpretation and enactment of CBE within their school contexts

Whereas the imaginaries that the competency reform embodied resonated with existing social imaginaries of quality education and development at the state level in Durango and were generally rejected in Michoacan, the processes of meaning-making of the reform by teachers were even more complex. In both states, three types of interpretations of CBE could be distinguished, although these interpretations were not equally distributed in the two states.

In Durango, most teachers interpreted competencies in ways similar to the national and state MoE. According to this mainstream interpretation, competencies were thought of as an integrated set of knowledge, skills and attitudes, and it was about putting knowledge into practice. Moreover, for these teachers, CBE aimed to move away from traditionalist banking education, was centred on the learner, and it was not necessarily associated with competition. The social imaginaries of quality education and development that the reform embodied resonated with their hopes for Mexico, and, although most teachers argued that they had not participated in the development of the reform, they perceived space for participation in the translation of the reform to their classrooms. As such, they argued that they could make the reform more contextually relevant.

However, contrary to the Durango state scale, about one-third of the teachers interviewed were less positive about CBE. They expressed that their voices had not been included, and that instead the dominant actors and influences in the competency reform had been international and national organizations. Therefore, they considered the reform to be irrelevant for the Durango context. The following quotes clearly illustrate this sentiment:

> I do not think they have taken us into account, they did not listen to us. I think those who wrote the reform are sitting behind a desk, they do not see the needs of this community. I wished the people who designed this reform could come and have a look at these communities. (I-SC33, Mezquital, 31 May 2013)
>
> They never asked me if I wanted a reform. Mexico looks at other country were the education system works, and they appropriate it and adopt it in Mexico. As if you buy a dress and it is too big and you adjust it so it fit's you well. But it is not a Mexican reform, it is a reform that comes from Chile, or Japan, I do not know where. (GI-SC2, El Oro, 7 February 2013)

A very small group of the teachers in Durango rejected CBE, on the basis of the same critical discourse as the dissident teachers' union CNTE. These teachers argued that CBE favoured a set of imposed narrow work skills, favoured competition among students, was irrelevant for Mexico, and was part of a neoliberal policy package. It clashed with their ideas about a socialist Mexico.

By contrast, in Michoacan, about half of the teachers interviewed adopted a similar critical discourse of CBE as the dissident teachers' union CNTE. Thus, these teachers perceived competencies negatively. The following quote from a rural teacher illustrates how CBE clashed with these teachers' socio-economic imaginaries:

Fundamental to our resistance is the idea: what country do we want? So, it is not just about education, it is about deciding where we want to go as a country. (I-SC10, Morelia, 9 May 2013)

A second group of Michoacan teachers (which was also very numerous) similarly believed the reform did not arise from the needs of Mexicans. However, they argued that there was space for them to adapt the reform to their context of practice, and make the reform more participatory as such. For example, one head teacher argued that

I cannot change the expected learning goals but the flexibility in the style of teaching. If they say: do twenty activities, maybe I can do five or ten, that's where the flexibility is. (I-SC11, Morelia, 9 June 2014)

A third group of teachers (the smallest group) interpreted CBE more positively, in ways that were more aligned with the mainstream discourse that could be found within the teachers' union SNTE and national MoE.

The different interpretations of CBE by teachers also led to different processes of adoption, rejection and enactment of the reform at the school level. For example, whereas the curricular reform was claimed to be rejected by the dissident teachers' union CNTE at the Michoacan state, the influence of these key interpreters at the state scale was limited at the school level, and many teachers expressed that they had to teach something in their classrooms. They explained that although they politically and discursively rejected CBE, most teachers were in fact working with the textbooks of the new reform.

Another example shows how the interpretation of CBE by teachers in their schools was shaped by education actors at the national and state scales. In Michoacan, those teachers who wanted to adopt the reform worked within a context that was not supportive of the reform, and they experienced a lack of information about CBE and how to enact this in practice. In Durango, despite the political and discursive support at the state scale, teachers sometimes experienced that this remained at the level of talk, and that they did not actually receive much practical support. Teachers were caught within this lack of information, and they had to find creative ways to enact the reform on their own, for example by acquiring additional literature about competences.

The research also revealed how within this scarcity of information, teachers between and within both states enacted the development of similar knowledge outcomes differently. One way in which the diversity of interpretations was evidenced was by the different ways in which teachers used different teaching techniques to develop the same knowledge goals (as stated in the curricular texts), for example relating to the Mexican Independence. A teacher in a rural indigenous school explained:

When we look at the Independence, I do not dictate stories, or give them questionnaire, because I feel like that it does not stick, they confuse the Revolution with Independence. As you can see in my planning I now work with 'staging'.[5] So I say: 'I was Morelos and I did this and that' and then the children remember that Morelos is the one with the head band, Hidalgo is the bald one. This is what putting knowledge in practice means. (I-SC1, Zitacuaro, 2 May 2013)

This teacher thus tried to develop students' knowledge of the Mexican Independence by 'acting out' the information and exercises from the textbooks in a narrative way. In contrast, another teacher from an urban school enacted the goal to develop knowledge of the independence by having her students make classroom presentations. Thus, in the processes of the re-contextualization of the competency-based curricular reform, teachers' personal teaching styles and preferences, but also their knowledge of pedagogy and didactics, training, and dedication, affected the ways in which they interpreted and enacted the reform at the school scale. This further explains the heterogeneous ways in which the competencies that were expected by the reform were developed.

Teachers' local interpretations of CBE were also shaped by other policies that were part of its policy ensemble. For example, although the reform texts emphasized the importance of the development of intercultural and gender competencies, these transversal skills were not measured by the yearly standardized evaluation ENLACE. Teachers argued that as much of their time was spent in preparing their students for this exam, this implied the enactment of a narrow version of CBE at the school scale.

The ways in which teachers were able to develop competencies were furthermore shaped differently between contexts in which teachers had access to education materials, education infrastructure (electricity, internet) or teacher training, a difference mainly seen between rural and urban areas. For example, in the light of global advances in ICT (see Chapter 1, this volume), central to the reform was the development of ICT skills, for which schools and teachers were required to use audiovisual and multimedia materials and the internet. However, for those schools without access to the internet, which were mainly located in rural and peri-urban areas, the development of ICT skills was complicated, as the following quote illustrates:

The textbook refers to a web page, but we barely have television, let alone Internet. (I-SC1, Zitacuaro, 2 May 2013)

Another rural teacher in the north of Durango explains how his ability to develop English-language competencies was constrained by his material context:

We are doing an English project, we've got the material, the yellow books, the ones you see over there, but they come with a cd and well ... there's no electricity, so how do we work with them? (GI-SC3, El Oro, 7 February 2013)

The competency-based curriculum also required teachers to develop students' presentation skills. However, the enactment of this competency was shaped differently in contexts where teachers had access to projectors, compared to contexts where they did not have access. For example, one teacher in a rural bilingual school enacted the development of presentation skills by having his students recite from their textbooks, whereas another teacher in an urban school stimulated the use of the online programme Prezi, computers and projectors.

Together, these examples suggest that in addition to the different re-contextualization of the reform *between* the states the reform also re-contextualized differently in rural and urban locations *within* the states.

Conclusion

This chapter has analysed the politics of the re-contextualization of CBE as a GEP idea, at the Mexican national, state and school scales, and in different socio-economic and political contexts. The chapter has argued that in the case of the curricular reform of primary education, CBE can be interpreted as a floating signifier. This means that CBE has been simultaneously interpreted within contrasting discourses: a discourse, which envisions competencies as narrow skills and training for work backed up by a neoliberal imaginary, and a holistic discourse, which perceives competencies as being about the development of an integrated set of knowledge, skills and attitudes necessary for living and working in modern societies.

Moreover, the chapter has argued that the policy space that allows the circulation of either discourse is unevenly distributed across the scales and between the contexts of the policy trajectory of the 2008–2011 competency-based curricular reform of Mexican primary education. On the one hand, for education actors operating at the international scale, the Mexican Ministry of Education at the national scale and the Durango state scale, and some groups of teachers in both Durango and Michoacan operating within neoliberal imaginaries, CBE meant 'the educational hope for Mexico'. On the other hand, actors operating at the Michoacan scale and groups of teachers in both Durango and Michoacan ascribed to a discourse of CBE as the 'Trojan horse of neoliberalism'. This interpretation of competencies is similar to that of groups of teachers and unions in for example Brazil and Chile, who equally argued that CBE would not improve education on the basis that it was a foreign and imposed policy idea (Bourgonje and Tromp 2011).

The chapter has also illuminated the politics of the re-contextualization of education policies as 'ideological work'. Key interpreters actively tried to define the meaning of the CBE floating signifier. For example, the national MoE did this by promoting the use of certain words that did not invoke the connotation of competition in the texts around the reform. By contrast, in the state of Michoacan the dissident union CNTE played the role of key interpreter on the basis of its dominant position in the state congress and ability to mobilize teachers. Critics of CBE were portrayed by the national MoE as uninformed and change-adverse people, which is a delegitimation strategy similar to that applied during the implementation of CBE in Turkey (Altinyelken 2012). This also illustrates how the power of different actors to shape the reform and promote their interests is constituted differently between the scales of the policy trajectory, as argued by Lingard et al. (2005, cited in Chapter 1, this volume).

The situation at the level of teachers was even more heterogeneous: contrary to the state government level, the reform was not interpreted positively by all teachers in Durango, nor was it interpreted negatively and rejected by all teachers in Michoacan. The interpretation of CBE was also influenced by actors operating at other scales. For example, whereas teachers found the space to reinterpret the meaning of CBE in their classrooms, Mexican national policy-makers had the power to define the meaning of CBE at a distance through the application of standardized competency-based tests. Research in other countries similarly shows how despite its holistic potential, CBE is too often interpreted in a narrow way, overly focusing on standardized exams (cf. Biemans et al. 2004; Dello-Iacovo 2009). Thus, the actor who could perform the role of key interpreter during the re-contextualization of CBE in the curricular reform was different across the scales and between the contexts. Such variation in roles was to a great extent related to actors' different positionalities.

The different interpretations had consequences for the enactment of the reform, which explains the heterogeneous trajectories that the global policy idea CBE took on in Mexico. Whereas the reform was supported at the state scale in Durango, by providing teachers with education and resources, it was resisted at the state scale in Michoacan, for example by preventing reformed textbooks to be distributed among teachers. Importantly, the chapter had also shown how CBE played out in practice was shaped by elements from their contexts, such as the resources that were available to enact the reform. Overall, the analysis of the messiness of the policy processes has illuminated the different trajectories CBE took on at subnational Mexican scales, which ultimately points to heterogeneous patterns of local meanings, adoptions, rejections and effects of GEP ideas. These research findings fit with similar studies which suggest that while we witness a global convergence of policy ideas, local contingencies shape a divergence of policy practices.

Questions for discussion

1 Why is the discourse of CBE expanding globally? What is its appeal for international and national education policy actors?

2 Who are the key policy actors that, usually operating at different scales, have defined the meaning of CBE in Mexico? Discuss some examples of their ideological work.

3 How do the contextual realities of classrooms (e.g. resources available) influence the enactment of CBE differently?

4 In your opinion, could CBE increase the quality of education?

Notes

1 That is, liberalization, privatization and deregulation, policies which are continued until today Arnaut and Giorguli (2010).

2 The CNTE is a teachers' movement within the Mexican national teachers' union SNTE. They draw on left-wing and Marxist imaginaries (throwing over state power) and imaginaries of popular democracy, and they challenge the power of the SNTE (Street 2003: 180).

3 The DeSeCo project aimed to specify the key competencies that all students, towards the end of basic education, should possess as a reference points for assessing and measuring the output of educational processes Rychen and Salganik (2001).

4 This, despite the fact that Durango was headed by the right-of-centre PRI, a political party different from the PAN that ruled the national scale in the beginning of the CBE reform.

5 *Escenificación.*

References

Altinyelken, H. K. (2012). 'A converging pedagogy in the developing world? Insights from Uganda and Turkey'. In A. Verger, M. Novelli and H. K. Altinyelken (Eds.), *Global education policy and international development: New agendas, issues and policies.* New York: Continuum.

Ananiadou, K. and Claro, M. (2009). '21st century skills and competences for new millennium learners in OECD countries', OECD Education Working Papers (41).

Anderson-Levitt, K. M. (2012). *Anthropologies of education: A global guide to ethnographic studies of learning and schooling*. New York and Oxford: Berghahn Books.

Appadurai, A. (1996). *Modernity at Large: Cultural dimensions of globalization*. Minneapolis: University of Minnesota.

Apple, M. W. (2008). 'Foreword'. In M. B. Weaver-Hightower (Ed.), *The politics of policy in boys' education: Getting boys right*. New York: Palgrave.

Argüelles, A. (2000). *Competency based education and training: A world perspective*. Mexico: Editorial Limusa.

Arnaut, A. and Giorguli, S. (2010). *Los grandes problemas de México. VII Educacion*. Mexico: El Colegio de México.

Ball, S. (1994). *Education reform: A critical and post-structural approach*. Buckingham: Open University Press.

Ball, S. (1998). 'Big Policies/Small World: An introduction to international perspectives in education policy'. *Comparative Education*, 34 (2), 119–130.

Biemans, H., Nieuwenhuis, L., Poell, R., Mulder, M. and Wesselink, R. (2004). 'Competence-based VET in the Netherlands: Background and pitfalls'. *Journal of Vocational Education and Training*, 56 (4), 523–538.

Bourgonje, P. and Tromp, R. (2011). *Quality educators: An international study of teacher competences and standards*. Brussels: Education International/Oxfam Novib.

Braun, A., Ball, S., Maguire, M. and Hoskins, K. (2011). 'Taking context seriously: Towards explaining policy enactments in the secondary school'. *Discourse: Studies in the Cultural Politics of Education*, 32 (4), 585–596.

Brown, C. A. (2015). *Globalization, international education policy and local policy formation: Voices from the developing world*. Dordrecht: Springer.

Buenfil-Burgos, R. N. (2000). 'Globalization, education and discourse political analysis: Ambiguity and accountability in research'. *International Journal of Qualitative Studies in Education*, 13 (1), 1–24.

Burbules, N. C. and Torres, C. A. (2000). *Globalization and education: Critical perspectives*. New York: Routledge.

Commission/EACEA/Eurydice, E. (2012). *Developing key competences at school in Europe: Challenges and opportunities for policy. Eurydice report*. Luxembourg: Publications Office of the European Union.

Cowen, R. (2009). 'The transfer, translation and transformation of educational processes: And their shape-shifting?'. *Comparative Education*, 45 (3), 315–327.

de Anda, M. L. (2011). 'Implementing competence frameworks in Mexico'. *Journal of Education and Work*, 24 (3–4), 375–391.

Dello-Iacovo, B. (2009). 'Curriculum reform and "Quality Education" in China: An overview'. *International Journal of Educational Development*, 29 (3), 241–249.

Diaz-Barriga, F. and Barrón M. C. (2014). 'Curricular changes in higher education in Mexico (2002–2012)'. *Journal of Curriculum and Teaching*, 3 (2), 58–68.

Esquivel Hernandez, G. (2015). *Extreme inequality in Mexico concentration of economic and political power*. Mexico City: Oxfam Mexico.

Farstad, H. (2004). 'Las competencias para la vida y sus repercusiones en la educación', 47ª reunión de la Conferencia Internacional de Educación de la UNESCO: Ginebra.

Gale, T. (1999). 'Policy trajectories: Treading the discursive path of policy analysis'. *Discourse: Studies in the Cultural Politics of Education*, 20 (3), 393–407.

Griffith, W. and Lim, H. (2014). 'Introduction to competency-based language teaching'. *MEXTESOL Journal*, 38 (2), 1–8.

IMF (2014). *World Economic Outlook Database*. Washington, DC.

Keating-Chetwynd, S. (2009). *How all teachers can support citizenship and human rights education: A framework for the development of competences*. Bruxelles: Conseil de l'Europe.

Kouwenhoven, G. W. (2003). *Designing for competence in Mozambique: Towards a competence-based curriculum for the Faculty of Education of the Eduardo Mondlane University*. Enschede: University of Twente.

Mausethagen, S. (2013). 'Governance through concepts: The OECD and the construction of "competence" in Norwegian education policy'. *Berkeley Review of Education*, 4 (1), 161–181.

Miranda López, F. (2004). 'La reforma de la política educativa: gestión y competencia institucional frente a la tradición corporativa', *Sociológica*, 19 (54), 77–123.

Navarro Gallegos, C. (2009). 'La Alianza por la Calidad de la Educación: pacto regresivo y cupular del modelo educativo neoliberal'. *El Cotidiano*, 24 (154), 25–37.

Navarro Gallegos, C. (2011). *El secuestro de la educación: el sexenio educativo de Elba Esther Gordillo y Felipe Calderón*. Mexico: La Jornada Ediciones.

Ngok, K. and Chan, C. K. (2015). *China's social policy: Transformation and challenges*. London: Routledge.

OECD (2005). *The definition and selection of key competencies: Executive summary*. Paris: OECD.

Opertti, R. and Murueta, M. C. (2010). *Herramientas de Formación para el Desarrollo Curricular. Módulo sobre Enfoques Curriculares basados en Competencias*. UNESCO/OIE.

Ornelas, C. (2004). 'The politics of privatisation, decentralisation and education reform in Mexico'. *International Review of Education*, 50 (3/4), 397–418.

Ornelas, C. (2008a). 'El SNTE, Elba Esther Gordillo y el gobierno de Calderón'. *RMIE Revista mexicana de investigacion educativa*, 13 (37), 445–469.

Ornelas, C. (2008b). *Política, poder y pupitres Crítica al nuevo federalismo educativo*. México: Siglo XXI.

Power, S., Whitty, G., Gewirtz, S., Halpin, D. and Dickson, M. (2004). 'Paving a "third way"? A policy trajectory analysis of education action zones'. *Research Papers in Education*, 19 (4), 453–475.

Quezada Ortega, M. (2001). 'Política educativa y reforma curricular en la escuela primaria: las lecciones de 1993'. *Tiempo de Educar*, 3 (6), 98–127.

Rear, D. and Jones, A. (2013). 'Discursive struggle and contested signifiers in the arenas of education policy and work skills in Japan', *Critical Policy Studies*, 7 (4), 375–394.

Reyes, R. and Pech Campos, S. J. (2007). 'Preocupación de los Profesores ante la Reforma Integral de la Educación Secundaria en México'. *REICE. Revista Electrónica Iberoamericana sobre Calidad, Eficacia y Cambio en Educación*, 5 (3), 173–189.

Rizvi, F. (2006). 'Imagination and the globalisation of educational policy research'. *Globalisation, Societies and Education*, 4 (2), 193–205.

Rothman, S. and Nugroho, D. (2010). *Evaluación de la Reforma Curricular de Educación Secundaria 2006 en México. Reporte Final*: El Consejo Australiano para la Investigación Educativa.

Rychen, D. S. and Salganik, L. H. (2001). *Defining and selecting key competencies*. Ashland: Hogrefe & Huber Publishers.

SEP (2004). *Programa de Educación Preescolar 2004*. México, DF: Secretaría de Educación Pública.

SEP (2007). *Programa Sectorial de Educación 2007–2012*. Mexico, DF: Secretaría de Educación Pública.

SEP (2008). *Educación Básica. Primaria. Plan de estudios 2009. Etapa de prueba*. México, DF: Secretaría de Educación Pública.

SEP (2011). *Plan de estudios 2011. Educación Básica*. México, DF: Secretaría de Educación Pública.

Smith, J. and Patterson, F. (1998), 'Positively bilingual: Classroom strategies to promote the achievement of bilingual learners'. *Nottingham, England: Nottingham Education Authority*.

Steiner-Khamsi, G. (2012). 'The global/local nexus in comparative policy studies: Analysing the triple bonus system in Mongolia over time'. *Comparative Education*, 48 (4), 455–471.

Street, S. (2003). 'Teachers' work revisited. Mexican teachers' struggle for democracy and the anti-neoliberal alternative'. In S. Ball, G. E. Fischman and S. Gvirtz (Eds.), *Crisis and hope. The educational hopscotch of Latin America*. New York: RoutledgeFalmer.

Tromp, R. (2016). 'The Politics of Competencies. A policy trajectory study of the re-contextualisation of the 2009–2011 competency-based curricular reform of Mexican primary education', PhD thesis, University of East Anglia Norwich.

Urciuoli, B. (2008). 'Skills and selves in the new workplace'. *American Ethnologist*, 35 (2), 211–228.

Verger, A., Novelli, M. and Altinyelken, H. K. (2012). *Global Education Policy and International Development: An Introductory Framework*. London: Bloomsbury Academic.

Vidovich, L. (1997). 'A "Quality" Policy Trajectory: From Global Homogenisation to Localised Differentiation', Australian Association for Research in Education Conference: Brisbane.

Vidovich, L. and Sheng, Y. M. (2007). 'The "Global Schoolhouse": A cautious confluence of privatization and internationalisation policies in Singaporean education', Refereed paper presented at the Australian Association for Research in Education conference: Fremantle.

Further reading

Ball, S., Maguire, M. and Braun, A. (2012). *How schools do policy: Policy enactments in secondary schools*. London: Routledge.

Buenfil-Burgos, R. N. (2000). 'Globalization, education and discourse political analysis: Ambiguity and accountability in research'. *International Journal of Qualitative Studies in Education*, 13 (1), 1–24.

Rizvi, F. (2006). 'Imagination and the globalization of educational policy research', *Globalization, Societies and Education*, 4 (2), 193–205.

9

The 2030 Global Education Agenda and the SDGs: Process, Policy and Prospects

Yusuf Sayed and Rashid Ahmed
with Rada Mogliacci

Chapter Outline

This is a revised version of a paper by Sayed, Y. and Ahmed, R (2015) 'Education quality, and teaching and learning in the post-2015 education agenda'. *International Journal of Educational Development (IJED)*, 40, 330–338.

Introduction

A new global development framework encompassing new goals, targets and indicators including for education were adopted in September 2015 at the United Nation General Assembly meeting (UN 2015). This formally marked the ending of the Millennium Development Goals (MDGs) and the Education for all Goals (EFA) adopted in 2000, which has cast its long shadow on research, policy and practice including how and for what aid monies were disbursed and what the academic and research agenda was. The Sustainable Development Goals (SDGs) agreed to in September 2015 set the scene for arguably a renewed and ambitious development framework in a global context of widening inequalities within and between countries, global economic crises, conflict and climate change. It lays out a foundation for an ambitious plan to eradicate poverty, promote social and economic inclusion, tackle climate change, promote equity and provide access to quality education encompassing both the Global North and the Global South.

Several texts in particular mark the shape of the global education and development relationship in general and the education agenda in particular. In this chapter, we provide an analysis of some of these documents by exploring the processes, participation and contents of these texts, examining how the education agenda has evolved, how quality is conceptualized and the location of teachers in the new agenda. Of these the texts listed below are the focus of this chapter:

- UNESCO and UNICEF (2013) *Making Education A Priority In The Post-2015 Development Agenda: Report of the Global Thematic Consultation on Education in the Post-2015 Development Agenda*. The World We Want. (61 pages)

- UNESCO (2014c) *Position Paper on Education Post-2015*. ED-14/EFA/POST-2015/1. (12 pages) and UNESCO (2014a) *GEM Final Statement and The Muscat Agreement*, ED-14/EFA/ME/3. (4 pages)

- WEF (2015) Education 2030, *Incheon Declaration and Framework for Action: Towards inclusive and equitable quality education and lifelong learning for all*. (51 pages)

- UN (2015) *Transforming Our World: The 2030 Agenda for Sustainable Development*, sustainabledevelopment.un.org A/RES/70/1. (41 pages).

Taken together these documents raise some of the key issues to be addressed in the 2030 education agenda.

In undertaking this analysis of policy texts, we conceive of policy as referring to stated intentions and providing a normative framework for conception of what the global world and national states should aspire to and what is valued. Policy formation and implementation is therefore not a neutral process but is understood as the authoritative allocation of values. Rizvi (2006) argues that policies have real effects as they enable particular practices through seeking to secure legitimacy. In so doing they enable people at all levels to develop a shared understanding of the identified problems which policies are meant to 'solve'.

Policies transcend national boundaries leading various authors such as Ball (2013); Verger et al. (2012); Lingard and Rawolle (2011); and Lingard, Rawolle and Taylor (2005) to talk about global education policy by which is meant policies which operate at the supranational level and which shape what nation states are able to do. Ball (2013, pp. 114–115) describes this as a process of 'policy transfer, policy colonisation and policy convergence' whereby 'through the writing of policy, policy consultancy and recommendations, policy influence, the selling of management and improvement products, and the growth and spread of multinational service providers with standardised methods and contents' a global education discourse is constituted which reflects the neoliberal hegemony in education. A globalized education policy discourse results in a 'rescaling of politics' whereby political authority is orientated 'outward toward supranational entities and inward toward subnational groups' (Lingard and Rawolle 2011, p. 490). The manifestation of this global education policy is described by Verger et al. (2012, p. 3) as ideas and examples such as '[C]hild-centred pedagogies, school-based management, teachers' accountability' (p. 3), which set the parameters for the global education agenda. In this chapter, the 2030 SDGs generally, and the education goal and targets in particular, are conceptualized as elements of the Global Education Policy which seeks to create a convergence of ideas and practices about what is valued and desirable in education. This approach frames the analysis of the specific policy texts in relation to the 2030 agenda in this chapter.

The post-2015 education and development route map: Consultation and ownership of the process

The post-2015 education and development discussion that led to the SDGs was an intense and wide-ranging process. The debate that preceded the adoption of the SDGs was intense and marked by a flurry of policy texts, think pieces, blogs and opinion surveys and galvanized by many interest groups with a stake in setting the agenda, including non-governmental organizations

(NGOs), civil society actors, consultancy firms, academics and vested interest groups. Unlike the generation of MDGs and the EFA goals in 2000, this process was by all account, far more extensive, far more inclusive, and far more transparent. It involved several multiple and interrelated processes, and four main processes are described.

The first involves the United Nations (UN) High-Level Panel (HLP). This panel was initiated by UN Secretary General, Ban Ki-moon, and consisted of twenty-seven eminent persons whose task was to make recommendations for the development of the post-2015 agenda. At the 2010 MDG Summit, UN member states stipulated inclusive and open consultations that brought together representatives of civil, private and research organizations from all the regions. The Secretary General's HLP of Eminent Persons on the Post-2015 Development Agenda entailed dialogue with researchers from various disciplines, 5,000 civil society organizations, and 250 chief executive officers of various corporations. Consultations took place during the panel meetings in New York, London, Monrovia and Bali (HLP 2013). The panel produced a report entitled, *A New Global Partnership: Eradicate Poverty and Transform Economies through Sustainable Development* (2013).

The second set of consultations was led by the United Nations Development Group (UNDG), chaired by the United Nations Development Programme (UNDP), leading a 'global conversation' on post-2015 including about 100 national consultations and 11 global thematic consultations as well as online and targeted consultations. The overall global thematic consultation on education was co-led by the United Nations International Children's Emergency Fund (UNICEF) and the United Nations Educational, Scientific and Cultural Organization (UNESCO), with support from the Government of Canada, the Government of Germany and the Government of the Republic of Senegal. The UNDG as noted above released the report of its consultations entitled, *A Million Voices: The World We Want: A Sustainable Future with Dignity for All* (UNDG 2013).

The third set of consultations and which specifically focused on the education agenda in relation to the EFA goals were directly led by the UNESCO in consultation with its member states, UNESCO National Commissions and stakeholder groups. There were several conversations about the post-2015 education agenda and EFA, including the *UNESCO Position Paper on Education Post-2015* (UNESCO 2014c) and the *UNESCO Muscat Global Education Meeting (GEM) agreement* (UNESCO 2014a). The UNESCO consultations as well as the discussions under the umbrella of the UNDG resulted in the World Education Forum (WEF) held in South Korea in Incheon, at which the near-final set of education goals and targets were agreed as well as the Framework of Action (WEF 2015) which represents the education roadmap for the 2030 SDGs.

The fourth process includes the work of the Open Working Group on Sustainable Development, which started officially at the Rio + 20 conference in 2012 and released its *Outcomes Document* in July 2014 (UN 2014) (http://sustainabledevelopment.un.org/owg.html). The same group released a draft of the *Proposed Goals and Targets on Sustainable Development* (http://sustainabledevelopment.un.org/content/documents/4523zerodraft.pdf).[1]

Collectively these processes led to the final SDG report adopted by the UNGA in September 2015.

Table 9.1 summarizes the consultation processes as represented in the official texts.

Table 9.1 Participation process in developing the agenda

Report	Participation process as described in the report
High-Level Panel	1) *The United Nations, as directed by the Secretary-General in our terms of reference. This includes national and global thematic consultations under the aegis of the United Nations Development Group (UNDG), regional consultations undertaken by the Regional Commissions, consultations with businesses around the world under the guidance of the UN Global Compact, and the views of the scientific and academic community as conveyed through the Sustainable Development Solutions Network.*
2) Education Thematic Consultations	3) *Global meeting of the thematic consultation; UN member states briefing; EFA regional meetings (Arab, Africa, Latin American Caribbean Region, Asia and Pacific Region); EFA Side meeting; Collective consultation of NGOs on EFA; Consultation with the private sector and donor agencies Thematic e-discussions moderated by education experts; Ongoing dialogue on education and a global outreach using social media platforms such as Twitter and Facebook, the World We Want 2015 platform*
4) UNESCO Position Paper and UNESCO MUSCAT Gem Document	5) *Ministers, heads of delegations, leading officials of multilateral and bilateral organizations, and senior representatives of civil society and private sector organizations*

Report	Participation process as described in the report
6) WEF (Incheon)Document plus Framework for Action	7) *1,600 participants from 160 countries, including over 120 Ministers, heads and members of delegations, heads of agencies and officials of multilateral and bilateral organizations, and representatives of civil society, the teaching profession, youth and the private sector*
8) SDG (Final Published Document)	9) *"Civil society and other stakeholders around the world, which paid particular attention to the voices of the poorest and most vulnerable. This consultation included valuable work done by the General Assembly Open Working Group on SDGs and by the United Nations, whose Secretary General provided a synthesis report in December 2014"*

As is clear, even for these, selected process there has been extensive engagement with the post-2015 development and education agenda. Across all the reports and public discussions on the post-2015 agenda there was agreement that education is important, that education should be core to any future development framework and that education quality is central to education change and transformation. They also argue, with different degrees of emphasis, for a more expansive view of education beyond providing basic literacy and numeracy including access to secondary, ECCE and higher education. While the formulations of goals in the various documents vary slightly,[2] the overarching goal 'Equitable and Quality Lifelong Learning for All', which emerges from the UNESCO and UNICEF education thematic consultations has received wide consensus and captures the essence of the conversation (UNESCO and UNICEF 2013).[3] The importance of education is underscored by the online My World survey, where the majority of people voted for a good education as one of the most important aspirations for a post-2015 future (My World 2013).

While the consultations were wide ranging and extensive, there are several aspects of the processes of participation in the development of the new global framework which warrant attention. First, it was not always clear how widespread these consultations really are. In their analysis of the consultation process thus far, King and Palmer (2013b) argue that it is largely driven by powerful Northern actors and represents the Northern voice. They question whether the global agenda is based on equal global participation. They point to the very limited interest expressed by many countries in the Global South, including larger countries like China and Brazil. They suggest that even Southern consultations can often be Northern-led and that the primary interest group may be stakeholders connected to overseas financial aid.

Second, participation is not simply about greater involvement by the Global South, but also which Southern voices are heard. While there are certainly structural limitations to how extensive the consultations can be, it is crucial to foreground whether the global agenda is 'for' rather than 'with' the marginalized. Even the consultations from the Global South represent a particular 'privileged' constituency already well resourced and connected to a global policy community. In this regard as well, all these processes relied on the extensive use of social media which enabled many more voices to be heard. The leveraging of social media as, for example, in the online voting reflected the widespread adoption of new technologies of consultations which were in their nascent stages in 2000. Yet, like other forms of consultations, they reflected divisions between those that were able to access them and those unable to do so as discussed later.

Third, participation is intimately connected to accountability. The symbolic power of global education discourse to mobilize constituencies for a future common agenda is unlikely to be realized if the uneven processes of participation also reflects a lack of ownership and accountability. Accountability for and ownership of the SDGs and the associated education agenda is a key concern of the new global framework. Groups not substantially involved in policy-making, who do not feel ownership of the defined goals, may comply formally to access donor funds or attempt to demonstrate the meeting of targets without investing efforts to transform all the education processes the goals imply. The uneven processes of participation above may be pointing to Northern-led or particular privileged constituencies dominance. There is therefore unlikely in this scenario to be truly global ownership of the 2030 agenda, and, more importantly, the new education agenda may not accurately reflect the concerns of the most marginalized.

The unfinished agenda: A reaction to the MDG and EFA frameworks of 2000

The adoption of the MDGs and the EFA goals in 2000 marked arguably a significant turning point in international education and development. It set a new regime of goals, target and indicators which galvanized political will and financial support for the attainment of agreed goals. Vandemoortele persuasively describes the strengths of the MDG framework as follows:

Nevertheless, it can be argued that the impact of the MDGs has been positive. It has mostly been in terms of mobilizing stakeholders and informing the public about human development, broadly defined. Many acronyms see the light of day but not all stay around. The MDGs have been an exception.

Their power stems from a combination of three factors: (i) the charm of simplicity; (ii) their integrated and synergetic nature; and (iii) their measurability. They express key outcomes for human well-being in health, education, nutrition, water and sanitation, and gender equality. By focusing on outcomes, they are intuitively easy to understand. Sectoral specialists and development practitioners, however, tend to focus on the complexity of human development. (Vandemoortele 2011, p. 7)

Vandermoortele's (2011) argument succeeds in capturing the impact of these frameworks. As a global discourse of progress, the MDGS and the EFA goals 'provided strategic direction to educational planning and budgeting; are important to monitor progress; and have encouraged focused and sustained support from development partners' (UNESCO and UNICEF 2013, p. 7). Clearly, to an extent, they succeed in driving forward development programmes and to a large extent stimulated development discourse to focus on poverty (Fukuda-Parr 2016). Crucially the setting of targets and goals reflected the emergence of a social compact between all actors, particularly international donors and financing agencies, national governments and civil society.

Notwithstanding their impact, there are several salient criticisms which point to inherent conceptual and practical limitations of this ambitious agenda. First, conceptually the agenda has a narrow conception of poverty focusing mainly on the reduction of poverty (Carant 2016; Fukuda-Parr 2016). Such an approach fails to see poverty in relation to inequality, as poverty as Tawney (1979) argues, is simply the unacceptable face of inequality. A more comprehensive and relational account would account for the dynamics of inequality between and within countries and tackle poverty as part of a comprehensive approach to tackling and eroding inequality. In this respect, the HLP panel also notes that the MDGs fail in 'reaching the very poorest and most excluded people' (HLP 2013, p. 5). In not foregrounding inequality, the agenda then focused mainly on countries in the Global South. As such it was perceived as an agenda that was not applicable to the countries in the Global North. Such an approach tended to also downplay the dynamics of dependency between the Global North and Global South.

Second, the 2000 MDG and EFA agenda whilst expansive was framed in a context when two dimensions of the global order, whilst present, were not sufficiently accommodated. In particular, the issue of the environment and countries and regions in conflict were remarkably absent. The HLP panel notes, 'They were silent on the devastating effects of conflict and violence on development.' It is partly these aspects which framed the new development vision (HLP 2013, p. 5).

Third, in education in particular the goals were ineffectively narrowed to a focus on primary education and physical access. Whilst it is argued that the education agenda has commitments to quality in earlier global documents, the vision was reduced with the MDGs. Moreover, at Dakar, no clear and measurable targets for quality were set. Whether the lack of targets in past agreements is a result of policy omission or default, the consequence has been that the driver of the global agenda and the consequent policy attention and aid funding has been targeted to increasing physical access. A narrow vision of education access (at the expense of quality and ignoring inequality) framed the agenda (Unterhalter 2014). A narrow vision, it is argued, led to an approach which did not deal with education in a holistic and comprehensive manner privileging easy to reach and monitor goals such as increasing enrolment to primary schooling.

Fourth, it is argued that the simultaneous existence of both the education MDGs and EFA goals resulted in a dual education architecture with rival planning processes, rival organizational commitment and rival organizational processes. The result of this was increasing fragmentation, lack of coordination and undue parallel demands made on national government by international organizations. It can be argued that these two processes rather than magnify the focus on education, may have potentially diluted the education agenda.

On balance, there was progress but in education, as Education Thematic Consultations noted, the MDG and EFA agenda remained unfinished and constitute 'unfinished business'. But a critical appraisal of the MDG agenda needs to be balanced by the caution of Vandemoortele (2011), who notes:

> The fundamental purpose of the MDGs is not for each and every country to meet the global targets, which would be utopian. Their ultimate aim is to help align national priorities with the MDG agenda so as to foster human well-being. Therefore, the intended users are primarily politicians, parliamentarians, preachers, teachers and journalists. It cannot be emphasized enough that development practitioners and policy makers do not need the MDGs to carry out their work. The MDGs have little to do with defining the nuts and bolts of macroeconomic or sectoral policies or with designing technical interventions. (Vandemoortele 2011, p. 7)

He cautions against reading the agenda with dual idolatry of as 'literalism and ideology'. By literalism he means that all work begins and ends with the MDGs arguing that

> if all aspects of development were to be included, the MDGs would become overloaded and incomprehensible to their primary users. While the literalists believe in the perfectibility of the MDGs, the reality is that their

success is due to their conciseness and measurability. This group refuses to accept that the MDGs can be used to make the case for their particular topic even if it is not mentioned specifically. (Vandemoortele 2011, p. 8)

He further argues against an ideology reading by which he means

that the MDGs specify outcomes without spelling out the process of achieving them. In this way, many have not only tried to misappropriate the global targets to gain support for their own development paradigm, they have also sanitized them by making the MDGs less offensive and more acceptable for the conventional view of development. The fact of the matter is that the MDGs were never meant to promote a certain development strategy. They focus on ends, not on means, on the destination and not on the journey. This distinction is important because all development is context-specific. (Vandemoortele 2011, p. 8)

Notwithstanding this persuasive defence, the reality is that the development framework, like any global set of goals, does promote a particular normative ideology of development. In the case of the MDGs this framework arguably promoted a conservative and narrow approach to poverty reduction failing to tackle inequality. The potential for a social justice framework and an alternative development vision and development strategies argued by Vandermoortele (2011) to be possible did not materialize. To characterize them as an unfinished agenda would therefore not be inaccurate.

A new development vision?

The new development framework is rooted in an assessment of the previous MDG approach as well as an outcome of the consultations processes as noted above. At its core is the idea of sustainable development captured in the notion of the four Ps: people, planet, partnership and peace (UN 2015). This notion succeeds in capturing a potentially broader development vision. At the heart of the SDGs is a focus on poverty and inequality. This is indeed a welcome break from the past as it situates a focus on tackling inequality as a core development priority. The SDG frameworks presents an expansive understanding of poverty that is linked to sustainable development and identifies it as a key global challenge:

Eradicating poverty in all its forms and dimensions, including extreme poverty, is the greatest global challenge and an indispensable requirement for sustainable development. (UN 2015, p. 6)

Similarly, the HLP (HLP 2013) notes that it is important to commit to 'Sustainable development integrating social, economic, and environmental dimensions in order to eradicate extreme poverty.' In both these frameworks, both a commitment to eliminating poverty and a more comprehensive conceptualization of poverty is present. Furthermore, the twin focus on eliminating poverty and reducing inequality provides a more sound conception of equity as noted above (Freistein and Mahlert 2016). However, whilst there is a strong commitment to eradicating poverty (Goal 1), a weaker commitment is made to inequality. The HLP goals do not have a specific goal on inequality and the SDG goal on inequality only mentions a reduction in inequality (Goal 10) with no specification about eliminating or even halving inequality.

Unlike the MDGs, the SDGs focus on sustainable development and inequality is intended to outline a development approach which is far more applicable to the Global North and the Global South. As such it significantly commits all countries and not just those classified as poor. This allows for an agenda which is far more encompassing and applicable to all contexts. In both documents, there is a strong focus on sustainable development as the overarching framework in which the development paradigm is expanded to understand the environment and its impact on living and vice versa. As such, economic growth, it is argued, cannot be at the expense of the environment. Additionally, it recognizes climate changes and its impact on humans as key features of the enhancing global context, a glaring absence in the previous MDGs.

As has been argued above, Table 9.2 reveals a far more extensive and ambitious development agenda. Of the two, the SDG agenda is more ambitious in scope than the goals articulated by the HLP in several areas. For example, the narrow focus on jobs and growth in the HLP is expanded as decent work and inclusive growth in the SDGs. The SDGs also bring into focus the need for peace which is not clear in the framing of the HLP goals. However, in spite of these differences both succeed in addressing some of the unfinished agenda from the past and a more holistic vision for the future.

Education as the heart of the new agenda

The documents being oriented towards education put the educational agenda in the centre of sustainable development. They all argue that education is closely tied to other aspects of the development agenda, such as inequalities, social well-being and sustainable society. Furthermore, some of the documents offer a far more comprehensive understanding of development by including the notion of a 'just' and 'inclusive' society. As Table 9.2 indicates, like the

Table 9.2 Main/overarching development goals

	Overarching Education Goals
Education Thematic Consultations	Education as a developmental priority connected to addressing inequalities and expanding sustainable development and promoting health and nutrition. pp. 13–14
UNESCO Position Paper	10) Education, as a key lever for development, is understood as a way of achieving social well- being, sustainable development and good governance. p. 1
11) UNESCO MUSCAT Gem Document	12) Education at the centre of global development agenda since 'it contributes to the reduction of inequalities and the eradication of poverty by bequeathing the conditions and generating the opportunities for just, inclusive and sustainable societies'. p. 2
13) WEF (Incheon) Document plus Framework for Action	14) 'Education is at the heart of the 2030 Agenda for Sustainable Development and essential for the success of all SDGs.' p. 6

more extensive and ambitious development agenda, the expanded version of education sets the parameters for a far more expansive education agenda. A comprehensive and holistic vision of education is positioned as a key lever for the 2030 agenda. Through an analysis of the overarching education goals, the evaluation of targets and teachers in the 2030, the sections that follow review both the extension of the previous education agenda, but also areas still requiring attention.

Unpacking the overarching education goal in the 2030 SDG agenda

While there is still debate about whether single or multiple goals are needed (UNESCO and UNICEF 2013), the advantage of a single overarching goal with an emphasis on quality is that it succeeds in framing the post-2015 education agenda as a 'quality' agenda. Unlike the previous EFA goals, which separated the access and quality agendas, a single goal suggests that there is only one united agenda. Furthermore, though quality was identified previously among the EFA goals, the absence of clear targets for quality in the EFA goals may have served to delegitimize the quality agenda. This 'quality turn' is of the most significant shifts in the new agenda. This section unpacks the notions of quality embedded within these documents and the extent to which the new education agenda succeeds in this 'quality turn'.

The formulation of the overarching goal to include the word *quality* for the post-2015 education framework is a significant achievement. It cements the quality turn and suggests that, in spite of the unfinished agenda, educational policy is not narrowly confined to physical access to schooling. It is not only an acknowledgement of some of the adverse consequences of the MDG access agenda, but also an opportunity to hold all stakeholders accountable to the quality agenda. While some argue that quality has long been part of the global agenda dating back to Jomtien and Dakar (King and Palmer 2013a), the driver of the global agenda and the consequent policy attention and aid funding has been targeted to increasing physical access. A single goal with quality at its heart affords an opportunity to correct the previous narrow focus of education reach.

Table 9.3 sets out the evolution of the overarching goals and the notion of quality remains central in these goals. The overarching goal specifies the notion of quality as 'equitable quality education' in the Position Paper on Education post-2015 (UNESCO 2014c) and as 'equitable and inclusive quality education' in the Muscat GEM agreement (UNESCO 2014a), as well as in SDG agenda (UN 2015). This is cemented by numerous references to equity in all the documents. The position paper explicitly acknowledges that 'A focus on equity is paramount and particular attention should be given to marginalised groups' (UNESCO 2014c, p. 3). Whether equity is positioned as a dimension of quality (Barrett et al. 2006; Sayed and Ahmed 2011), or outside a definition of quality, is less relevant at this point. What is crucial is that the inclusion of equity substantially expands the quality agenda and is consistent with broad conceptualizations of quality (cf. Tikly and Barrett 2009). The Muscat GEM agreement and SDG agenda extend this even further with the reference to 'inclusive'. Both formulations are similar to the UNESCO and UNICEF education thematic consultations where the overarching goal is formulated as 'Equitable, Quality Education and Lifelong Learning for All' (UNESCO & UNICEF 2013).

The terms 'inclusive', 'equitable' and 'lifelong learning' are significant in that they suggest a potentially broad conceptualization of quality. The reference to 'inclusive quality education' appears to be an attempt to emphasize quality as social justice. However, the use of inclusive quality education is somewhat ambiguous and contested, reflecting both a narrow (disability) and broader (all forms of exclusion) focus. While the term 'inclusive' may be ambiguous, the numerous references to equity clearly cement social justice as part of the education agenda. The conjoining of the words 'equity', 'inclusive' and 'for all' is a striking feature of the overarching goal. Clearly, they are not all necessary as equitable education is also inclusive and education for all by definition implies equity and inclusion. The repetition of the ideas contained in the goals is intended to signify a strong focus on equity as a significant departure from the previous global agenda.

The notion of lifelong learning is intended to signal a focus on education at all levels expressing a holistic understanding of education systems signalling a sharp break with the narrow focus on primary education in the MDG agenda (cf. Regmi 2015). This shift is significant for it indicates that secondary and higher education are as important as primary education. More importantly, it could also be understood as learning in multiple and diverse contexts, not necessarily restricted to secondary and tertiary education. For many countries in the Global South, the previous MDG agenda has inadvertently downplayed and marginalized the tertiary sector as well as created a context where many primary school leavers were unable to progress to secondary education. Moreover, secondary and post-secondary education is crucial to develop the skills and knowledge necessary for sustainable and inclusive equitable growth (UNESCO 2014a).

The notion of quality as articulated in the 2030 agenda is suggestive of, on the one hand, a focus on learning and specifically literacy and numeracy. Thus, education quality is positioned as an effort to improve learning and the experiences of students. On the other hand, by seeking to conjoin it with social justice, it positions education quality as a concept which if it is to be achieved must bridge inequities in society in respect of learning attainment. As such, a public education system cannot be characterized as possessing quality if it is not also equitable. This would discount systems of education quality such as elite private schools which may attain high levels of learning attainment of students but which exclude the majority. While this foregrounding of, and extension of the quality agenda is crucial, like the previous education agenda, it is the operationalization and implementation of the agenda that will determine the extent to which this agenda is realized. The subsequent section reviews how the targets operationalize the education agenda.

Table 9.3 Evolution of overarching goals

	Overarching Education Goals
High-Level Panel	15) Provide Quality Education and Lifelong Learning p. 36
16) Education Thematic Consultations	17) Equitable, Quality Education and Lifelong Learning for All p. 39
18) UNESCO Position Paper	19) Ensure equitable quality education and lifelong learning for all by 2030 p. 4

	Overarching Education Goals
20) UNESCO MUSCAT Gem Document	21) Ensure equitable and inclusive quality education and lifelong learning for all by 2030 p. 3
22) WEF (Incheon) Document plus Framework for Action	23) Ensure inclusive and equitable quality education and promote lifelong learning opportunities for all p. 8
24) SDG (Final Published Document)	Ensure inclusive and equitable quality education and promote lifelong learning opportunities for all p. 18

Unpacking the education targets in the 2030 SDG agenda

The education targets reflected much debate and argument in the operationalization of an agenda which has quality at its heart and which sought to develop a comprehensive and holistic education framework (Sayed and Ahmed 2011). Notwithstanding the debate about the nature of the targets in different processes, they signal a commitment to four agreed priorities which have been somewhat delegitimated in the previous agenda. First, the targets signal a strong commitment to ECCE in the form of guaranteeing learners access to pre-primary education.

Second, the agenda was expanded to include access to and completion of both primary and secondary education linked to education quality which was operationalized as 'measurable and recognizable learning outcomes'. The commitment to the completion of a full cycle of education marks a significant change in the agenda away from a narrow focus on primary education recognizing that secondary education is crucial to developing cognitive and affective skills crucial to economic growth and tolerant societies.

Third, gender equality as a core education and development priority is captured in the targets. In Target 2 of the UNESCO Muscat GEM agreement and in Targets 4.3 and 4.5, access to girls and women to all levels of education and the elimination of gender disparities in education is clearly expressed. The two targets of the SDG agenda relating to gender equity focus on two different aspects. Target 4.3 speaks to equal access (gender parity), whilst Target 4.5 more expansively argues for the elimination of gender disparities as well as eliminating inequities faced by persons who are disabled, indigenous and in vulnerable situations (SDG UN 2014).

Notwithstanding a more extensive and comprehensive review of the targets, certain observations can still be gleaned. As argued above, consistent with the broader conceptualization of quality in the texts, the targets represent an extension of the previous agenda. There is a greater educational reach, a recognition of multiple learning outcomes, a foregrounding of gender equality, a clear link to just, inclusive and sustainable societies and a recognition of the teachers in the success of the new agenda. While these are significant gains, several areas of concern remain. First, like the previous agenda, there is a concomitant narrowing of the quality agenda as well. Literacy and numeracy are elevated at the expense of a more comprehensive focus on affective outcomes such as peace, consequently reducing the more comprehensive quality vision (Schweisfurth 2015). Second, in spite of the greater ambition certain contradictions and gaps remain. For example, a more substantive commitment to early years care and education is lacking in the specification of the target. Similarly, the more ambitious elimination of gender disparities also implies equal access to education. Further, whilst the agenda may seek to link education quality, equity and inclusion it fails to, in policy terms, explain the trades-offs and compromises which are likely to result. For example, focusing on the marginalized requires more targeted interventions and funding which may require reducing support for the wealthy (Sayed 2016). Finally, a significant concern, discussed below, is the extent to which there is very little space for teachers in the final version of the agenda.

Teachers and the 2030 agenda

Teachers feature prominently in the new education agenda and the Mckinsey report (2007) goes as far as to state that a quality of an education system cannot exceed the quality of its teachers. Given then that some accord central importance to teachers to what extent do the goals and targets reflect this. The focus on quality in 2030 agenda rightly emphasizes a concern with teachers, teaching and teacher education.[4] Moreover, the specification in HLP of a 'sufficient number' starts to indicate that learning outcomes are also associated with teacher–pupil ratios and provides an opportunity to unpack the target in this direction. It is also quite clear in all the texts that it is also the type of teaching and the learning environments that also matter. While terms like 'well trained', 'qualified' and 'motivated' can be contested and need to be operationalized, they all indicate that it is both getting the teacher into the classroom and what the teacher does that matter. The strength of the ETC and UNESCO formulations as well as the extent to which they indicate that the context of teaching and learning is central. The UNESCO formulation in particular unpacks several factors like 'safety' and mother tongue medium of instruction that influence learning outcomes. While these aspects do represent advance on the quality agenda several, concerns remain.

Of particular concern in the discourse of teachers in the post-2015 agenda is that a vast and broad range of expectations and knowledge are then expected of teachers – life skills, citizenship and peace education, moral and ethical education, child protection, human rights, skills for sustainable livelihoods, challenging gender inequalities, practising learner-centredness (Sinclair 2002; Barrett et al. 2015) to name but a few. While these are important concerns, such an ambitious variety of responsibilities runs the real risk of overstating the potential of schools and their teachers to effect broad social transformations. In this context, it is sobering to note that, in a survey of ten countries, only 23 per cent of teachers thought they had influence over policy and practice (UNESCO 2014b). Teacher agency, as envisaged in the post-2015 agenda, is not a realistic possibility nor is agency possible when faced with multiple and conflicting demands subject to narrow accountability measures. It is therefore necessary to balance teacher agency with appropriate training to equip teachers to fulfil new roles.

An important omission in the construction of the target is the lack of a robust focus on equity. The key issue is not that all learners should be taught by qualified, professionally trained, motivated and well-supported teachers, but how to get such teachers in hard-to-reach areas. In South Africa for example, the inequities in education and the existence of two systems of education (Badat and Sayed 2014) can partly be attributed to the fact that good teachers working in an enabling learning environment are clustered in the wealthier school sector which, when added to the cultural capital of learners, creates a double privilege (Sayed and Ahmed 2015). To overcome inequities in South Africa would require positive discrimination in favour of learners in disadvantaged contexts through the distribution and payment of teachers. Moreover, it is not clear why, if equity and social justice are key goals underpinning the teacher targets, more attention is not paid to attracting the best candidates to teach from diverse and under-represented groups, including female teachers, as the initial goals in the position paper suggested.

The inclusion of teachers in the post-2015 agenda will also require increased and more strategic investments in education. It will also require rethinking the macroeconomic models that structure teacher salaries in low-income countries (ActionAid 2007). This is why the targets on aid in earlier discussions of the agenda are welcomed, although this becomes muted in the HLP report and the final SDG document. Furthermore, an important slippage is that the unit of the aid target shifts from groups to countries in that the UNESCO position paper states ' prioritizing groups most in need' while the Muscat GEM agreement states 'prioritizing countries most in need'. Similarly, in the SDG

Table 9.4 Evolution of teacher target

HLP	ETC	UNESCO	SDG
The quality of education in all countries depends on having a sufficient number of motivated teachers, well trained and possessing strong subject-area knowledge.	Equitable lifelong education requires attention to enabling conditions – conducive learning environments with the proper and necessary infrastructure; the presence of sufficient numbers of trained and motivated teachers; and participatory governance structures that empower parents and local communities to be effectively involved in school decision-making	'(a) recruiting and retaining well-trained and motivated teachers who use inclusive, gender-responsive and participatory pedagogical approaches to ensure effective learning outcomes, (b) providing content that is relevant to all learners and to the context in which they live, (c) establishing learning environments that are safe, gender responsive, inclusive and conducive to learning, and encompass mother tongue-based multilingual education, (d) ensuring that learners reach sufficient levels of knowledge and competencies according to national standards at each level, (e) strengthening capacities for learners to be innovative and creative, and to assimilate change in their society and the workplace and over their lifespans, and (f) strengthening the ways education contributes to peace, responsible citizenship, sustainable development and intercultural dialogue' (UNESCO 2014c, p. 8). T Target 6: By 2030, all governments ensure that all learners are taught by qualified, professionally trained, motivated and well-supported teachers.	4.C By 2030, substantially increase the supply of qualified teachers, including through international cooperation for teacher training in developing countries, especially least-developed countries and small island developing states

agenda, the unit of aid target is reduced to 'developing countries, especially least developed countries and small island developing States' (UN 2015, p. 20). This slippage runs the risk of ignoring the fact that inequality is as much within as between countries; therefore, aid must target both countries and groups most in need. Finally, no mention is made of better pay for teachers, a priority in many countries with the biggest education challenges (UNESCO 2014b).

Conclusion

It has been argued that, partially in response to the previous agenda, the 2030 agenda represents a more expansive and ambitious agenda. However, as is clear from the preceding analysis, there are several aspects that warrant attention. First, whilst there is strong commitment to the SDG as evidenced in all countries in the UNGA agreeing to them, they are of course not legally binding. The key question is what are the incentives and leverage mechanisms to ensure that all countries do implement them. It is also crucial that, there needs to be global ownership rather than North-led ownership. Second, while the final SDG document does include commitments to funding, it remains to be seen whether this will be realized in practice. Some of the changes made over time also raise concern about the extent to which lesser importance is accorded to funding to achieve the ambitious agenda. More importantly, funding must be considered within current macro-economic models of austerity that constrain a more ambitious education agenda. Third, much of the achievement of the goals depends on political will and capacity amongst donor and national government. When the dust has settled, national governments in developing countries in 2015 are no different and donor agendas remain the same. The success of the agenda then is inextricably linked to shifts in political will, capacity and current agendas. Fourth, what gets measured gets done could arguably sum up much of the debate about the education SDG framework (Schweisfurth 2015). This is evident in the fact the education goal (Goal 4) of the SDGs is to be measured by 11 global indicators. In addition, as agreed at the WEF, forty-four thematic indicators are proposed for the education goal. In reality though, there are more than forty-four, as many includes multiple indicators. In this respect a key issue is the extent to which national governments have the data necessary for the various thematic and global indicators. Notwithstanding the data availability challenge, there is a real risk of confining the quality agenda to literacy and numeracy and what can be measured quantitatively. The risk is that this process in correctly trying to assess and monitor success, runs the risk of substantially reducing and even erasing an agenda that focuses on quality and equity. Finally, the acknowledgement of the importance of teachers in the new agenda must be matched by a substantive engagement of how and what is necessary for teachers and teaching to realize this agenda. The ambition of the education agenda is not aligned to the challenges and priorities of teachers and teacher education that mitigate against the success of the quality agenda. While normative international frameworks like the SDGs are effective in terms of their ability to create new policy discourses, which in turn open up space for actors to pursue their conflicting agendas in new ways, there is a real risk that the notion of education quality and the role of teachers in the new agenda may be so thinned out in practice, that a robust social justice–orientated approach to education is not possible.

Questions for discussion

1 Discuss the main shifts in the development frameworks from the MDGs to the SDGs.

2 What are the strengths and weaknesses of the education goals and targets in the SDG framework? To what extent do they address equity and quality?

3 Discuss the proposition that the new SDG framework is too ambitious and unlikely to be achieved by 2030.

4 What are some of the challenges to ensuring a supply of well-trained, motivated teachers with strong subject-area knowledge?

Notes

1 This chapter does not analyse, as indicated, all the different processes and reports. However, it is important to note that the OWG Outcomes Document includes a target for teachers which is by '2030 increase by x% the supply of qualified teachers, including through international cooperation for teacher training in developing countries, especially LDCs and SIDS'.

2 The different degrees of emphasis across the goals and targets are discussed below.

3 For example, the High-Level Panel Report formulates the overarching goal as '*Provide Quality Education And Lifelong Learning*' while the Open Working Group on Sustainable Development identified the overarching goal as '*Ensure inclusive and equitable quality education and promote life-long learning opportunities for all*'.

4 See Sayed and Ahmed (2015) for a more extensive discussion.

References

ActionAid (2007). 'Confronting the Contradictions The IMF, Wage Bill Caps and the Case for Teachers'. ActionAid. http://www.actionaid.org/sites/files/actionaid/aaconf_contradictions_final2.pdf.

ActionAid (2012). *Righting the MDGs: Contexts and opportunities for a Post-2015 development framework*. London: ActionAid.

Badat, S. and Sayed, Y. (2014). 'Post-1994 South African education: The challenge of social justice'. *The ANNALS of the American Academy of Political and Social Science* 652 (March), 127–148. doi:10.1177/0002716213511188.

Ball, S. J. (2012). *Global education Inc.: New policy networks and the neo-liberal imaginary*. Oxon: Routledge.

Ball, S. J. (2013). *Education, justice and democracy: The struggle over ignorance and opportunity* (A social state for 2015). London: Centre for Labour and Social Studies.

Barrett, Angeline M., Yusuf, S., Michele, S. and Leon, T. (2015). 'Learning, pedagogy and the post-2015 education and development agenda'. *International Journal of Educational Development*, 40, 231–236.

Barrett, Angeline M., Chawla-Duggan, R. K., Lowe, J., Nikel, J. and Ukpo, E. O. (2006). 'The Concept of Quality in Education – A Review of the "international" Literature on the Concept of Quality in Education'. *Bristol, EdQual*, EdQual Working Paper no. 2.

Brookings (2013). 'Toward Universal Learning: Recommendations from the Learning Metrics Task Force'. UNESCO Institute for Statistics; Centre for Universal Education at Brookings.

Carant, Jane Briant (2016). 'Unheard voices: A critical discourse analysis of the millennium development goals' evolution into the sustainable development goals'. *Third World Quarterly* 0 (0), 1–26. doi:10.1080/01436597.2016.1166944.

Commonwealth Ministerial Working Group (2012). *Commonwealth recommendations for the post-2015 development framework for education*. London: Commonwealth Secretariat.

Engelbrecht, P. and Green, L. (Eds.) (2001). *Promoting learner development: Preventing and working with barriers to learning*. Pretoria: Van Schaik Publishers.

Freistein, Katja and Bettina, M. (2016). 'The potential for tackling inequality in the sustainable development goals'. *Third World Quarterly*, 37 (12), 2139–2155. doi:10.1080/01436597.2016.1166945.

Fukuda-Parr, Sakiko (2016). 'From the millennium development goals to the sustainable development goals: Shifts in purpose, concept, and politics of global goal setting for development'. *Gender & Development*, 24 (1), 43–52. doi:10.1080/13552074.2016.1145895.

GCE (2014). *Equitable, inclusive & free: A collective vision for quality education beyond 2015*. Global Campaign for Education.

HLP (2013). *A new global partnership: Eradicate poverty and transform economies through sustainable development. The report of the high-level panel of eminent persons on the post-2015 development agenda*. New York: UN.

King, Kenneth and Palmer, Robert (2013a). 'Education and skills post-2015: What evidence, whose perspectives?' NORRAG.

King, Kenneth and Palmer, Robert (2013b). 'Post-2015 agendas: Northern tsunami, southern ripple? The case of education and skills'. *International Journal of Educational Development* 33 (5), 409–425. doi:10.1016/j.ijedudev.2013.06.001.

Lingard, B. and Rawolle, S. (2011). New scalar politics: Implications for education policy. *Comparative Education*, 47 (4), 489–502.

Lingard, B., Rawolle, S. and Taylor, S. (2005). Globalizing policy sociology in education: Working with Bourdieu. *Journal of Education Policy*, 20 (6), 759–777.

My World (2013). 'MY World. The United Nations Global Survey for a Better World. Results Report'. UN.

Regmi, Kapil Dev (2015). 'Can lifelong learning be the post-2015 agenda for the least developed countries?' *International Journal of Lifelong Education*, 34 (5), 551–568. doi:10.1080/02601370.2015.1070209.

Save the Children (2012). 'After the Millennium Development Goals: Setting Out the Options and Must Haves for a New Development Framework in 2015'. Save the Children.

Sayed, Y. (2016). 'The governance of public schooling in South Africa: Social solidarity for the public good vs. class interest?' *Transformation* (91).

Sayed, Yusuf and Soudien, C. (2003). '(Re)Framing education exclusion and inclusion discourses'. *IDS Bulletin*, 34 (1), 9–19. doi:10.1111/j.1759-5436.2003. tb00055.x.

Sayed, Yusuf and Ahmed, R. (2011). 'Education quality in post-apartheid South African policy: Balancing equity, diversity, rights and participation'. *Comparative Education*, 47 (1), 103–118. doi:10.1080/03050068.2011.541680.

Sayed, Yusuf and Ahmed, R. (2015). 'Education quality, and teaching and learning in the post-2015 education agenda'. *International Journal of Educational Development (IJED)*, 40, 330–338.

Schweisfurth, Michele (2015). 'Learner-centred pedagogy: Towards a post-2015 agenda for teaching and learning'. *International Journal of Educational Development*, 40 (January): 259–266. doi:10.1016/j.ijedudev.2014.10.011.

Sinclair, Margaret (2002). *Planning education in and after Emergencies*. Paris: UNESCO: International Institute for Educational Planning.

Tawney, R. H. (1979). *Equality*. 4. London: Allen & Unwin.

Tikly, Leon P. and Barrett A. M. (2009). 'Social Justice, Capabilities and the Quality of Education in Low Income Countries'. *EdQual, Bristol* Working Paper Series (September).

UN (2014). 'Open working group proposal for sustainable development goals'. UN.

UN (2015). 'Transforming our world: The 2030 agenda for sustainable development'. A/RES/70/1. UN.

UNDG (2013). 'A million voices: The world we want. A sustainable future with dignity for all'. UNDG.

UNESCO (n.d.). 'Education: Inclusion in education'. http://www.unesco.org/new/en/education/themes/strengthening-education-systems/inclusive-education/browse/4/.

UNESCO (2014a). '2014 GEM Final Statement: The Muscat Agreement'.

UNESCO (2014b). *EFA global monitoring report 2013/4 – Teaching and learning: Achieving quality for all*. Paris: UNESCO.

UNESCO (2014c). *Position paper on education post-2015*. ED-14/EFA/POST-2015/1. Paris: UNESCO.

UNESCO & UNICEF (2013). *Making education a priority in the Post-2015 development agenda. Report of the global thematic consultation on education in the post-2015 development agenda.* Paris: UNESCO & UNICEF.

Unterhalter, Elaine. (2014). Measuring education for the millennium development goals: Reflections on targets, indicators, and a post-2015 framework'. *Journal of Human Development and Capabilities* 15 (2–3), 176–187. doi:10.1080/19452 829.2014.880673.

Vandemoortele, Jan (2011). 'The MDG story: Intention denied'. *Development and Change*, 42 (1), 1–21.

Verger, A., Novelli, M. and Altinyelken, H. K. (2012). *Global education policy and international development new agendas, issues and policies.* London: Bloomsbury Publishing.

WEF (2015). 'Education 2030, Incheon Declaration and Framework for Action: Towards Inclusive and Equitable Quality Education and Lifelong Learning for All'. ED-2016/WS/2.

Further reading

Jolly, R. (2010). 'The MDGs in historical perspective'. *IDS Bulletin*, 41 (1).

The Lancet (2012). A manifesto for the world we want. Available at: http://www .thelancet.com/journals/lancet/article/PIIS0140-6736(12)62092-3/fulltext.

UN System Task Team on the Post-2015 UN Development Agenda (2012d). Review of the contributions of the MDG agenda to foster development: Lessons for the post-2015 UN development agenda, *Discussion note*. Available at: http://www.un.org/en/development/desa/policy/untaskteam_undf/ mdg_assessment.pdf.

Vandemoortele, J. (2012a). On irrational exuberance about MDG progress. Retrieved from: http://www.beyond2015.org/sites/default/files/ OnirrationalexuberanceaboutMDGprogress.pdf.

Vandemoortele, J. and Delamonica, E. (2010). 'Taking the MDGs beyond 2015: Hasten slowly'. *IDS Bulletin*, 41, 60–69.

10

A Converging Pedagogy in the Global South? Insights from Uganda and Turkey

Hülya Kosar Altinyelken

Chapter Outline

Introduction

This chapter focuses on child-centred pedagogy (CCP) as a global education policy and examines how it was diffused globally, redefined by national policy-makers, and implemented by teachers in two very distinct contexts, Uganda and Turkey. By doing so, the chapter will highlight the importance of context in education policy implementation, teacher agency, and the extent to which teachers welcome or resist global education policies.

In recent decades, school pedagogy has assumed central importance in education reforms that are designed to enhance the quality of education. It has been increasingly linked to economic growth, international competitiveness (Alexander 2008), and political democratization (Tabulawa 2003). Particularly after the 1990s, the global political discourse on pedagogy has been progressively shaped by approaches that are based on constructivism. Such approaches have become 'part of a discursive repertoire of international rights and quality education' (Chisholm and Leyendecker 2008, p. 4). Donor agencies have also proven influential in placing the notions of constructivism on the international reform agenda (Tabulawa 2003; Ginsburg and Megahed 2008). Indeed, an overview of policy documents by influential international organizations reveals that skills-based and learner-centred curricula have increasingly become the default position internationally.

Over the years, constructivism has largely influenced educational reforms in low-income countries as many have endorsed reform programmes that are couched in the rhetoric of constructivism. It has been characterized differently in diverse contexts as CCP, student-centred pedagogy (SCP), learner-centred pedagogy, active learning or collaborative learning. By the late twentieth century, reforms introducing CCP, student participation, democracy in the classroom, hands-on learning and cooperative learning groups have become globally ubiquitous (Anderson-Levitt 2003; Altinyelken 2015). Constructivism has been 'increasingly taken for granted as part of notions of educational quality' (Ginsburg and Megahed 2008, p. 106).

There are several examples of countries endorsing such pedagogical reforms in recent history. In Asia, examples include China (Carney 2008; Dello-Iacovo 2009), Russia (Schweisfurth 2002), Kyrgyzstan (Price-Rom and Sainazarov 2009) and Taiwan (Yang et al. 2008); in sub-Saharan Africa, South Africa (Nykiel-Herbert 2004), Botswana (Tabulawa 2003), Namibia (O'Sullivan 2004; Chisholm and Leyendecker 2008), Ethiopia (Serbessa 2006), Malawi (Croft 2002) and Tanzania (Barrett 2007); in the Middle East, Egypt (Ginsburg and Megahed 2008) and Jordan (Roggemann and Shukri 2009); and in Latin America, Brazil (Luschei 2004), Guatemala, Nicaragua and El Salvador (de Baessa et al. 2002).

The spread of pedagogical approaches based on constructivism has rekindled the debate on globalization and curriculum, as scholars enquired whether convergence around discourses and national education policies has resulted in the convergence of educational practices around the world (Anderson-Levitt 2003, 2008; Carson 2009). In other words, has the convergence at the level of global policy talk on pedagogy led to convergence at the classroom level? And, to what extent have the global and the official national discourse on pedagogy reshaped teaching and learning practices in classrooms? This chapter aims to reflect on such questions and seeks to provide an empirical examination of the practice of global education policy, by focusing on the implementation of pedagogical reforms in Uganda and Turkey.

These two countries are similar in terms of undergoing major curriculum review processes within similar timeframes and scope, and for being 'late adopters' of pedagogical approaches couched in the rhetoric of constructivism, defined as CCP in Uganda and SCP in Turkey (CCP shall be used to refer to both of them throughout the chapter). However, they differ significantly in many other ways, including their geographical size, population, history, political economy, donor involvement and education system. Choosing cases that are very different from one other is considered appropriate, since the chapter is aimed at analysing how context (structural aspects) and agents (teachers) mediate 'global' policies, and what kind of indigenized implementation profiles emerge as such policies are implemented at school level. In other words, the nature and type of pedagogical reforms that Uganda and Turkey have recently experienced offered sufficient similarities to warrant comparison, with large differences to help highlight the influence of contextual factors and teacher agency.[1]

Constructivism

In its most basic understanding, pedagogy refers to the knowledge of teaching, and often used as a synonym for teaching. Yet, 'Teaching is an act while pedagogy is both act and discourse. Pedagogy encompasses the performance of teaching together with the theories, beliefs, policies and controversies that inform and shape it' (Alexander 2001a, p. 540).

Constructivism is not a pedagogical approach but a theory regarding how people learn. It associates knowledge directly with individual learners and considers it to be the product of students' activities. Through processes of accommodation and assimilation, knowledge is constructed by students as they relate the new information to their already-existing cognitive structures (Bruer 1993). In other words, learning is conceived as 'an active process in which learners are active sense makers who seek to build coherent and organized knowledge' (Mayer 2004, p. 14). Accordingly, knowledge is created by undergoing, researching and actively experiencing reality. Since learning is perceived as a self-regulated activity, emphasis is placed on providing students with ample opportunities for discovery and the interpretation of events. Learning to learn is perceived to be as important as mastering content. The role of teachers in this context is mainly geared towards stimulating and coaching students in their learning activities. New paradigms of learning and teaching based on the principles of constructivism are characterized by minimal teacher lecturing or direct transmission of factual knowledge, individual and small-group activities, and frequent student questions and extensive dialogue among students (Leu and Price-Rom 2006).

The global diffusion of CCP

Why do different countries around the world seem to be engaging in a similar dialogue on how pedagogy should be reformed? Why are official discourses converging around the same pedagogical model? Different and often competing answers have been provided to these questions. According to modernization theorists, countries borrow educational reforms from elsewhere because they are superior. The emerging global curriculum (and the pedagogical approach as an integral part of the curriculum) is a response to the demands of globalized economies and knowledge societies (Anderson-Levitt 2008). Hence, from this perspective, pedagogical approaches based on constructivism have become popular since they represent the best way of organizing teaching and learning in schools in the contemporary world. However, the outcomes of such pedagogies are contested, or the results are perceived as inconclusive in many developed countries where these pedagogies had a better chance of being implemented because of resource availability, smaller class sizes, and improved teacher training (Alexander 2001b; Gauthier and Dembele 2004; Mayer 2004; UNESCO 2005).

A second view is proposed by World Culture Theorists. According to them, countries have more or less freely adopted a global culture of schooling because a set of ideas and practices are perceived as the best and the most modern way, even though they may not actually be the best way to run schools. In other words, nations adopt ideas not because they are truly better, but because policy-makers perceive them as modern, progressive and inevitable (Meyer and Ramirez 2000). For instance, constructivism is perceived as effective in improving learning achievements and preparing children and young people for the labour market. In the current globalized, increasingly competitive knowledge economy, the business community demands employees who think creatively, adapt flexibly to new work demands, identify and solve problems, and cooperate with colleagues in effective ways to create complex products (Windschitl 2002).

Therefore, the assumption that constructivist learning environments are superior in developing and reinforcing such skills and competencies appears to have contributed to its greater appeal. Indeed, research has shown that approaches rooted in constructivism have been endorsed in many countries on the assumption that such approaches would better prepare workers for the global economy, in which 'the new rules of wealth creation are replacing the logic of Fordist mass production with new "knowledge-based" systems of flexible production' (Ball 1998, p. 120). Moreover, constructivism is associated with educating citizens who would effectively participate in democratic politics (Ginsburg 2009; Altinyelken 2015), and with creating more capable consumers through education.

The two theories presented above assume that countries import education policies more or less voluntarily, and they downplay the power asymmetries among them. Furthermore, the World Culture Theory, due to its structuralist ontology, fails to recognize the role of particular international actors who have been involved in disseminating such pedagogies in different parts of the world. These include bilateral organizations (e.g. DANIDA and USAID), international organizations (e.g. the World Bank and UNICEF) and other agencies (e.g. the Aga Khan Foundation and some international NGOs) that had different motives and agendas in promoting CCP.

The World System Theory, in contrast, considers power central to the discussion. Here, convergence represents power, rather than progress. Hence, if pedagogical practices are converging around the world (at least in the official curricula), it is because a certain pedagogical approach is in the interests of powerful states or international organizations (Guthrie 1990; Tabulawa 2003; Carney 2008). These perspectives emphasize imposition or coercion as educational transfer mechanisms and highlight the role of international aid agencies (such as USAID) as major players that have contributed to the spread of constructivism by advocating it as a prescription through educational projects and consultancies they funded (Tabulawa 2003). Although aid agencies frame their interest by focusing on the assumed effectiveness of constructivism in improving learning outcomes, this perspective points to a hidden agenda which is disguised as 'better' teaching. According to this view, the efficacy of constructivism lies in its political and ideological nature. Although the World System Theory captures some of the complexities ignored by the World Culture Theory, it overemphasizes the role of international actors, disregards the agency of the recipient countries and overstates imposition and coercion as policy transfer mechanisms.

Furthermore, Steiner-Khamsi underlines the importance of the 'politics' and 'economics' of educational borrowing and lending (Steiner-Khamsi 2010). The politics of educational transfer is relevant for both the lender and the borrower, and implies political reasons for exporting and disseminating specific education policies or reforms (e.g. by donor agencies, NGOs and consultants), as well as political motives at the local level for importing a set of education reforms. Steiner-Khamsi argues that borrowing can work as a means to decontextualize and deterritorialize educational reforms that are contested in a given country (Steiner-Khamsi and Quist 2000; Steiner-Khamsi 2004). She suggests that 'borrowing does not occur because reforms from elsewhere are better, but because the very act of borrowing has a salutary effect on domestic policy conflict' (Steiner-Khamsi 2006, p. 671). The economics of policy borrowing and lending, on the other hand, points to the economic reasons for borrowing a specific education reform. The economics of policy borrowing is particularly salient for low-income countries that are dependent on external aid. Indeed, the time has come for a specific reform when international funding for implementing that particular reform is secured (Steiner-Khamsi 2006). The economics of policy lending and borrowing also helps to explain why education reforms in low-income countries increasingly bear a resemblance to those in developed countries.

Educational transfer: Why and how are Western pedagogies imported?

The rationale

In both Turkey and Uganda, the CCP was imported within the framework of improving the quality of education, and pedagogical renewal constituted an integral part of broader curriculum review and change processes. While adopting CCP, both countries have also instigated changes in curriculum content and student assessment.

In Uganda, following a one-year pilot phase, the Thematic Curriculum for primary schools was implemented nationwide in February 2007 (NCDC 2006). Likewise, in Turkey, Curriculum 2004 was piloted for a year in a select number of schools and has been implemented nationwide since September 2005 (Educational Reform Initiative 2005). In Uganda, the content has been reorganized according to a number of thematic areas, and in Turkey, the content load has been reduced and a thematic approach has been considered in content organization. Both curricula have adopted a 'competency-based' approach as opposed to the traditional knowledge-based curriculum approach, and have emphasized the development of specific competencies and skills. In terms of student assessment, both countries attempted to move beyond testing, and adopted continuous assessment (see Altinyelken 2010a, 2011).

The official account as to why new pedagogies are adopted points to dissatisfaction with student learning achievements, the inefficiency of the education system and the urge to restructure pedagogical practices in line with the imperatives of the knowledge-based economy. In Uganda, the primary concern is related to the very low achievement levels in literacy and numeracy (UNEB 2005) and to the inefficiencies of the system as indicated by high dropout and repetition rates (Read and Enyutu 2005). CCP appears to have been embraced as an antidote to traditional teaching in the hope that learning achievements and competencies will consequently improve, particularly in literacy and numeracy. A literate and numerate population is seen as critical to economic growth, sustainable development and poverty reduction.

In Turkey, on the other hand, globalization, the knowledge-based economy, the European Union (EU) membership process and harmonization with the EU education system, the changing social and economic needs of Turkish society, concerns with low student motivation, and disappointment with the results of Turkish students in international tests (particularly PISA) are highlighted as important motives. SCP is considered to be 'progressive' and 'advanced', and viewed as the only alternative to the traditional teaching practices in both countries (see Altinyelken 2011). Furthermore, the discourses on the rationale for a new pedagogy reflect the primacy of economic considerations in both contexts. This does not come as a surprise, since such considerations have come to characterize many of the education policies initiated in different parts of the world.

Mechanisms

Both in Uganda and Turkey, the perceptions and the assumptions linking CCP with improved student learning and better preparation of workers for the contemporary labour markets appear to have strongly influenced education policy-makers. Furthermore, Uganda exemplifies a country where the 'economics of education transfer' have proven critical. The Ugandan education system is highly dependent on external assistance, as more than half of the budget is paid for by donors (DGIS 2003). In turn, this creates 'a situation in which "voluntary policy transfer" is enmeshed with "coercive policy transfer"' (Dolowitz and Marsh 2000, p. 6). Donor aid is often accompanied by the lending of reform ideas, and even with the wholesale transfer of a comprehensive reform package formulated by the lender (Steiner-Khamsi 2006). Indeed, in Uganda, USAID and the Aga Khan Foundation have been actively involved in disseminating and institutionalizing CCP in primary schools. For this purpose, they have developed and implemented projects in primary schools and teacher training institutes in different parts of the country. According to some accounts, they have been very influential during the curriculum change process and in endorsing CCP as the official pedagogical approach in the new curriculum (see Altinyelken 2010b).

The case of Turkey is interesting in terms of understanding both the politics and economics of educational transfer. The restructuring of the Turkish economy in line with neoliberalism was initiated in the 1980s, and the influence of such policies was also felt in the education system. However, an adaptation of the content of the primary school curriculum to the market was achieved by means of Curriculum 2004 (Akkaymak 2010). The curriculum change was initiated in the two years after the Justice and Development Party (JDP) came to power, so the adoption of SCP coincides with significant political change in Turkey. The political change is noteworthy in the sense that the JDP is the only party with Islamist roots that came to power as a single party in the history of the Republic. They had their own distinct vision of Turkish society and the education system. Even prior to their rise to power, they announced that they would bring about wide-ranging structural changes to the education system, which included changing the primary school curriculum. Since they were able to form a single-party government, they also had the political power to instigate fundamental changes (Akkaymak 2010).

In addition, accession to the EU has constituted another strong political motive in Turkey at that time. In this sense, 'harmonisation' as a mechanism of policy transfer (Dale 1999) appears to have been influential in the adoption of SCP. Education, training and youth are considered to be the responsibilities of the member states; however, the European Community contributes to developing the quality of education in EU countries (Commission of the European Communities 2004). The EU's 2002 annual progress report considered the principles of the Turkish education system to be generally consistent with those of the EU. However, the report pointed towards reviewing the curricula and teaching methods as 'major issues to be addressed to increase the efficiency of the education system' (Commission of the European Communities 2002, p. 104).

Furthermore, the role of TÜSİAD (the largest corporate lobby in the country) merits attention. TÜSİAD has published a number of reports on education since the 1990s, urging governments to initiate major changes in the education system. Their reports have often formulated the role of education in economic terms and suggested that the education system's primary responsibility is to produce an adequate workforce for the labour market. As early as in their 1990 Report, SCP was highlighted as the pedagogical model to be adopted, since it was considered to facilitate learning to learn and to develop important skills such as problem-solving, teamwork, research and entrepreneurship (TÜSİAD 1990). Indeed, the role of TÜSİAD or the market in general has been considered strong in changing the curriculum and the pedagogical approach (Akkaymak 2010).

The economics of policy transfer is also highly relevant in the Turkish case, since the curriculum review was funded by the EU through 'the Support to Basic Education Programme'. It was initiated in 2002 and phased out in 2007, with a budget of around €100 million. It aimed at improving access to good-quality education. Financing of a review process and the development of a new curriculum were not included (MONE 2008; Nohl and Somel 2015). The funding raised questions among teachers, as they enquired whether the funding was accompanied by lending of educational ideas. These teachers were convinced that financing from the Westerners was almost always coupled with 'foreign ideas'. Yet, such a possibility was strongly discounted by policy-makers, arguing that the EU funded the curriculum development process but did not intervene or influence the reform process in any way. This sentiment was confirmed by Ziya Selcuk, the president of the Board of Education, the institution within the Ministry of National Education responsible for developing and accrediting curricula and textbooks. In an interview, Selcuk argued that the European Commission only had a supportive role through funding and consultancies (mostly on the design of textbooks), and did not have a 'decisive role in the curriculum development process' (Nohl and Somel 2015, p. 74).

Indeed, both in Uganda and Turkey, the implications of 'outside imposition' appeared to touch a raw nerve among policy-makers who appeared defensive and were keen to highlight the degree of national ownership in curriculum reform processes. Yet, at the same time, 'Look West' and 'learning from West' have been historically powerful metaphors. It is noteworthy to add that this has dramatically changed in Turkey in recent years. In fact, there are increasingly very little references to the Western countries in the narratives of educational change discourses used by policy-makers (Onursal-Besgul 2016). Moreover, 'the post-2005 period has been marked by a downturn in EU-Turkey relations and growing disenchantment on both sides' (Aydin-Duzgit and Kaliber 2016, p. 1).

Main features of the new pedagogies

Despite their different characterizations, the new pedagogical approaches in Uganda and Turkey present several common features. The Ugandan curriculum interprets CCP as: interaction among children, and between children and their teacher; emphasizing classroom activities that enable children to handle materials and learn by doing; encouraging greater use of learning and teaching materials during lessons; advising that lessons be organized around the interests, concerns and abilities of children; and giving them the opportunity to influence the direction of the lessons. Active student participation in lessons, student talking time, and group and pair work are underlined. Learning by way of exploring, observing, experimenting and practising are highlighted. In the Turkish curriculum, SCP is also defined along very similar lines as student participation, classroom activities, the use of learning aids, hands-on-learning, and cooperative learning. Curriculum documents in both countries clearly suggest that the majority of lesson time should be spent on classroom activities. The four discernible differences with the Turkish case relate to the emphasis in Turkey on research activities, project-based learning (project and performance assignments), the use of information and communication technology (ICT) in classrooms, and the integration of learning activities in and outside school, which anticipates and requires greater involvement of parents in education (Altinyelken 2013a).

In both countries, the curriculum focuses on the development of specific competencies, and it is believed that CCP would prove highly conducive to this goal. The Ugandan curriculum focuses on the development of six life skills, which should occur in every theme and sub-theme. They include effective communication, critical thinking, decision-making, creative thinking, problem-solving and self-esteem (NCDC 2006). The Turkish curriculum, on the other hand, prioritizes the development of eight competencies: critical thinking, creativity, communication, problem-solving, research, using information technologies, entrepreneurship and language skills in Turkish (MONE 2005). The common features among the selected competencies are particularly notable, as four (out of six) competencies prioritized in the Ugandan curriculum are also prioritized in the new Turkish curriculum, that is, critical thinking, problem-solving, creative thinking and effective communication skills. In addition, decision-making and self-esteem, two other competencies targeted by the Ugandan curriculum, are also highlighted throughout revised educational programmes in Turkey. In both countries, CCP also aims at stimulating teamwork, cooperation and dialogue.

These findings support the idea that there is an international convergence in curriculum policy. The similarities in curriculum content (e.g. thematic organization and the focus on the development of specific competencies), student evaluation (e.g. the introduction of alternative assessment methods that evaluate learning processes) and pedagogical approach (e.g. an emphasis on classroom activities, student participation, cooperation and hands-on-learning) give credit to World Culture Theorists (Ramirez 2003). Does this evidence then point to a single global curriculum model or pedagogical approach? Indeed, it indicates the prevalence of pedagogical reforms couched in the rhetoric of constructivism and convergence around how education policies are formulated in this area. However, since official curricula and mediated curricula tend to differ substantially, it cannot be taken as proof of convergence at the level of practice.

Teachers' views: Is CCP desirable?

CCP alters the role of teachers and appears to have wide-ranging implications for their profession. According to this pedagogical approach, teachers are expected to play 'facilitating' roles within classrooms. Their primary role is no longer to convey knowledge but to mediate students' learning processes, and provide adequate guidance and support to these supposedly 'autonomous learners' as they embark on constructing their knowledge. The students' role has become critical to educational processes since they are expected to assume much more responsibility in their learning and to be active in classroom processes. More importantly, it is now students who are required to direct learning (e.g. their interests, needs, learning styles, capacities, motivation and readiness), not teachers.

Since the 'old' was critiqued and discredited in an effort to glorify and legitimize the 'new', having teachers at the 'centre' was increasingly claimed to be authoritarian, uncaring, inefficient and morally wrong. Several teachers gave credit to this discourse both in Turkey and Uganda, arguing that education is about children, so they are the legitimate 'centres' of schooling. The majority of them also believed that increased student activism in learning processes would lead to higher learning achievements and better outcomes in competencies and skills; and greater student involvement would improve motivation, concentration and attendance. A pedagogical approach based on the transmission model has been attacked in both countries to the extent that some Turkish teachers appeared uncomfortable during interviews when they disclosed that they occasionally lectured in their classes. Yet, as Alexander (2008, p. 79) insists: 'Transmission teaching is ubiquitous [...] because there are undoubtedly circumstances in which the transmission of information and skill is a defensible objective, in any context.' Both in Uganda and Turkey, a polarized understanding of pedagogy was prevalent, not only among teachers but also among other key stakeholders. Such an approach appeared to have forced teachers to align with either the 'old' teacher-centred (or subject-centred) approach or the 'new' child/student-centred approach. Only a few dared to suggest that educationalists could instead move beyond such a dichotomous perspective.

In both countries, the proposed pedagogical approaches enjoyed a high level of receptiveness. In Uganda, CCP was viewed as the 'modern' and 'progressive' pedagogical approach. With the exception of one, none of the teachers appeared to be critical of the pedagogical approach and they seemed to shy away from questioning its underlying assumptions and main principles. It was simply perceived as a much more 'superior' pedagogical approach to traditional teaching. In other words, the Ugandan teachers did not question the desirability or the appropriateness of the new pedagogical approach, and appeared to welcome it as an example of Western 'best practice', but were overwhelmed by its implementation.

Likewise, SCP was perceived as the more 'advanced' and 'progressive' pedagogical approach by the majority of Turkish teachers. Some even explicitly noted that 'no one could be against it as no one can openly oppose development and improvement'. Furthermore, like Ugandan teachers, SCP was perceived by many as the only alternative to the traditional teaching methods that were criticized by policy-makers, teachers and parents alike for being ineffective and boring. Some earlier studies have also identified overwhelmingly positive opinions and attitudes among Turkish teachers towards constructivism (Çınar et al. 2006; Işıkoğlu and Basturk 2007). Such a positive attitude was mainly based on the belief that SCP was the dominant pedagogical approach in schools across Western Europe. The West was viewed as advanced, developed, rich and successful. Implicit assumptions were made about the link between Europe's level of development and school pedagogy. Although research studies have not established a clear link between economic development and teaching and learning approaches (Alexander 2008), teachers as well as policy-makers believed that SCP could potentially stimulate economic development and boost the competitiveness of the Turkish economy. Adopting a Western 'best practice' was also deemed to be logical and practical. After all, in the past three centuries, Turkey has often turned to the West to modernize and reform its military, legal, economic, political or educational system (Ulusoy 2009). In fact, teachers' accounts in both countries suggest that the West was viewed as the 'reference society' (Schriewer and Martinez 2004). Hence, the pedagogical approach the Westerners might be using had credibility, legitimacy and enjoyed a certain reputation (see Altinyelken 2015).

Nevertheless, Turkish teachers' accounts are not so uniform, as strong criticism was also voiced by them. Indeed, some teachers expressed explicit resentment at and frustration with trying out foreign ideas. These teachers believed that educational ideas might work well in the countries of origin, but might fail when they were transplanted into new contexts. In this respect, teachers also pointed out that Turkish society is very different to Western European societies with regard to its vast socio-economic disparities between urban and rural citizens, the competitiveness of the education system, the hierarchical nature of relationships that involve an element of authority, the dynamics of parent–child relationships, the status attached to having a university degree, parental involvement in education, and so on.

Classroom practices: A case for convergence or divergence?

An examination of how the new pedagogical approaches imported from the West were re-contextualized and adapted locally in Uganda and Turkey reveals convergence at a superficial level around new rituals and practices, such as greater efforts to employ learning aids, or to involve children during lessons. However, the findings point more strongly to the persistence of divergences across nations. Divergence was not only manifest when the implementation profiles of the two countries were compared, but was also persistent when schools within a country or even classrooms within a school were compared. In other words, significant differences across schools and classrooms were noted as reform practices were embraced unevenly, interpreted differently and adaptations to classroom realities and student backgrounds have given rise to distinct implementation practices.

An overview of implementation profiles in Uganda and Turkey points to distinct as well as some common features. In Uganda, the three most common indicators of change in classrooms included student talking time, the use of learning materials and group seating arrangements. However, these changes were often formalistic and interpreted differently to the manner intended by policy-makers. For instance, student participation was regularly praised by teachers, and has become a buzzword among them. Although teachers reported increased student talking time, during classroom observations, students were observed as giving answers in chorus to teachers' questions. The lessons were often dominated by teachers' questions, which were limited to basic information recall, requiring one- or two-word answers. Likewise, a formalistic adoption of group work was observed in classes visited in Uganda. Studies in other sub-Saharan African countries have shown that changes in seating arrangements were the first – and in many cases the only – sign that teachers were implementing CCP (Nykiel-Herbert 2004). In the majority of Ugandan classrooms, children were seated in very large groups (up to thirty students in one group) and conducting meaningful learning activities proved difficult in such large groups. Furthermore, singing was a very common practice in Ugandan classrooms, as in several other sub-Saharan African countries (Croft 2002). It was often used as a strategy to separate learning areas, to introduce children to new themes, and to improve their motivation and concentration.

In Turkey, similar to Uganda, student talking time and the use of aids were common indicators of change. However, unlike Uganda, there was also much emphasis placed on classroom activities, the use of ICT, project, performance and research assignments. During lessons, teachers devoted the greater part of lesson time to activities listed in student workbooks. The activities were varied, and needed to be carried out individually, in pairs or in groups. Teachers suggested that the noise level in classrooms has risen on account of such activities, and challenges associated with classroom management have increased. Turkish teachers demonstrated great enthusiasm as to the benefits yielded by the use of ICT. The ICT tools concerned were used to screen documentaries, to practise using educational programmes for teaching language skills or mathematics, and for teacher and student presentations. Moreover, project and performance assignments were expected to stimulate learning through discovery and hands-on learning. Although some teachers appreciated their value in terms of stimulating creativity and learning, several others complained that students delegated such assignments to their parents so the objectives of the assignments were not achieved in practice. Parents' excessive involvement in project/performance assignments has become such a phenomenon that many referred to the new curriculum as 'parent-centred education' (Altinyelken 2013b).

Although student talking time and the use of aids appear to be common implementation practices in both countries, the way they are interpreted and practised differed significantly. As explained above, in Uganda, student talking time often meant posing questions to students that required one or two-word responses in chorus. In Turkey as well, teacher questions and short student answers were common, yet students were also given more opportunities to tell stories, or to talk about their experiences, such as their background, families, hobbies and so on. Likewise, the use of learning aids conveyed different meanings and practices in Uganda and Turkey. In Uganda, it often meant making use of printed materials (flash cards and wall charts), demonstrating specific objects while teaching words in English or literacy lessons, or counting with natural objects in Mathematics. In Turkey, on the other hand, it often meant the use of stationery for frequent classroom activities involving cutting and pasting, drawing and colouring, and the use of TV, computers or the internet.

Such implementation differences inform us a great deal about context (teachers and structural realities), as they are highly indicative of local circumstances. Indeed, Steiner-Khamsi and Quist (2000) suggest that understanding how a transferred education model or policy has been re-contextualized and locally adapted conveys much about the local conditions and realities. For instance, resource availability predetermines what kind of learning materials will be used in classrooms and how. Likewise, culture, student language proficiency and class size exert a considerable influence on the nature, frequency or duration of student talking time and participation. Moreover, teachers' own interpretations and choices lead to differences, as in the case of grouping and group work. For instance, while in Uganda, all teachers organized group seating arrangements, while only two teachers out of a larger sample in Turkey followed suit. For Ugandan teachers, group seating was a pragmatic way of dividing a large class characterized by significant differences in children's ability levels. In Turkey, even though group seating was not popular, teachers also organized ad hoc groups for specific classroom activities. In addition, group work also involved group activities and cooperation between children outside of lesson hours.

Implementation challenges: Is CCP feasible?

The classroom realities observed in Uganda and Turkey differed significantly in terms of resource availability and class sizes. For instance, although some classrooms had computers and internet access in Turkey, Uganda showed deficiencies in even the most basic needs, such as adequate chairs for students. Nevertheless, the Ugandan and Turkish teachers appeared almost equally puzzled and overwhelmed by the implementation of CCP. The majority of teachers in both countries considered the new approach complex, and viewed its implementation in their national contexts as highly problematic. They believed that the implementation process was constrained by a multitude of issues and problems, raising critical questions with regard to its feasibility. These included inadequate teacher training, large classes, the shortage of material, the examination system, language proficiency in English (in Uganda), teacher-related factors and parental opposition. These challenges should be borne in mind since they have shaped the indigenized versions of CCP in Uganda and Turkey. They are briefly outlined below (see Altinyelken 2010a, 2010b, 2011, 2013a for a broader discussion on them).

Most Ugandan and Turkish teachers received ten days of training prior to the piloting, which enabled them to be only minimally acquainted with the main features of the new curricula. Teachers in both contexts appeared very critical of teacher training because of its short duration and low quality. The lack of a sound and thorough basis for CCP led to confusion, frustration and wide discrepancies in interpretation and teacher practices. Moreover, class size was mentioned as one of the biggest implementation challenges in both countries. In Uganda, the average class size in visited schools was seventy, and some classrooms had up to 108 students. In Turkey, the average class size was thirty-six in visited schools, and the maximum was forty-nine. Teachers described the difficulties of teaching in such overcrowded classes, and suggested that CCP has intensified those challenges, as the recommended teaching methods, such as student participation, learning by doing, and group work were time consuming and difficult to organize. The expectations of policy-makers regarding the implementation of CCP in large classes were simply perceived to be unrealistic.

Furthermore, CCP appeared to step up the demand for learning aids in both countries. Nevertheless, teachers were frustrated over the lack of adequate materials, even though they were in a more advantageous situation as pilot schools in comparison to other public schools. Material needs were framed differently since Ugandan teachers were more concerned over the lack of textbooks, visual and storybooks, while Turkish teachers made frequent references to computers, the internet, TV, digital learning materials and stationery needs. Ugandan teachers complained about the high cost of materials, the limited supply of printed materials, the inadequacy of the school budget allocation for the purchase of learning aids, the inability of students to provide some of the basic materials, and the time and effort expended by teachers on developing learning aids. Teachers in Turkey also commented on insufficient school budgets for providing learning aids and the implications of resorting to parents to provide for the material needs. Indeed, despite the rhetoric on free public education at primary level, parents have been increasingly required to provide financial means for a range of items, including desks, seats, curtains, storybooks and ICT hardware. Such practices have not only raised the financial burden of education on family budgets but also created new forms of inequality within the education system. This has led to great discrepancies in school conditions and has led to visible differences and inequalities between schools or even between classrooms in a single school.

Nationwide entrance exams to post-primary education pose an important challenge to the implementation of CCP in many contexts because of contradictions between the objectives of a constructivist curriculum (e.g. the development of skills and competencies) and what is assessed during exams (knowledge acquisition). Such contradictions and tensions persist in both Uganda and Turkey, pointing to a lack of educational policy alignment (Altinyelken 2013b). In both countries, success is defined by exam performance. So, even if school management, teachers and parents value the development of abilities, skills and competencies, if students cannot make the transition to good-quality post-primary educational institutions, then the intrinsic value of such competencies becomes questionable.

The language of instruction was raised as an important concern among Ugandan teachers. Similar to several other African countries, Uganda adopted the colonial language, English, as the official language and the language of instruction in schools. The Thematic Curriculum introduced the use of local languages as the language of instruction at lower grades; however, all schools continued to teach in English in Kampala due to the city's ethnic and linguistic diversity. The use of English was perceived as an obstacle to practising CCP since several children, particularly those who had migrated from rural areas, had a poor level of English. Consequently, their participation and interaction with teachers and other students were limited (Altinyelken et al. 2014). In observed classrooms, some students appeared to be fluent in English, while some others had had no prior exposure to English. Children who had been to nursery schools spoke better English, and those who migrated from the North or the East had the most difficulty in comprehending it.

In Uganda, teacher-related issues that hindered the implementation of CCP include low teacher motivation and morale, inadequate salaries, low teacher status and unfavourable living conditions. Ugandan teachers indicated that CCP made further demands on teachers by asking them to engage children in learning to a greater extent, and by being more innovative and creative in their teaching. However, teachers suggested that many of them lacked the motivation and energy to engage fully in educational change processes. In Turkey, few teachers raised such issues as a challenge to curriculum implementation, yet they alluded to teacher resistance to change proposals as a critical issue (Altinyelken 2013a). Resistance to change was typically attributed to teachers who were relatively senior in age and who had many years of experience (more than twenty years). Some teachers argued that instead of organizing classroom activities, senior teachers continued to rely on more traditional methods of direct teaching, because they viewed change as tiring and demanding. These teachers were also 'problematised' during interviews with policy-makers, who openly suggested that once senior teachers had left the system, constructivism would be more widely endorsed. However, interview accounts have shown that extensive reliance on classroom activities and overemphasis on competencies were criticized by teachers of all ages. Indeed, the majority of them did not approve of the substantial reductions in content load and tended to supplement it with direct teaching due to concerns with students' academic success, nationwide examinations, the increasing demand for private tutoring and deepening educational inequalities. Therefore, these teachers demonstrated *principled resistance* (Achinstein and Ogawa 2006), since they perceived curriculum change proposals as detrimental to their students and to society in general.

Furthermore, in both countries, teachers encountered some parental opposition to the revised curriculum and concerns associated with the CCP. In Uganda, partly because of inadequate raising of public awareness prior to the implementation, parents were reported to be confused, ambivalent or displeased with the new curriculum. Parental complaints involved a number of issues, such as the replacement of a subject-based system with learning areas, the overlap with early-childhood education and the assessment system. For these parents, the new curriculum was a simplified version of the previous one; hence, it was viewed as less challenging. In addition, since the new approach encouraged active learning, learning by doing, group activities and play, children were less involved with copying things from the blackboard. However, for several parents written exercises were primary indicators of teaching and learning. In Turkey, teachers also reported some parental dissatisfaction with the new curriculum. Several parents appeared to be concerned with the quality of education: they were critical of the new curriculum for overemphasizing competencies and paying inadequate attention to knowledge acquisition. Parents believed that children did not learn much, as an excessive amount of classroom time was spent on classroom activities. Some parents openly challenged the teachers, arguing that 'children are empty, they do not learn', and they endeavoured to exert pressure on teachers to supplement the curriculum with additional information and to spend more time on lecturing. This kind of pressure particularly came from parents who perceived education as an important social mobility mechanism, and who seemed to be concerned over the incongruity between mainstream schooling and secondary school entrance exams.

Conclusion

This chapter attempted to provide a critical and empirical analysis of how a 'global' policy (pedagogical approaches based on constructivism) is adapted locally in two different country contexts, that is, Uganda and Turkey. The chapter provided an analysis on how context and local actors mediated education policies that are imported from the West.

The educational transfer process appears to entail distinct forces and mechanisms in the case study countries, involving a combination of the global and the local. In Uganda, the active role of some international donors (USAID and the Aga Khan Foundation) and the dependence on external aid (which is often accompanied by the lending of reform ideas) seem to be critical to the adoption of CCP. The case of Turkey, on the other hand, demonstrates 'harmonisation' as the policy transfer mechanism, because of the role of the EU, the most influential international organization in Turkey (Dale 1999). Since the EU also provided funding for the curriculum change process, both the mechanism of harmonization and imposition operated simultaneously. In Turkey, the 'enchantment' with the West, the 300 years of the policy borrowing tradition from Western countries and the status of EU countries as 'reference societies' (Schriewer and Martinez 2004) have also contributed to educational borrowing. The interplay of different factors in both cases gives credit to diverse theories that explain the relationship between globalization and educational transfer, yet in different degrees.

Educational policies are adapted and re-contextualized through multiple processes (Dale 1999); therefore, at the level of practice, there appears to be some convergence and many divergences in Uganda and Turkey. In both countries, CCP enjoyed a high level of receptiveness among teachers as the 'modern' and 'progressive' pedagogical approach. At the level of practice, implementation profiles reveal palpable differences because CCP is framed differently in curricular documents by accentuating different aspects of the pedagogy (e.g. research and ICT in Turkey and group work in Uganda), and, more importantly, because it is practised differently by Ugandan and Turkish teachers. Therefore, CCP assumed different forms in the case study countries. This is not surprising as an implementation process always involves the application and distortion of what is formally proposed by policy-makers and curriculum designers (Lopes and De Macedo 2009), and leads to discernible differences, even within the same country. Historical and comparative evidence suggests that continuities, especially at the level of pedagogy, prevail through successive education reforms (Schweisfurth 2002). 'Convergence often occurs exclusively at the level of policy talk, in some instances also at the level of policy action, but rarely at the level of implementation' (Steiner-Khamsi and Stolpe 2006, p. 9), because global policies are mediated and re-contextualized (sometimes beyond recognition), undermined or openly resisted by local actors.

It is also important to note that a one-size-fits-all approach to pedagogy fails to recognize that pedagogy is 'both the act of teaching and the discourse in which it is embedded' (Alexander 2001b, p. 507). Since teaching and learning are contextualized activities, there can be indeed no justification for a universal and homogenizing pedagogy (Tabulawa 2003). Furthermore, positioning the notions of teacher-centred and student-centred learning in opposite locations and making bipolar comparisons between them poses the risk of oversimplification (Edwards and Usher 2008). As Alexander (2001b) suggests, the pedagogical models should be as far removed as they can be from the crude and normative polarizing of 'teacher-centred' and 'child-centred teaching'. Therefore, mainstream comparative research should abandon this dichotomy. According to Alexander (2001b, p. 512), 'Perhaps the most damaging residue of this sort of thinking can still be found in the reports of some development education consultants, who happily commend Western "child-centred" pedagogy to non-Western governments without regard for local cultural and educational circumstances.'

Questions for discussion

1 Describe in what ways pedagogical practices have been homogenizing around the world, at least in the official curriculum. In other words, what are the main characteristics of these reform trends?

2 From the perspectives of the major theories on why educational ideas travel around the world, how can we explain this homogenization trend in pedagogy?

3 Discuss how teacher-related factors and teachers' perceptions of contextual realities (e.g. class size and resource availability) influenced re-contextualization of child-centred pedagogy in diverse contexts.

4 How do you think the increasing focus on standardization worldwide influences teachers' pedagogical choices?

5 Do you think CCP is the most appropriate pedagogy, particularly in resource-scarce contexts of the world? Why?

Note

1 The chapter is based on fieldwork in both countries: data collection took place in June–July 2007 in Uganda and February–May 2009 in Turkey. In both countries, public schools that were selected to pilot the new curriculum in the capital cities were chosen as research sites, and eight schools were visited per country, in Kampala and Ankara, respectively. Two forms of data collection, interviews and classroom observation, were used. At the school site, interviews were conducted with head teachers and deputy head teachers, and classroom teachers from Grades One and Two in Uganda and Grades One, Two and Five in Turkey. Interviews with school management amounted to a total of 24 (10 in Uganda and 14 in Turkey), and those with teachers to 103 (34 in Uganda and 69 in Turkey). Interviews were also conducted with key informants within the field of education, including ministry officials, international organizations, academics, teacher unions and educational institutions. Furthermore, lessons were observed in Primary One and Two in Uganda (in total 28) and Primary One, Two and Five in Turkey (76 in total), by using a checklist which included items on the level of interaction between students and teachers, student talking time, classroom management and atmosphere.

References

Achinstein, B. and Ogawa, R. T. (2006). '(In)fidelity: What the resistance of new teachers reveals about professional principles and prescriptive educational policies'. *Harvard Educational Review*, 76 (1), 30–63.

Akkaymak, G. (2010). 'Neoliberalism and education: Analysis of representation of neoliberal ideology in the primary school Social Studies curriculum in Turkey', MA thesis, Koç University, Istanbul.

Alexander, R. (2001a). *Culture and pedagogy: International comparisons in primary education.* London: Blackwell.

Alexander, R. (2001b). 'Border crossing: Towards a comparative pedagogy'. *Comparative Education*, 37 (4), 507–523.

Alexander, R. (2008). *Essays on pedagogy.* London: Routledge.

Altinyelken, H. K. (2010a). 'Curriculum change in Uganda: Teacher perspectives on the new thematic curriculum'. *International Journal of Educational Development*, 30 (2), 151–161.

Altinyelken, H. K. (2010b). 'Pedagogical renewal in sub-Saharan Africa: The case of Uganda'. *Comparative Education*, 46 (2), 151–171.

Altinyelken, H. K. (2011). 'Student-centered pedagogy in Turkey: Conceptualisations, interpretations and practices'. *Journal of Education Policy*, 26 (2), 137–160.

Altinyelken, H. K. (2013a). 'Teachers' principled resistance to curriculum change: A compelling case from Turkey'. In A. Verger, H. K. Altinyelken and M. De Koning (Eds.), *Global education reforms and teachers: Emerging policies, controversies and issues.* Brussels: Education International.

Altinyelken, H. K. (2013b). 'The demand for private tutoring in Turkey: Unintended consequences of curriculum reform'. In M. Bray, A. E. Mazawi and R. Sultana (Eds.), *Private tutoring across the mediterranean: Power dynamics and implications for learning and equity.* Rotterdam: Sense Publishers.

Altinyelken, H. K. (2015). 'Democratising Turkey through Student-centred Pedagogy: Opportunities and pitfalls'. *Comparative Education*, 51 (4), 484–501. In special issue 'Turkey at a Crossroads: Critical Debates and Issues in Education, edited by H. K. Altinyelken, K. Cayir and O. Agirdag.

Altinyelken, H. K., Moorcroft, S. and Van der Draai, H. (2014). 'The Dilemmas and complexities of implementing language-in-education policies: Perspectives from urban and rural contexts in Uganda'. *International Journal of Educational Development*, 36, 90–99.

Anderson-Levitt, K. (2003). 'A world culture of schooling?'. In K. M. Anderson-Levitt (Ed.), *Local meanings, global schooling: Anthropology and world culture theory.* New York: Palgrave Macmillan, pp. 1–26.

Anderson-Levitt, K. (2008). 'Globalization and curriculum'. In F. M. Connelly (Ed.), *The Sage handbook of curriculum and instruction.* London: Sage, pp. 349–368.

Aydın-Düzgit, S. and Kaliber, A. (2016). 'Encounters with Europe in an era of domestic and international turmoil: Is Turkey a De-Europeanising candidate country?' *South European Society and Politics*, 21 (1), 1–14.

Ball, S. J. (1998). 'Big policies/small world: An introduction to international perspectives in education policy'. *Comparative Education*, 34 (2), 119–130.

Barrett, A. (2007). 'Beyond the polarization of pedagogy: Models of classroom practice in Tanzanian primary schools'. *Comparative Education*, 4 (2), 273–294.

Bruer, J. T. (1993). *Schools for thought: A science of learning in the classroom.* Cambridge: MIT Press.

Carney, S. (2008). 'Learner-centred pedagogy in Tibet: International education reform in a local context'. *Comparative Education*, 44 (1), 39–55.

Carson, T. R. (2009). 'Internationalizing curriculum: Globalization and the worldliness of curriculum studies'. *Curriculum Inquiry*, 39 (1), 145–158.

Chisholm, L. and Leyendecker, R. (2008). 'Curriculum reform in the post-1990s sub-Saharan Africa'. *International Journal of Educational Development*, 28 (2), 195–205.

Çınar, O., Tefur, E. and Mehmet, E. (2006). 'İlköğretim okulu öğretmen ve yöneticilerinin yapılandırmacı eğitim yaklaşımı ve programı hakkındaki görüşleri'. *Eğitim Fakültesi Dergisi*, 7 (11), 47–64.

Commission of the European Communities (2002). *2002 Regular report on Turkey's progress towards accession.* Brussels: Commission of the European Communities.

Commission of the European Communities (2004). *2004 Regular report on Turkey's progress towards accession.* Brussels: Commission of the European Communities.

Croft, A. (2002). 'Singing under a tree: Does oral culture help lower primary teachers be learner-centred?' *International Journal of Educational Development*, 22 (3–4), 321–337.

Dale, R. (1999). 'Specifying globalization effects on national policy: A focus on the mechanisms'. *Journal of Education Policy*, 14 (1), 1–17.

de Baessa, Y., Chesterfield, R. and Ramos, T. (2002). 'Active learning and democratic behaviour in Guatemalan rural schools'. *Compare*, 32 (2), 205–218.

Dello-Iacovo, B. (2009). 'Curriculum reform and "Quality Education" in China: An overview'. *International Journal of Educational Development*, 29, 241–249.

DGIS (2003). *Local solutions to global challenges: Towards effective partnership in basic education, country study report-Uganda.* Joint evaluation of external support to basic education in developing countries. The Hague: DGIS.

Dolowitz, D. P. and Marsh, D. (2000). 'Learning from abroad: The role of policy transfer in contemporary policy-making'. *Governance: An International Journal of Policy and Administration*, 13 (1), 5–24.

Educational Reform Initiative (2005). 'Yeni Öğretim Programlarını İnceleme ve Değerlendirme Raporu' [Online]. Available at: http://www.erg.sabanciuniv.edu.tr/ (accessed on 17 August 2010).

Edwards, R. and Usher, R. (2008). *Globalisation and pedagogy: Space, place and identity*, 2nd edn. London and New York: Routledge.

Gauthier, C. and Dembele, M. (2004). 'Quality of teaching and quality of education: A review of research findings', paper commissioned for the EFA Global Monitoring Report 2005 'The Quality Imperative'. Available at: http://unesdoc.unesco.org/images/0014/001466/146641e.pdf (accessed on 25 April 2010).

Ginsburg, M. (2009). 'Active-learning pedagogies as a reform initiative: Synthesis of case studies' [Online]. Available at: http://www.equip123.net/docs/e1-ActiveLearningSynthesis (accessed on 7 April 2010).

Ginsburg, M. B. and Megahed, N. M. (2008). 'Global discourses and educational reform in Egypt: The case of active learning pedagogies'. *Mediterranean Journal of Educational Studies*, 13 (2), 91–115.

Guthrie, G. (1990). 'To the defence of traditional teaching in lesser-developed countries'. In V. D. Rust and P. Dalin (Eds.), *Teachers and teaching in the developing world.* New York and London: Garland, pp. 219–232.

Işıkoğlu, N. and Basturk, R. (2007). 'İlköğretim öğretmenlerinin yapılandırmacı yaklaşımla ilgili öğretim stratejileri hakkında görüşleri', paper presented to IV Eğitimde Yeni Yönelimler Sempozyumu, Ankara, 17 November.

Leu, E. and Price-Rom, A. (2006). *Quality of education and teacher learning: A review of the literature.* Washington, DC: USAID.

Lopes, A. C. and De Macedo, E. F. (2009). 'A critical perspective on managing curriculum'. *Curriculum Inquiry,* 39 (1), 57–74.

Luschei, T. F. (2004). 'Timing is everything: The intersection of borrowing and lending in Brazil's adoption of Escuela Nueva'. In G. Steiner-Khamsi (Ed.), *The global politics of educational borrowing and lending.* New York and London: Teachers College Press, pp. 154–167.

Mayer, R. (2004). 'Should there be a three-strikes rule against pure discovery learning? The case for guided methods of instruction'. *American Psychologist,* 59 (1), 14–19.

Meyer, J. W. and Ramirez, F. O. (2000). 'The world institutionalization of education'. In J. Schriewer (Ed.), *Discourse formation in comparative education.* Frankfurt: Peter Lang, pp. 111–132.

MONE (2005). *İlköğretim 1–5 sınıf programları tanıtım el kitabı.* Ankara: Ministry of National Education.

MONE (2008). 'Temel Eğitime Destek Programı' [Online]. Available at: http://projeler.meb.gov.tr/pkm1/index.php?view=article&catid=22:yaptik&id=63:tem el-eitime-destek-programtedp&option=com_content&Itemid=64 (accessed on 20 March 2010).

NCDC – National Curriculum Development Centre (2006). *The National Primary School Curriculum for Uganda, Teacher's Guide Primary 1.* Kampala: NCDC.

Nohl, A. M. and Somel, R. N. (2015). *Education and social dynamics: A Multilevel analysis of curriculum change in Turkey.* New York: Routledge.

Nykiel-Herbert, B. (2004). 'Mis-constructing knowledge: The case of learner-centred pedagogy in South Africa'. *Prospects,* XXXIV (3), 249–265.

Onursal-Besgul, O. (2016). Policy transfer and discursive de-Europeanisation: Higher education from Bologna to Turkey. *South European Society and Politics,* 21 (1), 91–103.

O'Sullivan, M. (2004). 'The re-conceptualisation of learner-centred approaches: A Namibian case study'. *International Journal of Educational Development,* 24 (6), 585–602.

Price-Rom, A. and Sainazarov, K. (2009). *Active-learning pedagogies as a reform initiative: The case of Kyrgyzstan,* Washington, DC: American Institutes for Research.

Ramirez, F. O. (2003). 'The global model and national legacies'. In K. Alexander-Levitt (Ed.), *Local meanings, global schooling: Anthropology and world culture theory.* New York: Palgrave Macmillan, pp. 239–254.

Read, T. and Enyutu, S. (2005). *Road map for the implementation of the curriculum reforms recommended by the primary curriculum review report and approved by the Ministry of Education and Sports.* Kampala: Ministry of Education and Sports.

Roggemann, K. and Shukri, M. (2009). *Active-learning pedagogies as a reform initiative: The case of Jordan.* Washington, DC: American Institutes for Research.

Schriewer, J. and Martinez, C. (2004). 'Constructions of internationality in education'. In G. Steiner-Khamsi (Ed.), *The global politics of educational borrowing and lending*. New York: Teachers College Press, pp. 29–53.

Schweisfurth, M. (2002). *Teachers, democratisation and educational reform in Russia and South Africa*. Oxford: Symposium books.

Serbessa, D. D. (2006). 'Tension between traditional and modern teaching-learning approaches in Ethiopian primary schools'. *Journal of International Co-operation in Education*, 9 (1), 123–140.

Steiner-Khamsi, G. (2004). 'Conclusion: Blazing a trail for policy theory and practice'. In G. Steiner-Khamsi (Ed.), *The global politics of educational borrowing and lending*. New York and London: Teachers College Press, pp. 201–220.

Steiner-Khamsi, G. (2006). 'The economics of policy borrowing and lending: A study of late adopters'. *Oxford Review of Education*, 32 (5), 665–678.

Steiner-Khamsi, G. (2010). 'The politics and economics of comparison'. *Comparative Education Review*, 54 (3), 323–342.

Steiner-Khamsi, G. and Quist, H. O. (2000). 'The politics of educational borrowing: Reopening the case of Achimota in British Ghana'. *Comparative Education Review*, 44 (3), 272–299.

Steiner-Khamsi, G. and Stolpe, I. (2006). *Educational import: Local encounters with global forces in Mongolia*. New York: Palgrave Macmillan.

Tabulawa, R. (2003). 'International aid agencies, learner-centred pedagogy and political democratisation: A critique'. *Comparative Education*, 39 (1), 7–26.

TÜSİAD (1990). 'Türkiye'de eğitim: sorunlar ve değişime yapısal uyum önerileri' [Online]. Available at: http://www.tusiad.org/FileArchive/turkiyedeegitim.pdf (accessed on 10 April 2010).

Ulusoy, K. (2009). 'The changing challenge of Europeanization to politics and governance in Turkey'. *International Political Science Review*, 30 (4), 363–384.

UNEB – Uganda National Examinations Board (2005). *The achievements of primary school pupils in Uganda in English and Numeracy*. Kampala: UNEB.

UNESCO (2005). *Education for all global monitoring report 2005 – The quality imperative*. Paris: UNESCO.

Windschitl, M. (2002). 'Framing constructivism in practice as the negotiation of dilemmas: An analysis of the conceptual, pedagogical, cultural, and political challenges facing teachers'. *Review of Educational Research*, 72 (2), 131–175.

Yang, F., Chang, A. and Hsu, Y. (2008). 'Teacher views about constructivist instruction and personal epistemology: A national study in Taiwan'. *Educational Studies*, 34 (5), 527–542.

Further reading

Alexander, R. J. (2000). *Culture and pedagogy: International comparisons in primary education*. Oxford: Blackwell.

Schweisfurth, M. (2013). *Learner-centred education in international perspective: Whose pedagogy for whose development? Series: Education, poverty and international development*. London: Routledge.

Tabulawa, R. (2013). *Teaching and learning in context: Why pedagogical reforms fail in sub-saharan Africa*. Dakar: CODESRIA.

11

Education in Emergencies: Tracing the Emergence of a Field

Mieke Lopes Cardozo and Mario Novelli

Introduction

This chapter seeks to chart the evolution of the field of research and practice known as 'education in emergencies' (EiE) since 2000 and to hone in on one key player, the International Network for Education in Emergencies (INEE[1]). In line with the book's overall objective, we are seeking to understand how a global 'education in emergencies'[2] agenda emerged within the field of international education and development and the role of INEE within this process, as a key global governance in education actor. While much contemporary research has been done relating to the transfer of ideas and policies and the role of the World Bank, the IMF and other powerful states, from various perspectives (c.f. Cammack 2004, 2007), less is written about the role of network organizations in these processes – either as catalysts for the spread of the global education agenda or as mediators.

The chapter will proceed as follows: first, we will reflect on the rise, expansion and ongoing transformation of the emerging field of research and practice known as 'Education in Emergencies.' We will do this through locating the field within the broader context of shifting post–Cold War and post-9/11 contexts. The second part of the chapter will develop an analysis of the INEE, which emerged in the run-up to the Education For All (EFA) Dakar Meeting in 2000, and has become a central player in the development of the field of EiE. The network brings together key policy and practice actors, as well as academics, and is located at the centre of the global architecture of international engagement in education in contexts of humanitarian crisis, armed conflict and post-conflict reconstruction.

Our aim in this chapter is to reflect on the role and position of INEE in the global governance of education, emergencies and conflict, linking the chapter back to broader debates contained in this book. We first discuss the foundational characteristics of the network in its current state, and, secondly, we will turn to explore the less visible, underlying mechanisms that drive decision-making and governance of this network, asking, *who is facilitating/ funding, and who or what is driving specific thematic areas of focus and why?*

Methodologically, we inform our analysis by a review of (online available) documentation on the network, including annual reports and publicly available material, as well as a review of relevant exiting studies. As part of our exercise to trace the emergence of the field, we were inspired to reflect on *the role and positionality of INEE*, not least because of our own engagement as members of the network. Rather than external observers, we consider ourselves as critical friends, and this work as a partly self-reflective exercise.

Global governance and inter-agency actors: Theoretical and epistemological reflections

Before mapping out the history of the emergence of EIE and exploring the role of INEE therein, we want to begin by outlining some of the theoretical tools that underpin our analytical approach. These are rooted in critical (cultural) political economy approaches to understanding education which recognize the need to understand education – not within itself – but in relation to the broader economic, political, cultural and social processes within which it is embedded (Robertson and Dale 2015). What we would call a shift from 'educationism' to the 'political economy of education' or what Roger Dale (2005) has called a shift from 'education politics' to the 'politics of education'.

Secondly, and in relation to this, we are also seeking to understand the complex relationship between agency and structure in international development and education governance and policy. That is to say we are interested in the role of the INEE, as a network-actor, that draws together key agencies and individuals that work on the field of 'Education in Emergencies'.

To what extent is INEE an agent of broader global geopolitical power relations, reproducing unequal global political relationships or acting as a buffer, mediator, and seeking to challenge these unequal relationships? We find the work of Bob Jessop on the strategic relational approach, as a helpful framework through which to understand the complexities of both structures and agents (Jessop 2005; see also our adaptation of this work to the field of education: Lopes Cardozo and Shah 2016a,b; Lopes Cardozo et al. 2016). The Strategic Relational Approach (SRA) allows us to go beyond both structuralism and the teleological arguments therein and agential idealism, which reifies agency and fails to adequately theorize the role of structures in shaping the limits of the possible:

> we can analyze ... structure as strategic in their form, content, and operation; and analyze actions, in turn, as structured, more or less context-sensitive, and structuring. This involves examining how a given structure may privilege some actors, some identities, some strategies, some spatial and temporal horizons, some actions over others; and the ways, if any, in which actors (individual and/or collective) take account of this differential privileging through 'strategic-context' analysis when choosing a course of action. In other words, one should study structures in terms of their structurally-inscribed strategic selectivities and actions in terms of (differentially reflexive) structurally-oriented strategic calculation. (Jessop 1999)

Thirdly, while recognizing that SRA was developed in relation to the 'state', in our work on International Development and Education and the 'governing' institutions therein, we also recognize that they possess certain types of 'state-like' behaviour and activities in terms of governing populations, setting up rules and regulations, delivering services and so on. In many ways they go beyond the parameters of state behaviour by setting global rules, agendas, standards, which allow for transnational influence.

Fourthly, we also want to recognize the particularities of the field of international development itself, which is overwhelmingly both a Western-led 'industry' rooted in the decolonization processes that took off since the 1940s and a contradictory process that expresses both the utopian idea of 'the rest' catching up with 'the West' and the architecture to ensure that highly unequal North–South relationships are maintained (Novelli 2016). In the rest of the chapter we endeavour to apply some of this thinking to the analysis of the emergence of the field of EiE.

Understanding the rise of interest in conflict, development and education

In this section, we seek to tell the story of the rise, expansion and ongoing transformation of the field of EiE. As Winthrop and Matsui (2013) note in a recent historical review of the field:

> While a common refrain among experts is that education and fragility is a new field, the practice of providing schooling and non-formal education to children and youth affected by conflict dates back at least to World War II, when communities provided schooling for evacuee and refugee children in Europe and the United States invested heavily in rebuilding European education systems through the Marshall Plan, perhaps the largest and most successful post-conflict education program to date.

It is in these practices of delivering education in refugee camps that the seeds of knowledge on the particularities of delivering education in contexts of conflict and insecurity begin to emerge. However, while education for refugees and displaced communities did take place, this was often at the initiative of the affected communities themselves, whilst the international community focused on 'life-saving' interventions in housing, food and health. For Winthrop and Matsui (2013), this was a period that represented a 'proliferation' of grass-roots attempts to provide education support to communities affected by conflict.

In order to understand the shift from a 'proliferation' of initiatives to the emergence of a coherent field of 'education in emergencies', we need to hone in on the early 1990s, in the period immediately after the end of the Cold War where the foundations of contemporary geopolitics were reset. This period marked the end of US/Russia bipolarism in international relations, which in turn resulted in a drop in overall development aid, but also a shift of focus in development policy and education policy towards the least-developed countries and population groups. The removal of Cold War geopolitics produced a noticeable, albeit partial, shift away from the overwhelmingly partisan and highly political allocation of aid during the Cold War (Lundborg 1998; Wang 1999; Christian Aid 2004).

These post–Cold War shifts led to an increased focus on sub-Saharan Africa and joint donor efforts to improve the coordination of international development policy. The first evidence of this shift in education was the 1990 'Education for All' commitments that emerged out of a high-profile meeting in Jomtien, Thailand. These efforts were, a decade later, integrated in the Millennium Development Goals – with aspects of the EFA objectives as part of an overall set of development targets. As part of a global education agenda, in 2005 donors agreed in the Paris Declaration to 'harmonise' their aid efforts in developing contexts, for instance through mechanisms such as the Sector-Wide Approaches (SWAPs) to education, ensuring ownership and alignment with aid recipients development strategies (Mundy 2002; Mundy 2006; King 2007; OECD 2005/2008). While not without both critics and critiques, there was a feeling that the architecture of aid was becoming more coherent and being targeted towards those areas of most need (Cosgrave 2005), even if the rhetoric often outpaced the financing (GCE 2009).

On the other hand, the post–Cold War period (from 1991 onwards) also represented the rise of US hegemony and the broader consolidation of the neoliberal political project (see Harvey 2007). This had the effect in the field of education and development of globalizing a set of neoliberal-inspired education policy recipes including decentralization, privatization, new public management and so on. These policies were initiated in the heat of the Cold War under World Bank-/IMF-sponsored structural adjustment policies but continue on to the present in different forms (Robertson et al. 2007).

Parallel to these post–Cold War developments of increased donor coordination and consensus and neoliberal hegemony was also a rise in Western interventionism, often under the leadership of the United States, in high-profile conflicts from the Balkans to Rwanda, Somalia, Sudan, Iraq and Afghanistan. The post–Cold War peace dividend appeared to be ending before it had really begun. Importantly, Western interventions in these conflicts were also discursively framed as 'humanitarian interventions' (Fearon 2008, p. 52), drawing on issues of human security, human rights, democracy and freedom for their justification (Roberts 2000; Forsythe 2000). The previous UN gospel of non-interventionism in the sovereign affairs of member states became tempered by the right of the international community to intervene in cases where the 'human security' of the population was at risk. Some critics saw this new humanitarianism as a new mode of imperialism (Chomsky 1994; Chossudovsky 1997; Chomsky 1999; Chossudovsky 2002).

The fallout from the 9/11 attacks in New York also catalysed increased intervention into conflict zones. Suddenly the insecurity and conflict occurring outside of the core global powers were recognized as producing insecurity at home (Duffield 2007). This led to an increased push to merge issues of international development with national security concerns – the merging of security and development – a logic that had of course been present throughout the Cold War. Almost immediately, the United States and other Western powers began to prioritize concerns over 'terrorism' and sought to integrate all other aspects of government policy under this overarching objective of security. During the Bush administration (2001–2009), development and humanitarian organizations were often simplistically treated as 'force multipliers' (Novelli 2010), and while the language softened under the Obama administration (2009–January 2017), the central thrust of linking development aid to national security objectives has remained intact (Southern Aid Effectiveness Commission 2010).

Back in 2008, USAID released their 'civil military cooperation policy' (2008), explaining their 3-D approach, incorporating defence, diplomacy and development and stating: 'Development is also recognized as a key element of any successful whole-of-government counterterrorism and counter-insurgency effort' (USAID 2008, p. 1). While the United States was and remains the most vigorous agent in the process of merging security and development, the EU and other donors (including, for instance, DFID, AUSAID, Japan and the Dutch) have maintained similar policies (EU 2003, p. 13). In 2015, the minister of foreign trade and development cooperation of the Netherlands, Liliane Ploumen, reflected on this merging of security and development in an interview in the *Guardian* newspaper:

Some worry that talking about peace and conflict prevention in the context of development will put too much emphasis on security, but I believe the opposite: bringing a development perspective to issues of conflict prevention and peace will allow us to focus better, and earlier, on emerging conflict and instability. [...] With the adoption of the global goals, the world has turned the mutual importance of peace and development into an agenda for action. Let's show that we are serious about leaving no one behind. We cannot allow fragile and conflict-affected areas to become the ghettoes of our world.[3]

While the renewed commitment of Western governments to the importance of international development might be welcomed as an expression of global solidarity, the 'joined up' whole-of-government 3-D approach has brought with it dangers for the development and humanitarian community of being taken over by the generally more powerful security wing of national governments. Moreover, mixing development cooperation with other policies or commercial, security or geopolitical interests undermines the possibilities of aligning overseas development assistance with internationally agreed aid effectiveness principles, like the Paris agenda.

While the dynamics and nature of the development and conflict agenda remain hotly debated, what is less contested is the fact that conflict and emergencies are at the centre of the development policy and debate. Since the 1990s there has been a massive increase in the number of UN peacekeeping troops and humanitarian and development actors operating in conflict situations. By 1995, humanitarian agencies were responding to a total of twenty-eight complex emergencies around the world, increasing from just five in 1985 (Bradbury 1995; Slim 1996). By the mid-1990s, emergency spending had increased by over 600 per cent from its mid-1980s point to over US\$3.5 billion and has continued to rise (Fearon 2008). Since 1999, the number of personnel had increased by over 700 per cent, to 110,000, with a budget of US\$7 billion in 2008. According to the 2008 Reality of Aid Report (2008, p. 8): 'Aid allocations to the most severely conflict-affected countries increased from 9.3% of total ODA in 2000 (for 12 countries) to 20.4% (for 10 countries) in 2006'. Coupled with a general increase in Overseas Development Assistance (ODA) during the same period, aid to conflict-affected countries nearly tripled in real terms between 2000 and 2006. Since 2007, 53 per cent of total ODA has gone to countries on the 2015 Organization for Economic Co-operation and Development (OECD) fragile state list (see OECD 2015, p. 22). What is also clear from the literature is that the distribution of aid among severely conflict-affected countries was, and remains, highly unequal, reflecting geopolitical interests rather than human need. Between 2002 and 2012, 22 per cent of all ODA to fragile states went to Iraq and Afghanistan (OECD 2015, p. 23).

Dynamics in the evolution of education in emergencies

Since the late 1990s and in tandem with the expansion of development and humanitarian intervention in conflict zones, there has been a parallel increase in interest and recognition of the importance of education delivery in emergency, protracted crisis, ongoing conflict and post-conflict zones. This, we argue, has been the result of at least four key drivers, linked to the geopolitical shifts outlined above.

First, education, like food and shelter, has come to be seen as part of the core building blocks of human development and a necessary and vital part of humanitarian response in conflict situations in particular (Save the Children 2010). One factor often identified as a catalyst within this process was the 1996 Machel Report on 'The Impact of Armed Conflict on Children', which identified the damaging effects of wars on the lives of children, with a particular emphasis on the role and importance of education. The report provided the foundation for the beginnings of an important debate about the 'life-saving' potential of education during and after armed conflicts, and the negative effects of depriving young people of access therein.

Since 2008, there has been a Global Education Cluster, headed by UNICEF and the International Save the Children Alliance that coordinates the educational response in emergency situations, as part of the Inter-Agency Standing Committee (IASC) that assumes overall coordination, and develops policy involving UN and non-UN humanitarian partners operating in conflict zones. Central to the rise in prominence of education within conflict situations has been the actions of Save the Children, INEE, UNICEF and others to successfully lobby for an expansion of their own mandates and activities in education – within a growing conflict and development funding regime.

Secondly, the success of these linked organizations and practitioners in placing education, emergencies and conflict firmly on the international development agenda has been aided, since 2000, by a recognition from bilateral donors that a large proportion of the world's out-of-school children are located in conflict and post-conflict countries. Thus, this issue needs to be addressed if global education targets, such as the EFA goals, and now the more recently adopted Sustainable Development Goals (SDGs) are to be achieved (Save the Children 2007, 2008; GMR 2011). This has also led to a growing awareness of the relationship between education and conflict, and its potentially catalytic and preventative roles (Bush and Saltarelli 2000; DFID 2003), though we would argue that the technical politics of delivering education in contexts of conflict rather than its political nature continues to dominate donor engagement.

UNICEF's Peacebuilding, Education and Advocacy (PBEA) Programme, with financial support from the Netherlands government, between 2012 and 2015,[4] has instigated a new push to understand and support education's crucial role in processes of peacebuilding. This sits at one end of a continuum of ways of thinking within the field at present, ranging from (1) a more humanitarian (EiE) approach, to (2) a conflict-sensitive education (CSE) approach that mainly aims to *do no harm*, and (3) an approach that recognizes education's role in transforming societies through processes of peacebuilding that can address the drivers of conflict and their links to education (Smith 2014).

Thirdly, the merging of security and development outlined above has also penetrated the field of education and development. In education this emerges as a process of reinterpreting both the purposes and the practices of both education and development – as having potential 'security benefits'. An illustration of this is the prevalence of references to the role of education in the US counterterrorism strategies elaborated in their 'Country Reports on Terrorism'.[5] As an example, the 2007 report, in Chapter 5, 'Terrorist Safe Havens', subsection 7 focuses on basic education in Muslim countries. In this section, it notes:

> The Department of State, USAID, and other U.S. agencies continued to support an increased focus on education in predominantly Muslim countries and those with significant Muslim populations. The United States' approach stresses mobilizing public and private resources as partners to improve access, quality, and the relevance of education, with a specific emphasis on developing civic-mindedness in young people. (US State Department 2008, p. 243)

Similarly, as part of the US military's counterinsurgency strategy in places such as Iraq and Afghanistan, 'humanitarian and civic assistance' included 'such non-emergency services as constructing schools, performing dental procedures, and even vaccinating the livestock of farmers' (Brigety 2008). Crucially for us, it appears that educational provision (particularly for girls) became a key discursive justification for the military intervention in Afghanistan, and educational progress as a means of demonstrating the alleged success of the occupation. The blurred lines between military and aid workers discussed above is also directly observable in the field of education, conflict and emergencies through the ongoing attempts to foster intersectoral collaboration between development workers, peacebuilders and humanitarian aid workers – amongst others (Winthrop and Matsui 2013).

Fourthly, and linked to the increasing politicization of education in debates linked to the 'war on terror', there has been a rise of direct attacks on education systems and communities, particularly in Afghanistan, Pakistan and Nigeria. The Global Terrorism Database notes a significant increase in violent and extremist attacks on educational institutions since 2005.[6] Furthermore, there has also been an increased interest on the educational links to processes of radicalization, and a growing awareness that there is a need to better understand, and address, the root causes of violent extremism in order to prevent future violent attacks targeting learners, educators, education facilities and societies at large. This was, for instance, highlighted in the UN Secretary General's Plan of Action to Prevent Violent Extremism, which was presented to the UN General Assembly in January 2016.[7]

These combined reasons have led to a growing commitment to the area of education and conflict and have, not surprisingly, led to increased calls for funding to education in conflict zones. However, what should be noted is that as with the general aid disbursements to conflict and fragile states, the distribution of educational aid between countries is highly uneven with several high-profile countries such as Iraq, Pakistan, Sudan and Afghanistan receiving large portions of the cake (UNESCO GMR 2011). In addition, the main players in the field hardly recognize the role of education, either positively and negatively, in relation to persistent and growing forms of urban (gang) violence (Carapic and Lopes Cardozo 2016).[8] While Save the Children and several other actors have lobbied hard – and continue to do so – to increase the volume of spending and see current spending as insufficient to meet the challenges ahead (Save the Children 2007, 2008, 2010), the funds allocated have increased significantly over the past decade. DFID, in its latest development strategy paper (DFID 2015), aspires to spend 50 per cent of its aid budget in conflict-affected contexts, and 50 per cent of all to education spending, a commitment present in their education strategy since 2010 (see DFID 2010, Education Strategy Paper).[9]

The recently launched fund for EiE, the 'Education Cannot Wait Fund', is the most recent and visible attempt to 'bridge the humanitarian-development divide' and aims to support coordination and collaboration between public and private actors.[10] The overall five-year fundraising ambition of *Education Cannot Wait Fund* is to raise $3.85 billion, while it aims to scale up its resource mobilization over the first five years, commencing with an aim to raise approximately $150 million in the first year and with an ambition to bring funding to a level of $1.5 billion in the fifth year. INEE writes how, during the launch event in May 2016 at the World Humanitarian Summit in Istanbul,

> donor representatives from the United Kingdom, the United States, Norway, the European Union and the Netherlands stepped up and pledged $87.5 million or just over half of the $150 million needed to fully fund year one. Non-state pledges for the first year included a $2.5 million contribution from Dubai Cares to support initial set-up of the Education Cannot Wait secretariat bringing the total to more than $90 million. The Global Business Coalition for Education also committed to mobilize $100 million in financial and relevant in-kind contributions.[11]

INEE clearly played an important role in the emergence and foundation of this latest fund, but what do we know about the major driving forces behind this attempt to create a more robust, coordinated effort to support education interventions in emergencies and conflict? How should we understand the role of INEE as a network, and/or as a player in the field? The next section develops these questions further in an attempt to sketch/explore the latest developments in the field.

In conclusion to this section, the education and conflict agenda has been facilitated by the convergence of a range of external and internal factors of a very different nature: by post–Cold War and post-9/11 geopolitical realities and intentions; by EFA goals, MDG and SDG; by the advocacy of organizations like Save the Children, UNICEF and INEE – pushing for the humanitarian and human rights agenda of education; and, finally, also through the agency of military and security sectors that see building schools and strengthening education in certain conflict zones as part of their military strategy to win the hearts and minds of the civilian populations. Many of these issues and actors appear to clash with each other and produce unlikely bedfellows, and, interestingly, many of these players come together under the INEE umbrella. To further explore this interplay, in the next section we will begin to unravel in more detail what role INEE has played in this complicated picture.

The International Network of Education in Emergencies (INEE)

INEE is a network created to improve inter-agency communication and collaboration within the context of EiE, and has gained recognition as an effective lobbying, advocacy and policy coordination and development institution. There are some relevant prior studies undertaken that have evaluated the emergence of the network (Anderson and Mendenhall 2006; Bromley and Andina 2010) as well as some evaluative studies of the minimum standards (MS) tools (including Kirk and Cassidy (2007), a USAID study of Uganda by Sullivan-Owomoyela (2006), an INEE/UNICEF case study of Uganda by Karpinska (2008) and an OID/IIEP/INEE study by Mendizabal and Hearn (2011)). Nevertheless, there is not an extensive body of literature we can draw on for this analysis. Hence, we highlight insights from other studies where relevant, and build our further discussion on an analysis of available online resources as well as our own participation as members of the network during the past decade.

Founded in 2000, its membership has increased to about 11,000 members, and includes a mix of practitioners, students, teachers, staff from UN agencies, non-governmental organizations (NGOs), donors, governments and universities from most countries around the world.[12] Drawing on INEE's own analysis of its membership, about one-third of its members are working within NGOs, around 8 per cent in UN organizations, and another one-fifth in educational or academic institutions. Zooming into the two organizations that 'deliver' most members, Save the Children (138 members) is followed closely by UNICEF (114 members).[13] This is perhaps somewhat unsurprising, considering that both these organizations also co-lead the Education Cluster, which was started in 2007 by the Interagency Standing Committee (IASC) to ensure education – as a basic human right – is a core element of humanitarian response.[14]

As argued by Mendizabal and Hearn, 'As a network, INEE's structure is wholly different from that of a typical organisation' (2011).

So, *how is INEE governed and what is its modus operandi?* As a network organization, selected member organizations are involved in the operational structure, organized in the Steering Group, Secretariat, Working Groups and Language Communities, which are all discussed below. As part of its governance structure, the Steering Group

> provides strategic vision and overall governance for the network. In consultation with the wider membership and in line with the INEE Strategic Plan, the INEE Steering Group sets goals and plans for the network; approves new working groups and task teams; and provides strategic guidance to the INEE Secretariat staff. Steering Group members are senior representatives of organizations actively engaged in education in emergencies.[15]

The INEE *Secretariat* consists of a director, three coordinators for the respective *working groups* (more below), an administrative officer and a senior communications officer. Together, the secretariat aims to ensure

> effective coordination; convene and supports the members; build linkages and connections; strengthen commitment, collaboration, and partnerships within the network; filter and share information; enhance knowledge and capacity within and beyond the membership; and provide overall project management for network activities.[16]

The three dedicated Working Groups 'are formalized structures which help develop and promote specific work within INEE. Participation in Working Groups is on an institutional basis with individual representatives for each agency'. Within the working groups, focusing respectively on (1) *Standards and Practice* (2) *Education Policy* and (3) *Advocacy*,[17] there are specific *Working Groups Task Teams* in which individual members collaborate on specific areas of interest. Finally, the *Language Communities* facilitate access to resources, tools and experience in the non-English working languages of INEE (Arabic, French, Portuguese and Spanish).

The recent change in leadership in 2014 went hand in hand with a process of developing a new strategic plan (2015–2017). The plan was the result of a year-long process of consultation with members, both those within working groups and beyond, and has following as it mains goal: '*To enable quality, safe, and relevant education for all in emergencies and crisis contexts through prevention, preparedness, response, and recovery.*'[18] While the biannual INEE working group meetings were largely used to collectively draw out the main lines of the plan, the steering group played a decisive role in its final formulation as well as the new names given to the working groups, according to their main functions. As an entire network, the strategic plan established the following core functions: community building, convening, knowledge management, amplifying, advocating, facilitating, learning and providing.

Having established some of the foundational characteristics of the network as it functions at the moment of writing, we now turn to our discussion of the less-visible, underlying mechanisms that drive decision-making and governance of this network. In other words, *who is facilitating/funding, and who or what is driving specific thematic areas of focus and why?*

To start with the first question of who is funding, resources available on INEE's webpage illustrate how a range of institutions have provided financial and/or institutional support to the network. While current donors include Dubai cares,[19] Education Above All,[20] Mercy Corps,[21] UNICEF[22] and USAID,[23] further support is provided by the International Rescue Committee, the Norwegian Refugee Council, the RET and UNHCR as they hire and host INEE Secretariat staff. In addition, the INEE Steering Group member organizations provide annual financial membership contributions. [24] As the full list of donors (between 2001 and 2015) on INEE's webpage illustrates, there is a somewhat heavier involvement of institutions based in or directed from the 'western' part of the world, often equated with 'traditional' donor countries, as well as considerable support from UN agencies.[25]

While some colleagues in former studies usefully highlighted the challenge and dilemma's of working on a 'tightrope of promoting international understandings of EiE situations while being attentive to the local context of each crisis' (Bromley and Andina 2010, p. 586), instead we now turn to discuss *who or what is driving specific thematic areas of focus and why.*

First, following our comments above on where the funding comes from, there is a connected argument to be made about where this money consequently flows. Especially when it concerns the strategic planning and activities of the working groups, there seems to be an observable connection between the priorities of institutions that deliver the funding, and the thematic focus areas these working groups mostly focus on – establishing what we could perhaps term a form of intellectual or thematic dependency (e.g. the funding provided by one of the major donors, USAID, to the Education Policy

Working Group, and its respective focus on CVE/PVE fits neatly with its interests).

Secondly, and coming back to our earlier historical analysis of the rise of EiE, it pays off at this stage to bring back to mind the integrated approach/3-D approach, adopted by major (Western) donors. The fact that many of the funding agencies supporting INEE are at the same time committed to this integrated foreign policy strategy potentially means there is limited space for a more critical inquiry or even counter-voice towards the role these same 'western' powers historically have played, or perhaps still play, in conflict-affected regions. In other words, is there a space for INEE (members) to question Western interventionism in, for instance, the Middle East – as these same powers are also the main funders for the work that INEE aims to do to counterbalance the effects of conflict?

Thirdly, in this line of thinking, we would like to accentuate one more time a question raised earlier in this chapter, of whether INEE is an agent of broader global geopolitical power relations, reproducing unequal global political relationships or acting as a buffer, mediator, seeking to challenge these unequal relationships? In attempting to formulate a possible answer, recognizing that many responses are available, we return to insights from the SRA presented earlier on to shed light on the interrelations between structures and agents, as well as discursive and material realities. In a way, adapting insights from the SRA, we contend that INEE could be analysed through both the lens of a strategic selective *structure* and seeing it as a *strategic actor* in the field of education and development/emergencies. So, if we consider INEE as a network structure, it entails strategic selectivity's in its own existence. The governance of the network, and decisions on who is to be included/excluded in the active working groups, on paper aims for diversity. Exceptions that serve this purpose are left aside, due to limitations of material resources, language barriers and geographical remoteness, and the active membership is largely selectively enabled only for those usually already well connected to 'the field' with the institutional resources to fulfil these obligations.

When we consider INEE through the analytical lens of a strategic 'agent' – following the dominantly employed discourse and activities of INEE over the past fifteen years, a shift seems to have happened in the identity/character of what INEE is, and what course of action(s) it should take. Looking at INEE's mandate, a shift seems to have emerged of INEE functioning mainly as a network, to a more conventional umbrella organization, following a process of professionalization – and institutionalization – and in part also becoming more concerned with service delivery.

At the same time, from an initial focus on the role of EiE situations, a move was made to incorporate protracted crisis, conflict and post-conflict recovery and peacebuilding in subsequent years. These shifts can be seen as a process of (self-)identification of INEE as a strategic actor in the field it operates in. This process of identity building, of who INEE is/represents and what its roles are, is closely related to the mechanisms of governance and finances discussed above. Put simply, who is included and who pays also have the biggest say in what the networks stands for, and how it relates to the broader field of work. This then leads to the reflection that existing power relations are mostly reproduced through the ways in which the network is governed structurally, funded materially and expressed discursively by and beyond its active membership.

Conclusion

Reflecting on the global governance of 'Education in Emergencies' what we can see is a field that has been catapulted to prominence through a combination of factors that have emerged out of the broader challenges of post–Cold War geopolitics, where both development and conflict – and within that security – have merged in complex and often contradictory ways. On the one hand, the recognition that more than half of the world's out-of-school children live in conflict-affected contexts provided a rights-based justification for the consolidation of a subfield of international education and development. This subfield focused on technical solutions to the provision of education in complex emergencies, and served to legitimize the discourse of seeing education as life saving and worthy of a seat at the humanitarian table.

On the other hand, its focus on conflict and crisis-affected contexts placed it in the orbit of a range of high-stakes global political processes and actors, particularly since 9/11, which have shaped its evolution in line with broader US-led geopolitical priorities, which have focused disproportionately on those zones and regions designated as part of the 'war on terror'. These tensions between technical solutions, political priorities and security interests remain at the heart of the field's ongoing evolution. The growing attention in the realm of development, security and humanitarian policy and practice for the role of education in conflict and emergencies has also been mirrored in a rapidly emerging field of study. The increasing number of panel sessions in international conferences, such as, for instance, the recently established Special Interest Group on Education, Conflict and Emergencies at the Comparative and International Education Societies (CIES) conferences is illustrative of such a trend.[26] Nevertheless, recent reviews of the literature connected to this field refer to a lack of, and hence further need for, research and evidence (Smith et al. 2011; Burde et al. 2015; Horner et al. 2015; Lopes Cardozo et al. 2015; Smith and Ellison 2015).

Exploring the key role of the INEE within this emerging field highlights the way that this network has provided a coordinating forum for a range of powerful agencies to come together, develop common projects, share experiences, develop capacity and build a common identity and purpose. The network form and the open membership process have also facilitated broad participation from a wide range of policy actors and practitioners, students and researchers, providing the semblance of common purpose and mission. However, its apparent horizontal network and open membership structure is tempered through mechanisms that filter whose voices get heard and whose interests and priorities are embraced. Engagement in the various working groups, which represent a higher tier of governance and agenda setting, is dependent on being both selected by the steering committees and having an institutional backer that can cover the necessary expenses to attend the global meetings. Similarly, the funding priorities and focus of those institutions that provide resources to INEE seem to, at least partly, determine the agenda of the network and limit its openness to a wider plurality of voices and perspectives. Hence, the horizontal network structure is tempered by the 'real politik' of power and money.

This critique is not to downplay the many excellent achievements of INEE over the last two decades in facilitating the provision of education to children in some of the most complex contexts on our planet and in facilitating a far more collegial approach and common mission by practitioners and policy actors whose institutions often operate in silos that frequently undermine inter-agency collaboration and cooperation. Nor is it to downplay the deeply felt and genuine commitment of many of its members to promoting sustainable peace and development. More so, it seeks to provide an avenue for reflection on the way soft-power operates, uncover often under-represented mechanisms of geopolitics and both material (funding) and discursive (agenda-setting) hegemonies that influence the field's development. In revealing these imbalances and inequities, we can then better think through alternative, and complementary, mechanisms and strategies to ensure a plurality of perspectives and interests get represented in INEE and in the field of EiE more broadly.

Questions for discussion

1 Can you explain what were the major geopolitical events that have influenced the shift from a 'proliferation of initiatives' to the emergence of a coherent field of 'education in emergencies' since the 1990s?

2   In what specific ways do you see INEE as a key network actor within the field of EiE?:

(a) As a possible reproducing force of unequal global political relationships
(b) As a potential mediating force, functioning as a broker or bridge between different sectors and stakeholders
(c) As a potentially transformative entity seeking to challenge (unequal) relationships

3   What are the potential strategies or mechanisms that might enable a network actor – including, yet not limited to, INEE – to play a transformative role, and at what scales do you see the most important engagement of such a network actor?

Notes

1   Formerly known as the Inter-Agency Network for Education in Emergencies.

2   Using the language 'education in emergencies' does not reflect the authors' acceptance of the term. There have been a variety of debates and disputes over the years since INEE's foundation over the term 'education in emergencies' which we believe serves to conflate issues related to education in conflict-affected contexts with issues related to education in contexts affected by natural disasters. It also implies that the field – and INEE itself – works primarily in the emergency phase, while the field itself explores issues related to prevention and recovery – both short and long term – of education systems and societies affected by conflict and natural disasters. Our main focus in this chapter is on conflict-affected contexts, which is where our own area of expertise lies.

3   Ploumen, 17 November 2015, The Guardian: http://www.theguardian.com/global-development/2015/nov/17/without-rule-of-law-conflict-affected-areas-will-become-poverty-ghettoes?CMP=share_btn_tw (accessed 15 July, 2017).

4   http://learningforpeace.unicef.org/pbea/about-pbea/what-is-pbea/ (accessed 16 June 2017).

5   See http://www.state.gov/j/ct/rls/crt/ (accessed 16 June 2017).

6   See https://www.start.umd.edu/gtd/ (accessed 16 June 2017) and http://www.ineesite.org/en/preventing-violent-extremism (accessed 16 June 2017).

7   https://www.un.org/counterterrorism/ctitf/en/plan-action-prevent-violent-extremism (accessed 16 June 2017).

8   See http://old.norrag.www438.your-server.de/fileadmin/Working_Papers/Working_Paper__10_Carapic_Lopes_Cardozo.pdf (accessed 16 June 2017).

9   We consider 'fragile states' as a complicated and value-laden concept, and

while emphasizing its problematic nature (what state would be willing to be called 'failed' by others?), we chose to use the term for this chapter in order to stay close to the discourse used in the global environment.

10 Resources: http://www.educationcannotwait.org/the-fund/ and http://www.ineesite.org/en/education-cannot-wait (accessed 16 June 2017).see also https://www.government.nl/latest/news/2016/05/23/the-netherlands-pledges-extra-educational-support-for-refugee-children (both accessed 18 July 2016).

11 *Donor commitments made at the 23 May 2016 launch event:* the United States = $20 million; the United Kingdom = £30 million over two years; European Union = €5 million; Norway = $10 million; the Netherlands = €7 million; Dubai Cares = $2.5 million, source: http://www.unicef.org/media/media_91132.html (accessed 16 June 2017). For commitment of the GBC see http://gbc-education.org/private-sector-to-mobilize-100-m/ (accessed 16 June 2017)

12 For more resources on the evolution of INEE as a network, see also the work of Anderson and Mendenhall (2006), Bromley and Andina (2010), Mendizabal and Hearn (2011).

13 INEE webpage, http://www.ineesite.org/en/who-we-are (accessed 16 June 2017). For a visual representation of this data, see https://drive.google.com/file/d/0B2ZJ2C7BqezFSjJIYWp5dWh0Tm8/view (last accessed 17 November 2016).

14 http://educationcluster.net (accessed 16 June 2017).

15 INEE webpage: http://www.ineesite.org/en/how-we-work (accessed 16 June 2017).

16 INEE webpage: http://www.ineesite.org/en/who-we-are#INEESecretariat (accessed 16 June 2017).

17 INEE webpageL http://www.ineesite.org/en/working-groups (accessed 16 June 2017).

18 The plan included four strategic priorities, including:

Strategic Priority 1: To serve as a global advocate and thought leader, promoting education for all and in all circumstances. **Strategic Priority 2**: To foster the strengthening of the evidence base through partnerships that inform research, policy, and practice across humanitarian and development contexts. **Strategic Priority 3**: To increase the availability and accessibility of knowledge and information which builds upon and improves capacities to deliver education for all. **Strategic Priority 4**: To foster an engaged, inclusive and diverse membership, and build strategic partnerships to achieve all other strategic priorities.

Source: http://www.ineesite.org/en/how-we-work
(accessed 16 June 2017).

19 No data available at the time of writing.

20   6 per cent from total in 2015, and 4 per cent from total in 2014.

21 $69,499 in 2015.

22   28 per cent from total in 2014, 28 per cent from total in 2013, 13 per cent from total in 2012, 23 per cent in 2011, 38 per cent from total 2010, 35 per cent from total in 2009, 33 per cent from total in 2008, 44 per cent from total in 2007.

23   39 per cent from total in 2015, 19 per cent from total in 2013, 20 per cent from total in 2012, 27 per cent from total in 2011.

24   http://www.ineesite.org/steering-group (accessed 16 June 2017), the webpage does not specify what amounts are concerned here.

25   http://www.ineesite.org/en/donors (accessed 16 June 2017), see for instance the considerable funding from UNICEF and USAID as detailed in endnotes 22 and 23.

26   For more info see http://www.cies.us/?page=TopicSigs and https://www.facebook.com/CIES.ECE/?fref=ts (accessed 16 June 2017).

References

Anderson, A. and Mendenhall, M. (2006). Inter-agency network for education in emergencies, *Forced Migration Review Supplement (Education and Conflict: Research Policy and Practice)*.

Bradbury, M. (1995). *Aid under fire: Redefining relief and development*, London: HMSO.

Brigety REI (2008). *Humanity as a weapon of war*. Sustainable Security and the Role of the US Military. Washington, DC: Center for American Progress.

Bromley, P. and Andina, M. (2010). 'Standardizing chaos: A neo-institutional analysis of the INEE minimum standards for education in emergencies, chronic crises and early reconstruction'. *Compare*, 40 (5), 575–588.

Burde, D. Guven, O., Kelcey, J., Lahmann, H. and Al-Abbadi, K. (2015). *What Works to Promote Children's Educational Access, Quality of Learning, and Wellbeing in Crisis-Affected Contexts*, Education Rigorous Literature Review. Department for International Development. Available at: http://www.ineesite .org/en/lit-review-what-works-in-eie (accessed 16 June 2017).

Bush, J. and Saltarelli, D. (2000). *The two faces of education in ethnic conflict*. New York: UNICEF.

Cammack, P. (2004). 'What the World Bank means by poverty reduction, and why it matters'. *New Political Economy*, 9 (2), 189–211.

Cammack, P. (2007). 'Imperial nature: The World Bank and struggles for social justice in the age of globalization'. *Progress in Human Geography*, 31 (1), 124–126.

Carapic and Lopes Cardozo. (2016). Education, urban violence, and youth: Exploring pathways or roadblocks for 'peace' in the city, NORRAG Working Paper #10, March 2016. Available at: http://old.norrag.org.www438.your -server.de/fileadmin/Working_Papers/Working_Paper__10_Carapic_Lopes _Cardozo.pdf (accessed 16 June 2017).

Chomsky, N. (1994). *World orders, old and new*. London: Pluto.

Chomsky, N. (1999), *The new military humanism: Lessons from Kosovo*. London: Pluto.

Chossudovsky, M. (1997). *The globalisation of poverty: Impacts of IMF and World Bank reforms*. London: Zed Books, Penang: Third World Network.

Chossudovsky, M. (2002). *War and globalisation: The truth behind September 11*. Shanty Bay, ON: Global Outlook.

Christian Aid (2004). *The politics of poverty: Aid in the new cold war*. London: Christian Aid.

Cosgrave, J. (2005). *The impact of the war on terror on aid flows*. London: Action Aid.

Dale, R. (2005). Globalisation, knowledge economy and comparative education. *Comparative Education*, 41 (2), 117–149.

DFID (2003). *Education, conflict and development*. London: DFID.

DFID (2010). *Learning for all: DFID's education strategy 2010–2015*. London: DFID.

DFID (2015). *UK aid: Tackling global challenges in the national interest*. DFID: London. https://www.gov.uk/government/publications/uk-aid-tackling-global-challenges-in-the-national-interest (accessed 16 June 2017).

Duffield, M. R. (2007). *Development, security and unending war: Governing the world of peoples*. Cambridge: Polity.

EU (2003). *A secure Europe in a better world*. Brussels: European Union.

Fearon, D. (2008). 'The rise of emergency relief aid'. In M. N. Barnett and T. G. Weiss (Eds.), *Humanitarianism in Question*. Ithaca, NY: Cornell University Press, 49–72.

Forsythe, D. P. (2000). *Human rights in international relations*. Cambridge: Cambridge University Press.

GCE (2009). *Education on the brink: Will the IMF's new lease on life ease or block progress towards education goals?* Johannesburg: Global Campaign for Education.

Harvey, D. (2007). *A brief history of neoliberalism*. Oxford: Oxford University Press.

Horner, L., Kadiwal, L., Sayed, Y., Barrett, A., Durrani, N. and Novelli, M. (2015). 'Literature review: The role of teachers in peacebuilding'. Research Consortium Education and Peacebuilding, University of Sussex. Available at: https://educationanddevelopment.wordpress.com/rp/outputs-research-consortium/ (accessed 16 June 2017).

Jessop, B. (1999). 'The strategic selectivity of the state: Reflections on a theme of Poulantzas'. *Journal of the Hellenic Diaspora*, 25 (1–2), 1–37.

Jessop, B. (2005). 'Critical realism and the strategic-relational approach'. *New Formations*, 56, 40–53.

Karpinska, Z. (2008). *An evaluation of the INEE minimum standards for education in emergencies, chronic crises and early reconstruction: A Uganda case study*. London: The Inter-Agency Network for Education in Emergencies.

King, K. (2007). 'Multilateral agencies in the construction of the global agenda on education'. *Comparative Education*, 43 (3), 377–391.

Kirk, J. and Cassidy, E. (2007). Minimum standards for quality education for refugee youth. *Youth Studies Australia*, 26 (1), 50–56.

Lopes Cardozo, M. T. A. and Shah, R. A. (2016a). 'The fruit caught between two stones': The conflicted position of teachers within Aceh's independence

struggle', *Globalisation, Societies and Education*, 14 (3), 331–344. http://dx.doi.
org/10.1080/14767724.2016.1145572.

Lopes Cardozo, M. T. A. and Shah, R. A. (2016b). A conceptual framework to
analyse the multiscalar politics of education for sustainable peacebuilding.
Comparative Education, pp. 1–22. http://dx.doi.org/10.1080/03050068.2016.12
20144.

Lopes Cardozo, M. T. A., Higgins, S. and Le Mat, M. L. J. (2016). Youth agency
and peacebuilding: An analysis of the role of formal and non-formal education.
Synthesis report on findings from Myanmar, Pakistan, South Africa and
Uganda, Research Consortium on Education and Peacebuilding, University of
Amsterdam.

Lopes Cardozo, M. T. A., Higgins, S., Maber, E., Brandt, C. O., Kusmallah, N. and
Le Mat, M. L. J. (2015). Literature Review: Youth Agency, Peacebuilding and
Education, Research Consortium Education and Peacebuilding, University of
Amsterdam. Available at: https://educationanddevelopment.wordpress.com/
rp/outputs-research-consortium/ (accessed 16 June 2017).

Lundborg, P. (1998). 'Foreign aid and international support as a gift exchange'.
Economics and Politics, 10 (2), 127–142.

Machel, G. (1996). *Impact of armed conflict on children*. United Nations.

Mendizabal, E. and Hearn, S. (2011). *Not everything that connects is a network*.
ODI Background Note.

Mundy, K. (2006). 'Constructing education for development: International
organizations and education for all'. *Comparative Education Review*, 50 (2),
296–298.

Mundy, K. E. (2002). 'Retrospect and prospect: Education in a reforming World
Bank'. *International Journal of Educational Development*, 22 (5), 483–508.

Novelli, M. (2010). 'The new geopolitics of aid to education: From cold wars to
holy wars'. *International Journal of Educational Development*, 30, 453–459.

Novelli, M. (2016). Capital, inequality and education in conflict-affected contexts.
British Journal of the Sociology of Education, 37 (6) September, 848–861.

OECD (2015). *States of Fragility 2015: Meeting Post-2015 Ambitions*, OECD
Publishing, Paris. doi:http://dx.doi.org/10.1787/9789264227699-en.

OECD/DAC (2005/2008). *The Paris Declaration on Aid Effectiveness and the
Accra Agenda for Action*. Available at: http://www.oecd.org/dac/effectiveness/
parisdeclarationandaccraagendaforaction.htm (accessed 16 June 2017).

Reality of Aid Network (2008). *The reality of aid 2008: An independent review of
poverty reduction and development assistance*. Quezon City: Ibon Books.

Roberts, A. (2000). 'Humanitarian issues and agencies as triggers for international
military action'. *International Review of the Red Cross*, 839, 673–698.

Robertson, S. and Dale, R. (2015). 'Toward a critical cultural political economy of
the globalisation of education', *Globalisation, Societies and Education*, 13 (1),
149–170.

Robertson, S., Novelli, M., Dale, R., Tikly, L., Dachi, H. and Ndebela, A. (2007).
*Education and development in a global era: Ideas, actors and dynamics in the
global governance of education*. London: DFID.

SAEC – *Southern Aid Effectiveness Commission* (2010). *Towards more effective
Aid Assessing reform constraints in the North*, April 2010, facilitated by
Eurodad and the Reality of Aid.

Save the Children (2007). *Last in line, last in school: How donors are failing
children in conflict-affected fragile states*. London: Save the Children.

Save the Children (2008). *Last in line, last in school 2008: How donors can support education for children affected by conflict and emergencies.* London: Save the Children.

Save the Children (2010). *The future is now, education for children in countries affected by conflict.* London: Save the Children.

Slim, H. (1996). 'Military humanitarianism and the new peacekeeping: An agenda for peace?' *IDS Bulletin*, 27 (3), 86–95.

Smith, A. (2014), 'Contemporary challenges for education in Conflict affected countries', *Journal of International and Comparative Education*, 3 (1). Available at: http://crice.um.edu.my/downloads/Smith14.pdf (accessed 16 June 2017).

Smith, A. and Ellison, C. (2015). The Integration of Education and Peacebuilding: A Review of The Literature, Research Consortium on Education and Peacebuilding/University of Ulster. Available at: https://educationanddevelopment.wordpress.com/rp/outputs-research-consortium/ (accessed 16 June 2017).

Smith, A., McCandless, E., Paulson, J. and Wheaton, W. (2011). *Education and peacebuilding in post-conflict contexts: Literature review*, United Nations Children's Fund, New York. Available at: https://www.unicef.org/protection/files/EEPCT_Peacebuilding_LiteratureReview.pdf (accessed 16 June 2017).

Sullivan-Owomoyela, J. (2006). Inter-Agency Network for education in emergencies minimum standards for education in emergencies, chronic crisis, and early reconstruction: A Uganda case study. *Prepared by Creative Associates International, Inc. for USAID. Overseas Development Institute, 111.*

UNESCO/GMR (2011). The Hidden Crisis: Armed Conflict and Education. EFA Global Monitoring Report 2011. Paris: UNESCO.

US State Department (2008). *Country reports on terrorism 2007.* Washington, DC: United States Department of State Publication Office of the Coordinator for Counterterrorism.

USAID (2008). *Civilian-Military Cooperation Policy.* [pdf]. Washington, DC: USAID. Available at: pdf.usaid.gov/pdf_docs/PDACL777.pdf (accessed 16 June 2017).

Wang, T. Y. (1999). 'US foreign aid and UN voting: An analysis of important issues'. *International Studies Quarterly*, 43, 199–210.

Winthrop, R. and Matsui, E. (2013). *A new agenda for education in fragile states.* Center for Universal Education at Brookings.

Further reading

Davies, L. (2004). *Education and conflict: Complexity and chaos.* London: Routledge.

Novelli, M., Valiente, O., Higgins, S. and Ugur, M. (2014). *The political economy of education systems in conflict affected states.* London: DFID.

Shah, R. A. and Lopes Cardozo, M. T. A. (2015). The politics of education in emergencies and conflict. In T. McCowan and E. Unterhalter (Eds.), *Education and international development: An introduction.* London: Bloomsbury Academic, pp. 181–200.

Winthrop, R. and Matsui, E. (2013). *A new agenda for education in fragile states.* Center for Universal Education at Brookings.

12

Constructing Low-Fee Private Schools as an Educational Model for the Global South: From Local Origins to Transnational Dynamics

Antoni Verger, Clara Fontdevila
and Adrián Zancajo

Chapter Outline

This work has been developed with the support of a research grant from *Education International* and in the context of the Marie Curie project 'Public–Private Partnerships in Educational Governance' (EDUPARTNER, ref. GA-2012-322350). This piece develops and updates the chapter *Privatization by Default in Low-Income Countries* from the book *The Privatization of Education: A Political Economy of Global Education Reform* (NY: Teachers College Press, 2016), written by the same authors.

Introduction

Private-sector involvement in education is growing in most countries, but for reasons that are very different and context specific. We tend to think about education privatization as the main result of neoliberal or pro-market education reforms. However, in many Southern countries, private schools are growing not necessarily because governments are openly promoting them through explicit policy programmes and instruments, but because governments face restrictions of an economic, administrative and/or political nature in responding to education expansion pressures. Thus, in these countries, the fact that the state does not properly attend an increasing educational demand opens a big window of economic opportunity for private education providers. This privatization-*by-default* mechanism seems to be especially relevant in southern regions such as sub-Saharan Africa, Latin America, and Southeast Asia. As shown in Figure 12.1, these three regions have witnessed a constant and significant expansion of enrolment in private schooling in the last fifteen years.[1]

The main modality of private schools that are expanding in southern contexts are the so-called low-fee private schools (LFPSs). *Low-fee private schools* are defined as private schools that have been set up and are owned by an individual or group of individuals for the purpose of making a profit, and are supposed to be 'affordable' for low-income families (adapted from Phillipson

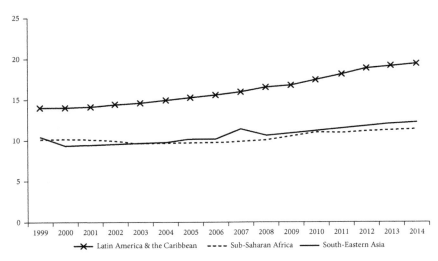

FIGURE 12.1 *Percentage of enrolment in primary education in private institutions (%) by region, 1999–2014*

Source: Adapted from the UNESCO Institute of Statistics (UIS) database.

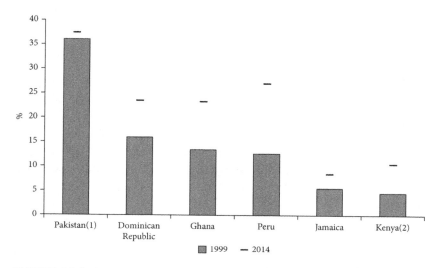

FIGURE 12.2 *Percentage of enrolment in primary education in private institutions (%), 1999–2014. (1) The first year with data available is 2004 instead of 1999. (2) The data covers the 2005–2009 period*

Source: Adapted from data from UNESCO Institute of Statistics (UIS).

2008). According to existing research, LFPSs are a growing phenomenon in countries such as Malawi, Nigeria, Kenya, Ghana, India, Pakistan, Peru, Dominican Republic and Jamaica. Figure 12.2 shows how the percentage of enrolment in primary education has increased significantly in most of these countries in the last years, predictably through the expansion of the LFPS sector.[2]

However, there are different perspectives when it comes to determining the real size of the LFPS phenomenon, with its promoters eager to exaggerate its dimensions (see Pearson 2015; Tooley 2013) and sceptics downsizing it (Lewin 2007). One of the main reasons why it is difficult to quantify the real dimension of LFPSs is that many of these schools are not registered and, consequently, cannot be properly quantified and tracked through official data (Srivastava 2008; Härma 2011; Härma and Adefisayo 2013; Dahal and Nguyen 2014).

Another reason why it is difficult to quantify LFPSs as a schooling sector is that it represents a relatively new phenomenon whose definition and boundaries are contentious in conceptual terms. Specifically, it is difficult to determine which private schools are included and excluded from the *low-fee* category. The meaning of *low cost* or *low tuition fee* is especially unclear and highly subjective, and the point at which a private school stops being considered as low fee or low cost cannot be defined universally. The determination of such a threshold will be contingent on the socioeconomic structure of the contexts in which these schools operate, as well as on the economic circumstances of particular families.

In any case, most scholars agree on the existence of a new privatization trend that, despite its heterogeneity, is different from more conventional forms of privatization. LFPSs are different from traditional elite private schools in the sense that the latter are selective by definition and generally do not target the poor. LFPSs are also different from private schools run by non-government organizations (NGOs), communities, or churches, in that the latter also target the poor, but they are usually established on the basis of social, communitarian, or religious motivations, and not necessarily economic or for-profit ones.

This chapter focuses on the reasons, agents, and other type of drivers behind the emergence and expansion of LFPSs in the Global South, and discusses the policy and socio-educational implications of such an expansion. Among other things, this chapter shows that a phenomenon that first emerged spontaneously, at a local level and, apparently, *by default*, is now strongly promoted by several influential international players in the education-for-development field, including international organizations, donors and transnational corporations. In fact, as will be observed, these actors are actively constructing LFPSs as an appropriate partner to achieve the current global development goals. Accordingly, more and more governments and other key stakeholders are integrating (or considering to integrate) this type of schools into their education expansion plans, policies and strategies.

To build this argument, we structure the chapter in three main sections. In the first section we reflect on the role that poor families exert in the expansion of LFPSs, and reflect on the different reasons why they resort to these types of schools. In the second part of the chapter, we explore what are the main international agents, rationales and strategies behind the promotion of low-fee schooling in the Global South. In the third and last part of the chapter, we show how, in part as a result of international promotion, some LFPSs operators are scaling up their activity significantly, and numerous southern governments have started subsidizing and/or partnering with this sector as a way to expand education more efficiently.

Methodologically, the chapter is based on a systematic review approach (Gough et al. 2012), which is a type of literature review that has allowed us to systematize numerous pieces of research focusing on how and why education privatization happens in Southern countries. For the production of this piece, a total of seventy publications have been reviewed (although not all of them are included in the list of references). These publications were selected on the basis of their thematic fit, out of a larger pool of studies compiled from different sources (electronic databases, grey literature, and recommendations from key informants), and screened against quality and relevance criteria.[3] At the theoretical level, a *cultural political economy* framework has guided the review. This framework has permitted us to observe and to analyse how drivers of a different nature (agentic and structural, global and local, material and semiotic, etc.) interact in the production of pro-private sector transformations at different stages and through different mechanisms (Jessop 2010; see also introductory chapter in this volume).

Inquiring into poor families' demand for LFPSs

Are LFPSs better than public schools? A contentious debate

Researchers supportive of privatization consider that LFPSs are 'mushrooming' in numerous developing countries (cf. CfBT 2011; Tooley 2013), and that this is happening because of poor families' school choice decisions. According to them, poor families would make the economic effort to put their children in LFPSs because they consider that these schools offer higher-quality education than public schools and, as a consequence, 'will better increase their children's opportunities and potential' (Tooley 2013, p. 460). Their research argues that LFPSs are better managed than public schools, and that teachers in LFPSs are more committed and, more importantly, children would learn more than in public schools. On the basis of research conducted in poor areas of India (Delhi and Hyderabad), Kenya (Nairobi), Ghana (Ga, near Accra) and Nigeria (Lagos State), James Tooley, a well-known LFPS advocate, concludes the following:

> On quality, we tested a total of 24,000 children in mathematics, English, and one other subject and found that children in the low-cost private schools significantly outperformed those in government schools, even after controlling for family background variables and possible selectivity biases. (Tooley 2016, p. 64)

These authors also argue that poor families are aware of and well informed about the apparent superiority of LFPSs to public schools (e.g. Dixon et al. 2013). According to them, poor families have sufficient information to distinguish 'good-quality' education and make schooling decisions accordingly. In their own words, 'The choices favoring low-cost private schools made by parents in the slums are based on quality considerations, like those made by wealthier parents' (Dixon et al. 2013, p. 102).

Nonetheless, other scholars challenge studies that reflect on the 'quality advantage' of LFPSs on the basis of parental perceptions of education quality. For instance, according to Shailaja Fennell (2013), most poor parents in low-income countries lack the baseline personal experience in schooling to judge the quality of a school or teachers at the moment of choosing the school – this is why many of them would postpone their (more accurate) judgements until their children are already in school. Similarly, Balarin (2015) shows that poor Peruvian parents' discernment of school quality, when arguing about their preference for LFPSs, tends to be quite precarious. According to many of the parents she interviewed, LFPSs are perceived as better than the public alternative because they give more subjects, workbooks and homework to children. Thus, these families would perceive discipline and traditional forms of education as a proxy for the quality of education, despite the fact that current pedagogical and didactical theories clearly challenge these perceptions.

Overall, the superior quality of LFPSs is a highly contested subject in the existing literature. In fact, this theme has generated one of the most controversial debates in the 'education for development' field in the last several years. A rigorous review funded by the UK Department for International Development (DFID) on the impact of private schools in developing countries recently concluded that evidence on the potential contribution of LFPSs to achieving quality education for all is still inconclusive in many aspects (see Ashley et al. 2014). The belligerent reaction of James Tooley (see Tooley and Longfield 2015) to this report is very illustrative of the battle for evidence that surrounds this theme. In a similar vein, the publication of a study drawing on experimental evidence and calling into question the added value of LFPSs in terms of learning outcomes[4] (Muralidharan and Sundararaman 2015) was almost immediately revisited by James Tooley (Tooley 2016) – who re-examined and reframed the results in order to make the case for this modality of schooling and for its promotion through the use of publicly funded vouchers.

Critical scholars, but also teachers' unions and civil society organizations, tend to point to teachers' qualifications and labour conditions as the main challenge of LFPSs from a quality perspective. According to them, LFPSs often hire unqualified teachers (who may receive very little training, are trained in-house, or both) and pay them very low wages (Andrabi et al. 2008; Aslam and Kingdon 2011; Riep, 2014; Edwards et al. 2017). *Other scholars* argue that LFPSs are not better than public schools in abstract terms, but they tend to be more intensive when it comes to teaching hours, with some having classes on Saturdays, and are more strategic when it comes to teaching students how to do well on standardized tests (Riep 2014).

The DFID review on education privatization in low-income contexts mentioned above concluded that private schools are better than public schools in terms of more teacher presence, pupil attendance and teaching activity. However, evidence of the superiority of the private sector in terms of learning outcomes is far beyond question yet (Ashley et al. 2014). According to this review, even though there is a body of research showing that students from low-income countries attending private schools tend to achieve better learning results, most of this research does not 'adequately account for social background differences of pupils' (Ashley et al. 2014, p. 45). This review also challenges the assumption that private schools are more accountable than public ones.

Are LFPS affordable?

To make it easier for poor families to attend LFPSs, many of these schools tend to operate a daily payment system. They establish this daily fee-paying formula (which some call the 'pay as you learn' model) because they are aware that poor people also earn money on a daily basis rather than having a certain weekly, monthly or yearly income, and that their saving capacity is limited (Riep 2014). In a way, some level of tolerance with delayed or missing payments is a necessary condition for schools having a regular enrolment of families with financial difficulties (Edwards et al. 2017).

Nonetheless, many challenge the idea of LFPSs being really affordable and/ or attended exclusively by the poor. Empirical research on the theme shows that, in many contexts, 'the reliance on LFPSs charging school fees is likely to be prohibitive for poor households' (Härmä and Rose 2012, p. 256; see also Ashley et al. 2014; Govinda and Bandhyopadhyay 2008; Riep 2014). Among other things, these doubts on the affordability of LFPSs could mean that one of the 'comparative advantages' of this type of schools is related to the social origin of their students. LFPSs might attract relatively poor families, but they do attract those families among the poor that have a higher level of education, more expectations for their children's education, or a combination (Fennell and Malik 2012; Akyeampong and Rolleston 2013; Härma and Adefisayo 2013). It is, therefore, no coincidence that, as mentioned earlier, many of the researchers who point to better learning outcomes in this type of private school do not properly account for students' socio-economic status (Ashley et al. 2014).

Interestingly, the school composition factor in part explains the growing demand for LFPSs in different settings. This seems to be the case in those countries, especially in sub-Saharan Africa, that have abolished school fees in government schools in the last few decades. These countries have witnessed an increasing educational demand from the poorest sectors and have not increased the number of public schools accordingly. As a reaction to the massification of classrooms in government schools, but also as a way to distinguish themselves from the new (and academically less skilled) pupils entering the system, a significant number of the less-disadvantaged population have abandoned public schools and populated all types of private schools, including LFPSs (Bold et al. 2010). One of the results of this 'exit' dynamic is that public education has become 'a ghettoised option of last resort for the poorest and most marginalized in society' (Härmä 2010, p. 38).

Other dimensions of LFPS choice

Even though the evidence about the superior quality of private versus public education is inconclusive, there is a widespread social perception in many places that private schools are better than public schools (see Akyeampong and Rolleston 2013). This perception is reinforced by the fact that public schools in remote or slum areas are more likely to be under-resourced or poorly managed than those in better-established urban areas (Mehrotra and Panchamukhi 2007; Rose and Adelabu 2007). In fact, many LFPSs are emerging in remote rural areas or in new (and usually unofficial) urban settlements where public schools do not even exist yet. Thus, parents from these settings do not send their kids to LFPSs because they prefer them as a first choice, but because there are no decent free public school alternatives close enough to their homes (Heyneman and Stern 2014). Similar dynamics can be observed in cities of the Global South where a relatively rapid demographic growth has not been matched by public investment in education (Flores 1997; Guzmán and Cruz 2009).

Not all poor families choose LFPSs because they consider them as superior forms of education provision. Closeness to home is one of the main school choice criteria for many poor families. Choosing an LFPS that is close to home is convenient for families because it makes schooling more compatible with the parents' domestic and work duties, and because it saves money in transportation. But it is also important for security reasons. The closeness of the school to home 'allows parents to be more vigilant of their children – taking them and picking them up from school – in precarious urban contexts that are perceived by their dwellers as being very high risk' (Balarin 2015, p. 18).

Finally, religious and cultural aspects also explain the demand for LFPSs in vulnerable contexts and, especially, among minority groups. For instance, the Indian Muslim community educational choices often favour LFPSs run by Muslims because they consider that their religion is not sufficiently recognized in the predominantly Hindu public education system (Sarangapani and Winch 2010). Something similar has been documented in the case of linguistic minorities and their school choice strategies (Walford 2013), or in situations of internal political conflict – since, in conflict situations, some families may decide not to send their children to government schools when these families and the government have adopted different positions within the conflict (Caddell 2006).

In a nutshell, LFPS demand is likely to be driven by the accumulation of unsatisfied demand for education resulting from state passivity and/or limited capacity when it comes to expand or improve school provision. Nonetheless, the reason behind the increasing demand for LFPSs cannot be reduced to education quality issues; any poor families opt for LFPSs not only because these schools are perceived as superior in terms of learning outcomes, but because the curriculum, religious option or language of instruction in these schools is more aligned with their own cultural or political identities and preferences. Last but not least, in many instances parents choose LFPSs for social distinction and security reasons as well.

Beyond the demand from poor families, the following section reflects on the multiple forces that contribute to the growth of the LFPS phenomenon. Specifically, we focus on the role of international aid actors and transnational education corporations in the promotion of this controversial schooling modality.

The global promotion of LFPSs

Traditionally, 'individual village entrepreneurs' have been considered the main agents behind the LFPS phenomenon (Walford 2015). The owners of LFPSs tend to be described as local 'edupreneurs' that have detected a business opportunity in the education sector, usually in their own community (Tooley 2013). These edupreneurs are usually the owners of a single school that has been built with their own resources and, in some instances, even located in their own home (Härma and Adefisayo 2013). Because of this, several authors refer to the growth of LFPSs as a sort of 'grassroots privatization' phenomenon (Tooley 2013; Miller et al. 2014).

However, in recent years, other actors, very different in nature to these local edupreneurs, have entered the LFPS sector and are promoting and offering this type of private schooling in the Global South. These include public and private organizations and policy entrepreneurs operating on a transnational geographical scale.

Most of these actors promote LFPSs with arguments of government failure and the potential efficiency gains of this education model. According to them, LFPSs need to be seen as a strategic option for both the governments of low-income countries and the international community because they facilitate more efficient access to education (at least, from the perspective of public spending). This type of argument is especially prevalent among the international aid community, whose focus is on widening education access in the context of global development goals such as Education For All (EFA), the Millennium Development Goals (MDGs) and, more recently, the Sustainable Development Goals (SDGs). As we develop below, the development compact constituted by these global goals lends itself to a certain tactical use, given its ambiguity (or lack of a clear statement) concerning the expected role of the public and the private sectors regarding the funding and delivery of education.

Perceiving the role of the private sector in such an instrumental way is far from a new development. Conventionally, the promotion of private schools has been seen as a cost-efficient measure because the private consumption of education (by those who can afford it) increases the total resources available for education and relieves the pressure on public budgets (Bray 2002). In other words, by enrolling their children in private schools, middle-class families contribute to freeing up government resources that can be invested in improving public schools attended by the poor. Nevertheless, the LFPS phenomenon is altering – and somehow radicalizing – the pro-private schools discourse by proposing and celebrating that poor families can also 'afford' private education. In this respect, LFPSs, by enlarging the target population of those who can attend private schools, have challenged the prevailing reasoning on private school consumption.

The World Bank is, in fact, one of the global actors that have recently started to perceive LFPSs as a desirable option for the poor; to that end, it began supporting this concept through different lines of credit in Bangladesh, Pakistan and Haiti. In the *2020 Education Sector Strategy*, released in 2011, the World Bank acknowledges that private schools can be an affordable option for the poor and a method of overcoming 'state failure' in education (Verger and Bonal 2012). The *2020 Education Sector Strategy* considers that the International Finance Corporation (IFC), the World Bank Group agency that deals directly with the private sector, should play a bigger role in financing, through lending operations, private school organizations that 'target poor populations' (World Bank 2011, p. 32). In fact, the IFC has started approving important loans for LFPS chains that operate in sub-Saharan Africa, such as Bridge International Academies. Furthermore, as a way of promoting this line of credit and to explore how to bring private education to more people globally, every two years, the IFC organizes the IFC Private Education Conference, an international meeting on private education that gathers education entrepreneurs, investors and consultancy firms. In the recent past, the LFPS sector has been widely represented at these events.[5]

Bilateral aid agencies, such as those from Australia, Canada, the United States and the United Kingdom, have also joined the list of international actors explicitly supporting LFPSs for the poor as part of their education development strategy (Niemerg 2013). Of all of them, the DFID is one of the most active in LFPS promotion. This aid agency is currently committed to 'expanding access to and educational outcomes for poor children, including through low-fee private schools' (DFID 2013, p. 19), and supports the expansion of LFPSs in countries like Kenya, Nigeria and Pakistan (Niemerg 2013; Junemann et al. 2016). DFID is also 'funding the Center for Education Innovations (2012–2016), to document market-based education innovations that can 'increase access to quality, affordable and equitable education for the world's poor' (CEI website) with the aim of 'collaborating more closely with the private sector in development' (DFID 2013)' (Junemann et al. 2016, p. 544).

Nonetheless, the UN's Committee on the Rights of the Child has disputed the support of DFID to LFPS. A recent resolution adopted by this committee expresses its concern about the international cooperation policy of the United Kingdom promoting LFPS.[6] For the committee the increase in LFPSs threatens the quality and equity of education systems in Southern countries. In response to this resolution, DFID has stated that they only support LFPSs where there is weak or non-existent government provision (Balch 2016).

The appeal exerted by LFPS on the education for development community can be partially explained by its apparent compatibility with what is perceived as 'noble goals' – such as the EFA goals or, more recently, the SDGs. As observed by Srivastava (2010, p. 523), the fact that the EFA movement has not agreed on a specific education policy or governance agenda has created an 'unscrutinized space' in which different actors tactically use the globalization discourse to advance their particular agendas, including those involving further education privatization. Similarly, the SDGs agenda addresses the role of the private sector in a rather ambiguous way, what could again allow for a certain instrumentalization in favour of the LFPS cause. In fact, the *Education 2030 Framework for Action* recognizes the private sector as 'a contributor with significant potential to complement resources for education and increase synergies' (UNESCO 2016, p. 34) and, at the same time, leaves open to interpretation the specific arrangements through which this collaboration with the private sector is expected to materialize.

On a different note, and beyond the 'education for development' community, the increasing expansion and profit potential of the LFPS sector has contributed to private corporations and finance entities stepping into the sector as well. The most well-documented case in this respect is that of Pearson, a giant player in the global education industry that has created the Pearson Affordable Learning Fund (PALF) to especially target the LFPS sector. PALF was launched in July 2012 with $15 million of initial capital, and was expended with $50 more million in 2015. Pearson sees this initiative as a way 'to demonstrate how a for-profit approach can scale and solve education in developing countries'.[7] However, for this corporation, PALF is not only an economic tool; it is also part of a broader political strategy to promote and construct LFPS as a sector. As Sir Michael Baber, chief education advisor to Pearson, stated in an interview:

> What we want to demonstrate [with PALF] is that with an injection of capital and the governance that goes with it – and we will take minority stakes in businesses that are developing, either chains of schools or providers of support services to chains of schools – we can demonstrate that you could improve the quality of that sector and you could build the sector. (Santori et al. 2016, p. 200)

Similar funding initiatives to that of Pearson can be found, for example, in the Rising Schools Program and in the Orient Global Education Fund (Srivastava 2014). The Rising Schools Program is a microfinance initiative for LFPS owners in Ghana launched in 2009 by the Innovation Development Progress (IDP) Foundation and the Sinapi Aba Trust. Rising Schools' mission is 'developing innovative, scalable, and replicable programs through sustainable initiatives that move away from aid-based models and lead to greater progress in the achievement of Education for All for the most deprived'.[8] So far, the Rising Schools programme self-report reaches more than 500 primary schools and 123,000 pupils and continues to resort to global goals as a master frame to justify further private investment in the low-fee schooling sector – highlighting, for instance, its alignment with SDGs:

> Since the release of the Sustainable Development Goals (SDGs), the IDP Rising Schools Programme has identified that much of its work intersects at goals 1, 4, 5, 8 and 17. With the SDGs set forth, the programme is continuing to effectively grow and measure its impact, while supporting this rapidly growing sector. While the focus may be to build more public schools to replace private schools, governments can leverage the cost-savings provided by existing schools and identify policies needed to support their improvement so that all children have access to quality education, thus breaking the cycles of illiteracy and poverty.[9]

Finally, it is important to mention that the international promoters of LFPSs, including international organizations, aid agencies, private foundations and international consultants, regularly meet with private school owners and other types of edupreneurs at a number of international events, conferences and seminars held regularly in different locations, although recently they have had a bigger presence in the Gulf states. They include the IFC Private Education Conference mentioned previously, the International and Private Schools Education Forum, the Qatar Foundation's World Innovation Summit for Education (WISE) and the Global Education and Skills Conference. Interestingly, these two latter events see themselves as 'the Davos of Education'. According to Junneman et al. (2016), conferences like these provide opportunities for 'talk and touch', which produce and consolidate trust. Through the social relations that participants establish in these events, ideas are shared and borrowed, stories about 'best practices' and local edupreneurs are told, and visits are organized (Santori et al. 2015). Overall, these international events contribute to expanding and strengthening networks and to closing business deals. At a more symbolic level, these spaces also contribute to entrenching a discourse in the international education arena on the desirability of including both the private sector and for-profit motives in educational development policies.

Recent developments in the sector

Due largely to the external support received from foreign investors and donors, some LFPSs are scaling up their operations and developing into chains of schools. These include Innova Schools, Bridge International Academies (BIA), LEAP Science and Maths Schools, the Omega schools and the APEC schools. Some of the main selling points of these school chains are that they are expected to generate economies of scale, but also to standardize their educational products and services – for example, by strongly prescribing teaching–learning content and processes. Standardization is meant to control all aspects of the education process to reduce the risk of schools not delivering 'results'. It is also meant to generate an identifiable chain's brand and, by doing so, help families to overcome the usual information problems that they face when choosing a school for their kids. It is quite illustrative of this standardization ambition that some of these companies state that they are creating an easily replicable 'school-in-a-box' model (Riep 2014).

Some LFPS chains have started internationalizing their operations or are planning to do so in the coming years. Among them, BIA, an LFPS chain based in Kenya that has expanded to Uganda and Nigeria and is preparing to expand to India, stands out. By 2025, BIA expects to 'be operating in at least a dozen countries, and have 10,000,000 pupils coming to class every day'.[10] BIA is also convinced of the potential of the standardization and vertical integration of educational processes within its chain and, in fact, considers itself as the 'Starbucks' of schools in developing countries (Srivastava 2016). A wide range of transnational investors has supported BIA when it came to scaling up its activity. These investors include the Omidyar Network, Pearson, the

Deutsche Bank Foundation, Gray Ghost Ventures, the W.K. Kellogg Foundation and, more recently, the IFC (Junemann et al. 2016; Srivastava 2016). When it comes to networks and influences, BIA has connections with the US charter school movement or Teach for America, with which it has common ideological commitments and modes of operation (Junemann et al. 2016).

As shown above, an important barrier preventing the LFPS sector from advancing more quickly is that many poor families, especially those with several children or from the lowest-income quintile, cannot afford this or any other type of private schooling. To overcome this barrier, LFPS advocates are recommending that governments adopt voucher schemes or related demand-side interventions as a way of facilitating access to these types of schools and, by doing so, provide poor families with more school choice opportunities (Dahal and Nguyen 2014, p. 27). These types of recommendations imply the establishment of formal contracts or public–private partnerships (PPPs) between governments and LFPSs. In fact, the inclusion of LFPSs in PPP frameworks is already being discussed, piloted and even adopted on a larger scale in low-income countries such as Uganda (Brans 2013; Srivastava 2016), India (Srivastava 2010; Verger and VanderKaaij 2012), Pakistan (Barber 2013) and Liberia. The government of the latter country surprised the international education community in 2015 when it announced *Partnership Schools for Liberia*, an ambitious charter school reform that sought to put BIA in charge of managing all the public schools of the country (although, after much of a stir, not all Liberian schools will be *charterised*, and BIA will not be the single private provider). [11]

Using PPPs *with* LFPSs is a policy approach that is expected to become increasingly central in the education for development agenda because it apparently addresses two key concerns: on the one hand, the efficiency criteria that many donors and financial international organizations are looking for when promoting the expansion of education and, on the other hand, the equity concerns that most privatization policies generate (in the sense that the public subsidy would provide more opportunities for the poor to attend private schools that, even if they are meant to be low fee, the poorest cannot afford). However, this new trend is not without potential risks and challenges at the regulatory and accountability levels. According to Srivastava (2014, p. 2):

> Lessons emerging from countries with longer histories of PPP-friendly institutional frameworks [reflect] that large-scale PPP arrangements are not only more risky for the public sector, as there are fewer actors to bear the risk, but also that they operate with vested interests against those of the public, can lead to more complicated regulatory frameworks not less, and that they have the potential of becoming 'abusive' if the stronger partner dominates.

Thus, the biggest question that models of PPPs with LFPSs generate concerns the extent to which the governments of low-income countries will have the capacity to enforce and enact the necessary regulations and accountability mechanisms to ensure that this type of private schools respect public education principles and, accordingly, do not discriminate against the most disadvantaged students with their school admission procedures or expulsion policy, or do not charge uncovered fees that the poorest families cannot afford to pay.

Conclusion

LFPS represent a modality of private schooling that is becoming more central in educational provision in many low-income countries. It is portrayed as a grass-roots privatization movement in the sense that these schools have been traditionally initiated by local edupreneurs who have detected a business opportunity in their communities, usually because of insufficient or inadequate public education. To a great extent, the advancement of LFPSs due to economic restrictions at the country level, which often merge with administrative challenges around planning education properly or with a lack of political will on the part of Southern countries' governments to invest more resources in public education.

Privatization advocates consider that LFPSs are expanding because they offer better-quality education and achieve higher learning outcomes than public schools. Nonetheless, numerous scholars challenge these assumptions from both the perspectives of the supply and the demand. Thus, from the supply-side perspective, these authors argue that teachers in LFPSs are insufficiently trained and paid, and evidence on better learning outcomes in LFPSs is far from conclusive. On the demand side, existing research shows that many families choose LFPSs not only as a matter of giving more learning opportunities to their children, but also as a matter of security and control, linguistic and religious recognition, and, more importantly, social distinction (i.e. a way for low-income parents to distance themselves from even more disadvantaged families).

Despite its locally situated origins, the LFPS phenomenon is being increasingly globalized, with international organizations, donors, philanthropists and private investors further promoting and investing in them in various contexts. Thus, an initiative that was initiated by poorly resourced individuals at the community level is becoming more and more embedded in transnational networks of influence, capital and ideas. Many international players perceive LFPSs as a cost-efficient and profitable way of promoting access to education for the poor. The LFPS sector is increasingly attractive to a broader range of private actors because it fits neatly in the philanthrocapitalist idea (see Bishop and Green 2008) that profit is compatible with – and can even become a driver of – more noble goals, such as EFA and the SDGs.

The international network of LFPS advocates, which tends to crystallize and meet in conferences, philanthropy encounters, award ceremonies and other international events, is eager to demonstrate that this schooling modality can benefit the poor in different ways. In the context of this network, the idea of the inherent superiority of the private sector over public education tends to be constructed via the selective use of evidence (Srivastava 2016). Nonetheless, beyond the articulations of ideas and discourses pro-private education, the international community is also using a mix of finance mechanisms, like private funds coming from international investors or voucher schemes funded by aid agencies, as a way to promote LFPSs.

The promotion that LFPSs are benefiting from at different scales is translating into two emerging developments in the sector. First, LFPS chains, like BIA or Omega, despite still being a minority compared to stand-alone schools, are emerging, but expanding massively in countries such as Liberia. These chains are able to standardize their education services and open similar schools in different locations (even in different countries). Second, PPPs in education increasingly include the LFPS sector as a way to give more educational choice to the poor. These new developments have generated new policy debates and concerns. For instance, research on teaching and learning practices casts considerable doubt on the adequacy of the pedagogical approaches frequently adopted by LFPSs. There is evidence that the need to minimize costs and scale up profits is likely to translate into the use of standardized methods such as the use of scripted lessons, an emphasis on rote learning and the use of technology as a substitute of trained teachers (GCE 2016). These practices tend to have a negative impact in terms of curriculum and learning relevance, and challenge the concept of teachers as professionals with the necessary knowledge to adapt their teaching to different situations and contexts. From the governance perspective, the main question that models of PPPs with LFPSs generate concerns the extent to which the governments of low-income countries will be able to persuade and regulate for-profit actors to work in the public interest, and to avoid PPPs generating further educational inequalities.

In a nutshell, LFPSs are moving from being considered *de facto* privatization to being a significant part of the 'strategy of design' by the international development community (Srivastava 2010, p. 3). This shift brings forward new and important challenges for the governance of education systems and the achievement of equity and learning goals in low-income contexts.

Questions for discussion

1 Why are LFPSs expanding in so many developing countries? What are the institutional conditions that favour LFPS expansion?

2 Can you differentiate between local and external drivers in LFPS promotion?

3 How would you define the population attending LFPSs? Are LFPSs affordable for the poor?

4 What are the main concerns that the expansion of LFPSs generates from an educational equity perspective?

5 In your opinion, could a voucher scheme address some of the equity concerns that LFPSs generate?

Notes

1 Private enrolment is also growing in countries of the Southern Asia, particularly in India and Pakistan (Dahal and Nguyen 2014). Unfortunately there is not sufficient comparable data to estimate the value of this indicator for this region.

2 Private enrolment in primary education has also increased dramatically in recent years in many other Southern countries such as Congo, Gambia Guinea-Bissau, Guinea, Morocco, Mauritania, Gabon and Thailand (see UNESCO 2015). Although such an increase in private enrolment could be attributed to LFPSs expansion, we have not identified literature focusing on this phenomenon for these countries.

3 The research strategy in electronic datasets was based on the combination of search-terms focusing on the following dimensions: (1) political economy, (2) privatization reforms/policies, (3) policy actors, and (4) general education terminology.

4 Although highlighting their cost-effectiveness.

5 See for instance: www.ifc.org/wps/wcm/connect/industry_ext_content/ ifc_external_corporate_ site/industries/health+and+education/news/ bridgeschools_feature.

6 UN Committee on the Rights of the Child (CRC/C/GBR/CO/5). Concluding observations on the fifth periodic report of the United Kingdom of Great Britain and Northern Ireland. Available online: http://tbinternet.ohchr .org/layouts/treatybodyexternal/Download.aspx?symbolno=CRC/C/GBR/ CO/5&Lang=en (accessed 30 September 2016).

7 See: https://www.affordable-learning.com/content/corporate/global/palf/en/ about/vision.html (accessed 5 October 2016).

8   See www.idpfoundation.org/about (accessed 23 September 2016).

9   http://www.idpfoundation.org/blog/low-fee-private-schools-closing-the-education-gap-in-ghana (accessed 23 September 2016).

10 http://www.bridgeinternationalacademies.com/company/mission/ (accessed 21 September 2016).

11 http://www.nytimes.com/2016/06/14/opinion/liberia-desperate-to-educate-turns-to-charter-schools.html?r=0 (accessed 5 October 2016).

References

Akyeampong, K. and Rolleston, C. (2013). 'Low-fee private schooling in Ghana: Is growing demand improving equitable and affordable access for the poor?'. In P. Srivastava (Ed.), *Low-fee private schooling: Aggravating equity or mitigating disadvantage?*. Oxford: Symposium Books, pp. 37–64.

Andrabi, T., Das, J. and Khwaja, A. I. (2008). *A dime a day: The possibilities and limits of private schooling in Pakistan* (World Bank Policy Research Working Paper 4066). Washington, DC: World Bank.

Ashley, L. D., Mcloughlin, C., Aslam, M., Engel, J., Wales, J., Rawal, S.,... Rose, P. (2014). *The role and impact of private schools in developing countries: A rigorous review of the evidence. Final report* (EPPI-Centre Education Rigorous Literature Review Reference Number 2206). London: DfID.

Aslam, M. and Kingdon, G. (2011). 'What can teachers do to raise pupil achievement?'. *Economics of Education Review*, 30 (3), 559–574.

Balarin, M. (2015). The default privatization of Peruvian education and the rise of low-fee private schools: Better or worse opportunities for the poor? (Open Society Foundations/Privatisation in Education Research Initiative – Education Support Program Working Paper 56). London, UK: OSF.

Balch, O. (2016, June 14). 'UN criticises UK for spending aid money on for-profit private schools'. *The Guardian*.

Barber, M. (2013). *The good news from Pakistan: How a revolutionary new approach to education reform in Punjab shows the way forward for Pakistan and development aid everywhere*. London: Reform.

Bishop, M. and Green, M. (2008). *Philanthrocapitalism: How the rich can save the world*. New York: Bloomsbury Press.

Bold, T., Kimenyi, M., Mwabu, G. and Sandefur, J. (2010). Does abolishing fees reduce school quality? Evidence from Kenya (CSAE Working Paper WPS/2011-04). Oxford: Centre for the Study of African Economies – University of Oxford.

Brans, B. J. (2013). 'Public private partnerships in Uganda: More perils than promises for universal secondary education'. In A. Verger, H. K. Altinyelken and M. de Koning (Eds.), *Global managerial education reforms and teachers: Emerging policies, controversies, and issues in developing countries*. Brussels, Belgium: Education International, pp. 74–90.

Bray, M. (2002). *The costs and financing of education: Trends and policy implications* (Education in Developing Asia, Volume 3). Manila/Hong Kong: Asian Development Bank/Comparative Education Research Centre – The University of Hong Kong.

Caddell, M. (2006). 'Private schools as battlefields: Contested visions of learning and livelihood in Nepal'. *Compare*, 36 (4), 463–479.

CfBT. (2011). *Preliminary study into low-fee private schools and education – Final report*. Reading, PA: CfBT/DfID.

Dahal, M. and Nguyen, Q. (2014). Private non-state sector engagement in the provision of educational services at the primary and secondary levels in South Asia: An analytical review of its role in school enrollment and student achievement (World Bank Policy Research Working Paper 6899). Washington, DC: World Bank – South Asia Region, Education Unit.

Department for International Development (DfID). (2013). *Education position paper: Improving learning, expanding opportunities*. London: Department for International Development.

Dixon, P., Tooley, J. and Schagen, I. (2013). 'The relative quality of private and public schools for low-income families living in slums of Nairobi, Kenya'. In P. Srivastava (Ed.), *Low-fee private schooling: Aggravating equity or mitigating disadvantage?*. Oxford: Symposium Books, pp. 83–104.

Edwards, B. Jr., Klees, S. J. and Wildish, J. L. (2017). 'Dynamics of low-fee private schools in Kenya: Governmental legitimation, school-community dependence, and resource uncertainty'. *Teachers College Record,* 119 (7), pp. 1–42.

Fennell, S. (2013). 'Low-fee private schools in Pakistan: A blessing or a bane?' In P. Srivastava (Ed.), *Low-fee private schooling: Aggravating equity or mitigating disadvantage?*. Oxford: Symposium Books, pp. 65–82.

Fennell, S. and Malik, R. (2012). 'Between a rock and a hard place: The emerging educational market for the poor in Pakistan'. *Comparative Education*, 48 (2), 249–261.

Flores, R. (1997). *La escuela básica en la zona marginal de Santo Domingo. Un estudio comparativo de la organización industrial del servicio de educación en la República Dominicana*. Washington, DC: Inter-American Development Bank.

Global Campaign for Education (GCE) (2016). *Private Profit, Public Loss. Why the push for low-fee private schools is throwing quality education off track*. Johannesburg: Global Campaign for Education.

Gough, D., Thomas, J. and Oliver, S. (2012). 'Clarifying differences between review designs and methods'. *Systematic Reviews*, 1 (28).

Govinda, R. and Bandyopadhyay, M. (2008). *Access to elementary education in India: Analytical overview* (CREATE Working Paper). Brighton: University of Sussex – Centre for International Education.

Guzmán, R., y Cruz, C. (2009). *Niños, niñas y adolescentes fuera del sistema educativo en la República Dominicana*. Santiago: Foro Socioeducativo.

Härmä, J. (2010). *School choice for the poor? The limits of marketisation of primary education in rural India* (CREATE–Pathways to Access Research Monograph Number 23). Brighton: University of Sussex–Centre for International Education; Consortium for Educational Access, Transitions, and Equity.

Härmä, J. (2011). Low-cost private schooling in India: Is it pro poor and equitable? *International Journal of Educational Development*, 31 (4), 350–356. doi:10.1016/j. ijedudev.2011.01.003

Härmä, J. and Rose, P. (2012). 'Is low-fee private primary schooling affordable for the poor? Evidence from rural India'. In S. L. Robertson, K. Mundy, A. Verger and F. Menashy (Eds.), *Public-private partnerships in education: New actors and modes of governance in a globalizing world*. Cheltenham/Northampton: Edward Elgar, pp. 243–258.

Härmä, J. and Adefisayo, F. (2013). Scaling up: Challenges facing low-fee private schools in the slums of Lagos, Nigeria. In P. Srivastava (Ed.), *Low-fee private schooling: Aggravating equity or mitigating disadvantage?*. Oxford: Symposium Books, pp. 129–152.

Heyneman, S. P. and Stern, J. M. B. (2014). 'Low-cost private schools for the poor: What public policy is appropriate?' *International Journal of Educational Development*, 35, 3–15.

Jessop, B. (2010). 'Cultural political economy and critical policy studies'. *Critical Policy Studies*, 3 (3/4), 336–356. doi:0.1080/19460171003619741.

Junemann, C., Ball, S. and Santori, D. (2016). Joined-up policy: Network connectivity and global education governance. In K. Mundy, A. Green, R. Lingard and A. Verger (Eds.), *Handbook of global policy and policy-making in education*. West Sussex: Wiley-Blackwell, pp. 535–553.

Lewin, K. M. (2007). *The limits to growth of non-government private schooling in sub-Saharan Africa* (CREATE–Pathways to Access Research Monograph Number 5). Brighton: University of Sussex–Centre for International Education.

Mehrotra, S. and Panchamukhi, P. R. (2007). 'Universalizing elementary education in India: Is the private sector the answer?' In P. Srivastava and G. Walford (Eds.), *Private schooling in less economically developed countries: Asian and African perspectives*. Oxford: Symposium Books, pp. 129–153.

Miller, P., Craven, B. and Tooley, J. (2014). Setting up a free school: Successful proposers' experiences. *Research Papers in Education*, 29 (3), 351–371.

Muralidharan, K. and Sundararaman, V. (2015). The aggregate effect of school choice: Evidence from a two-stage experiment in India. *Quarterly Journal of Economics*, 130, 1011–1066.

Niemerg, M. (2013). *International support to low-cost private schools*. Chicago, IL: INP Foundation Inc.

Pearson PLC. (2015). Where are the low-cost schools? Retrieved from www. affordable- learning.com/resources/where-are-the-low-cost-schools.html.

Phillipson, B. (2008). *Low-cost private education: Impacts on achieving universal primary education*. London: Commonwealth Secretariat.

Riep, C. B. (2014). 'Omega schools franchise in Ghana: "Affordable" private education for the poor or for-profiteering?'. In I. Macpherson, S. Robertson and G. Walford (Eds.), *Education, privatisation, and social justice: Case studies from Africa, South Asia, and South East Asia*. Oxford: Symposium Books, pp. 259–278.

Rose, P. and Adelabu, M. (2007). 'Private sector contributions to education for all in Nigeria'. In P. Srivastava and G. Walford (Eds.), *Private schooling in less economically developed countries: Asian and African perspectives*. Oxford: Symposium Books, pp. 67–88

Santori, D., Ball, S. J. and Junemann, C. (2015). 'Education as a site of network governance'. In W. Au and J.J. Ferrare (Eds.), *Mapping corporate education: Power and policy networks in the neoliberal state*. New York: Routledge, pp. 23–42.

Santori, D., Ball, S. J. and Junemann, C. (2016). Financial markets and investment in education'. In A. Verger, C. Lubienski and G. Steiner-Khamsi (Eds.), *World yearbook of education 2016: The global education industry*. New York: Routledge, pp. 193–207.

Sarangapani, P. M. and Winch, C. (2010). 'Tooley, Dixon, and Gomathi on private education in Hyderabad: A reply'. *Oxford Review of Education*, 36 (4), 499–515.

Srivastava, P. (2008). 'The shadow institutional framework: Towards a new institutional understanding of an emerging private school sector in India'. *Research Papers in Education*, 23 (4), 451–475.

Srivastava, P. (2010). 'Privatization and education for all: Unravelling the mobilizing frames'. *Development*, 53 (4), 522–528.

Srivastava, P. (2014, March). Contradictions and the persistence of the mobilizing frames of privatization: Interrogating the global evidence on low-fee private schooling. Paper presented at the annual conference of the Comparative & International Education Society (CIES), Toronto, Ontario, Canada.

Srivastava, P. (2016). 'Questioning the global scaling up of low-fee private schooling: The nexus between business, philanthropy, and PPPs'. In A. Verger, C. Lubienski and G. Steiner-Khamsi (Eds.), *World yearbook of education 2016: The global education industry*. New York: Routledge, pp. 248–263.

Tooley, J. (2013). 'Challenging educational injustice: "Grassroots" privatisation in South Asia and sub-Saharan Africa'. *Oxford Review of Education*, 39 (4), 446–463.

Tooley, J. (2016). 'Extending access to lo-cost private schools through vouchers: An alternative interpretation of a two-stage 'School Choice' experiment in India'. *Oxford Review of Education*, 42 (5), 579–593.

Tooley, J. and Longfield, D. (2015). *The role and impact of private schools in developing countries: A response to the DFID-commissioned 'rigorous literature review'*. London: Pearson.

UNESCO (2015). *Education for all 2000–2015: Achievements and challenges*. Paris: UNESCO Publishing.

UNESCO (2016). *Education 2030. Incheon Declaration and Framework for Action. Towards inclusive and equitable quality education and lifelong learning for all*. Available at: http://www.uis.unesco.org/Education/Documents/incheon -framework-for-action-en.pdf (accessed 20 September 2016)

Verger, A. and Bonal, X. (2012). "All things being equal?" Policy options, shortfalls, and absences in the World Bank education strategy 2020. In S. J. Klees, J. Samoff and N. P. Stromquist (Eds.), *The World Bank and education: Critiques and alternatives*. Rotterdam, the Netherlands: Sense Publishers, pp. 125–142.

Verger, A. and VanderKaaij, S. (2012). 'The national politics of global policies: Public-private partnerships in Indian Education'. In A. Verger, M. Novelli and H. K. Altinyelken (Eds.), *Global education policy and international development: New agendas, issues, and policies*. London/New York: Bloomsbury Academic, pp. 245–266.

Walford, G. (2013). 'Low-fee private schools: A methodological and political debate'. In P. Srivastava (Ed.), *Low-fee private schooling: Aggravating equity or mitigating disadvantage?*. Oxford: Symposium Books, pp. 199–213.

Walford, G. (2015). 'The globalisation of low-fee private schools'. In J. Zajda (Ed.), *Second international handbook on globalisation, education and policy research*. Dordrecht, the Netherlands: Springer Netherlands, pp. 309–320.

World Bank (2011). *Learning for all: Investing in people's knowledge and skills to promote development: World Bank Group education strategy, 2020*. Washington, DC: World Bank.

Further reading

Ashley, L. D., Mcloughlin, C., Aslam, M., Engel, J., Wales, J., Rawal, S. and Rose, P. (2014). *The role and impact of private schools in developing countries: A rigorous review of the evidence. Final report* (EPPI-Centre Education Rigorous Literature Review Reference Number 2206). London: DfID.

Junemann, C., Ball, S. and Santori, D. (2016). 'Joined-up policy: Network connectivity and global education governance'. In K. Mundy, A. Green, R. Lingard and A. Verger (Eds.), *Handbook of global policy and policy-making in education*. West Sussex: Wiley-Blackwell, pp. 535–553.

Mcloughlin, C. (2013). Low-cost private schools: Evidence, approaches and emerging issues. Available at: http://www.enterprise-development.org/wp-content/uploads/Low-cost_private_schools.pdf (accessed 25 September 2016).

Srivastava, P. (Ed.) (2013). *Low-fee private schooling: Aggravating equity or mitigating disadvantage?*. Oxford: Symposium Books.

Srivastava, P. (2016). Questioning the global scaling up of low-fee private schooling: The nexus between business, philanthropy, and PPPs. In A. Verger, C. Lubienski and G. Steiner-Khamsi (Eds.), *World yearbook of education 2016: The global education industry*. New York: Routledge, pp. 248–263.

13

Measuring and Interpreting Re-Contextualization: A Commentary

Gita Steiner-Khamsi

The re-contexualization of global education policy is a recurrent theme in this book. Several authors draw on studies in Brazil, El Salvador, Kenya, South Africa, Turkey and Uganda to make a case that global education policy means different things to different actors, is embraced by these actors for different reasons and is, depending on context, implemented differently. In my commentary on this inspiring book, I scratch at the surface of such statements that at first sight appear to be commonsensical but at closer examination lend themselves as a starting point for developing novel approaches to measuring and understanding policy change. My commentary offers a methodological thought and a few theoretical observations on the challenges and the gains associated with the study of re-contextualization.

How to trace global education policy methodologically

How does one measure global education policy? Is it sufficient to provide evidence that the reform resembles – in design or in rhetoric – policies in other countries or, even more telling, in the majority of countries of this world? Is the occurrence of a traveling reform, which surfaces in different corners of the globe, indicative of a global policy? These types of methodological questions are key concerns in globalization studies. They are hardly new, and three of the most common replies are briefly sketched in the following: neo-institutionalist theory, diffusion/social network analysis and policy-borrowing/lending research.

Scholars with a neo-institutionalist world view tend to draw on a large number of cases, countries or institutions, over a long time period (50–150 years), but only a few variables, to draw conclusions that there is nowadays a shared global understanding of particular beliefs such as social justice and equity. Decision-makers align the national with the educational and promote educational practices that are in line with these shared beliefs and global standards. This is a bird's-eye view on social development, in that similarities are observed and recorded at a supranational or cross-national level. From such a distance, re-contextualization does exist but has little conceptual relevance. In fact, loose coupling is a metaphor that is frequently used by scholars in institutional theory and organizational sociology to denote the discrepancies between the various levels or activities of an organizational field. Gili Drori et al. (2003), for example, apply the concept to demonstrate that despite the [universal] 'belief that science is a tool for achieving development' (Drori et al. 2003, p. 159), international organizations have developed a variety of 'solutions'.

According to the authors, the solutions vary from IMF-type to UNESCO-type solutions, the former promoting technology parks and the latter school science education programmes for young children. Similar to discrepancies between attitude and behaviour, intention and action, policy and practice, loose coupling is, depending on the author, seen as irrational, idiosyncratic or particularistic and therefore yields few insights for understanding bigger, long-term changes at societal level. In comparative and international education, Francisco Ramirez (2003) and David Baker and LeTendre (2005) revert to loose coupling as an explanation whenever they encounter profound differences between a universal standard (e.g. student-centred teaching, gender awareness) and its local manifestation. For example, Baker and LeTendre (2005, p. 177) insist that the 'classroom in Seoul, Paris, Santiago, Cleveland or Tunis will be remarkably similar' and add, drawing on the argument of loose coupling, '[w]hat differences remain will be mostly across schools within nations for intentional reasons and some idiosyncratic variation introduced by teachers'.

The second method of inquiry emphasizes and measures transnational interaction. Diffusion of innovation studies date back to the 1920s, were revived in the 1970s (see Rogers 1995, first 1962) and refined in the new millennium as part of social network analysis (Watts 2003). The quintessential question of diffusion/social network analysis is best illustrated in the classic example of the spread of the stone axe (see Rogers 1995): Is the fact that the stone axe was discovered in different locations at about the same time an expression of maturation (trial and error) or an expression of interaction (borrowing from others)? More than 3,000 years later, only a few researchers wonder whether conditional transfer programmes (CCT), implemented in over forty countries, represents a 'best practice' that matured over time, based on trial-and-error methods for attracting and retaining children from poor families in school. The majority of researchers assume transnational interaction and acknowledge that CCT programmes, actively propagated, funded and disseminated by development banks, have been transferred from one context to another, and were subsequently re-contextualized.

Finally, borrowing/lending research is genuinely interested in understanding the disjunctures that occur between global education policy and local re-contextualization. I share this critical, contextual or culturalist perspective with many authors of this book. Indeed, it is the social, political and economic conflicts, the power differentials and the legitimacy issues within a particular context, country or case that facilitate the circulation of global education policy. Unsurprisingly, one of the key questions is: Why does a global education policy resonate in a particular context? The analytical unit of policy borrowing/lending researchers is the local policy context. Concretely, references to other countries, other subsystems within a country (notably the economy) or, more broadly, to 'globalization', 'inter- national standards' or 'best practices' are interpreted as political manoeuvres to build policy coalitions in situations of protracted policy conflict. In line with the theory of self-referential systems (Luhmann 1990; Schriewer 1990), a group of us argue that externalization provides, literally translated, 'additional meaning' (German: *Zusatzsinn*).

Without going into too much depth here about the Advocacy Coalition Framework in policy studies (see Steiner-Khamsi 2010), 'additional meaning' is actually exactly what it takes to make adverse interest groups come together in unison or at least temporarily build a coalition to bring about change. Precisely because the act of externalization takes a best practice or a lesson learnt from other countries out of context, it is amenable to adoption by groups with divergent policy agendas. Indicator research and statistical measurements help neutralize and provide a stamp of scientific rationality on policies that in reality are politically charged. The different local actors selectively borrow aspects or rhetoric of a global education policy that best fits their own political agenda. The theory explains why liberal and progressive groups selectively borrow certain aspects of conditional cash transfer (CCT), public–private partnerships (PPP), new public management (NPM) and other neoliberal reforms. The de-contextualized best practices, lessons learned from others or international standards, present themselves (or more accurately are actively promoted) as neutral and thereby allow for all kinds of projections, speculations and ultimately broad support (see Takayama 2010; Waldow 2010, 2012).

Not to be overlooked in this volume is the fascinating analysis of Camilla Addey and Sam Sellar on why national governments participate in international large-scale assessments (ILSAs). Their study breaks radically with commonsensical explanations of why national policy actors agree to participate in a PISA, TIMSS or other ILSA study. The most commonsensical ones are lesson drawing or learning from comparing over time or across educational systems. In contrast, their analytical approach takes into account political, economic, social and technical dimensions. Their contextual focus enables them to identify a wide range of reasons of why national policy actors find ILSAs useful. The rationale for participation in ILSAs includes the better-known ones, such as (1) coalition building or, more precisely, for generating or alleviating reform pressure, (2) mobilizing financial sources for the education sector, (3) demonstrating internationality, (iv) learning technical skills of how to measure student outcomes and system performance. Having examined several countries that participated in PISA, LAMP and PISA-D, Addey and Sellar identify a total of seven categories of reasons that explain a country's participation in these three ILSAs.

Having briefly sketched the main features of three widely referenced theories on globalization in education, it is now possible to situate the contributions made in this book. None of the authors takes on a neo-institutionalist research agenda: nobody in this book assumes that global education policy spreads because it represents a 'best practice' or because it fits into a universally shared understanding of what constitutes 'good education'. To put it politely, the theory is of limited value for understanding re-contextualization because for neo-institutionalist theory loose coupling *is* the explanation (Latin: *explanans*) rather than the issue that begs for an explanation *(explanandum)*.

Without any doubt, the contributions in this book help advance theories in diffusion/social network analysis and in policy borrowing/lending research. The place allocated for this commentary is too short to get caught up in the narcissism of petty differences. The distinctive feature between the two related yet distinctive interpretive frameworks is the act of externalization. For researchers of borrowing/lending it matters a great deal whether an explicit reference to another educational system, to another sector or to an international standard has been made. The emphasis is on agency and on agenda-driven policy borrowing and lending and not on diffusion alone. Thus, it is not sufficient to state the resemblances between various policies and interpret them *a posteriori* as a case of policy borrowing. This said, many studies in this book are about diffusion and fewer about policy borrowing/ lending.

Arguably there is a reason why there are more studies on diffusion than on policy borrowing/lending. Peter Hall's distinction between three types of policy learning helps to explain the methodological differences between diffusion/social network analysis and policy borrowing/lending research. Hall (1993) differentiates between first-order policy change (incremental change), second-order policy change (policy goals are maintained but the instruments are changed) and third-order policy change (policy goals and instruments are changed). He applies the classification to explain why the emergence of the monetarist, neoliberal thought in the 1980s and 1990s represented a Kuhnian-type paradigm shift or a third-order change in the United Kingdom. Incremental or first-order changes constitute the most common type of policy learning, but naturally most scholars are more interested in understanding bigger changes in the form of second-order and third-order changes. Most chapters in this book deal with third-order policy change (see Hall 1993) and document radical or fundamental policy alterations in the direction of neoliberalism (privatization, school-based management, decentralization) or individualism (student-centred teaching, life-long learning, human rights). Several chapter authors observe the diffusion of these travelling reforms in two or more countries and analyse how they were locally adapted.

It would be wrong to assume that this book is only about diffusion and translation. It is also to some extent about reception, resonance and cross-national policy attraction, all issues that are prototypical for policy borrowing/ lending research. The co-editors of this volume have reframed the issue in the following fascinating research question: 'Why do policy-makers *buy* global education policy?' (Verger, Novelli and Altinyelken, Chapter 1 of this volume). For example, Antoni Verger, Clara Fontdevila and Adrián Zancajo (in this volume) deconstruct the myth that low fee private schools (LFPSs) have experienced an exponential growth over the past few years because parents see them as the better alternative – in terms of quality of education – than free public schools. They start out by calling into question the very definition of LFPSs. Does the count of LFPSs only represent registered schools or does the figure include a rough estimate on the large number of LFPSs that are not registered? What is the fee threshold, that is, at which fee level should a school simply be considered a (fee-based) private school rather than an LFPS? Their chapter calls for a nuanced analysis of LFPSs that helps to disaggregate the cluster of schools nowadays lumped together under the term. In the same vein, they show that, depending on the context, LFPSs resonate with parents for different reasons, ranging from geographic proximity or non-availability of nearby public schools, respectively, to linguistic and cultural reasons for choosing LFPSs, sometimes operating as a community school. It is important to acknowledge that the global education industry is currently actively promoting the expansion of LFPSs. The profit potential for such schools is great, especially in an era when countries in the Global South are starting to pass legislation on the Right to Education. Even though the surge in LFPSs is most likely smaller than commonly reported and the reasons for favouring LFPSs over free public schools multifaceted, the global dimension is not to be underestimated. As Verger, Fontdevila and Zancajo astutely point out, global actors of the education industry, including, for example, Pearson, Omega Schools, Bridge International Academies, have entered the arena and are therefore likely to advocate for this particular type of PPP as a superior form of education as compared to free public schools. Different from PPPs in Organization for Economic Co-operation and Development (OECD) countries, it is international donors (notably Department for International Development (DFID) and the World Bank) rather than national governments, which provide the financial source for subsidizing businesses.

As well as scrutinizing in great detail the interaction between local and global actors and the timing of externalization, several studies identify the economic and political reasons why local decision-makers buy into global education policy (see also Verger 2012). Besides political gains – coalition building – there are, in particular in the interaction between global donors and recipient governments, economic benefits. Economically, the 'purchase' of a particular reform programme is closely associated with the 'terms of agreement' (programmatic conditionality) for receiving a loan or a grant from a global player. For the donor, in turn, lending a portfolio of (their own) 'best practices' presumably reduces transfer cost, makes it managerially easier for them to monitor and evaluate expected outcomes, and helps them to strengthen their visibility and ascertain their position vis-à-vis competing donors.

Re-contextualization: So what?

Not all studies on re-contextualization contribute to theory building. The great bulk of re-contextualization studies document in minute detail – sometimes across vertical levels, multiple sites and spatial scales – how the same global education policy plays out differently in two or more contexts. Such case studies or vertical ethnographies are 'thick' in description but 'thin' with regard to generalizations. The question becomes: What does the act of re-contextualization tell us about the policy process and, in particular, about policy change in an era of globalization?

Brent Edwards and Stephen Klees (in this volume) examine the inflationary usage of 'participation' in development and, drawing from reforms in El Salvador, convincingly show that the same label served not only diverse but also opposing political agendas. They compare in particular the neoliberal agenda (manifested in EDUCO), the liberal programme (exemplified in Plan 2021) and the progressive programme (illustrated in Popular Education in Santa Marta). The neoliberal proponents and free-market believers, represented by USAID and the World Bank, were enamoured with the concept because individual participation in the market and community participation in school councils fitted their larger agenda of parental choice and school-based management. The liberal spin on participation also included civil society organizations and advanced, among others, participatory poverty assessments. The progressive approach to participation finally used a far-reaching definition that implied transformative change and change in power relations. According to Edwards and Klees, 'EDUCO schools reflect neoliberalism's preoccupation with a narrow version of efficiency and effectiveness through community-based accountability relations' (Edwards and Klees, in this volume). At the heart of an EDUCO school is the Community Education Association (ACE, in Spanish) which is in charge of hiring, firing and managing teachers.

There is no doubt that EDUCO, similar to CCT, PPP, NPM, life-long learning and a host of other programmes discussed in this book, qualifies as a global education policy or a travelling reform. The study by Edwards and Klees is so compelling because only a few scholars shed light on the origins of a global education policy. Most studies deal with re-contextualization and compare how early versus late adopters of a global education policy, years later, redefine or modify the imported reform. Let me explain why it is important to differentiate between the initiators, early adopters and late adopters of a global education policy. The study of initiators, as presented by Edwards and Klees, helps us to understand that there always exist several competing policy options, some backed with massive financial capital and strong government support, and others only supported by civil society organizations or smaller advocacy groups. In El Salvador, the new government, with backing from USAID and then the World Bank, introduced EDUCO as a means to regain control over schools. The neat distinction that Edwards and Klees make in their case, whereby one political group promotes one particular reform, however, evaporates at a later stage of a global education policy. It disappears when we deal with global policy borrowing. Once a policy goes global – in this case EDUCO – the policy takes on different meanings and therefore resonates with different political groups for different reasons. EDUCO ceases to be associated only with neoliberal groups and is, for reasons utterly unrelated to its original context, selectively adopted by different political camps.

The study of early or late adopters of EDUCO in Central America and in other continents (see Poppema 2012) shows little similarity with the initial context for a particular reason: every reform programme, including EDUCO is, figuratively speaking, an octopus with several arms. For neoliberal groups, the social accountability arm might have been appealing because it helps to improve financial management at school levels, whereas for progressive groups parental involvement and community participation were – to lean on Verger's great metaphor – the 'selling point'.

Without going into too much detail here, the chapter on Global Education Policy Networks (Avelar, Pavlina Nikita, and Ball; in this volume) is a powerful exemplar of determining situated knowledge and discursive power. Applying ethnographic network analysis, they investigated what participants contributed to a meeting (held in Brazil) in terms of what they actually said but also in terms of how they relate to each other. As with other chapters in this volume, the study by Avelar, Pavlina and Ball pays great attention to context. Laying bare the relation between actors, as illustrated in the ethnographic network analysis, entails bringing back the institutional context in which something is said, argued, promoted and – if business interests are involved – sold.

The ambition to interpret the findings on the various re-contextualization studies for a larger theory on policy change makes it necessary to lay bare the theoretical assumptions underlying one's work. One of the assumptions that I invoked in the previous paragraph relates to the lifespan of a global education policy. As discussed in other publications (e.g. Steiner-Khamsi 2010), I find it important to acknowledge the continuous deterritorialization and decontextualization process that accompanies a global education policy over the course of its lifespan. A global education policy ends up becoming nobody's and everyone's policy within a short period of time, making its import or adoption increasingly likely. I therefore suggested that we distinguish between the designers, early adopters and late adopters of a global education policy. In social network analysis, the three distinctive phases are labelled slow growth, exponential growth and burnout. They are typically illustrated in the shape of a lazy S-curve (see Steiner-Khamsi 2010). There is nothing more practical than having a theory: for example, the assumption of a policy lifespan helps us to differentiate between the various time periods of a global education policy and explain why local policy-makers at some point – typically during the exponential growth phase – refer to a particular global education policy as a 'best practice' or 'international standards'. The example of the lifespan of a policy only served as an appeal for making one's theoretical assumption transparent.

Naturally, many attempts have been made to label various assumptions and categorize them into a larger framework. This book presents one of the most persuasive frameworks that I have read to date. Susan Robertson's brilliant synopsis, published in this volume, categorizes different strands of thought that attempt to locate the 'global' in education policy. The following list reiterates Robertson's categorization (presented in italics) and adds kin constructs used by others in globalization and education research. The term 'global' captures a wide range of social phenomena including the following:

- *condition of the world*, labelled by most authors as globalization

- *discourse*, also known as 'semantics of globalisation' (Jürgen Schriewer)

- *project,* popularized with the term 'globalisation optique' (Stephen Carney)

- *scale*, typically addressed with terms such as 'global players/actors'

- *reach*, in this book referred to as global education policy

Robertson's thoughtful categorization enables us to dig deeper into the question of how re-contextualization studies help advance theories on globalization and the policy process. It helps us to identify the areas under scrutiny. For example, several of us have made it a vocation to challenge the current nationalistic and parochial theories on policy change. The conviction has to do with our particular angle: we see a global map underlying national policy agendas. This particular *globalization optique* makes us interpret national or local education policies in a particular manner. For us, 'globalisation' is – to use Robertson's terminology – a 'project' that helps us to see and interpret local education policy in its larger context. Globalization is the relatively new terrain of reforms or, as Verger, Novelli and Altinyelken (in this volume) phrased it, the 'context of contexts' of education policy.

Robertson's categorization of how scholars localize the 'global' is multidimensional, relational and, without any doubt, the opposite of flat. The relational feature of critical globalization research is pointed out by many (see, e.g., dos Santos and Soeterik in this volume), yet rarely empirically investigated. I find in particular the notions of 'positionality' and 'audience' key for understanding the relational nature of global education policy. In my earlier work on global education policy in Mongolia, I noticed that government officials frequently engage in double-talk. One talk is directed towards donors ('global speak') and is instrumental for securing external funding, and another, printed in party action programmes, funded from the national education budget, and distributed over the media, is addressed to a Mongolian audience ('local speak'). The first one is published in English and recycled in technical reports, education sector reviews and strategies that are funded by international donors. In contrast, the local speak is in Mongolian and is barely accessible to international consultants and researchers, leading donors to perpetuate the myth that the only reform projects that the Government of Mongolia is carrying out are the ones funded by international donors. It was in this context that I suggested that we examine policy bilingualism, that is, the two different scales or 'spaces' from which one and the same policy actor or state institution speaks or operates.

In his research, Tavis Jules takes the distinction a step further and analyses the different audiences that one and the same Caribbean government addresses in different policy documents (Jules 2012). He finds that the same government addresses different reform priorities and strategies, depending on whether the audience is a national, regional or international entity. His work on policy triangulism represents a fascinating study on the spatial or scalar dimension of globalization studies.

Theoretical debates on policy bilingualism, multiscalarity or multi-spatiality of policy actors are crucial for abandoning the frequently made distinction between global (out there) and local (in here). It appears that the twin notion of 'positionality' and 'audience' helps to soften the dichotomy between external and internal that has afflicted globalization research. The twin notion first surfaced in the era of postmodern theories in the 1990s and nowadays also holds a prominent place in postcolonial and post-development studies.

The relational nature between the global, regional and local is not to be underestimated. The most dazzling phenomenon is that local politicians periodically invoke globalization as a discourse and present the condition of globalization towards their local audience as a quasi-external force for the sole purpose of generating reform pressure in their local context. The fact that a series of similar global education policies circumvent the globe is often taken as proof that national educational systems are converging towards the same reform package or global education policy. Note the circularity of the argument: local politicians first create the phantom of (vaguely defined) international standards to generate reform pressure; then they use the existence of such (self-produced) standards as proof that all educational systems, including their own, must be aligned with them. To put it differently, 'globalisation' is a reality but also a phantom that is periodically mobilized for political and economic purposes. Robertson's distinction between globalization as a condition (real) and a discourse (imagined) comes to mind here (see Steiner-Khamsi 2004).

For all the reasons listed in this commentary, it is important to study re-contextualization and interpret why particular features of a global education policy have resonated in a particular policy context. Our interest does not lie with describing the global education policy (often reduced to a meaningless label when analysed comparatively) but rather with understanding the re-contextualized versions of the policy. It is the re-contextualized versions of one and the same global education policy that tells us something about context but also about the policy process and change.

References

Baker, D. P. and LeTendre, G. K. (2005). *National differences, global similarities. World culture and the future of schooling.* Stanford, CA: Stanford University Press.

Drori, G. S., Meyer, J. W., Ramirez, F. O. and Schofer, E. (2003). *Science in the modern world polity. Institutionalization and globalization.* Stanford, CA: Stanford University Press.

Hall, P. A. (1993). 'Policy paradigms, social learning, and the State: The case of economic policymaking in Britain'. *Comparative Politics*, 25 (3), 275–296.

Jules, T. D. (2012). *Neither world polity nor local or national societies: Regionalization in the Global South – The Caribbean Community.* Berlin: Peter Lang.

Luhmann, N. (1990). *Essays on self-reference.* New York: Columbia University Press.

Poppema, M. (2012). 'School based management in Post-Conflict Central America: Undermining Civil Society and making the Poorest Parents Pay'. In A. Verger, M. Novelli and H. Kosar-Altinyelken (Eds.), *Global education policy and international development: New agendas, issues and policies.* London: Continuum, 296 pp.

Ramirez, F. O. (2003). 'The global model and national legacies'. In K. Anderson-Levitt (Ed.), *Local meanings, global schooling.* New York: Palgrave Macmillan, pp. 239–255.

Rogers, E. M. (1995). *Diffusion of innovations,* 4th edn. New York: Free Press.

Schriewer, J. (1990). 'The method of comparison and the need for externalization: Methodological criteria and sociological concepts'. In J. Schriewer and Holmes (Eds.), *Theories and methods in comparative education.* Frankfurt-am-Main: Peter Lang, pp. 25–83.

Steiner-Khamsi, G. (2004). 'Globalization in education: Real or imagined?'. In G. Steiner-Khamsi (Ed.), *The global politics of educational borrowing and lending.* New York: Teachers College Press, pp. 1–11.

Steiner-Khamsi, G. (2010). 'The politics and economics of comparison'. *Comparative Education Review*, 54 (3), 323–342.

Takayama, K. (2010). 'Politics of externalization in reflexive times: Reinventing Japanese education reform discourses through "Finnish success"'. *Comparative Education Review*, 54 (1), 51–75.

Verger, A. (2012). 'Framing and selling global education policy: The promotion of public-private partnerships for education in low-income contexts'. *Journal of Education Policy*, 27 (1), 109–130.

Waldow, F. (2010). 'Der Traum vom "skandinavisch schlau Werden" – Drei Thesen zur Rolle Finnlands als Projektionsfläche in der gegenwärtigen Bildungsdebatte'. *Zeitschrift für Pädagogik*, 56 (4), 497–511.

Waldow, F. (2012). 'Standardisation and legitimacy: Two concentral concepts in research on educational borrowing and lending'. In G. Steiner-Khamsi and F. Waldow (Eds.), *Policy Borrowing and Lending*. London and New York: Routledge, pp. 411–427.

Watts, D. J. (2003). *Six degrees: The science of a connected age*. New York: Norton.

14

Global Education Policy: Creating Different Constituencies of Interest and Different Modes of Valorization

Roger Dale

Chapter Outline

From the opening page of the Introduction, the central unifying role of the idea of global education policy (GEP) and development in the volume is very evident. All authors seem comfortable to operate under its auspices. The very wide range of instances and foci that make up the volume instantiates the potential reach most effectively. This is indeed an impressive range of studies that can make a serious claim to represent the state of the art. However, the volume also shows, albeit without great fanfare, that the state of the art leaves quite a lot to be desired.

We can see this in two ways in particular.

From one side, what is striking is the fact that despite the very wide, rich and complex range of empirical cases, locations, objectives, sponsors, partnership models, levels of education, academic approaches and so on, the most consistent conclusion to be drawn from the separate projects and cases, and collectively across the projects and cases, is that most if not all of them appear to fail. Looking across the fascinating range of the projects and the varied and important detail reported in the various chapters, it is evident that what they have in common, besides involving 'outside' 'interventions', in typically national education systems, is that little, if any, net gain or successful achievement of objectives is reported. From the other side, what is significant for the central thrust of the project is that this level of failure occurs irrespective of governance and provenance of the projects that make up GEP. Or, to put it a different way, we are little closer to giving serious substance to the concept of GEP, except through reflection on its different paths to failure.

At the same time, equally notable are the similarities in the accounts of the very diverse range of projects and examples contained in the volume. On the one hand, there is a recurring account of what is seen as 'technical' failure, including inadequacy of conceptualization of the problem, ineffectiveness or inappropriateness of implementation mechanisms, lack of capacity, insufficient funding and so on. On the other hand, we find discourses of cultural disjunction, which are especially clearly and effectively reported in chapters that contrast two or more examples of the implementation of the same programme (Jakobi, Poppema, Altinyelken, Deventer-Wells and Sayed, for instance).

What is also notable about these accounts is not just that they undoubtedly shed light on the difficulties of 'doing development', but that we would not have been surprised to read similar accounts of doing development at almost any point in the last three decades and more. Over that period, perhaps the dominant accounts of the shortcomings of educational aid have been (largely from the right, e.g. Easterly 2006) that it is inefficient, ineffective and counterproductive, and from the left that it is a form of perpetuating colonial relationships between the West and the rest (Amin 2011). Now while there are more criteria for appraising and evaluating educational aid from the richer parts of the world to the poorer than are apparent in the simple conception of success implied by these accounts, and more dimensions to understanding the political relationships involved than are captured in 'colonialism' discourses, nevertheless that apparently continuity does – properly and importantly – generate the questions: (1) Why does GEP persist in these forms? (2) How has GEP, as an umbrella concept, adapted to its changing challenges and components, and reframed the questions of provenance and governance? (3) Who benefits from it, and how and under what conditions has this changed over the last decade or so?

In terms of the first of these questions it is clear from the wider critical literature around the topic that the aid relationship does generate a complex range of associations and affiliations between the multiple stakeholders and interests that it brings into being, which may be quite distinct from the formal goals of projects. And we might accept that it does satisfy some needs for all or most of the parties involved, even though these needs may not be directly related to the aims of the project or intervention itself. For donors, it is a means of demonstrating commitment. For recipients, aid provides means of accessing goods and services that would not otherwise be available, irrespective of their relationship to the aims of the project. However, the second question, about the difference that globalization makes, is the core concern of this volume, and I will try to unpick a little in this brief contribution. Finally, addressing the third question a little obliquely may enable us to take a small step towards understanding it.

The editors recognize the importance of the question of the difference GEP makes, and they address it head on in their Introduction. Quite rightly, and productively, they see it as what Jamie Peck and Nik Theodore (2010, p. 172) refer to as the 'context of context', the macro institutional patternings, ... scalar architectures, (and) broad-gauge regulatory variegation', in other words the broader structures and conditions that frame and give meaning to new forms of the discursive and material power of national and international institutions. They proceed to catalogue what they see as the main impacts of globalization in education policy, pointing to the multiple ways that policy is affected; that it generates new problems for education policy; alters the capacity of welfare states; implies the deterritorialization of the education policy process; revitalizes the role of international (*sic*) players and brings new ones in; benefits from ICT; transforms the legal framework of transnational education; creates a private transnational education market; as neoliberalism, frames education policy ideas; and, finally, and more positively, fosters the development of transnational social justice movements.

One useful way of putting this kind of list to work is to employ Bob Jessop 2002's categories of structural and strategic selectivity. Put very simply, structural selectivity might be seen to represent the 'context of context' through which the various cases of the 'impact' of GEP are framed: Why is this kind of 'development' occurring at this time, in these places, in these forms? Major elements of the 'context of context' are common to all the cases elaborated in the text, most importantly, though very broadly, elements of what is known as 'neoliberalism'. Strategic selectivity relates, equally broadly, to the perceived options open to the actors involved in the specific circumstances of a particular development relationship. What possible courses of action seem to be available to them, under what circumstances and with what likely outcomes? The value of such an approach is that it provides us with a means of drawing back somewhat from the particular cases, and potentially enables us to examine them in a comparative way, so as to be able to explain the differences between them. These differences are quite evident in the cases described in the text, but we do not have a means of comparing them, or bringing them into productive conjunction with each other. This is a theoretical as well as a methodological issue. It assumes that there may be explanations for the similarities and differences between the cases. For such comparison to be able to lead to explanation (of the different forms and roles of a hypothesized GEP), we would need to go beyond the restrictions of juxtaposition of cases, to look more closely at their constitution; this is not a matter of the number of cases; juxtaposing more cases does not take us closer to understanding what, if anything, makes them comparable. This entails a double analytic shift – from concrete to abstract, and from simple to complex.

One simple basis for doing this is to use what I have referred to as the 'Education Questions' (see Dale 2000, 2005), which, very briefly, shift from the observed practices of education, to the sociopolitical conditions that enabled (but did not require) them – the level of strategic selectivity – to the level referred to here as the context of context, or structural selectivity, where the broad conditions framing the possibilities of education policies are laid down.

The other main component of the context of context is what might be called the 'discursive context', and recent work in critical geography (e.g. Sheppard and Leitner 2010; Silvey and Rankin 2011) has shed valuable light on this through the changing nature of what might be called the 'development paradigm'. Sheppard and Leitner point to what they see as a 'continuous socio-spatial imagery' underlying all conceptions of development: 'one that presents capitalism as capable in principle of bringing development and prosperity to all ... It has repeatedly legitimized discourses of first world expertise even as the policies based in this expertise repeatedly fail' (186, 192). It is based on: (1) a Rostovian conception of a single trajectory of development 'that has the effect of presenting places with no choices about what development means, and of ranking (them) on a (single) scale of development' which has settler colonies at the top; (2) 'an imaginary of globalisation and capitalist development as process that is flattening out the world, creating a level playing field that equalises opportunities everywhere' (192), but which (3) does not mean a homogeneous world 'so much as one where differences need not be sources of inequality', and where 'cultural differences are recognised and valorised in terms of how they can be utilised in the market, ... (but) where social and cultural differences that are not regarded as commodifiable are dismissed as barriers to development, in need of modernisation' (2011). One of the key accompaniments of these changes in the post–Washington Consensus has been the 'governance turn', the shift away from one-size-fits-all approaches to one that recognizes the importance of local institutions. The key point here, of course, is that this shift does not signal or represent a shift away from neoliberalism, but an intensification of it; the move to governance essentially means eroding differences between state and market, as states themselves are led to operate according to market principles.

This is crucial to the understanding of the nature of the GEP and of the explanation of the differences between the cases presented in this book. For what they crucially point to is an assumption of sufficient similarity of condition for all cases to be subjected to the same 'treatment'. Key to the basis of the exceptions identified in the paradigm is the nature of the cultural and social differences, and whether, how far and in what ways they may be seen as commodifiable, or as obstacles to commodification that are to be overcome through modernization. We see here a broad but fundamental distinction between the logic of intervention to be employed in different cases. At one end are those countries whose cultural differences (from the West, let it be remembered) are such that they can be valorized – classic cases here, of course, are the 'Asian tigers' (a term that sounds oddly old-fashioned, as the possibilities of using them as a model for countries with other, less commodifiable differences, recedes). The problem here is how to valorize the differences. At the opposite end of the scale, the problem is how to remove, ignore or neutralize the differences in countries whose cultural patterns are not so supportive of capitalist marketization. This is a problematization to which the governance turn is a clear response, and creates a project in which education is effectively handed a dual role, as a process and as an outcome.

What we see here is the consistent application of a strategy – imposing Western capitalism as the model for all – which remains valid, but calls for different tactics as the relative commodification possibilities themselves are changed by changing global regional and local relations.

However, even this approach contains some extremely important potential lacunae. It tends to see 'commodification' as the only relevant outcome, and thus to see the donors, 'the West', as the definers of and the (thwarted) beneficiaries from local cultural and social differences. In addition, where they do not have the desired effects on 'local' situations, Western interventions are seen to have no (relevant) consequences for local social and cultural differences. This leads to consequences in the form of interventions being recognized only through a cost-effectiveness lens, and the assumption that the particular modes of intervention create, or recognize, only particular forms and beneficiaries of valorization.

The crucial point here is that as well as threats to existing groups, development projects necessarily generate new constituencies of interest, and produce a range of different opportunities for different groups – and not only for those designated as beneficiaries. What this means is that the balance sheet of development effects cannot be confined to that stated in the prospectus (and it is this that lies at the heart of the response to the question: Why do they keep doing it?) In a nutshell, the answer is that education development/GEP interventions produce a range of groups, constituencies, organizations and so on, with a powerful interest in maintaining those interests through the medium of the development paradigm as implemented in the 'traditional way'. These comprador groups run from national governments to village stores. The interventions also, of course, create new 'disadvantaged' groups and intensify the disadvantage of others, as well as creating new groups of beneficiaries. And a major consequence of this is that this uneven distribution of opportunities and beneficiaries itself changes the 'local' social and cultural differences and challenges in ways significant for the 'reception' of the next wave of interventions, with new commodifiable interests and barriers to development.

One example of this is the creation of comprador groups of intermediaries and go-betweens at national and local levels who facilitate and in many cases enable processes of international intervention. A good account – mutatis mutandis – of the nature and work of comprador groups can be found in the case of their role in making possible the transformation of former Communist countries in Eastern Europe.

The international environment in which transition and post-transition policy-making took place had indeed a crucial role in explaining final outcomes. But there is a missing link. The pressures of the transnational environment had first to be translated, embodied and expressed by key actors in the state – the comprador service sector. Domestic politics plays a crucial role in this process. Domestic politics, however, cannot be understood as completely internally determined. It must be treated as an instantiation of locally materialising transnational processes. Transnationally constituted domestic politics explains both the initial inward-oriented outcomes and later shifts toward the competition state. The emergence of externally oriented competition states has been conditioned upon the unfolding hegemonic role of the comprador service sector. This created a field of force that allowed this sector to come to the forefront as its interests become increasingly 'universal'. The role and agency of this sector, however, do not explain the policy as such. They work as a linking factor that influences when, in which way, and in what form such a shift toward the competition state takes place. The comprador service sector helped to translate the structural power of transnational capital into tactical forms of power that enabled agential power to work in sync with the interests of the multinationals. (Drahokoupil 2008, p. 176)

Though this example of the 'transnational constitution of domestic politics' is drawn from a quite specific time and place, the role of the 'transnational in the domestic' is clearly crucial in creating the chances of success of the transnational project. That project does not contain the conditions of its own success; it is dependent on the involvement of key domestic interests. It shows very clearly the need for local spaces to be opened up in which transnational projects can flourish, and which can be occupied and valorized by different social groups. We can see examples of this in several chapters in this volume (and note that this piece focuses on the chapters not discussed in Gita Steiner Khamsi's response), and I will refer to them very briefly now.

Though these points are not fully developed in the contributions, one 'big message' that characterizes the studies in the book is that local recipients of GEP are not passive, but active 'strategic selectors' from what is offered. We might say the preferred account of the nature and influence of the GEP in the volume is the 'mediating, recontextualising, even undermining or openly resisting' (Altinyelken) reception given by different groups to manifestations of the GEP within recipient countries. However, one element of these forms of response is that they tend to be reactive rather than responsive; that is, they might be seen to adjust to the existence of the GEP, rather than seeking to alter it more fundamentally. 'Re-contextualization' may be seen as an exception to that claim, though it might be noted that for a concept that is asked to carry a considerable burden in this volume, it is used rather loosely and imprecisely at times. More broadly, there is a tendency for the studies to concentrate their focus quite narrowly on matters that are obviously – and self-identifyingly – associated with education, sometimes quite narrowly conceived as schooling; they tend to be 'strategic *sectoral* selectors'. There can be no objection to the focus on the relationship between GEP and schooling, but this should not occur at the expense of recognizing the wider implications of education policy. It is interesting that in studying educational development, we tend to concentrate much more on things that are obviously directly related to access to schooling, for instance, rather than on the deeper solution relations with which access, for instance, is implicated, with rather less attention paid to the kinds of issues addressed in the sociology of Western education.

So we do find in the book a range of interesting and very different examples of forms of local brokering of opportunities. For instance, Altinyelken shows how the same reform of pedagogical approaches in the rather different cases of Uganda and Turkey allowed – possibly encouraged –the emergence of a distinct group of 'modern and progressive' teachers, a group likely to be identified as future educational leaders, while Unterhalter notes a similar phenomenon in her case study. A further example of particular groups retaining power in the face of policies intended – at least formally – to democratize education governance with a rhetoric of local participation is offered by Edwards (in this volume) and by Poppema (2012), through the example of the use of school-based management reforms. These reforms were hugely instrumental schemes, aimed at undermining 'politically dangerous' civil society organizations in El Salvador and Nicaragua, and at the depoliticization of socio-economic organizations and the building of new forms of socio-economic co-existence at local level.

Unterhalter's chapter on gender equality aspects of the Millennium Development Goals (MDGs) and Education For All (EFA) goals produces valuable evidence of the different levels of penetration – and perhaps immediate relevance of discourses of poverty, human rights and gender equality, with the more 'metropolitan' staff involved embracing such aspirations fully, but 'district education officers, primary school teachers and rural NGO staff' seeing poverty, rights, gender equality discourses as 'other people' projects. Similarly, Jakobi (2012)'s research on lifelong learning is a classic case of 'policy alignment without policy implementation'. Her research focuses on Africa, and in particular Nigeria and South Africa, but she finds neither country implementing the reform fully. However, this is an important and interesting example of how GEP might be seen to work. While neither country, and especially Nigeria, is fully engaged with lifelong learning in practice, both have made at least symbolic shifts of policy to be seen to align with it: South Africa through the development of a qualifications framework, and Nigeria with a concept of basic education (Jakobi 2012). Of particular significance here is that this major GEP effectively involves a major break with the philosophy, and especially the patterns, of education worldwide, from an activity spanning a number of years to one covering a lifetime.

This has, of course, been well recognized by students of education and development, but may now be entering a quite new phase, with the explicit creation of what amounts to comprador bourgeoisies in the traditional sense, of local representatives of international or global capital, in the form of public–private partnerships in education, discussed in several chapters of this volume. Rather than valorization of development education through other forms of capital, which is made possible because it is involved with both sides of the partnership – cultural, social, political, and so on – the privatization/commercialization of education, which is being very actively pursued by the World Bank – opens up opportunities for direct financial comprador operation in education. This is itself a very significant outcome of the governance turn, and one that opens up a wide range of possible consequences, outside the specific consequences for access, quality and control of education itself.

The emergence of low-fee private schools (LFPSs), described by Verger et al., is seen as a 'default mechanism', a relatively novel response to the increasing inequalities between nations driven by an increasingly unequal world system. While it clearly has comprador features, the authors suggest that the LFPS phenomenon is becoming 'more and more embedded in transnational networks of influence, capital and ideas'.

The concept of 'global education policy networks' deployed by Avelar et al. focuses on ways that such networks can be seen as means of moving outside and beyond, and possibly to a degree supplanting, national or even transnational, public education systems. Global Education Policy Networks (GEPN) are both financially *independent*, typically relying on funding from business-related foundations, and epistemologically *selective*. The chapter focuses on the ways that policy emerges through the process of 'meetingness' that evolves within the networks – though perhaps processes of 'inter-meetingness' might be equally powerful.

However, if Avelar et al.'s networks, and Verger et al.'s increasingly embedded LFPSs reflect a GEP operating with a considerable degree of independence, Addey and Sellar's account of international large-scale assessments (ILSAs) demonstrates the continuing significance of national governments, whose rationales for participation are very much related to reinforcing the national image, in what the authors refer to as a 'global ritual of belonging'. This develops to the point where, the authors argue, 'the sociopolitical contexts in which ILSAs are adopted are transforming the intended uses of ILSAs'.

If that is so, it is an important reminder of the need to retain clear conceptions of, and multiple and variegated interactions between the immensely complex ensembles of political, economic and cultural elements that underlie and compose any conception of a GEP.

Conclusion

As the editors make very clear, GEP raises serious conceptual issues. The volume itself underpins and illustrates the sense that 'global' talk entails recognition that that involves not just a quantitative increase in the diffusion of similar policies, but fundamental reappraisals of what is meant by 'global' 'education' and 'policy', that recognize and respond to qualitative political, economic and cultural changes that the GEP concept at its best and most rigorous summarizes and represents. So, for instance, 'good governance' is not 'a form of government by any other name', but a quite distinct phenomenon, a way of framing and constituting new and distinct problems, and of creating 'solutions' that go with rather than against the grain of the dominant neoliberalism, and of assembling new forms of education strategies, tactics and mechanisms. It has done this through a rich collection of closely observed case studies.

This brief contribution has aimed to suggest that it is not only through the framing and attempted implementation of its goals that GEP has effects beyond as well as within the education sector, but that it also has significant consequences, through the opportunities it offers to various kinds of groups to develop new modes of valorization, beyond as well as within the education sector.

Finally, I am writing these few words just hours after learning of the death of Fidel Castro, and it would be remiss in the extreme not to mention perhaps the most successful educational system in the world (see, e.g., Carnoy 2007), and to ask why, especially in an era besotted with notions of 'Evidence-Based Practice', the Cuban model is so rarely mentioned. Answering that question could shed extremely interesting and powerful light on the 'approved' and 'not-approved' roads followed, and not followed, by GEP.

References

Amin, S. (2011). *Maldevelopment: Anatomy of a global failure*, 2nd edn. Oxford: Pambazuka Press.

Carnoy, Martin (2007). *Cuba's academic advantage*. Stanford, CA: Stanford University Press.

Dale, R. (2000). 'Globalisation and education: Demonstrating "A Common World Educational Culture" or locating "A Globally Structured Educational Agenda"?'. *Educational Theory*, 50 (4), 427–449.

Dale, R. (2005). 'Globalisation, knowledge economy and comparative education'. *Comparative Education*, 41 (2), 117–149.

Drahokoupil, J. (2008). 'The rise of the comprador service sector: The politics of state transformation in Central and Eastern Europe'. *Polish Sociological Review*, 57 (2), 175–189.

Easterly, W. (2006). *The white man's burden*. New York: Penguin.

Jakobi, A. (2012). 'Implementing global policies in African countries: Conceiving lifelong learning as basic education'. In A. Verger, M. Novelli and H. K. Alitnyelken, *Global education policy and international development: New agendas, issues and policies*. London: Bloomsbury, pp. 119–140.

Jessop, B. (2002). *The future of the capitalist state*. Cambridge: Polity.

Peck, J. and Theodore, N. (2010). 'Mobilising policy: Models, methods and mutations'. *Geoforum*, 41 (2), 169–174.

Poppema, M. (2012). 'School-based management in post-conflict Central America: Undermining civil society and making the poorest parents pay'. In A. Verger, M. Novelli and H. K. Alitnyelken, *Global education policy and international development: New agendas, issues and policies*. London: Bloomsbury, pp. 161–180.

Sheppard, E. and Leitner, H. (2010). 'Quo vadis neoliberalism? The remaking of global capitalist governance after the Washington Consensus'. *Geoforum*, 41, 185–194.

Silvey, R. and Rankin, K. (2011). 'Development geography: Critical development studies and political geographic imaginaries'. *Progress in Human Geography*, 35 (5), 696–704.

List of Contributors

Camilla Addey is a researcher and lecturer at Humboldt University of Berlin, Germany, and co-director of the Laboratory of International Assessment Studies. She researches global educational policy and international large-scale assessments in lower- and middle-income countries. Her current research focuses on the OECD and PISA for Development. She has carried out research in Laos, Mongolia, Paraguay and Ecuador. She previously worked at UNESCO in the Literacy and Non-Formal Education section. She is author of *Readers and Non-Readers,* co-editor of *Literacy as Numbers* and has authored papers published in *Critical Studies in Education*, *Compare and Educação & Sociedade*.

Rashid Ahmed is currently employed as a senior lecturer in the Department of Psychology at the University of the Western Cape. He obtained his postgraduate teacher's diploma from the University of South Africa (UNISA), his professional qualification as a clinical psychologist from University of Cape Town and his doctorate from UNISA. His research interests are in community psychology and resilience; particularly community resilience in low-income contexts and advancing a human rights agenda for education. He has published in the area of resilience, contextualized clinical psychology training and community psychology and education policy. He is the Deputy Chair of the Psychology Department with an interest and involvement in community engagement initiatives.

Hülya Kosar Altinyelken is a senior lecturer and researcher at the Child Development and Education Department of the University of Amsterdam, the Netherlands. Her research interests cover a wide range of issues, including global education policies, curriculum change, child-centred pedagogy, reform implementation and teachers. She is currently involved in two research projects on Muslims in the Netherlands, looking at the pedagogy of mosque education as well as its influence on identity development and social integration of Muslim youth.

Marina Avelar is a PhD candidate at the University College London, Institute of Education, UK. Her research is focused on the work of private actors, such as new philanthropy, in education policy-making and global policy networks. Her research is funded by CAPES/Brazil and the IOE Centenary Research Scholarship, and she was the winner of the 2016 Peter Lang Young Scholars Competition in Education Studies. Prior to the PhD, she completed her bachelor's and master's degrees in education at the State University of Campinas, Brazil, with visiting periods at the Lund University, Sweden, and the UCL Institute of Education, UK.

Stephen J. Ball is Distinguished Service Professor of Sociology of Education at the University College London, Institute of Education, UK. He was elected Fellow of the British Academy in 2006; and is also Fellow of the Academy of Social Sciences and Society of Educational Studies, and a Laureate of Kappa Delta Phi; he has honorary doctorates from the Universities of Turku, Finland, and the University of Leicester, UK. He is co-founder and Managing Editor of the *Journal of Education Policy*. His main areas of interest are in sociologically informed education policy analysis and the relationships between education, education policy and social class. He has written twenty books and has published over 140 journal articles. Recent books: *Edu.Net* (2017) and *Foucault as Educator* (2017).

Xavier Bonal is Professor of Sociology at the Universitat Autònoma de Barcelona, Spain, and Special Professor of Education and International Development at the University of Amsterdam, the Netherlands. He is the director of the research group *Globalisation, Education and Social Policies* (GEPS) at the UAB and Coordinator of the GLOBED Project, an Erasmus Mundus Master on *Education Policies for Global Development*. He has widely published in national and international journals and is the author of several books on sociology of education, education policy and globalization, education and development. He has worked as a consultant for international organizations such as UNESCO, UNICEF, the European Commission and the Council of Europe.

Mieke Lopes Cardozo is Assistant Professor of International Development Studies at the University of Amsterdam, the Netherlands. Her academic research and teaching focuses on the role of education in processes of peacebuilding and social justice in the contexts of Sri Lanka, Aceh/Indonesia, Bolivia and Myanmar. She recently co-directed the Research Consortium on Education and Peacebuilding together with Professor Mario Novelli (University of Sussex, UK) and Professor Alan Smith (University of Ulster, UK) in collaboration with UNICEF. She is appointed as Advisor for the Security Council mandated Progress Study on Resolution 2250 on Youth, Peace and Security, and is a member of the Education Policy Working Group of the International Network for Education in Emergencies.

Roger Dale is Professor of Sociology of Education at the University of Bristol, UK. He was previously Professor of Education at the University of Auckland, New Zealand, and was Scientific Coordinator of the EU's Network of Experts in Sociology of Education (NESSE). His major interests focus on the critical cultural political economy of education. He is co-editor and co-founder of the journal *Globalisation, Societies and Education*.

D. Brent Edwards Jr. is Assistant Professor of Theory and Methodology in the Study of Education at the University of Hawaii, Manoa, USA. His work focuses on (1) the global governance of education; (2) education policy, politics and political economy, with a focus on low-income countries; and (3) critical and democratic alternatives to dominant neoliberal education models. He has two recent books: *The Trajectory of Global Education Policy: Community-Based Management in El Salvador and the Global Reform Agenda* and *The Political Economy of Schooling in Cambodia: Issues of Equity and Quality*.

Clara Fontdevila holds a degree in Sociology from the Universitat Autònoma de Barcelona, Spain, and is currently a PhD candidate at the Department of Sociology of the same university, with a thesis research project on the settlement of the post-2015 global education agenda through network analysis. Her areas of interest are private sector engagement in education policy, education and international development, and the global governance of education. She has previously participated in the evaluation of the Civil Society Education Fund, as well as in a research project on the role of the World Bank on the global promotion of teacher policies.

Rada Mogliacci is a postdoctoral research fellow at the Centre for International Teacher Education, Cape Peninsula University of Technology, South Africa. She obtained her degree in Primary Education at the University of Novi Sad (Serbia) and PhD in Human Development in Social and Cultural Research from Bielefeld University (Germany). Her work has been particularly focused on pre-service and in-service teacher education, and teacher policies formulation and implementation. Rada is currently engaged in research projects on newly qualified teachers, and teacher policy analysis.

Dimitra Pavlina Nikita is a PhD candidate at the University College London, Institute of Education, UK. Her research interests are in the fields of sociology of education and policy sociology. She is currently focusing on: changing modes of governance in education policy; neoliberalism and education policy-making; innovative social research methods in critical policy studies.

Mario Novelli is Professor of the Political Economy of Education and Director of the Centre for International Education (CIE) at the University of Sussex,

UK. His research explores the relationship between education, globalization and international development, with a specific focus on education delivery in conflict-affected contexts. He is currently working on issues related to the role of education in peacebuilding processes and has worked with UNICEF on a series of research projects.

Xavier Rambla is Associate Professor of Sociology at Universitat Autònoma de Barcelona, Spain. Currently, he is interested in the following research areas: education policy transfer between international organizations and governments, lifelong learning policies, and the implications of Europeanization for education policies. Previously, he has also worked on early school leaving, Education For All and inequalities in Latin America, education policies targeted to vulnerable social groups (in Southern Europe and the Southern Cone) and critical coeducational action research.

Susan L. Robertson is Professor of Sociology of Education, in the Faculty of Education, University of Cambridge, UK. She has a long-standing interest in state power and policy-making, transformations of the state, the state and spatiality, and the changing role of education in these dynamics. Susan has published extensively on these issues. She is also founding editor of the journal *Globalisation, Societies and Education*.

Yusuf Sayed is Professor of International Education and Development Policy at the University of Sussex, the South African Research Chair in Teacher Education, and the Founding Director of the Centre for International Teacher Education (CITE), at the Cape Peninsula University of Technology (CPUT), South Africa. He is also a Senior Research Fellow at the Institute of Social and Economic Research (ISER), Rhodes University, South Africa. Previously, Yusuf was Senior Policy Analyst at the EFA Global Monitoring Report, UNESCO, Team Leader for Education and Skills, the Department for International Development UK, and Head of Department of Comparative Education at the University of the Western Cape, South Africa. Yusuf is an education policy specialist with a career in international education and development research. His research focuses on education policy formulation and implementation as it relates to concerns of equity, social justice and transformation. He has published on various issues in international education and development including education quality and teacher education, exclusion and inclusion; education governance and the role of the state; and equity, financing and education. He is presently engaged in several research projects on teachers and teacher education including the ESRC/DFID funded project 'Engaging teachers in peacebuilding in post conflict contexts: evaluating education interventions in Rwanda and South Africa' and several large-scale studies about teacher professionalism, teacher education and continuing professional development in South Africa and globally.

Sam Sellar is Reader in Education Studies at Manchester Metropolitan University, UK, and a member of the Board of Directors for the Laboratory of International Assessment Studies. He has studied school systems in Australia, Canada and the United Kingdom to explore how educational data shape policy and practice in schools. He has published widely on the growing influence of data in education globally, including the education work of the OECD and its Programme for International Student Assessment.

Gita Steiner-Khamsi holds a dual academic affiliation as Professor of Comparative and International Education at Teachers College, Columbia University in New York, USA (fall semesters), and at the Graduate Institute of International and Development Studies in Geneva, Switzerland (spring semesters). She also serves as the Director of NORRAG. Her areas of research are policy borrowing and lending, globalization studies and public–private partnerships in education.

Aina Tarabini is an associate professor in the Sociology Department at Universitat Autònoma de Barcelona, Spain and researcher in the research groups GEPS (Globalization, Education and Social Policy) and GIPE (Interdisciplinary Group on Education Policies). She is specialist in sociology of education and on the analysis of educational inequalities. Her research is concerned with social inequalities and their educational repercussions at three levels: actors' subjectivities, educational practices and everyday actions; schools' practices and pedagogical devices; educational policies and programmes. Currently, she is co-PI of the R+D project: 'The construction of post-16 educational opportunities. An analysis of post-compulsory educational transitions in urban settings'.

Rosanne Tromp is a critical education policy researcher with the University of Amsterdam, the Netherlands. She is interested in the politics of education policy, international education policy transfer, education privatization and alternative education. She has worked for international organizations, such as Education International and UNESCO, Ministries of Education, as well as universities in the UK and Mexico. She is a board member of the Netherlands Association for Latin American and Caribbean Studies (NALACS), and a co-founder of the human rights organization the 'SMX Collective'.

Elaine Unterhalter is Professor of Education and International Development at the University College London, Institute of Education, UK. She works on gender, education and international development, most recently co-ordinating a number of research projects in this area in South Africa, Kenya, Tanzania, Nigeria and Ghana, and selected global organizations. She is the author of *Gender, Schooling and Global Social Justice* (2007) and co-author of works

Towards Equality? Gender in South African Schools during the HIV and AIDS Epidemic (2009) and *Global Inequalities and Higher Education. Whose Interests Are We Serving?* (2010).

Antoni Verger is an associate professor in the Department of Sociology at the Universitat Autònoma de Barcelona, Spain. A former postdoctoral fellow at the Amsterdam Institute for Social Science Research (University of Amsterdam, the Netherlands), Dr Verger's research analyses the relationship between global governance institutions and education policy. He has specialized in the study of public–private partnerships, quasi-market mechanisms and accountability policies in education, and has published extensively on these themes. Currently, he is coordinating the research project REFORMED – Reforming Schools Globally: A Multiscalar Analysis of Autonomy and Accountability Policies in the Education Sector (ERC StG, 2016–2021).

Adrián Zancajo holds a PhD degree in Sociology from the Universitat Autònoma de Barcelona, Spain, in 2017. He holds a degree in Economics and a Master of Educational Research, both from the Universitat Autònoma de Barcelona, Spain. His areas of research are education privatization, education quasi-markets and social inequalities within education systems. He has participated in different research projects on these matters, including 'The new quasi-market reforms in education in Latin America' (EDUMERCAL) and 'Public-Private Partnerships in Educational Governance' (EDUPARTNER).

Index

Lightning Source UK Ltd.
Milton Keynes UK
UKOW01n0930080218
317523UK00004B/264/P